Universal Human Rights
in Theory and Practice

International Human Rights, 4th ed. (2012)

Realism and International Relations (2000)

The Concept of Human Rights (1985)

Universal Human Rights in Theory and Practice

THIRD EDITION

Jack Donnelly

CORNELL UNIVERSITY PRESS | ITHACA AND LONDON

First published 2013 by Cornell University Press
First printing, Cornell Paperbacks, 2013

Printed in the United States of America

Library of Congress Cataloging-in-Publication Data

Donnelly, Jack.
    Universal human rights in theory and practice / Jack Donnelly. — 3rd ed.
        p. cm.
    Includes bibliographical references and index.
    ISBN 978-0-8014-5095-2 (cloth : alk. paper)
    ISBN 978-0-8014-7770-6 (pbk. : alk. paper)
    1. Civil rights.   2. Human rights.   3. Cultural relativism.   I. Title.
    JC571.D755 2013
    323—dc23   2012039604

Cornell University Press strives to use environmentally responsible suppliers and materials to the fullest extent possible in the publishing of its books. Such materials include vegetable-based, low-VOC inks and acid-free papers that are recycled, totally chlorine-free, or partly composed of nonwood fibers. For further information, visit our website at www.cornellpress.cornell.edu.

Cloth printing   10 9 8 7 6 5 4 3 2 1
Paperback printing   10 9 8 7 6 5 4 3

Contents

Part II. The Universality and Relativity of Human Rights

Part III. Human Rights and Human Dignity

Part IV. Human Rights and International Action

Part V. Contemporary Issues

Preface to the Third Edition

Pierre Vidal-Naquet, one of the great classicists of our time (although perhaps better known for his human rights work as a historian of French crimes during the Algerian war), observed that "for reasons that are my own and are probably not too 'rational,' in Greek studies the article is much easier for me than the book" (Vidal-Naquet 1986: xv). Much the same is true of my writings on human rights, which "naturally" seem to be more or less self-contained but interconnected units of about eight thousand words. The first edition of *Universal Human Rights in Theory and Practice* represented the coalescence of several essays written in the early and mid-1980s that were linked by their defense of a conception of "universal" human rights that acknowledges and incorporates the obvious historical contingency of both the idea of human rights and its dominant international expressions. The second edition represented both a continuation of the process of essay accumulation and a response to the aging of the first edition. This third edition is more of the same.

The first edition, which I delivered to the press in the fall of 1988, bore the unmistakable stamp of the Cold War. The second edition, delivered at the end of 2001, reflected its post–Cold War context. This edition, delivered in the middle of 2012, reflects, I hope, a more nuanced engagement with globalization and the special context it provides for discussions of universality. And this changing context is an important part of the book. Although primarily theoretical, it engages, both directly and indirectly, issues of immediate political significance.

I have deleted all or most of four chapters, added five that are largely or wholly new, radically reorganized the material in three others, and updated and refined most of the rest. The result is a third edition that is about half new. It is, however, a genuine third edition (rather than a fundamentally new book), with the same substantive focus, the same basic arguments, a similar structure, and much the same feel. Those who liked the first two editions will, I think, find this a rejuvenated version of the book they have known. Those who did not like them will, I am sure, find fresh provocations. With luck, this edition may attract some readers not familiar with the earlier editions.

Permission to reprint material that has appeared previously, in different form, has been granted by The Johns Hopkins University Press, which gave permission to reprint here as chapter 13 a revised version of "Human Rights, Democracy, and Development," *Human Rights Quarterly* 21 (August 1999), and MIT Press, which gave permission to reprint as chapter 12 a much shortened version of "International Human Rights: A Regime Analysis," *International Organization* 40 (Summer 1986).

This book has grown, almost organically, over the course of thirty years. Like most authors, I have accumulated numerous debts in writing (and rewriting) it. I am afraid, though, that I simply cannot adequately acknowledge them. Rather than rely on faulty memory and even worse record keeping, let me simply say thank you (you know who you are).

It is much easier to acknowledge my personal debts—to my wife Katy and son Kurosh. The first edition of this book was part of my introduction to Katy. The second edition appeared just when she arrived in this country. She has lived with me through the production of the third edition, without question the best decade of my life. And with her and our son—who although only fifteen months old has long since figured out that computers unfairly interrupt the essential work of paying attention to him—I am looking forward to the time between now and the fourth edition.

Universal Human Rights
in Theory and Practice

Introduction

This book aims to explicate and defend an account of human rights as universal rights. I do not, however, argue that human rights are timeless, unchanging, or absolute. Quite the contrary, I show that any list or conception of human rights—and the idea of human rights itself—is historically specific and contingent. Nonetheless, I argue that the particularity of human rights is compatible with a conception of human rights as universal rights.

The book is divided into five parts. Part I sketches the outline of a theory of human rights. Chapter 1 begins analytically, looking at the character of rights in general and human rights in particular. Chapter 2 then provides a largely descriptive sketch of the dominant contemporary understanding of human rights. Chapter 3 considers the two principal theoretical challenges to this dominant understanding, namely, the status of economic and social rights and the near complete absence of group human rights. Chapter 4 then offers a liberal, substantive justification of this model.

Part II turns to the issue of the universality and relativity of human rights. Rather than see this as an either-or choice, or even a matter of degree, I argue in chapter 6 that in some important senses of the term "human rights" these rights are universal but that in other, no-less-important senses they are not. I also argue that in some important senses of the term "human rights" these rights are relative, but in other, no-less-important senses they are not. These arguments build not only on the theory outlined in part I but also on chapter 5, which demonstrates that ideas and practices of human rights, in the Western and non-Western worlds alike, are an entirely modern (and in many ways a twentieth-century) phenomenon. Chapter 7 then explores some of the implications of this understanding, focusing on the issue of responsible advocacy of universal human rights in a world of particularity.

Part III continues the discussion of the historical particularity of human rights in the context of the foundational claim in contemporary international human rights law that human rights derive from the inherent dignity of the human person. Chapter 8 shows that in the West prior to the late eighteenth century, "dignity," rather than being a term of universalistic inclusion, was a particularistic term of hierarchical exclusion; only a small portion of the population was seen as having dignity. The contemporary notion of universal human rights, in other words, rests on a radical democratization of the notion of dignity, seen as an inherent attribute of all human beings rather than the achievement of a small elite. Chapters 9 and 10 develop similar arguments for Confucian China and Hindu India.

Part IV turns to the international politics of human rights. Chapter 11 provides an extended survey of multilateral human rights regimes. Chapter 12 considers bilateral foreign policy.

Part V concludes the volume by examining four contemporary areas of political controversy: the relationship between human rights, development, and democracy; Western attitudes toward economic and social rights; humanitarian intervention; and discrimination against homosexuals. In each case I try to show that a clear theoretical grasp of human rights and the particular character of their universality can make an important contribution to ongoing national and international policy debates.

Two general themes merit emphasis here. The first is methodological: the necessarily multidisciplinary character of the study of human rights. The second is more substantive: the interaction of theory and practice.

Consider the range of issues covered by the Universal Declaration of Human Rights, which recognizes personal rights to life, nationality, recognition before the law, protection against torture, and protection against discrimination on such bases as race and sex; legal rights to a fair trial, the presumption of innocence, and protections against ex post facto laws, arbitrary arrest, detention or exile, and arbitrary interference with one's family, home, or reputation; a comparable variety of civil liberties and political rights; subsistence rights to food and health care; economic rights to work, rest and leisure, and social security; social rights to education and protection of the family; and the right to participate in the cultural life of the community. A comprehensive account of these rights would require that we combine, at minimum, the perspectives of law, political science, economics, and sociology—plus philosophy, if we want to understand the conceptual foundations of human rights and the justifications for this particular list.

The study of human rights is an inherently multidisciplinary enterprise. One of my principal aims is to take seriously this often stated but rarely heeded methodological dictum. To do justice to the scope and complexities of human rights, and to increase understanding of human rights, material and perspectives from various disciplines and subfields are offered. Within my own discipline of political science, I draw principally from the subfields of political theory and international relations. I also draw heavily on work in philosophy, history, and international law. The result, I hope, concretely illustrates the fruitfulness, even necessity, of approaching human rights issues without regard to conventional disciplinary boundaries.

The importance of the interaction of theory and practice is especially striking when we consider the practical implications of the theoretical arguments of relativism considered in part II. The way in which we think about a problem does not determine how we act. It may, however, influence behavior. The way problems are conceptualized may also be important for justifying actions and policies. For example, if it can be established that the sacrifice of human rights is not an imperative of development, but merely a convenience for those who control development policy (or even simply a cover for their self-enrichment), then repressive regimes are deprived of one important defense of their human rights violations.

Clear thinking about human rights is not the key to the struggle to implement them. It may not even be essential to successful political action on their behalf. In fact, such a utopian belief in the power of ideas is itself a dangerous impediment to effective political action. Nonetheless, conceptual clarity, the fruit of sound theory, can facilitate action. At the very least it can help to unmask the arguments of dictators and their allies.

This book thus aspires not merely to analyze the interaction of theory and practice but also to contribute in some small way to improving practice. Such a hope underlies, and perhaps even justifies, not only this book but also much of the scholarly literature on human rights.

Part I

Toward a Theory
of Human Rights

I

The Concept of Human Rights

uman rights—*droits de l'homme, derechos humanos, Menschenrechte,* "the rights of man"—are literally the rights that one has because one is human. What does it mean to have a right? How are being human and having rights related? The first four sections of this chapter consider these questions, examining how human rights work and how they both rest on and help to shape our moral nature as human beings. The final three sections consider the problem of philosophical foundations of substantive theories of human rights.

1. How Rights Work

What is involved in having a right to something? How do rights, of whatever type, work?

A. Being Right and Having a Right

"Right" in English, like equivalent words in several other languages, has two central moral and political senses: rectitude and entitlement. In the sense of rectitude, we speak of "the right thing to do," of some*thing* being right (or wrong). In the narrower sense of entitlement we typically speak of some*one* having a right. To have a right to x is to be entitled to x. It is owed to you, belongs to you in particular. And if x is threatened or denied, right-holders are authorized to make special claims that ordinarily trump utility, social policy, and other moral or political grounds for action (Dworkin 1977: xi, 90).

More precisely, rights are prima facie trumps. All things considered, rights may themselves be trumped by weighty other considerations. Claiming a right, however, in effect stops the conversation and both increases and shifts the burden of proof to those who would argue that this right in this particular case is itself appropriately trumped.[1]

Both rectitude and entitlement link right and obligation but in systematically different ways. Claims of rectitude (righteousness)—"That's wrong," "That's not right," "You really ought to do that"—focus on a standard of conduct and draw attention to the duty-bearer's obligation under that standard. Rights claims, by contrast, focus on the right-holder and draw the duty-bearer's attention to the right-holder's special title to enjoy her right. Rights in this sense thus are sometimes called "subjective rights"; they focus on the subject (who holds them) rather than an "objective" standard to be followed or state of affairs to be realized.

Rights create—in an important sense are—a field of rule-governed interactions centered on, and under the control of, the right-holder. "A has a right to x (with respect to B)" specifies a right-holder (A), an object of the right (x), and a duty-bearer (B). It also outlines the relationships in which they stand. A is entitled to x (with respect to B), B stands under correlative obligations to A (with respect to x), and, should it be necessary, A may make special claims upon B to discharge those obligations.

Rights are not reducible to the correlative duties of those against whom they are held. If Anne has a right to x with respect to Bob, it is more than simply desirable, good, or even right that Anne enjoy x. She is entitled to it. Should Bob fail to discharge his obligations, besides acting improperly (i.e., violating standards of rectitude) and harming Anne, he violates her rights, making him subject to special remedial claims and sanctions.

Neither is having a right reducible to enjoying a benefit. Anne is not a passive beneficiary of Bob's obligation. She is actively in charge of the relationship, as suggested by the language of "exercising" rights. She may assert her right to x. If he fails to discharge his obligation, Anne may press further claims against Bob, choose not to pursue the matter, or even excuse him, largely at her own discretion. Rights empower, not just benefit, those who hold them. Violations of rights are a particular kind of injustice with a distinctive force and remedial logic.

B. Exercising, Respecting, Enjoying, and Enforcing Rights

"Claiming a right makes things happen" (Feinberg 1980: 150). When Anne exercises her right, she activates Bob's obligations, with the aim of enjoying the object of her right (which in some cases may require coercive enforcement). Exercise, respect, enjoyment, and enforcement are four principal dimensions of the practice of rights.

---

1. For a good discussion of the attractions and limitations of the trump metaphor, see Zivi (2012: 24–42).

When we consider how rights work, though, one of the more striking facts is that we talk about rights only when they are at issue. If I walk into the supermarket and buy a loaf of bread, it would be odd to say that I had a right to my money, which I exchanged for a right to the bread. Only in unusual circumstances would we say that those who refrained from stealing my money or bread were respecting my rights. Rights are actually put to use, and thus important enough to talk about, only when they are at issue, when their enjoyment is questioned, threatened, or denied.

Three major forms of social interaction involving rights can be usefully distinguished.

1. "*Assertive exercise*": the right is exercised (asserted, claimed, pressed), activating the obligations of the duty-bearer, who then either respects the right or violates it (in which case he is liable to enforcement action).
2. "*Active respect*"[2]: the duty-bearer takes the right into account in determining how to behave, without the right-holder ever claiming it. The right has been respected and enjoyed, even though it has not been actively exercised. Enforcement may have been considered by the duty-bearer but is otherwise out of the picture.
3. "*Objective enjoyment*": rights apparently never enter the transaction, as in the example of buying a loaf of bread; neither right-holder nor duty-bearer gives them any thought. The right—or at least the object of the right—has been enjoyed. Ordinarily, though, we would not say that it has been respected, and neither exercise nor enforcement is in any way involved.

Objective enjoyment must be the norm. For society, the costs associated with even active respect of a right must be the exception rather than the rule. Right-holders too would prefer not to have to exercise their rights. In an ideal world, rights would remain both out of sight and out of mind.

Nonetheless, the ability to claim rights, if necessary, distinguishes having a right from simply being the (rights-less) beneficiary of someone else's obligation. Paradoxically, then, "having" a right is of most value precisely when one does not "have" (the object of) the right—that is, when active respect or objective enjoyment is not forthcoming. I call this the "possession paradox": "having" and "not having" a right at the same time—possessing it but not enjoying it—with the "having" being particularly important precisely when one does not "have" it.

2. In the first edition, I used the label "direct enjoyment," which now seems to me misleading in drawing attention to the right-holder's enjoyment rather than the duty-bearer's respect for the right.

We thus should be careful not to confuse having a right with the respect it receives or the ease or frequency with which it is enforced. In a world of saints, rights would be widely respected, rarely asserted, and almost never enforced. In a Hobbesian state of nature, rights would never be respected. At best, disinterest or self-interest would lead duty-bearers to not deny the right-holder the object of her right. Only the accidental coincidence of interests (or self-help enforcement) would allow a right-holder to enjoy (the substance of) her right.

Differing circumstances of respect and enforcement tell us nothing about who *has* what rights. To have a right to x is to be specially entitled to x, whether the law that gave you a legal right is violated or not, whether the promise that gave rise to the contractual right is kept or not, whether others comply with the principles of righteousness that establish your moral right or not. I have a right to my car whether it sits in my driveway, is borrowed without my permission (for good reason or bad), is stolen but later recovered, or is stolen, never to be seen again by me (whether or not the thief is ever sought, apprehended, charged, tried, or convicted). Even if the violation ultimately goes unremedied and unpunished, the nature of the offense has been changed by my right.

2. Special Features of Human Rights

Human rights are literally the rights that one has simply because one is a human being. In section 3 we will consider the relationship between being human and having (human) rights. Here I focus on the special characteristics of human rights.[3]

Human rights are *equal* rights: one either is or is not a human being, and therefore has the same human rights as everyone else (or none at all). Human rights also are *inalienable* rights: one cannot stop being human, no matter how badly one behaves or how barbarously one is treated. And they are *universal* rights, in the sense that today we consider all members of the species *Homo sapiens* "human beings" and thus holders of human rights.

Much of this book explores the political implications of human rights being equal, inalienable, and universal. In this section I stress the implications of their being rights (in the sense discussed above) and their special role in enabling progressive political change.

A. Human Rights as Rights

The substance of human rights—what is on a defensible list of human rights— will be addressed in chapters 2 and 4. Here I focus on the fact that human rights

---

3. I emphasize the differences between (human) rights and other social practices and grounds for action. The similarities are perceptively discussed and emphasized in Nickel (2006).

are not just abstract values. They are rights, particular social practices to realize those values. A human right thus should not be confused either with the values or aspirations underlying it or with enjoyment of the object of the right.

For example, protection against arbitrary execution is an internationally recognized human right. The fact that people are not executed arbitrarily, however, may reflect nothing more than a government's lack of desire. Even active protection may have nothing to do with a right (title) not to be executed. For example, rulers may act out of their sense of justice or follow a divine injunction that does not endow subjects with any rights. And even a right not to be arbitrarily executed may be a customary or statutory (rather than a human) right.

Such distinctions are more than scholastic niceties. Whether citizens have a right (title) shapes the nature of the injury they suffer and the forms of protection and remedy available to them. Denying someone something that it would *be* right for her to enjoy in a just world is very different from denying her something (even the same thing) that she is entitled (*has* a right) to enjoy. Furthermore, whether she has a human right or a legal right that has been contingently granted by the state dramatically alters both her relationship to the state and the character of her injury.

B. Human Rights, Legal Change, and Political Legitimacy

Human rights traditionally have been thought of as moral rights of the highest order. They have also become, as we will see in more detail below, international (and in some cases national and regional) legal rights. The object of many human rights can be claimed as "ordinary" legal rights in most national legal systems. Many local jurisdictions also have human rights statutes.

Armed with multiple claims, right-holders typically use the "lowest" right available. For example, in the United States, as in most countries, protection against racial discrimination in employment is available on several grounds. Depending on one's employment agreement, a grievance may be all that is required, or a legal action based on the contract. If that fails (or is unavailable), one may be able to bring suit under a local ordinance or a state nondiscrimination statute. Federal statutes and the Constitution may offer remedies at still higher levels. In unusual cases, one may (be forced to) resort to international human rights claims. (In Europe, the European Court of Human Rights provides an intermediate stage between national and international law. See section 11.3.A.) In addition, a victim of discrimination may claim moral (rather than legal) rights—as well as appeal to non-rights-based considerations of justice or righteousness.

One can—and usually does—go very far before explicit appeals to human rights become necessary. The "higher" claims are always available; one still *has* those rights. In practice, though, they rarely are appealed to until lower-level remedies have been tried (if not exhausted). An appeal to human rights usually testifies to the absence of enforceable positive (legal) rights and suggests that everything else has been tried and failed, leaving one with nothing else (except perhaps violence).[4] For example, homosexuals in the United States often claim a human right against discrimination because US courts have held that constitutional prohibitions of discrimination do not apply to sexual orientation. If rights are a sort of last resort, claimed only when things are not going well, human rights are a last resort in the realm of rights; no higher rights appeal is available.

Claims of human rights thus ultimately aim to be self-liquidating, giving the possession paradox a distinctive twist. Human rights claims characteristically seek to challenge or change existing institutions, practices, or norms—especially legal practices. Most often they seek to establish (or bring about more effective enforcement of) a parallel "lower" right. For example, claims of a human right to health care in the United States typically aim to create a legal right to health care. To the extent that such claims are politically effective, the need to make them in the future will be reduced or eliminated; the human rights claim will be replaced by a claim of ordinary legal rights.

A set of human rights thus can be seen as a standard of political legitimacy. The Universal Declaration of Human Rights, for example, presents itself as a "standard of achievement for all peoples and all nations." To the extent that governments protect human rights, they are legitimate.

No less importantly, though, human rights authorize and empower citizens to act to vindicate their rights, to insist that these standards be realized, and to struggle to create a world in which they enjoy (the objects of) their rights. Human rights claims express not merely aspirations, suggestions, requests, or laudable ideas, but rights-based demands for change.

We must therefore not fall into the trap of speaking of human rights as demands for rights; as what Joel Feinberg calls rights in a "manifesto sense" (1980: 153). Human rights do imply a manifesto for political change. That does not, however, make them any less truly rights. Claiming a human right, even when it also involves a demand to create or better enforce a parallel legal right, involves exercising a (human) right that one already has. And in contrast to other grounds on which legal rights might be demanded—for example, justice, utility, self-interest, or beneficence—human rights claims rest on a prior moral (and international legal) entitlement.

---

4. In some places, especially Europe, human rights have been incorporated into national law with the label "human rights." In such cases, we need to distinguish what we might call nationally legalized human rights from "human rights" as I am using the term here. The point I am making is the tendency for human rights to function as "above" ordinary national law.

Legal rights ground legal claims to protect already established legal enti-tlements. Human rights ground "higher," supra-legal claims (which often seek to strengthen or add to existing legal entitlements).[5] This makes human rights neither stronger nor weaker than other kinds of rights, just different. They are human (rather than legal) rights. If they did not function differently from legal rights there would be no need for them.[6]

3. Human Nature and Human Rights

Let us now turn from the "rights" to the "human" side of "human rights." This involves charting the complex relationship between human rights and "human nature."

Legal rights have the law as their source. Contracts create contractual rights. Human rights would appear to have humanity—"human nature"—as their source. With legal rights, though, we can point to statute or custom as the mechanism by which the right is created. With contractual rights we have the act of contracting. How does being human give one rights?

A. Needs and Capabilities

Human needs are a common candidate: "needs establish human rights" (Bay 1982); "a basic human need logically gives rise to a right" (Green 1981: 55); "it is legitimate and fruitful to regard instinctoid basic needs . . . as *rights*" (Maslow 1970: xiii).[7] Unfortunately, "human needs" is almost as obscure and controversial a notion as "human nature."

Science reveals a list of empirically validated needs that will not generate anything even approaching an adequate list of human rights. Even Christian Bay, probably the best-known advocate of a needs theory of human rights, admits that "it is premature to speak of any empirically established needs beyond sustenance and safety" (1977: 17). Conversely, Abraham Maslow, whose expansive conception of needs comes closest to being an adequate basis

---

5. Viewing human rights as international legal (rather than moral) rights requires adding "municipal" or "national" before "legal" in this and the preceding sentence.
6. This discussion, along with the earlier discussion of the possession paradox, implicitly criticizes the "legal positivist" claim that there are no rights without remedies and no remedies except those provided by law or the sovereign. The classic locus of this argument, which goes back at least to Hobbes, is Austin (1954 [1832]). Whatever the grounds for stipulating such a definition, it is inconsistent with ordinary usage and understandings. We have no difficulty understanding, and regularly make claims of, moral and unenforced (even unenforceable) rights. That a right is not legally enforceable often is an important fact about that right. It is a fact, though, about a right, not about some other kind of claim.
7. Compare Benn (1967), Pogge (2001 [1995]: 193), Gordon (1998: 728), Felice (2003: 45), Osiatynski (2007), London (2008: 68), and Miller (2011: 169).

for a plausible set of human rights, admits that "man's instinctoid tendencies, such as they are, are far weaker than cultural forces" (1970: 129; cf. 1971: 382–88).

Without grounding in hard empirical science, "needs" takes on a metaphorical or moral sense that quickly brings us back to philosophical wrangles over human nature.[8] There is nothing wrong with philosophical theory—as long as it does not masquerade as science. In fact, to understand the source of human rights we *must* turn to philosophy. The pseudoscientific dodge of needs will not do. In fact, it is positively dangerous to insist that rights are rooted in needs but then be unable to provide a list of needs adequate to produce an attractive set of human rights.

The idea of "human capabilities" has become increasingly popular in recent discussions of human rights.[9] There certainly are important links between rights and capabilities. "Human capabilities" may be somewhat less contentious than "human nature" (if only because somewhat narrower), but appeals to capabilities largely restate, rather than resolve, the problem of providing a source for human rights.

Leading proponents simply do not present capabilities as a ground for human rights. For example, Amartya Sen, who has done more than anyone to advance the idea of human capabilities, notes that "human rights and human capabilities have something of a common motivation, but they differ in many distinct ways" and argues that they "go well with each other, so long as we do not try to subsume either entirely within the other" (Sen 2005: 152, 163). Martha Nussbaum, the most prominent advocate of capabilities after Sen, argues for "defining the securing of rights in terms of capabilities" (Nussbaum 2003: 38; cf. Nussbaum 1997: 294). Capabilities, in other words, are a way to operationalize the enjoyment of human rights, not ground their substance. Polly Vizard (2007) even argues for defining capabilities in terms of human rights.

Many internationally recognized human rights simply are not fundamentally matters of capabilities. As Sen notes, many political rights "cannot be adequately analysed within the capability approach" (2005: 163). Human rights are fundamentally about human dignity not human capabilities—although it is plausible to see human capabilities as also rooted in human dignity, although derived from it by different means (Cf. Nussbaum 2000: 124, Vizard 2007: 247).

---

8. Needs have even been defined in terms of rights: "We can initially define human needs, in a *minimal* sense, as that amount of food, clean water, adequate shelter, access to health services, and educational opportunities to which every person is entitled by virtue of being born" (McHale and McHale 1979: 16).
9. See, for example, Nussbaum (1997, 2011), Sen (2004, 2005), Alexander (2004), Vizard (2007), Vizard, Fukuda-Parr, and Elson (2011), and Yao (2011: chap. 5).

The source of human rights is man's *moral* nature, which is only loosely linked to scientifically ascertainable needs and not adequately captured by the idea of human capabilities. The "human nature" that grounds human rights is a *prescriptive* moral account of human possibility. (Needs and capabilities are typically understood as descriptive.) The scientist's human nature says that beyond this we cannot go. The moral nature that grounds human rights says that beneath this we must not permit ourselves to fall.

Human rights are "needed" not for life but for a life of dignity, a life worthy of a human being. "There is a human right to x" implies that people who enjoy a right to x will live richer and more fully human lives—a notion that goes well beyond developing or realizing their "capabilities." Conversely, those unable to enjoy human rights will to that extent not merely see their capabilities diminished, they will be estranged from their moral nature.

B. Human Rights and the Social Construction of Human Nature

The scientist's human nature sets the "natural" outer limits of human possibility. Human potential, however, is widely variable: the world seems to be populated by at least as many potential rapists and murderers as potential saints. Society plays a central role in selecting which potentials—capabilities—will be realized.

Today this selection is significantly shaped by the practice of human rights, which are rooted in a substantive vision of man's moral nature. Human rights set the limits and requirements of social (especially state) action, but that action, guided by human rights, plays a major role in realizing that "nature." When human rights claims bring legal and political practice into line with their demands, they *create* the type of person posited in the underlying moral vision.

Just as an individual's "nature" or "character" arises from the interaction of natural endowment, social and environmental influences, and individual action, human beings create their "essential" nature through social action on themselves. Human rights provide both a substantive model and a set of practices to realize this work of self-creation.

"Human nature" is a social project rather than a pre-social given. Marx and Burke provide important examples of such a theory of human nature (see Donnelly 1985a: 37–44), clearly indicating that such a conception is not tied to any particular political perspective. Human rights theories and documents point beyond actual conditions of existence—beyond the "real" in the sense of what has already been realized—to the possible, which is viewed as a deeper human moral reality. Human rights are less about the way people are than about what they might become. They are about moral rather than natural or juridical persons.

The Universal Declaration of Human Rights, for example, tells us little about life in many countries. And where it does, that is in large measure because the rights enumerated in the Universal Declaration have shaped society in their image. Where theory and practice converge, it is largely because the posited rights have helped to construct society, and human beings, in their image. Where they diverge, claims of human rights point to the need to bring (legal and political) practice into line with (moral) theory.

The Universal Declaration, like any list of human rights, specifies minimum conditions for a dignified life, a life worthy of a human being. Even wealthy and powerful countries regularly fall far short of these requirements. As we have seen, though, his is precisely when, and perhaps even why, having human rights is so important: they demand, as a matter of entitlement (rights), the social changes required to realize the underlying moral vision of human nature.

Human rights are at once a utopian ideal and a realistic practice for implementing that ideal. They say, in effect, "Treat a person like a human being and you'll get a human being." They also, by enumerating a list of human rights, say, in effect, "Here's how you treat someone as a human being."

Human rights thus can be seen as a self-fulfilling moral prophecy: "Treat people like human beings—see attached list—and you will get truly human beings." The forward-looking moral vision of human nature provides the basis for the social changes implicit in claims of human rights. If the underlying vision of human nature is within the limits of "natural" possibility, and if the derivation of a list of rights is sound, then implementing those rights will make "real" that previously "ideal" nature.

Human rights seek to fuse moral vision and political practice. The relationship between human nature, human rights, and political society is "dialectical." Human rights shape political society, so as to shape human beings, so as to realize the possibilities of human nature, which provided the basis for these rights in the first place.

Human rights thus are constitutive no less than regulative rules and practices.[10] We are most immediately familiar with their regulative aspects: "No one shall be subjected to torture or to cruel, inhuman or degrading treatment or punishment"; "Everyone has the right to work, to free choice of employment, to just and favorable conditions of work and to protection against unemployment." No less importantly, however, human rights *constitute* individuals as a particular kind of political subject: free and equal rights-bearing citizens. And by defining the requirements and limits of legitimate government they constitute states of a particular kind.

In an earlier work (1985a: 31–43) I described this as a "constructivist" theory of human rights. One might also use the language of reflexivity. The

---

10. The classic formulation of this distinction is Rawls (1955), reprinted in Rawls (1999).

essential point is that "human nature" is seen as a moral posit rather than a fact of "nature" and as a social project rooted in the implementation of human rights. It is a combination of "natural," social, historical, and moral elements, conditioned, but not simply determined, by objective historical processes that it simultaneously helps to shape.

4. Human Rights and Related Practices

Human rights, as we have seen, are a particular type of social practice, founded on a particular conception of "being human," implemented by particular kinds of mechanisms. They must not be confused with other values and practices such as social justice, natural law, or moral duty.

We do not have human rights to all things that are good, or even to all important good things—and this is not only or even primarily because of the need to keep the Universal Declaration short. There are many good things that we not only *do* not but *should* not enjoy as matters of human rights. For example, we are not entitled—do not have (human) rights—to love, charity, or compassion. Parents who abuse the trust of children wreak havoc with millions of lives every day. We do not, however, have a human right to loving, supportive parents. In fact, to recognize such a right would transform family relations in ways that most people would find deeply unappealing, even destructive. Most good things simply are not the object of human rights.

The emphasis on human rights in contemporary international society thus implies selecting certain values for special emphasis. It also involves selecting a particular mechanism—rights—to advance those values.

As we saw above, human rights are not just abstract values such as liberty, equality, and security. They are rights, particular social practices to realize those values. A human right thus should not be confused with the values or aspirations underlying it or with enjoyment of the object of the right.

Human rights do not even provide a comprehensive account of social justice. Justice is particular as well as universal, and it is not entirely a matter of rights. Furthermore, as we will see in some detail below, human rights are but one historically very distinct way to conceptualize and attempt to realize social justice.

Human rights are a) the minimum set of goods, services, opportunities, and protections that are widely recognized today as essential prerequisites for a life of dignity, and b) a particular set of practices to realize those goods, services, opportunities, and protections. No more. But no less.

5. Analytic and Substantive Theories

The theory I have sketched so far is substantively empty—or, as I would prefer to say, conceptual, analytic, or formal. I have tried to describe the character of any human right, whatever its substance, and some of the basic features of the practice as a whole. I have yet to argue for the existence of even a single particular human right.

The obvious "solution" is to present and defend a theory of human nature linked to a particular set of human rights. Few issues in moral or political philosophy, however, are more contentious or intractable than theories of human nature. There are many well-developed and widely accepted philosophical anthropologies: for example, Aristotle's *zoon politikon*; Marx's "human natural being" who distinguishes himself by producing his own material life; Mill's pleasure-seeking, progressive being; Kant's rational being governed by an objective moral law; and feminist theories that begin by questioning the gendered conceptions of "man" in these and most other accounts. Each of us probably has a favorite that, up to a certain point, we would defend. There are few moral issues, though, where discussion typically proves less conclusive.

Philosophical anthropologies are much more like axioms than theorems. They are more assumed (or at best indirectly defended) starting points than the results of philosophical argument. This does not make substantive theories of human rights pointless or uninteresting. They are, however, contentious in ways, or at least to a degree, that a good analytic theory is not.

If we were faced with an array of competing and contradictory lists of human rights clamoring for either philosophical or political attention, failure to defend a particular theory of human nature might be a serious shortcoming. Fortunately, there is a remarkable international normative consensus on the list of rights contained in the Universal Declaration and the 1966 International Human Rights Covenants (the International Covenant on Economic, Social and Cultural Rights and the International Covenant on Civil and Political Rights). Furthermore, in the philosophical literature on lists of human rights there are really only two major issues of controversy (other than whether there are such things as human rights): the status of economic and social rights (which is addressed in section 3.1) and the issue of group human rights (addressed in section 3.2).

Finally, although it may sound perverse, let me suggest that the "emptiness" of a conceptual theory is one of its great attractions. Given that philosophical anthropologies are so controversial, there are great dangers in tying one's analysis of human rights to any particular theory of human nature. The account of human rights I have sketched above is compatible with many (but not all) theories of human nature. It is thus available to provide (relatively) "neutral" theoretical insight and guidance across (or within) a considerable range of positions.

A conceptual theory delimits a field of inquiry and provides a *relatively* uncontroversial (because substantively thin) starting point for analysis.[11] It also helps to clarify what is (and is not) at stake between competing substantive theories. Ultimately, however—in fact, rather quickly—we must move on to a substantive theory. And as soon as we do we must confront the notorious problem of philosophical "foundations."

6. The Failure of Foundational Appeals

In a weak, largely methodological sense of the term, every theory or social practice has a "foundation," a point beyond which there can be no answer to questions of "Why?" ("Because I'm the mom!") Usually, though, we talk about foundations in a strong, substantive sense as something "beyond" or "beneath" social convention or reasoned choice. A (strong) foundation can compel assent, not just ask for or induce agreement. In this sense, human rights have no foundation.

Historically, though, most human rights advocates and declarations have made foundational appeals. For example, both Locke and the American Declaration of Independence appealed to divine donation. The Universal Declaration of Human Rights makes an apparently foundational appeal to "the inherent dignity . . . of all members of the human family." Needs and capabilities, as we saw above, are often advanced today as an "objective" foundation.

Such grounds have often been accepted as persuasive. None, however, can through logic alone compel the agreement of a skeptic. Beyond the inevitable internal or "epistemological" challenges, foundational arguments are vulnerable to external or "ontological" critique.

Consider the claim that God gives us human rights. Questions such as "Are you sure?" or "How do you know that?" ask for evidence or logical argument. They pose (more or less difficult) challenges from within an accepted theoretical or ontological framework. The external question "What God?" raises a skeptical ontological challenge from outside that framework. To such questions there can be no decisive response.

"Foundational" arguments operate within (social, political, moral, and religious) communities that are defined in part by their acceptance of, or at least openness to, particular foundational arguments.[12] For example, all the major parties in the English Civil War took it for granted that God was a

---

11. A conceptual theory cannot be *entirely* empty. For example, "human" and "rights" are substantive moral concepts. They can, however, be effectively neutral notions in discussions across a considerable range of substantive theories.
12. The examples in this section are Western in part to emphasize that the issue has nothing to do with difference between cultures or civilizations (which are the subject of part 2).

central source of rights and that the Bible provided authoritative evidence for resolving political disputes. Their disagreements, violent as they ultimately became, were "internal" disputes over who spoke for God, when, and how, and what He desired. To English and Scottish Christians in the 1640s, asking whether God had granted political rights to kings, to men (and if so, which men), or both—and if both, how He wanted their competing claims to be resolved—was "natural," "obvious," even "unavoidable." But through argument alone they would have been unable to compel the assent of a skeptical atheist (had one dared raise a head).

Natural law theories today face much the same problem. For example, John Finnis's *Natural Law and Natural Rights* (1980) is a brilliant account of the implications of neo-Thomist natural law for questions of natural (human) rights. To those of us outside of that tradition, the "foundational" appeals to nature and reason are more or less attractive, interesting, or persuasive. But for Finnis, operating within that tradition, they are definitively compelling. Having accepted Finnis's starting point, we may be rationally compelled to accept his conclusions about natural rights.[13] But a skeptic cannot be compelled by reason alone to start there.

Consider Arthur Dyck's appeal to "the natural human relationships and responsibilities on which human rights are based" (1994: 13). His effort to ground human rights on "what is logically and functionally necessary, and universally so, for the existence and sustenance of communities" (1994: 123) fails because there is very little that is empirically universal about human communities, and almost nothing that is truly logically necessary for their existence. Dyck is really arguing about human communities *of a particular type*, specified in contentious normative—not empirical/descriptive—terms.[14]

Hadley Arkes, another contemporary natural law theorist, correctly identifies the situation when he writes of "The Axioms of Public Policy" (1998). Without accepting certain axiomatic propositions *that we are rationally free to reject*, no moral or political argument can go very far. Unfortunately, Arkes goes on to treat his axioms as if they were indisputable facts about the world.

Consider a very different example. The 1966 International Human Rights Covenants make a vague but clearly foundational appeal to "the inherent dignity of the human person." The very category "human being" or "human person," however, is contentious. Those who do not draw a sharp categorical distinction between *Homo sapiens* and other creatures (as, for example, in

13. More precisely, the debate shifts to internal ("epistemological") questions. For example, Maritain (1943) provides a somewhat different neo-Thomist derivation of human rights. Fortin (1982) offers a critique from within the Thomist camp that stresses the difference between natural rights and natural law. See also Fortin (1996).

14. Very similar problems are faced by efforts (e.g., Gewirth 1982; Griffin 2008) to root human rights in the capacity for agency, understood as an allegedly universal feature of human beings and human life.

classical Hindu cosmology and social theory) are not irrational, however sub-stantively misguided we may today take them to be. Neither are those who draw categorical moral distinctions between groups of human beings—as in fact most societies throughout most of history have done. Many societies have denied the moral centrality of our common humanity on grounds no less thoughtful or carefully justified than contemporary theories of univer-sal human rights. Even granting the moral category "human person," we face almost equally difficult problems specifying the nature and source of a per-son's putative "inherent dignity."

Moral and political arguments require a firm place to stand. That place appears firm, though, largely because we have agreed to treat it as such. "Foun-dations" ground a theory only through an inescapably contentious decision to *define* or *accept* such "foundations" as firm ground.[15]

"Foundational" arguments reflect contingent and contentious agreements to cut off certain kinds of questions. What counts as a "legitimate" question is itself unavoidably subject to legitimate (external) questioning. There is no strong foun-dation for human rights—or, what amounts to the same thing, there are multi-ple, often inconsistent "foundations," as we will see in more detail in section 4.2.

I will argue below that this is less of a practical problem than one might imagine. Nonetheless, it does counsel a certain degree of caution about the claims we make for human rights. Even if we consider ourselves morally com-pelled to recognize and respect human rights, we must remember that the simple fact that someone else (or another society) rejects human rights is not necessarily evidence of moral defect or even error.

7. Coping with Contentious Foundations

The common complaint that non-foundational theories leave human rights "vulnerable" is probably true but certainly irrelevant.[16] The "invulnerability" of a strong foundation is, if not entirely illusory, then conventional, a matter of agreement rather than proof. Foundations do provide reasoned assurance for moral beliefs and practices by allowing us to root particular arguments, rules, or practices in deeper principles. This reassurance, however, is a matter of internal consistency, not objective external validation.[17]

15. A useful analogy might be drawn with the "hard core" of a Lakatosian research program (1970, 1978).
16. See, for example, Freeman (1994), which gives considerable critical attention to my "relativist" position. I should perhaps note, though, that in conversation Freeman has indicated that he no longer holds these views in the strong form he presents them in this essay.
17. Even Alasdair MacIntyre, who remains committed to the idea of the rational superiority of particular systems of thought (1988: chaps. 17–19), in his Gifford Lectures (1990) speaks of Thomism as a tradition, and even titles one chapter of the book based on the lectures "Aquinas and the Rationality of Tradition." I take this to be very close to an admission that "foundations" operate only within discursive communities.

Chris Brown correctly notes that "virtually everything encompassed by the notion of 'human rights' is the subject of controversy. . . . the idea that individuals have, or should have, 'rights' is itself contentious, and the idea that rights could be attached to individuals by virtue solely of their common humanity is particularly subject to penetrating criticism" (1999: 103). But we can say precisely the same thing about all other moral and political ideas and practices. While recognizing that human rights are at their root conventional and controversial, we should not place more weight on this fact than it deserves. Problems of "circularity" or "vulnerability" are common to all moral concepts and practices. They are neither specific to human rights nor unusually severe in their case.

Human rights ultimately rest on a social decision to act as if such "things" existed—and then, through social action directed by these rights, to make real the world that they envision. This does not make human rights "arbitrary," in the sense that they rest on choices that might just as well have been random. Nor are they "*merely* conventional," in roughly the way that driving on the left is required in Britain. Like all social practices, human rights come with, and in an important sense require, justifications. Those justifications, however, appeal to "foundations" that ultimately are a matter of agreement or assumption rather than proof.

Moral arguments can be both uncertain in their foundations and powerful in their conclusions and implications. We can reasonably ask for good grounds for accepting, for example, the rights in the Universal Declaration of Human Rights. But such grounds—for example, their desirable consequences, their coherence with other moral ideas or practices, or the supporting authority of a revealed religious text—are not unassailable, and we must recognize that there are other good grounds not only for these principles and practices but also for different, even "competing," practices.

Faced with inescapably contending and contentious first principles, we not only can but should interrogate, evaluate, and judge our own. Working both "up" from "foundational" premises to particular conclusions and back "down" from particular practices, we can both explore the implications of foundational assumptions that have previously remained obscure and attempt to ascertain whether particular judgments and practices are "reasonable" or "well justified."[18] Through such work, moral progress, in a very real sense of that term, may be possible—consider the rethinking of slavery and colonialism in the Western world in the nineteenth and twentieth centuries—even if it is progress only within an ultimately conventional set of foundational assumptions.

The contentious nature of the foundations of substantive theories of human rights, however, does not make such theories any less necessary or

18. Compare John Rawls's notion of reflective equilibrium (Rawls 1971: 20–21, 48–51).

possible. Chapters 2 and 4 represent my effort to sketch the outlines of a substantive theory of human rights, thus providing substantive content to the analytic theory offered above. I do so by arguing that we have a variety of good (although not unassailable) moral and political reasons for accepting the system of human rights outlined in the Universal Declaration of Human Rights.

2

The Universal Declaration Model

This chapter begins to sketch a particular substantive theory of human rights that I call "the Universal Declaration model," in recognition of the central role of the 1948 Universal Declaration of Human Rights in establishing the contours of the contemporary consensus on internationally recognized human rights.[1] For the purposes of international action, "human rights" means roughly "what is in the Universal Declaration." I do not, for reasons outlined in the preceding chapter, attempt to give a philosophical account of human rights—let alone the "best" philosophical account. Rather, I treat the body of international human rights law as providing largely authoritative standards for all states in the contemporary world (compare sections 4.1 and 6.2.A). In this chapter I try to explicate the conceptual logic that underlies the Universal Declaration and the body of international human rights law to which it has given rise.

I. The Universal Declaration

Most of us today take human rights to be a normal and "obvious" part of international relations. In fact, however, such an understanding goes back only to the end of World War II.

The recognition of certain limited religious rights for some Christian minorities in the Peace of Westphalia (1648)—which brought the Thirty Years' War to an end and is usually seen as inaugurating modern international relations—can be seen, with the benefit of hindsight, as an early precursor of the idea of international human rights. In the nineteenth century, international campaigns against the slave trade and slavery had clear

---

1. The best study of the development and substance of the Universal Declaration is Morsink (1999). See also Samnoy (1993, 1999) and Eide et al. (1992).

overtones of what today we would call human rights advocacy. After World War I, workers' rights and minority rights were addressed by the newly created International Labor Organization and the League of Nations. Nonetheless, prior to World War II the very term "human rights" was largely absent from international discourse. For example, it is not mentioned in the Covenant of the League of Nations, which is usually seen as an expression of the "idealism" of the immediate post–World War I era. Even those who believed that all human beings had an extensive set of equal and inalienable rights—a distinctly minority idea in an era that had little trouble justifying colonialism—did not suggest that other states had rights or obligations with respect to those rights.

This changed decisively with the creation in 1945 of the United Nations, which took place in the shadow of not only an unusually vicious global war but also of the Holocaust. The preamble of the UN Charter lists as two of the four principal objectives of the organization "to reaffirm faith in fundamental human rights, in the dignity and worth of the human person, in the equal rights of men and women and of nations large and small" and "to promote social progress and better standards of life in larger freedom."[2] Likewise, Article 1 lists as one of the four purposes of the United Nations "to achieve international co-operation in solving international problems of an economic, social, cultural, or humanitarian character, and in promoting and encouraging respect for human rights and for fundamental freedoms for all without distinction as to race, sex, language, or religion." In 1946 the newly created United Nations Commission on Human Rights quickly began to give definition to these abstract statements of postwar optimism and goodwill.

The original commission was composed of eighteen elected members, generally representative of the then fifty-one members of the United Nations. Its first task was to draft an authoritative statement of international human rights norms, a task it undertook with both skill and speed. The initial drafts were written by John Humphrey, a young Canadian member of the commission's staff, and René Cassin, the French member of the commission. There was widespread participation, though, by non-Western representatives. The eight-member drafting committee included P.C. Chang of China (the vice chair of the commission), Charles Malik of Lebanon (the rapporteur of the commission), and Hernan Santa Cruz of Chile. Each, along with the commission chair, Eleanor Roosevelt of the United States, played a major role in shaping the Declaration.[3]

2. The other objectives are "to save succeeding generations from the scourge of war" and to establish conditions for the respect of international law.
3. See Morsink (1999: 28–34) and Samnoy (1990: chap. 7). On the important role of small and non-Western states, see Waltz (2001, 2002, 2004) and Glendon (2003).

After barely a year and a half of work, the commission had completed a short statement of principles, adopted as the Universal Declaration of Human Rights by the UN General Assembly on December 10, 1948. (December 10 is thus celebrated globally as Human Rights Day.) The vote was forty-eight in favor, none opposed, and eight abstentions.[4] Although most of Africa, much of Asia, and parts of the Americas were still under colonial rule, the Universal Declaration from the beginning had global endorsement. It received the votes of fourteen European and other Western states, nineteen states from Latin America, and fifteen from Africa and Asia. In other words, both African and Asian states and Western states provided just less than a third of the votes for the Universal Declaration. Furthermore, the countries that later achieved their independence were at least as enthusiastic in their embrace of the Declaration as those who voted for it in 1948.

There was no North-South split in 1948. Ashlid Samnoy (1990: 210) correctly notes that the debate in the United Nations in 1948 "gives an impression of a massive appreciation of the Declaration. The events were characterised as 'the most important document of the century' (Ecuador), 'a world milestone in the long struggle for human rights' (France), 'a decisive stage in the process of uniting a divided world' (Haiti), 'an epoch-making event' (Pakistan) and 'a justification of the very existence of the United Nations' (the Philippines)."

The 1966 International Human Rights Covenants—the International Covenant on Economic, Social and Cultural Rights (ICESCR) and the International Covenant on Civil and Political Rights (ICCPR)—give the force of treaty law to the Universal Declaration (which as a resolution of the UN General Assembly is not in itself directly binding in international law). A number of single-issue treaties have expanded considerably on particular rights (see section 11.4). The Universal Declaration, however, is unquestionably the foundational document of international human rights law. It establishes the basic parameters of the meaning of "human rights" in contemporary international relations—and (as I will argue in part 2) in national discussions as well.

2. The Universal Declaration Model

The Universal Declaration and the Covenants—together sometimes known as the International Bill of Human Rights—proclaim a short but substantial list of human rights. Table 2.1 identifies the rights recognized in these documents.

---

4. Saudi Arabia abstained principally because of provisions that allowed Muslims to change their religion. South Africa abstained because of the provisions on racial equality. The abstention of the six Soviet bloc states (USSR, Byelorussian SSR, Czechoslovakia, Poland, Ukrainian SSR, and Yugoslavia) was ostensibly because the document was insufficiently detailed and far-reaching.

In addition to the substance of these internationally recognized human rights, to which we will return in chapter 3, five structural features of the Universal Declaration model merit emphasis.

TABLE 2.1 INTERNATIONALLY RECOGNIZED HUMAN RIGHTS

The International Bill of Human Rights recognizes the rights to:
Equality of rights without discrimination (Dl, D2, E2, E3, C2, C3)
Life (D3, C6)
Liberty and security of person (D3, C9)
Protection against slavery (D4, C8)
Protection against torture and cruel and inhuman punishment (D5, C7)
Recognition as a person before the law (D6, C16)
Equal protection of the law (D7, C14, C26)
Access to legal remedies for rights violations (D8, C2)
Protection against arbitrary arrest or detention (D9, C9)
Hearing before an independent and impartial judiciary (D10, C14)
Presumption of innocence (D11, C14)
Protection against ex post facto laws (D11, C15)
Protection of privacy, family, and home (D12, C17)
Freedom of movement and residence (D13, C12)
Seek asylum from persecution (D14) Nationality (D15)
Marry and found a family (D16, E10, C23)
Own property (D17)
Freedom of thought, conscience, and religion (D18, C18)
Freedom of opinion, expression, and the press (D19, C19)
Freedom of assembly and association (D20, C21, C22)
Political participation (D21, C25)
Social security (D22, E9)
Work, under favorable conditions (D23, E6, E7)
Free trade unions (D23, E8, C22)
Rest and leisure (D24, E7)
Food, clothing, and housing (D25, E11)
Health care and social services (D25, E12)
Special protections for children (D25, E10, C24)
Education (D26, E13, E14)
Participation in cultural life (D27, E15)
A social and international order needed to realize rights (D28)
Self-determination (E11, C1)
Humane treatment when detained or imprisoned (C10)
Protection against debtor's prison (C11)
Protection against arbitrary expulsion of aliens (C13)
Protection against advocacy of racial or religious hatred (C20)
Protection of minority culture (C27)

Note: This list includes all rights that are enumerated in two of the three documents of the International Bill of Human Rights or have a full article in one document. The source of each right is indicated in parentheses, by document and article number. D = Universal Declaration of Human Rights. E = International Covenant on Economic, Social, and Cultural Rights. C = International Covenant on Civil and Political Rights.

First, human rights are rooted in a conception of human dignity. Section 3 looks briefly at this relationship, to which we will return in some historical detail in chapter 8.

Second, (universal) rights—entitlements—are the mechanism for implementing such values as nondiscrimination and an adequate standard of living. The implications of this choice have been discussed in chapter 1.

Third, all the rights in the Universal Declaration and the Covenants, with the exception of the right of peoples to self-determination, are rights of individuals, not corporate entities. Section 4 examines the logic behind this restriction and addresses some common misconceptions about individual human rights. The question of group (human) rights is taken up in section 3.2.

Fourth, internationally recognized human rights are treated as an interdependent and indivisible whole, rather than a menu from which one may freely select (or choose not to select). I discuss this idea briefly in section 5 and return to the most controversial aspect of this claim—namely, the equal status of economic, social, and cultural rights—in section 3.1.

Fifth, although these are universal rights, held equally by all human beings everywhere, states have near-exclusive responsibility to implement them for their own nationals. Sections 6 and 7 explore the special place of the state in the contemporary practice of human rights.

3. Human Dignity and Human Rights

Human dignity is the foundational concept of international human rights law, "the 'ultimate value' that gives coherence to human rights" (Hasson 2003: 83). The 1996 International Human Rights Covenants, in the second paragraphs of their preambles, proclaim that "these rights derive from the inherent dignity of the human person." The Vienna Declaration of the 1993 World Conference on Human Rights likewise affirms, also in its preamble's second paragraph, that "all human rights derive from the dignity and worth inherent in the human person." Such claims build on the opening words of the Universal Declaration: "recognition of the inherent dignity and of the equal and inalienable rights of all members of the human family is the foundation of freedom, justice and peace in the world." All of this can be traced back to the aim of the United Nations, as stated in the second paragraph of the preamble of the Charter, "to reaffirm faith in fundamental human rights, in the dignity and worth of the human person, in the equal rights of men and women and of nations large and small."

As one would expect from legal instruments, though, these documents are unclear as to the exact meaning of human dignity and how it gives rise to or grounds human rights. "We do not find an explicit definition of the expression 'dignity of the human person.' . . . Its intrinsic meaning has been left to intuitive understanding. . . . When it has been invoked in concrete situations, it has been generally assumed that a violation of human dignity can be recognized even if the abstract term cannot be defined" (Schachter 1983: 849; cf. Henkin 1992: 211; Beyleveld and Brownsword 2001: 11, 21). Although there are immense philosophical problems in grounding a conception of human dignity and deriving a list of human rights from it, for our purposes here—namely, understanding the logic of the Universal Declaration model— little more is required than noting this vague quasi-foundational appeal and explicating its basic terms.

Dignity indicates worth that demands respect. The first definition of "dignity" in the *Oxford English Dictionary* is "The quality of being worthy or honourable; worthiness, worth, nobleness, excellence." Other ethically and politically relevant senses include "honourable or high estate, position, or estimation; honour; degree of estimation, rank"; "*collect.* Persons of high estate or rank"; "an honourable office, rank, or title; a high official or titular position"; "*transf.* A person holding a high office or position; a dignitary"; and "nobility or befitting elevation of aspect, manner, or style; . . . stateliness, gravity."

As these definitions suggest—and as we will see in detail in chapter 8— dignity historically has usually been ascribed to an elite group. *Human dignity*—when linked with the idea that all members of the species *Homo sapiens* are human in the relevant sense—represents, in effect, the democratization of dignity. The claim of human dignity is that simply being human makes one worthy or deserving of respect; that there is an inherent worth that demands respect in all of us.

Human rights can thus be understood to specify certain forms of social respect—goods, services, opportunities, and protections owed to each person as a matter of rights—implied by this dignity. The practice of human rights provides a powerful mechanism to realize the dignity of the person. More precisely, as we will see below, human rights are one particular mechanism for realizing a certain class of conceptions of human dignity.

4. Individual Rights

With the exception of the right to self-determination, which I will ignore for the rest of this section, all the rights in the Universal Declaration and the Covenants are the rights of individuals. Enumerations typically begin "Every human being," "Everyone has the right," "No one shall be," and "Everyone is entitled." Even where we might expect groups to appear as right-holders, they do not. For example, Article 27 of the ICCPR reads, "In those States in which ethnic, religious or linguistic minorities exist, persons belonging to such minorities shall not be denied the right, in community with the other members of their group, to enjoy their own culture, to profess and practise their own religion, or to use their own language." Individuals belonging to minorities, not minorities (collective entities), have these rights. More generally, even where group membership is essential to the definition of a human right, the rights are held by individual members of protected groups— not the group as a collective entity. For example, individual workers (not workers as a group) hold workers' rights and individual women (not women as a group) are protected against gender discrimination.[5]

Society does have legitimate claims against individuals. Individuals do have important duties to society.[6] Many of those duties correspond to rights of society. From none of this, though, does it logically follow that society, or any social group, has *human* rights.

If human rights are the rights that one has simply as a human being, then only human beings have human rights. Because only individual persons are human beings, it would seem that only individuals can have human rights. Collectivities of all sorts have many and varied rights, but these are not human rights—unless we substantially recast the concept. It is worth taking seriously claims for radical revisions of the Universal Declaration model. This chapter, however, is restricted to explicating that model and beginning to lay out some of its attractions. (In the next chapter, I defend a strong general prejudice against group human rights.)

In addition to being separate persons, though, individuals are members of multiple communities and participants in many associations. Any plausible account of human dignity must include membership in society. To paraphrase Aristotle, outside of society, one would be either a god or a beast. As Hobbes put it, life would be solitary, poor, nasty, brutish, and short. Individual human rights no more require atomistic individualism than communitarianism requires reducing individuals to ciphers or cells that have no value apart from the organic whole of society. Quite the contrary, atomistic individuals cannot make for themselves a life worthy of human beings.

Rights-based societies can be, have been, and are societies, not aggregates of possessive, egoistic atoms.[7] Furthermore, the very ideas of respecting and

5. The partial exception (in addition to self-determination) is families, which are protected by a number of internationally recognized human rights. The human rights of families, however, apply only against the broader society. Furthermore, families may not exercise their rights in ways that infringe the human rights of their members (or any other persons). Families may not, for example, deny their adult members freedom of religion or the right to participate in politics.
6. These duties, however, are not a condition for the possession or even the enjoyment of human rights (except in some very limited instances, such as restrictions on the enjoyment of personal liberty of those convicted of serious crimes). One has the same human rights whether or not one discharges one's duties to society. One is a human being, and thus has the same human rights as any other human being, whether or not one is a good citizen or even a contributing member of society.
7. Howard (1995) emphasizes the compatibility of human rights and strong communities.

violating human rights rest on the idea of the individual as part of a larger social enterprise. Individual rights are a *social* practice that creates systems of obligations between individuals and groups of various sorts. A's right to x with respect to B establishes itself and operates through social relationships. Individual and group rights differ in who holds the right—individuals or corporate actors—not in their sociality.

The Universal Declaration envisions individuals deeply enmeshed in "natural" and voluntary groups ranging from families through the state. Furthermore, many individual human rights are characteristically exercised, and can only be enjoyed, through collective action. Political participation, social insurance, and free and compulsory primary education, for example, are incomprehensible in the absence of community. Freedom of association, obviously, is a right of collective action. Workers' rights, family rights, and minority rights are enjoyed by individuals as members of social groups or occupants of social roles.[8]

5. Interdependence and Indivisibility

The Universal Declaration model treats internationally recognized human rights holistically, as an indivisible structure of rights in which the value of each right is significantly augmented by the presence of many others. As Article 5 of the 1993 Vienna Declaration puts it, "All human rights are universal, indivisible and interdependent and interrelated."[9]

"Interdependence" suggests a functional relation between rights: they interact with one another to produce a whole that is more than the sum of its parts. For example, the right to life and the right to food are together worth far more than the sum of the two rights enjoyed separately. "Indivisibility" suggests that a life of dignity is not possible without something close to the full range of internationally recognized human rights. For example, having, say, 80 percent of your rights respected does not mean that you have pretty much a life of dignity but only that your dignity is being denied in a *relatively* narrow set of ways.

During the Cold War, this doctrine was regularly challenged. In particular, the relationship between civil and political and economic, social, and cultural rights was a matter of intense and lively, although not particularly productive or illuminating, controversy. Commentators and leaders in all Soviet bloc and most Third World countries regularly disparaged most civil

8. These rights, however, are universal in the sense that they refer to anyone who should happen to be in that class, the membership of which is in principle open to all (in the sense that it is not defined by achievement or ascription).
9. Whelan (2010) provides a thorough historical-theoretical survey of this idea. See also Nickel (2008).

and political rights. Conversely, many Anglo-American conservatives and philosophers—but, among states, significantly, only the government of the United States—disparaged most economic and social rights. Although such debates have largely receded from international discussions, in the United States a lingering suspicion of economic and social rights persists. For example, few mainstream politicians or commentators have addressed the ongoing crisis of health care in the United States in terms of a human right to health. Political discussions of "entitlements"—which are usually addressed to limiting, reducing, or eliminating them—usually treat social security, medical care, food, housing, and income assistance as matters contingently granted by the government rather than fundamental and overriding obligations imposed by universal human rights. I will thus address arguments against economic and social rights directly in section 3.1 and indirectly in chapter 14.

6. The State and International Human Rights

If human rights are held universally—that is, equally by all—one might imagine that they apply universally against all other individuals and groups. Such a conception is inherently plausible and in many ways morally attractive. It is not, however, the dominant contemporary understanding.

A. National Implementation of International Human Rights

Internationally recognized human rights impose obligations on, and are exercised against, sovereign territorial states. "Everyone has a right to x" in contemporary practice means that each state has the authority and responsibility to implement and protect the right to x within its territory. The Universal Declaration presents itself as "a common standard of achievement for all peoples and nations"—and the states that represent them. The Covenants create obligations only for states. And states have international human rights obligations only to *their own* nationals (and foreign nationals in their territory or otherwise subject to their jurisdiction or control).

Although human rights norms have been largely internationalized, their implementation remains almost exclusively national. As we will see in chapter 11, contemporary international (and regional) human rights regimes are supervisory mechanisms that monitor relations between states and citizens. They are not alternatives to a fundamentally statist conception of human rights. Even in the strong European regional human rights regime, the European Court of Human Rights regulates relations between states and their nationals or residents.

The centrality of states in the contemporary construction of international human rights is also clear in the substance of recognized rights. Some, most notably rights of political participation, are typically (although not universally) restricted to citizens. Many obligations—for example, to provide education and social insurance—apply only to residents. Virtually all apply to foreign nationals only while they are subject to the jurisdiction of that state.

Foreign states have no internationally recognized human rights obligation—or even a right—to protect foreign nationals abroad. They are not even at liberty to use more than persuasive means on behalf of foreign victims. Current norms of state sovereignty prohibit states from acting coercively abroad against virtually all violations of human rights—genocide being the exception that proves the rule (compare chapter 15).

This focus on state-citizen relations is also embedded in our ordinary language. A person beaten by the police has her human rights violated but we usually call it an ordinary crime, not a human rights violation, if she receives an otherwise identical beating at the hands of a thief or an irascible neighbor. Similarly, we draw a sharp categorical distinction when comparable suffering is inflicted on innocent civilians based on whether the perpetrator is (an agent of) one's own government or a foreign state—which produce, respectively, human rights violations and war crimes.

Although neither necessary nor inevitable, this state-centric conception of human rights has deep historical roots and reflects the central role of the sovereign state in modern politics. Since at least the sixteenth century, dynastic states, and later territorial nation-states, have struggled, with considerable success, to consolidate their internal authority over competing local powers. Simultaneously, early modern states struggled, with even greater success, to free themselves from imperial and papal authority. Their late modern successors have jealously, zealously, and (for all the talk of globalization) largely successfully fought attempts to reinstitute supranational authority.

With power and authority thus doubly concentrated, the modern state has emerged as both the principal threat to the enjoyment of human rights and the essential institution for their effective implementation and enforcement. Although human rights advocates have generally had an adversarial relationship with states, both sides of this relationship between the state and human rights require emphasis.

B. Principal Violator and Essential Protector

Early advocates of natural (human) rights emphasized keeping the state out of the private lives and property of its citizens. In later eras, workers, racial and religious minorities, women, and the colonized, among other dispossessed groups, asserted their human rights against states that appeared to them principally as instruments of repression and domination. In recent decades, most human rights advocates, as symbolized by the work of groups like Amnesty International, have focused on preventing state abuses of individual rights. Given the immense power and reach of the modern state, this emphasis on controlling state power has been (and remains) both prudent and productive.

The human rights strategy of control over the state has had two principal dimensions. Negatively, it prohibits a wide range of state interferences in the personal, social, and political lives of citizens, acting both individually and collectively. But in addition to carving out zones of state exclusion, human rights place the people above and in positive control of their government. Political authority is vested in a free citizenry endowed with extensive rights of political participation (rights to vote, freedom of association, free speech, etc.).

The state, though, precisely because of its political dominance in the contemporary world, is the central institution available for effectively implementing internationally recognized human rights. "Failed states" such as Somalia show that one of the few things as frightening as an efficiently repressive state is no state at all. Therefore, beyond preventing state-based wrongs, human rights require the state to provide certain (civil, political, economic, social, and cultural) goods, services, opportunities, and protections.

This more positive human rights vision of the state also goes back to seventeenth- and eighteenth-century social contract theories. Locke, for example, emphasizes that natural rights cannot be effectively enjoyed in a state of nature. In fact, society and government are not only essential to the enjoyment of natural or human rights, the legitimacy of a state, within the contractarian tradition, can largely be measured by the extent to which it implements and protects natural rights.

The essential role of the state in securing the enjoyment of human rights is, if anything, even clearer when we turn from theory to practice. The struggle of dispossessed groups has typically been a struggle for full legal and political recognition by the state, and thus equal inclusion among those whose rights the state protects. Opponents of racial, religious, ethnic, and gender discrimination, political persecution, torture, disappearances, and massacre typically have sought not simply to end abuses but to transform the state from a predator into a protector of rights.

The need for an active state has always been especially clear for economic and social human rights. Even early bourgeois arguments emphasizing the natural right to property stressed the importance of active state protection. In fact, the "classic" liberalism of the eighteenth and nineteenth centuries saw the state as in large measure a mechanism to give legal form and protection to private property rights. Since the late nineteenth century, as our conceptions of the proper range of economic and social rights have expanded, the politics of economic and social rights has emphasized state provision where market and family mechanisms fail to assure enjoyment of these rights.

A positive role for the state, however, is no less central to civil and political rights. For example, implementing the right to nondiscrimination often requires extensive positive actions to realize the underlying value of equality. Even procedural rights such as due process entail substantial positive endeavors with respect to police, courts, and administrative procedures. Free, fair, and open elections do not happen through state restraint and inaction.

Because human rights first emerged in an era of personal, and thus often arbitrary, rule, an initial emphasis on individual liberty and state restraint was understandable. As the intrusive and coercive powers of the state have grown—steadily, and to now frightening dimensions—an emphasis on controlling the state continues to make immense political sense. The language of human rights abuses and violations continues, quite properly, to focus our attention on combating active state threats to human rights.

Nonetheless, a state that does no active harm itself is not enough. The state must also protect individuals against abuses by other individuals and private groups. The right to personal security, for example, is about safety against physical assaults by private actors, not just attacks by agents of the state. The state, although needing to be tamed, is today the principal institution we rely on to discipline social forces no less dangerous to the rights, interests, and dignity of individuals, families, and communities.

Other strategies have been tried or proposed to control the destructive capacities of the state and harness its capabilities to realize important human goods and values. The virtue or wisdom of leaders, party members, or clerics, the expertise of technocrats, and the special skills and social position of the military have seemed to many to be attractive alternatives to human rights as bases of political order and legitimacy. But the human rights approach of individual rights and popular empowerment has proved far more effective than any alternative yet tried—or at least that is how I read the remarkably consistent collapse of dictatorships of the left and right alike over the past three decades in Latin America, Central and Eastern Europe, Africa, Asia, and (it now seems finally) the Middle East.

Most of the alternatives to human rights treat people, if not as objects (rather than as agents), then at best as beneficiaries (rather than right-holders). They rest on an inegalitarian and paternalistic view of the average person as someone to be provided for; a passive recipient of benefits, rather than a creative agent with rights to shape his or her life. Thus even if we overlook their naively benign view of power and the state, they grossly undervalue both autonomy and participation. To use the language that I develop in chapter 4, they fail to treat citizens with equal concern and respect. That requirement is the substantive core of the Universal Declaration model.

7. Respecting, Protecting, and Providing Human Rights

A different way to look at the special role of the state is in terms of the differential social allocation of the duties correlative to human rights. Slightly modifying Henry Shue's classic analysis (1980: 52–60, 1984), we can identify duties (1) to respect the right (or not to deprive the right-holder of the enjoyment of her right), (2) to protect against deprivation, (3) to provide what is necessary to ensure that right-holders are able to enjoy their rights, and (4) to aid the deprived.[10] Duties to respect (to not deprive) are held by all social actors. In the contemporary world, however, duties to protect, to provide, and to aid are assigned almost exclusively to states, creating the system of national implementation of internationally recognized human rights noted above.

The language of entitlement and claims draws our attention conceptually toward the duty to respect (to not deprive) and practically toward the duty to protect against deprivation. To the extent that duties to provide are contemplated, emphasis tends to be placed on adversarial processes that culminate in "legal remedy"—that is, a system of authoritative and effective adjudication. Even the most superficial reflection, however, reveals that most of the work of protection, and virtually all the work of provision, takes place far from courts. A social provision focus shifts our attention to the duty to provide (and where necessary to aid the deprived).

I do not mean to belittle the role of courts and legal remedy.[11] Rights are indeed likely to be well guaranteed where right-holders can challenge deprivations of their rights through fair and impartial courts whose judgments are reliably implemented. This, however, is only the tip of the iceberg. Even where law is arguably the single most important institution assuring the effective enjoyment of human rights, this is largely because "the law" is embedded in or built on top of a complex system of social provision of rights.

A social provision perspective also remains open to multiple mechanisms of provision. The state is required only to guarantee internationally

10. In international legal discussions of economic, social, and cultural rights, it has become conventional to talk of duties to protect, to respect, and to fulfill. See, for example, Guideline 6 of the 1997 Maastricht Guidelines on Violations of Economic, Social and Cultural Rights (University of Minnesota Human Rights Library, http://www1.umn.edu/humanrts/instree/Maastrichtguidelines_.html).
11. For a variety of perspectives on the "legalization" of human rights, see Meckled-Garcia and Cali (2005). The title of my essay in that volume, "The Virtues of Legalization" (Donnelly 2005), makes it clear that I am no critic of law as a mechanism to realize human rights. But law alone is never enough. And legal mechanisms have been given inordinate overrepresentation—or, perhaps more accurately, nonlegal mechanisms have not been given sufficient attention.

recognized human rights; that is, to create a system of social provision. It is not required—and in no society does it—directly perform all the work of protection and provision. Much the same is true of duties to aid the deprived (although in practice such duties tend to be discharged directly by the state).

Consider "the right to security in the event of unemployment, sickness, disability, widowhood, old age or other lack of livelihood in circumstances beyond his control" (Universal Declaration, Article 25[1]). Duties to not deprive will rarely be of much significance; active deprivation of social security is likely to occur only through violations of other rights (e.g., assault or theft). Even duties to protect from deprivation are of secondary significance. The right to social security is fundamentally about assuring that one has available—if necessary, is provided with—the financial and other resources needed to lead a minimally dignified life when confronted with unemployment, old age, etc.

How, though, is this to be accomplished? Different societies and states have had "social security systems" that have relied to varying degrees on family, society, state, and self-provisioning. Historically, the family has been the principal social security mechanism. "Society" often has an obligation—for example, through religious organizations or through a redistributive social norm obliging the wealthy to assist those in need. Patron-client relations are another common "societal" mechanism. Over the past half century, the state in many countries has played a central role. But even in countries with developed market economies, family provision is an essential element of the system of social guarantees. In many countries, self-provisioning, through savings and private insurance and investment schemes, is an important part of the picture. Employers, through "private" pension schemes, also sometimes play an important role.

The practical heart of the human right to social security is the obligation of the state to assure that some system of provision is in place that gives everyone a reasonable guarantee of social security. Whoever actually provides the necessary goods and services, the state is obliged to assure that citizens are provided with social security. The state, though, has a considerable margin of appreciation in allocating particular elements of the general duties to protect and to provide to different social actors.

Social provision is no less important for civil and political rights, many of which involve primarily duties to provide. Consider the right to a government chosen by "periodic and genuine elections" carried out with "universal and equal suffrage" (Universal Declaration, Article 21[3]). The principal duty correlative to this right is the obligation of the state to stage and to administer elections that are free, fair, and open (to all candidates and all voters). Other actors—e.g., poll watchers or international election monitors—may be incorporated into the process to strengthen its integrity. The state must vigilantly protect all citizens from private efforts to coercively discourage or prevent them from participating. For the most part, though, the state's basic obligation is to run—that is, to provide—clean elections.

Other civil and political rights emphasize protection. For example, Article 5 of the Universal Declaration declares, "No one shall be subjected to torture or to cruel, inhuman or degrading treatment or punishment." Citizens have not merely a right not to be tortured (correlative to the duty to not deprive) but also a right to be protected against deprivation. The practicalities of assuring such protection point also to the duty to provide—in this case, through institutions and practices that protect detained suspects against abuse.

Consider also the right to security of person (Article 3). In the contemporary world of states, duties to protect personal security are largely carried out by the police and courts. Nonstate societies, however, rely (by definition) on other social institutions, usually including a substantial element of "self-help." In all societies, families, neighbors, and friends play a supporting role and individual right-holders are expected to exercise a certain degree of prudence.

In the contemporary United States, for example, private security services and neighborhood watch organizations have become an important part of the system for those able to afford or to organize them. Urban gangs, in addition to their criminal activities and other social functions, often provide some elements of neighborhood security. Individuals have been forced to take a variety of personal measures—installing better locks and alarms, exercising more caution when walking in certain areas, choosing where one lives on the basis of neighborhood and building security—to "supplement" state efforts. Many large Third World cities reveal a similar dynamic. Rio de Janeiro is an often-cited example.

Such self-help or self-provisioning mechanisms sometimes operate effectively. Often—more often, I suspect—they do not. In thinking about the social provision of human rights, we need to be open to considering the full range, and various mixtures, of "private" and state provision. The results produced by the system of provision as a whole are the measure of whether a state is adequately discharging its human rights obligations.

Assuring effective enjoyment of one's rights is the bottom line for civil and political rights and economic and social rights alike. In most instances, this will require multiple social actors discharging a variety of duties. The state need not be, and often is not, the only or even the principal provider. Nonetheless, the state has primary and ultimate responsibility for implementing an effective system of universal (national) provision.

8. Realizing Human Rights and Human Dignity

The practice of human rights is about realizing the dignity that is inherent in us as human beings. Although none of this is independent of resources, every state, no matter how poor, can and must respect all internationally recognized human rights. What counts as, for example, "the guarantees necessary for [a criminal defendant's] defense" or "necessary social services" will vary with national resources, but each and every country—from Sweden to Somalia—can and must implement each and every human right.

The demands of human rights thus are constantly escalating. A quantity and quality of, say, health care or legal services appropriate for a country at one point in its history will not be adequate to meet the same human rights obligations of that same country when its government has access to substantially greater resources. Viewed from a more psychological perspective, what satisfied the demands for human rights of our great grandparents would in many ways be considered inadequate for us today, and what we accept today will probably appear to our great grandchildren as in many ways far too restricted.

Every state can make substantial progress at realizing human rights with its existing resources. But every state also always has more to do to realize human rights—and the underlying vision of a life of dignity.

3

Economic Rights and Group Rights

There have been two principal challenges to the Universal Declaration model. Many Anglo-American political conservatives, and some philosophers, have challenged the status of economic and social rights, and many, especially on the political left and in the global South, have challenged the restriction of internationally recognized human rights almost exclusively to individual rights. This chapter considers these two challenges. Readers who wish to get on with the further development of my argument—rather than pause to pursue the more controversial elements of the Universal Declaration model—may reasonably choose to skip this chapter, in whole or in part, or come back to it later.

I. The Status of Economic and Social Rights

In international discussions it has become almost a reflex to talk of "civil and political rights" and "economic, social, and cultural rights." Although I too occasionally use these categories, they are seriously misleading. A dichotomous division of any complex reality is likely to be crude and easily (mis)read to suggest that the two categories are antithetical. This is especially true because this particular dichotomy was born of political controversy, first in working-class political struggles in the nineteenth and early twentieth centuries and then in Cold War ideological rivalry. The argument against economic and social rights, however, has also been philosophical. And it is of considerable immediate political relevance, especially in the United States.

A. Universality and Paramountcy

Maurice Cranston offers the most widely cited argument that, whereas traditional civil and political rights to life, liberty, and property are "universal, paramount, categorical moral rights" (1964: 40), economic and social rights "belong to a different logical category" (1964: 54)—that is, are not truly human rights.[1] As chapter 1 suggests, I accept universality and paramountcy as central indicators of rights that might appropriately be considered human rights. Cranston, however, is simply wrong that internationally recognized economic, social, and cultural rights fail to meet these tests.

Cranston notes that the right to work, like many other economic and social rights, refers directly to a particular class of people, not to all human beings (1973: 67). Many civil and political rights, however, also fail such a test of universality. For example, only citizens who have attained a certain age and completed any necessary formalities of registration have the right to vote.[2]

As for lack of paramountcy, Cranston singles out the right to periodic holidays with pay (1973: 66–67). Such a right, however, is no less important than, say, the right of juveniles to separate prison facilities, which is recognized in the International Covenant on Civil and Political Rights. Questions concerning paramountcy arise in both cases because we are dealing with a small part of a much broader right. In the case of paid holidays, the full right recognized is a right to "rest, leisure, and reasonable limitation of working hours and periodic holidays with pay." Denial of this right would indeed be a serious affront to human dignity. It was, for example, one of the most oppressive features of unregulated nineteenth-century capitalism.

In any case, the right of periodic holidays with pay is hardly the typical economic and social right. For example, in an industrial or postindustrial economy, the right to work is as important as most basic civil and political rights; the psychological, physical, and moral effects of prolonged enforced unemployment may be as severe as those associated with denial of freedom of speech. A right to education may be as essential to a life of dignity as freedom of speech or religion. Economic and social rights to food and health care may be as essential for protecting life as the civil or political right to life.

Cranston's appeal to (im)practicality is more complex. "'Political rights' can be readily secured by legislation. The economic and social rights can rarely, if ever, be secured by legislation alone" (1964: 37).[3] In fact, however, no right can be reliably realized through legislation alone. Unless legislation is backed by enforcement, the right is likely to be legally and politically insecure.

Cranston claims that "there is nothing essentially difficult about transforming political and civil rights into positive rights," whereas realizing economic

1. Cranston goes so far as to claim that such rights "[do] not make sense," that claims of such rights probably are not even "intelligible" (1973: 65, 69).
2. These rights remain universal, however, in the sense that the class is in principle open to all human beings.
3. Cranston even claims that civil and political rights "generally . . . can be secured by fairly simple legislation" (1973: 66).

and social rights is "utterly impossible" in most countries (1973: 66). Similarly, an article in the *Economist* argues that "to guarantee civil and political rights is relatively cheap, whereas to guarantee economic and social rights is potentially enormously costly" (2001: 20). Hugo Adam Bedau likewise advances what he calls an "argument from indifference to economic contingencies" (1979: 36–37).

In fact, however, there are severe impediments to establishing an effective positive right to, say, freedom of speech, press, or assembly in North Korea, Zimbabwe, Cuba, or China. Only in particular kinds of political circumstances—for example, where there has already been considerable progress in implementing many internationally recognized human rights—are civil and political rights likely to be systematically easier to implement. Even then, the differences are more matters of degree than kind, and they vary considerably from right to right and with time and place.

If we insist on the standards of Sweden, it may not be false to say that realizing most economic and social rights is "impossible" in most countries. But northern European standards for civil and political rights would be nearly as "impossible." Furthermore, it seems odd to me to suggest that something is a real human right only if it is relatively easy to implement. Ease of implementation is certainly irrelevant to determining moral paramountcy.

Because rights impose correlative duties and, as the old moral maxim puts it, "ought implies can"—no one has an obligation to attempt what is truly impossible—Cranston argues that it is logically incoherent to hold that economic and social "rights" are anything more than utopian aspirations (1973: 68). But the "can" in "ought implies can" refers to physical impossibility; unless it is physically impossible, one may still be obliged to try to do something that proves to be "impossible." The impediments to implementing most economic and social rights, however, are political. For example, there is more than enough food in the world to feed everyone; widespread hunger and malnutrition exist not because of a physical shortage of food but because of political decisions about its distribution.[4]

B. "Positive" and "Negative" Rights

Underlying many criticisms of economic and social rights is the distinction between "negative" rights, which require only forbearance on the part of others, and "positive" rights, which require others to provide goods, services, or opportunities. Henry Shue (1979, 1980), however, has shown that this distinction is of little moral significance and in any case fails to correspond to the distinction between civil and political and economic and social rights.

---

4. In fact, contemporary famines occur in places where there is enough food for everyone within the borders of the famine-stricken country (Sen 1981; Dreze and Sen 1990).

The right to protection against torture is usually advanced as the archetypal negative right: it requires "nothing more" than that the state refrain from incursions on personal liberty and bodily integrity. But providing protection against torture always requires positive endeavors by the state. Guaranteeing this "negative" right as a practical political matter requires major "positive" programs to train, supervise, and control the police and security forces. In many countries this would be not only extremely expensive but also politically "impossible" (without changing the regime).

Conversely, in some circumstances government inaction may be the key to realizing the positive-sounding right to food. Consider development programs that have encouraged producing cash crops for export rather than traditional food crops for local consumption. In such cases, the right to food would have been better realized if the government had done "nothing more" than refrain from interfering with agricultural incentives.

All human rights require both positive action and restraint on the part of the state. Furthermore, whether a right is relatively positive or negative usually depends on historically contingent circumstances. For example, the right to food is more of a negative right in the wheat fields of Kansas than on the streets of East Los Angeles. Equal protection of the laws is more positive in the South Bronx than in Stockholm. In Argentina, protection against torture was a very positive right indeed in the late 1970s. Today it is a much more negative right.

But even if all civil and political rights were entirely negative they would not therefore deserve priority. Cranston (1964: 38) and Bedau (1979: 38) suggest that "negative" civil and political rights deserve priority because their violation involves the direct infliction of injury (an act of commission), whereas violating "positive" economic and social rights usually involves only the failure to confer a benefit (acts of omission). Even accepting this false description of the rights, Shue shows that often there is little moral difference.

Imagine a man stranded on an out-of-the-way desert island with neither food nor water. A sailor from a passing ship comes ashore but leaves the man to die. This act of omission is as serious a violation of human rights as strangling him, an act of commission. It is killing him, plain and simple—indirectly through "inaction" but just as surely, and perhaps even more cruelly (Shue 1979: 72–75). Doing it actively and directly may be in some ways worse, but doing it passively or indirectly is no less homicide—at least from a moral perspective and especially insofar as the killing is either intended, anticipated, or readily predictable.

C. The Right to Property

Finally, we can note that most critics of economic and social rights do not in fact reject all such rights. Quite the contrary, almost all accept a right to private property.

For example, Cranston, like Locke, offers a list of exactly three basic human rights, to life, liberty, and property ("estates" in Locke's older terminology).[5] But rather than challenge the status of the economic human right to private property,[6] Cranston concludes his property chapter by insisting that property "is inseparable from liberty" (1973: 50). Enough food to remain alive and guaranteed rest and leisure, however, are also inseparable from liberty, but Cranston denies human rights to these things. That x is essential to the enjoyment of y to which we have a human rights does not make y a human right.

Furthermore, there is no plausible theoretical ground that yields precisely this one economic right. For example, property is often defended because it provides needed resources and space for the effective exercise of liberty. A right to work, however, would seem at least as plausible a way to assure resources for every person, given what we know about the tendency of private property to be very unevenly distributed and readily alienated in most legal systems. A limited right to property can make an important contribution to a life of dignity. This single economic right alone, however, simply cannot provide economic security and autonomy for all. In fact, for many people—in the Western world, most people, whose principal "property" is their labor power or skills—other economic and social rights would seem to be a better mechanism to realize economic security and autonomy.

D. Transcending the Dichotomy

The conventional dichotomy also obscures the immense diversity within each of its two classes. Consider civil and political rights. Rights to life, protection against discrimination, prohibition of slavery, recognition before the law, protection against torture, and nationality protect the bodily, legal, and moral integrity of individuals. Rights to habeas corpus, protection against arbitrary arrest and detention, the presumption of innocence, and protection against ex post facto laws provide procedural guarantees for individuals in their dealings with the legal system. The rights to freedom of thought, conscience, speech, press, association, and assembly define both a private sphere of conscience and belief and a public space in which these "private" issues, as well as public concerns, can be freely discussed, criticized, and advocated. The right to popular participation in government, and many public aspects of

---

5. From a more explicitly libertarian perspective, Tibor Machan devotes considerable effort to arguing for "the nonexistence of basic welfare rights" (1989: 100–123, 193–205) while giving centrality of place in his scheme to the right to property. Cf. Boaz (1997: 60–68).
6. This suggests that Cranston, quite bizarrely, considers private property a civil or political right (cf. Machan 1999: 4, 86; Yates 1995: 123). But if private property is not an economic right—and an often extravagant one at that—it is hard to imagine what is.

civil liberties such as the freedoms of speech, press, and assembly, empower citizens to participate in politics and exercise some control over the state.

Economic, social, and cultural rights are no less varied. The rights to food and health care provide survival and minimal physical security against disease or injury. Rights to social security, work, rest and leisure, and trade unions reflect not only the material necessity of labor but also the fact that meaningful work often is central to personal dignity and development. The rights to education, to found and maintain a family, and to participate in the cultural life of the community provide social and cultural membership and participation.

There are also striking affinities across the conventional categories. The right to work, for example, is a right to economic participation that is instrumentally and intrinsically valuable in ways very much like the right to political participation. Cultural rights are perhaps most closely related to individual civil liberties, given the integral place of religion, public speech, and the mass media in the cultural life of most communities. The "social" or "cultural" right to education is intimately connected with the "civil" or "political" rights to freedom of speech, belief, and opinion.

Our lives—and the rights we need to live them with dignity—do not fall into largely separate legal-political and socioeconomic spheres. Economic and social rights usually are violated by, or with the collusion of, elite-controlled political mechanisms of exclusion and domination. Poverty in the midst of plenty is a political phenomenon. Civil and political rights are often violated to protect economic privilege. We must think about and categorize human rights in ways that highlight rather than obscure such central social realities.

How one thinks about human rights cannot determine political practice. Nonetheless, certain ways of thinking, such as the traditional dichotomy, can help to support widely prevalent patterns of human rights violations. In every country where ruling elites have been able to enforce such a dichotomization, the consequence has been the systematic violation of a wide range of internationally recognized human rights.[7] Conversely, well-conceived theory, even at the very basic level of classificatory schemes, can aid in the struggle for greater respect for human rights.

2. Group Rights and Human Rights

A standard complaint about human rights is that they are excessively individualistic. Group (human) rights are frequently advanced as a remedy.

---

7. As an American, I want to note explicitly that this includes the United States, where economic and social rights are systematically violated in significant measure because they still are seen as not really matters of basic rights but considerations of justice, charity, or utility.

In this section, I defend the restriction of internationally recognized human rights to individual rights, with only a few rare exceptions. Although group-based suffering is a very real and serious problem, I argue that individual rights approaches usually are capable of accommodating the legitimate interests of even oppressed groups—and that where they are not, group human rights rarely will be more likely to provide an effective remedy.

A. Individual Rights and Group Difference

Just as individual human rights do not presume atomized individuals, they do not presume either identical or merely abstract individuals. They are fully compatible with—and in fact regularly used to protect—individual and group difference. They simply do so in a particular way, relying on two principal mechanisms: nondiscrimination and freedom of association and participation.

Individual rights approaches to group difference rest on the idea that group affiliations—other than membership in the species *Homo sapiens*—ought to be irrelevant to the rights and opportunities available to human beings. Therefore, a central focus is protecting members of despised or disadvantaged groups against discrimination based on group membership. There are at least three general approaches to nondiscrimination, which I will call toleration, equal protection, and multiculturalism.

Toleration involves not imposing special legal burdens or disabilities on individuals based on voluntary, ascriptive, or imposed group membership or disapproved behavior associated with a group. Groups and their members may still be *socially* marginalized and even despised. Others are required merely to tolerate, not positively (or even neutrally) value the group or behavior in question.

Equal protection requires active efforts to insure that members of all groups enjoy the (equal) rights that they formally hold. At minimum this requires efforts to assure that people are not excluded from goods, services, and opportunities that would be available to them were they not members of despised or disadvantaged groups. In its stronger forms—"affirmative action" and certain kinds of "reverse discrimination"—equal protection seeks to assure that members of targeted groups achieve full legal and political incorporation into society.

Equal protection, however, allows a neutral, even negative, evaluation of diversity. "Multiculturalism" positively values diversity, implying policies that recognize, celebrate, preserve, or foster group differences. Rather than attempt to abstract from group differences, as in toleration and equal treatment, those differences are highlighted and positively valued, within a general context of equal concern and respect.

Each of these is a plausible (although controversial) interpretation of the concept of nondiscrimination.[8] Different states are free to choose among them, for a variety of reasons, and particular groups and their differences may reasonably be addressed by different approaches within a particular country. For example, it would be completely consistent with international human rights standards for a state to merely tolerate one minority religion while actively supporting the majority religion and a different minority religion. Such decisions fall within the margin of appreciation left to states by the broadly stated norms of the Universal Declaration (see section 6.3). States may choose to treat all religions identically—for example, no state support for any, as in the United States—but that is not required.

The general approach, as Michael Walzer nicely puts it in discussing liberalism, is "permissive, not determinative." It "allows for a state committed to the survival and flourishing of a particular nation, culture, or religion, or of a (limited) set of nations, cultures, and religions—so long as the basic rights of citizens who have different commitments or no such commitments at all are protected" (1994: 99–100). There is not merely a place for group difference within the structure of individual human rights, the protection of many forms of difference is one of the most important objectives of the Universal Declaration model—because (but only to the extent that) citizens value and seek to create for themselves lives that produce such diversity.

Nondiscrimination, however, is only one part of an individual rights approach to group difference. Remedying systematic discrimination usually requires collective action, which in the Universal Declaration model is enabled by rights to freedom of association and to economic, social, cultural, and political participation. Nondiscrimination protects a sphere of personal and group liberty and offers protection against suffering imposed for group membership. Freedom of association and rights of participation entitle individuals to act, alone or with others of their choosing, to realize their visions of the good life. Taken together they provide a wide-ranging and coherent set of protections for groups and individuals rooted in the core values of equality and autonomy, which are addressed in chapter 4.

Freedom of association, because it is a right of individuals, models group membership as a "voluntary" exercise of the protected autonomy of its members. Descriptively, this is obviously inaccurate for groups whose identity is in significant measure externally imposed. It may also be problematic for groups marked by biological signs such as skin color or sex—although, it must be emphasized, race and gender are social constructs not natural categories. Nonetheless, an individual rights approach has considerable leverage even in such cases. For all its problems, a vision of group membership as

8. I offer a broader discussion of the idea of interpretations of human rights concepts in section 6.3.

a voluntary exercise of protected individual autonomy challenges coercively imposed ascriptive identities, denies the naturalness of difference, and insists that group membership ought to be irrelevant to the concern and respect one receives from the state.

B. Group Rights and Group *Human* Rights

Even accepting the above arguments, one might still argue for augmenting individual human rights with group human rights. Group human rights thus understood would supplement, perhaps even complete, the Universal Declaration model by providing a more adequate vision of, and protections for, human dignity in the contemporary world. In the following sub-section I pose seven questions that I think should lead us to be extremely wary of such a move. Here I want to clarify the terms of reference.

Group rights, in any strong sense of that term, are rights held by a corporate entity that is not reducible to its individual members. A state, for example, has a corporate identity distinct from that of its citizens—the national interest is not the sum or the average of the interests of the nation's citizens—and states, as groups, have many rights. Business corporations similarly are not reducible to their stockholders or staff and have a considerable range of rights. Families, trade unions, NGOs, and bowling leagues also are irreducible groups with rights.[9]

For a group right to be a *human* right, it must be universal in the sense that all groups of the specified type have that right. Although few candidate groups meet this test, international human rights law does unambiguously recognize one group human right: the right of peoples to self-determination. I have stipulated international human rights law as providing an authoritative list of internationally recognized human rights. Therefore, I am committed methodologically to recognizing the right of peoples to self-determination.[10] But there is also a strong substantive argument to be made for a group right to self-determination.

In a system of national implementation of internationally recognized human rights, one enjoys one's human rights through the agency of "one's

---

9. It simply is empirically false to deny that many groups have a distinct corporate identity. "Methodological individualism"—the view that only individuals are real (and thus groups are reducible to their members)—is either an analytically convenient representation or a prescriptive philosophical position inconsistent with the manifest reality of groups as irreducible corporate entities.

10. More precisely, the so-called right of peoples to self-determination is, in practice, a right of peoples subject to colonization by a geographically noncontiguous and culturally or ethnically distinct power to a state with the same boundaries as the colonial entity. The duty correlative to the right of peoples to self-determination, as a matter of authoritative international practice, is the obligation to decolonize Western overseas empires (or at least allow those subject to Western imperialism a fully free choice of independent statehood).

own" state. Overseas colonialism has, in virtually every instance, failed to provide a state that protects the equal human rights of subjected peoples. Colonialism, in other words, is a well-recognized standard threat to human dignity. Decolonization thus is a practical prerequisite to the enjoyment of internationally recognized human rights. And it is the subjected people as a group that have this right. (This is part of the reason why decolonization, although a prerequisite for the enjoyment of other human rights, often did not produce or even improve enjoyment of internationally recognized human rights. It puts to an end a particular vile injustice but is only a first step on the way to the protection of human rights.)

There may be other group human rights. The rights of indigenous peoples are perhaps the strongest example. I address them below. A right to cultural heritage is, in my view, the other strong candidate that has been widely discussed internationally: it is irreducibly a group right, applies to all cultural heritages, and seems to be in the process of being widely recognized as a standard threat to human dignity that requires remedy. Nonetheless, I remain deeply skeptical of claims of group human rights—without in any way arguing against group rights (but not group *human* rights) as an appropriate mechanism in many particular circumstances to remedy historic injustices or to protect the current and future rights and interests of particular groups and their members.

C. Seven Skeptical Questions about Group Human Rights

I am not, to repeat, arguing categorically against group human rights. My concern instead is with the more practical question of which if any group human rights beyond the right of peoples to self-determination ought to be recognized. This is ultimately a question that must be handled on a case-by-case basis. Nonetheless, I think that there are at least seven reasons for strong prima facie skepticism toward claims for the recognition of group human rights.

1) How do we identify the groups that ought to hold human rights? Unless we can restrict the range of collective right-holders, we are likely to be swamped in a wild proliferation of human rights that would devalue the practical force of claims of human rights. Certainly not *all* groups ought to have human rights. Consider, for example, states, multinational corporations, gangs, and barbershop quartets.

Suppose that we were to agree that it would be desirable for, say, minorities to have group human rights. By what criteria could we legitimately grant rights to minorities but not to other groups? Although not an intractable problem, it is an important one that advocates of group rights have largely ignored.

The most obvious criterion, namely, a long history of ongoing, systematic suffering, would yield group human rights for women; racial, ethnic, religious, and linguistic minorities; indigenous peoples; homosexuals; disabled people; seniors; children; and poor people—to mention just some of the more prominent groups. Pretty much everyone except prosperous white Western males—and many of them as well—would have group human rights. Such a radical expansion of right-holders and associated claims of rights seems to me extremely problematic.

2) Having identified group x as a potential holder of human rights, what particular substantive rights does or should x have? Certainly it is not enough that x wants r in order to establish a (human) right of x to r. On what grounds can we say that others do or do not owe r to x—*as a matter of human rights*? This is another problem to which advocates of group human rights have given shockingly little attention.

The most limited move would be to recognize those rights needed to enjoy already recognized human rights. These, however, would be only temporary, remedial measures, and thus probably best seen as practical measures to achieve nondiscrimination.

A more interesting class of group rights would appeal instead to the particular character of the group or to values or attributes not already recognized. Such claims need to be evaluated on a case-by-case basis. Once more, though, in order to avoid debasing the currency of human rights with a flood of new, unregulated coinage, it seems appropriate to place a substantial burden of proof on advocates of such rights.

3) Who exercises group rights? As we saw in section 1.1.B, rights work not simply by being voluntarily respected by duty-bearers but, most importantly, by being exercised by right-holders. The rights of states are exercised by governments. The rights of business corporations are exercised by shareholders, directors, and managers. Who ought—and is able—to exercise, for example, minority rights, understood as rights of a group?

The problems of group agency may be modest for small, concentrated, and homogenous groups with a strong tradition of collective action. (Indigenous peoples come readily to mind.) When the group is largely voluntary (for example, some religious minorities) the officers of the association (e.g., a clerical hierarchy) may be a plausible agent. But where the group is "natural," ascribed, or coercively defined and maintained, agency is likely to be highly problematic, especially when the group is large, heterogeneous, or widely dispersed.[11] The "solution" of having group rights exercised by individuals or associations of group members, beyond its irony, raises serious questions as to

---

11. For a thoughtful and balanced philosophical discussion of the problem of group agency in the context of rights, see Nickel (1997).

whether such rights really are *group* rights, rather than collective exercises of individual rights.

4) How do we handle conflicts of rights? Although all rights conflict with at least some other rights or important social interests, group rights will not only increase the number of conflicts but also create unusually intense competition between qualitatively different kinds of rights. How should we respond, for example, to a native North American tribe that denies equal treatment to women if women challenge this discrimination? Related issues may be raised by defining who is (and is not) in the group. Especially problematic from a human rights perspective are efforts to block or punish exit from the group.

5) Are the purported group rights necessary? Is the problem a lack of group rights or rather inadequate efforts to implement individual human rights? Most often, it seems to me, it is the latter. Once more, the burden of proof ought to lie with advocates of group rights.

6) Why should we expect group rights to succeed where individual rights have failed? If a government refuses to respect the individual rights of a despised minority, it will usually (although perhaps not always) be hard to imagine it being convinced to treat those people better as members of a group. If the difference between "us" and "them" is emphasized by group rights, might this not lead to even worse treatment?

7) Are group *rights* the best way to protect or realize the interests, values, or desires of a group? "Proponents of collective rights . . . often seem to move in a rather cursory way from the claim that communities are good things to the claim that communities have rights" (Hartney 1995: 203). We must demand an argument for protecting the values in question through the mechanism of rights. In particular, we must ask whether recognizing a new group *human* right—which by definition would hold against all states for all groups of the designated type—is either necessary or desirable.

None of these problems is fatal. They do, however, suggest prima facie skepticism toward (although not automatic rejection of) most (but not necessarily all) group human rights claims. At the very least, we should insist on clarity in specifying the "gap" in the Universal Declaration model that is being addressed and how the group human right in question would provide an effective remedy. We should also pay careful attention to unintended consequences of the proposed group human rights remedy.

D. Indigenous Peoples

Indigenous peoples probably present an exception to the individual rights approach I have been defending. If indigenous communities are more or less globally subject to threats to their autonomy, equality, and dignity and if those threats cannot be countered by existing rights to nondiscrimination and freedom of association, then it may make sense to recognize international human rights of indigenous peoples. In other words, a plausible case can be made that this is a standard threat to human dignity that deserves recognition and protection through internationally recognized human rights. But, I will argue, many such rights should be seen as individual rights of members of indigenous communities. Furthermore, the special circumstances that justify recognizing these group rights merit emphasis. Internationally recognized human rights for indigenous people should be seen as an exception that proves the rule rather than a model for a new general approach to group rights.

To simplify the discussion, let us imagine an indigenous community that is small—if not a face-to-face society, at least one in which the lineages of most members are known to most other members. It is geographically and culturally separate from the mainstream society. Mainstream institutions thus appear alien to most members of the community. Because there are also regular contacts with the "outside" world, though, we can think of those who reside in the community as having chosen to stay. Finally, imagine that the indigenous community is fragile in the sense that well-established mainstream institutions (e.g., private property in land) would *as an unintended consequence* radically alter the community's way of life in a fashion that most members would reject if given a choice.

In such circumstances the threat to the community comes not principally from internal defection but from the external pressures of modern states and modern markets, and the individuals and social forces associated with them. The plight of indigenous people is thus surprisingly similar in its structure, however different it may be in its particulars, to that of "modern" individuals. As a result, the rights of the Universal Declaration model can provide considerable support and protection.

I would go further. The choice by an indigenous community of a particular way of life that is vulnerable in special ways to outside attack demands not merely respect from mainstream society and institutions but accommodation and protection. In the conditions I have outlined there would appear to be no effective alternative to group rights involving both considerable selfgovernment—which would be facilitated by the group's small size, geographical concentration, and cultural history—and restrictions on the activities of nonmembers (in light of the fragility of the indigenous community). Recognizing such rights is further facilitated by the fact that they would impose severe burdens on relatively few outsiders in return for immense benefits to the group and its members.

The broader significance of this exception bears noting. Even if most claims for group human rights are profoundly defective, no particular claim can be rejected without examining its merits. Even where skepticism is the appropriate general attitude, claims for recognizing new human rights, whether held by individuals or by groups, deserves careful scrutiny. Systematic threats to human dignity change over time. In addition, our understandings of the nature of the life worthy of a human being, and of the practical meaning of equal concern and respect, may change. Therefore, we must always be willing, even eager, to explore gaps in and needed additions to the Universal Declaration model. The Universal Declaration and the Covenants may be (for us, now) authoritative, even definitive. They are not, however, likely to be the last word on international human rights.

E. Protecting Group Identity in a Human Rights Framework

Membership and participation in a variety of social groups is an essential part of a life of dignity. Many groups appropriately have a variety of rights. My argument against group *human* rights should not obscure these important points.

Even in the modern West, where individualism seems to have reached the pinnacle of its historical development, almost no one defines herself entirely as an individual. Most Westerners see themselves as part of a family; some even see the family as their most important locus of personal identity. Many define themselves in significant measure by their religion. Most blacks see race as an important facet of both their self-definition and their definition by others in society. Gender functions similarly for many women. Most Westerners also have at least a weak sense of "national" pride that is in some cases a significant element of their self-definition. Outside the West, such group self-identifications are widely held to be even more important. Furthermore, in almost all contemporary societies, a wide range of collective groups—for example, families, private clubs, professional associations, charitable organizations, business corporations, religious communities, and states—hold legal, political, and moral rights.

Nonetheless, an individual rights approach to difference may, it must be acknowledged, lead to the weakening, even the demise, of some minority (and other group) identities. Group identities, however, are not now, and I think should not become, subjects of international human rights protection. Only individual autonomy gives rise, and value, to identities that must be respected by others. Neither individually nor collectively do others have a right to impose any particular identity on a resistant individual or group.

Identity is entitled to protection only where it is an autonomous expression of the rights and values of those who carry it. Others may choose to value difference for its own sake or for the social benefits that diversity provides. They are required, as a matter of human rights, only to respect the decisions that people choose to act on for themselves, within the limits of their rights.

Almost all adults have multiple identities. It is for such real, and realistically complex, human beings to balance the varied roles and histories that shape their life. Such choices are, of course, conditioned, and thus in some (relatively uninteresting) sense not "free," but if equal treatment and freedom of association are effectively realized, those choices can appropriately be seen as autonomous exercises of internationally recognized human rights.

In such a social and political environment, groups of all sorts have a fair opportunity to compete in shaping the identities of their members. If a particular identity is valued sufficiently, it will survive, perhaps even thrive. If not, then it will not. And that is the way it should be. For example, if young Amish men and women choose to retain their distinctive style of life, their communities are likely to be preserved. If not, the demise of the group will be their decision—a decision that only they have a right to make. The alternative would be to force group membership on those who see it not as a means to creative self-fulfillment but as an oppressive limitation of their existence and identity.

This does not preclude active state support for a threatened or declining group. Such support, however, reflects a more or less voluntary decision of justice or policy that a state or society is free (not compelled) to make for particular groups of its choosing. No group is entitled to such support simply because it is a group (or even a group of a particular type, such as a racial minority).

There is a real loss when a community dies out, but if its members freely choose another way of life we must be prepared to accept that loss. If a group's survival requires the systematic denial of the internationally recognized human rights of its members, it is unlikely to deserve even our toleration, let alone our respect or support.

4

Equal Concern and Respect

Chapter 2 described the Universal Declaration model. This chapter offers a series of increasingly deep and substantive—and thus increasingly controversial—justifications. I argue that the Universal Declaration model is rooted in an attractive moral vision of human beings as equal and autonomous agents living in states that treat every citizen with equal concern and respect. I will also argue that a certain kind of liberalism provides a good justification for this system of rights.

1. Hegemony and Settled Norms

I begin with a descriptive, empirical claim: human rights have become a hegemonic political discourse, or what Mervyn Frost (1996: 104–11) calls "settled norms" of contemporary international society; that is, principles that are widely accepted as authoritative within the society of states. Both nationally and internationally, full political legitimacy is increasingly judged by and expressed in terms of human rights.

The six leading international human rights treaties (on civil and political rights, economic, social, and cultural rights, racial discrimination, discrimination against women, torture, and the rights of the child) had an average of 172 parties in early 2012.[1] Even more notable is the penetration of human rights into bilateral, multilateral, and transnational diplomacy. In the 1970s, controversy still raged over whether human rights were even an appropriate concern of foreign policy. As late as 1980, only a handful of states had explicit international human rights policies. Today, however, human rights are a standard subject of bilateral and multilateral diplomacy.

---

1. Calculated from United Nations Treaty Collection, http://treaties.un.org/.

Most national societies are also increasingly penetrated by human rights norms and values. Both governments and their opponents appeal to human rights much more frequently and more centrally than just a few decades ago. Compare, for example, the terms of debate and the range of political options seriously considered nationally and regionally today in Latin America, Africa, and Asia with those of the 1960s and 1970s. The Arab Spring of 2011 indicates the substantial penetration of these ideas into the Middle East as well.

The collapse of the Soviet Union and its empire, and the retreat of dictatorial regimes in all areas of the world, suggests that, when given a chance, people in the contemporary world usually choose human rights. That choice has been made with varying degrees of enthusiasm and understanding. For many, human rights are a "default option," accepted only because the leading competitors have been delegitimized. Nonetheless, in contemporary international society there is no widely endorsed alternative.[2] When given a choice, experience suggests that people rarely choose the alternatives that dictators of various stripes claim that they prefer (but tellingly refuse to allow them the opportunity to choose freely).

Even China, where in the 1980s the very use of the term "human rights" could land one in jail, has reluctantly come to adopt that language. Such uses, to be sure, are often cynical. Nonetheless, the need to appear to be acting on behalf of human rights tells us much about dominant values and aspirations. Even cynical uses pay tribute to the moral imperative of a commitment to human rights. As the Helsinki process in central and eastern Europe suggests (see Thomas 2001), such norms can take on an independent life of their own, with consequences very different from those intended by cynical endorsers.

Even where citizens do not have a particularly sophisticated sense of what a commitment to human rights means, they respond to the general idea that they and their fellow citizens are equally entitled to certain basic goods, services, protections, and opportunities. The Universal Declaration, I would suggest, offers a good first approximation of the list that they would come up with, largely irrespective of civilization, after considerable reflection. More precisely, there is almost nothing in the Universal Declaration that they would not put there, although one might readily imagine a global constitutional convention coming up with a somewhat larger list.

The prominence of human rights in contemporary international society is not unrelated to their endorsement by the world's leading power, the United States, and its principal allies. Example, however, has been far more powerful

---

2. This is perhaps a modest exaggeration. Islamic fundamentalism is perhaps a real challenger in several countries, and one with genuinely universalistic aspirations. Xenophobic nationalism might also be seen as a recurrent challenger, but one that is fundamentally inegalitarian and rarely capable of universalization (and thus of less interest, for reasons discussed below).

than advocacy—which has often been clumsy, even insulting—or imposition. Human rights have moral and political authority that goes well beyond their backing by power (force). They dominate contemporary political discussions not only, or even primarily, because of the support of materially dominant powers but rather because they respond to some of the most important social and political aspirations of individuals, families, and groups in most countries of the world. Human rights have become internationally "hegemonic" in a Gramscian sense of the term.[3]

2. An Overlapping Consensus on International Human Rights

My claim that there is an international consensus on the system of human rights rooted in the Universal Declaration is *relatively* uncontroversial—although we will return to several elements of contention in parts 2 and 4. My more controversial argument that this consensus is more voluntary then coerced would be substantially strengthened if I could account for how it came about in the face of the considerable—at times profound—philosophical differences that exist between and within civilizations, cultures, and societies in the contemporary world. John Rawls's idea of an overlapping consensus offers a descriptively accurate and morally attractive explanation.

Rawls distinguishes "comprehensive religious, philosophical, or moral doctrines," such as Islam, Kantianism, Confucianism, and Marxism, from "political conceptions of Justice," which address the political structure of society, defined (as far as possible) independently of any particular comprehensive doctrine (Rawls 1996: xliii–xlv, 11–15, 174–76; 1999: 31–32, 172–73). Adherents of different comprehensive doctrines may be able to reach an "overlapping consensus" on a political conception of justice (1996: 133–72, 385–96). Overlapping consensus offers a plausible answer to the question "how is it possible that there can be a stable and just society whose free and equal citizens are deeply divided by conflicting and even incommensurable religious, philosophical, and moral doctrines?" (1996: 133). Although formulated initially for domestic societies, this idea has an obvious extension to international society, particularly a culturally and politically diverse, pluralist international society. Such a consensus, I am claiming, has come to develop on the rights of the Universal Declaration.

---

3. Gramsci's discussion is scattered through *Selections from the Prison Notebooks* and can be roughly followed using the index in that book (1971). For an extended secondary discussion, see Femia (1981: 1–129). Compare also Cox (1996: chaps. 6, 7). I use the term "hegemonic" here descriptively, and without any necessary implications of class domination (which is essential to Gramsci's own account), but in what I take to be the root sense—namely, ideological power arising from the effective exclusion of viable normative alternatives within the mainstream of a society.

An overlapping consensus is partial rather than complete; comprehensive doctrines converge but do not completely coincide. The consensus is political rather than moral or religious. It is not, however, *merely* political. In particular, it is more than a modus vivendi between irreconcilable views that are for practical reasons forced to coexist. Rather, it reflects a reasoned agreement despite many important differences at a deeper philosophical level.

An overlapping consensus on internationally recognized human rights means that there is a striking convergence on a vision of the limits of political legitimacy in the contemporary world. Looked at from the bottom up, there is a transnational normative convergence on the basic expectations that citizens may legitimately have of their societies and governments.

This strategy of "justificatory minimalism," as Joshua Cohen describes it, "aims to avoid imposing unnecessary hurdles on accepting an account of human rights (and justice), by intolerantly tying its formulation to a particular ethical tradition. It is left to different traditions—each with internal complexities, debates, competing and conflicting traditions of argument, and (in some cases) canonical texts—to elaborate the bases of a shared view of human rights within their own terms" (Cohen 2004: 213; cf. Lindholm 1999: 69–73). That shared vision represents, however, not a lowest common denominator but rather the robust set of human rights enumerated in the Universal Declaration. In other words, by allowing appeals to different sets of foundational values we have in effect discovered that, at least in the conditions of the contemporary world, otherwise very different peoples, traditions, individuals, and groups turn out to share something very much like the robust vision of the conditions for a life of dignity outlined in the Universal Declaration.

Human rights can be readily derived from a considerable variety of moral theories: for example, they can be seen as encoded in the natural law, as political means to further human good or utility, or political institutions designed to produce virtuous citizens. The increasing political prominence of human rights in recent decades has led more and more adherents of a growing range of comprehensive doctrines to endorse human rights—but only as a political conception of justice. For example, Muslims of various political persuasions in many parts of the Islamic world have in recent decades developed Islamic doctrines of human rights that are strikingly similar in substance to the Universal Declaration.

Human rights thus have no single philosophical or religious foundation. Instead they have many foundations—and thus much greater practical resonance than could be provided by any particular philosophy or religion. Christians, Muslims, Confucians, and Buddhists; Kantians, utilitarians, pragmatists, and neo-Aristotelians; liberals, conservatives, traditionalists, and radicals, and many other groups as well, come to human rights from their own particular paths. Today, almost all the leading paths to social justice and human dignity centrally involve human rights. For their own varied reasons, most leading comprehensive doctrines now see human rights as the political expression of their deepest values. As Jacques Maritain famously put it, "We agree about the rights but on condition no one asks us why" (UNESCO 1949: 10)—and this is not because there is no good answer but because there are many different good answers (and each tradition remains committed to its own).

Although internationally recognized human rights do not depend on any particular religious or philosophical doctrine, they are *not* compatible with all comprehensive doctrines. The link between human rights and comprehensive doctrines, although loose, is a matter of substance, not just procedural agreement. Claims such as those in the Covenants that "these rights derive from the inherent dignity of the human person" or in the Vienna Declaration that "all human rights derive from the dignity and worth inherent in the human person" limit the range of possible comprehensive doctrines within an overlapping consensus. Most importantly, human rights, because they are held equally by all human beings, are incompatible with fundamentally inegalitarian comprehensive doctrines, which are in principle excluded from the consensus.

Are inegalitarian comprehensive doctrines predominant, or even prominent, in contemporary African, Asian, Western, or Islamic civilizations? We will return to this question in part 2. For now I will simply assert that they are not.

In their past, *all* major regional civilizations have at times been dominated by views that treated some significant portion of human beings as "outsiders" not entitled to guarantees that could be taken for granted by "insiders." For example, there are few regions of the globe where slavery or similar forms of human bondage have never been practiced and widely justified. For most of their histories all literate civilizations have relied on inegalitarian, ascriptive characteristics such as birth, age, or gender to assign social roles, rights, and duties.

Today, however, the basic moral equality of all human beings is not merely accepted but strongly endorsed by all leading comprehensive doctrines in all regions of the world. This convergence on egalitarian comprehensive doctrines, both within and between civilizations, provides the foundation for a convergence on the rights of the Universal Declaration. In principle, a great variety of social practices other than human rights might provide the basis for politically implementing foundational egalitarian values. In practice, for reasons suggested in the next chapter, human rights have become the preferred option.

It is an exaggeration to say that "the conception of humanity as expressed in the Universal Declaration of Human Rights has become the only valid framework of values, norms and principles capable of structuring a meaningful and yet feasible scheme of national and international civilized life" (Weisstub 2002: 2). This claim, however, does contain a kernel of truth. The Universal Declaration may not be the *only* valid framework. It is, admittedly, an incomplete framework. Nonetheless, it does represent a realistically utopian cross-cultural vision of the demands and possibilities of our moral nature, a vision that has something like universal validity for us today.

The insight of the drafters of the Universal Declaration into some of the central social and political problems of modernity has proved immensely fruitful. "While protecting the ability of diverse consciences to disagree radically about the premises and principles of ethical theory, they found a way to emphasize a number of basic findings of practical reason, to which a sufficient majority of peoples around the world had been driven" (Novak 1999: 39)—and continue to be driven.[4] The hope of one of its drafters, Charles Malik of Lebanon, has indeed been realized, namely that the Declaration would "either bring to light an implicit agreement already operative, perhaps dimly and unconsciously, in the systems and ways of life of the various states, or consciously and creatively advance further and higher the area of agreement" (quoted in El-Hage 2004: 8). As a result, the Universal Declaration has become what it rather grandly claimed to be in 1948, namely "a common standard of achievement for all peoples and all nations."

3. Moral Theory, Political Theory, and Human Rights

This appeal to overlapping consensus suggests that human rights fall more in the domain of political theory (political conceptions of justice) than moral theory (comprehensive doctrines). This suggestion is reinforced by the place of human rights in modern Western moral theory.

It is conventional to distinguish deontological (duty-based) theories, such as Kant's categorical imperative, from teleological (ends-, goals-, or consequence-based) theories, such as Bentham's utilitarianism or (neo-Aristotelian) virtue-based theories. Deontological and teleological theories posit radically different relationships between the right and the good.[5]

Right is the moral primitive for deontological theories. We are required to do what is right (follow our duty), period, independent of the effects for

---

4. Thus I reject the suggestion of Anthony Langlois that the Universal Declaration makes "the implicit claim . . . that human rights has the authority to stand over and above the multiplicity of traditions, religions, cultures, political ideologies and metaphysical traditions existent throughout the world" (2005: 374). Quite the contrary, the drafters saw the Declaration as emerging out of deeper foundations. Internationally recognized human rights stand "above" these deeper foundations only in the sense that a house is "above"—that is, constructed upon—its foundation. This is particularly true given the above account of multiple foundations in an overlapping consensus.

5. Within Anglo-American philosophy, Ross (1930) provides a classic discussion.

good or bad produced by our actions. "Thou shalt not . . ." In teleological theories, by contrast, the moral primitive is the good. Duty depends on the consequences of our actions. We are morally required to, within the limits of our skill and resources, increase human happiness, virtue, or some other end (or reduce human suffering, vice, etc.).[6]

This common classification of moral theories, however, tells us little about human rights, which have played a vanishingly small part in the history of Western moral theory, even during the modern era. For example, rights play no significant role in Kant's *Grounding for the Metaphysics of Morals*. For utilitarians, rights are only second-order rules that save us the (often considerable) task of calculating utilities in particular cases. Although we might in principle imagine rights-based moral theories, in practice such a category has historically been largely an empty one.[7] Human rights logically may be, but in fact rarely have been, taken to be a moral primitive.

When we turn to *political* theory, however, human rights often become central.[8] For example, in part 1 of Kant's "Theory and Practice" (1983 [1793]), which deals with individual morality, rights make no significant appearance, but rights (entitlements) become central in part 2, which treats "political right." In fact, Kant's contractarian political theory is centered on the rights we have as human beings, as subjects, and as citizens. More generally, human rights are at the heart, and a defining feature, of contractarian political theories. And other political theories may endorse a human rights standard of political legitimacy by other routes.

The loose and weak link between human rights and leading moral theories is an attraction rather than a drawback, allowing for a considerable degree of *political* consensus despite moral divergences. By remaining open to many egalitarian moral and political theories, human rights may allow us to handle certain questions of political justice and right while circumventing difficult and usually inconclusive disputes over moral foundations.

This openness is particularly attractive in a "postmodern" world skeptical of the possibility of finding unassailable foundations. Political theorists have increasingly turned their attention to notions such as deliberative democracy

---

6. Deontological and teleological theories thus posit different accounts of the relationship between means and ends. Teleologists are concerned primarily with consequences, and thus ends. Actions ("means") are evaluated by their contribution to realizing the defining moral end (e.g., utility maximization). Deontological theories, while recognizing the instrumental value of actions, see the morality of an act as determined by its inherent nature rather than its consequences. For deontologists, moral acts are required because they are right, not because they produce some other effect in the world. They are not means to anything at all. They instantiate rather than cause or bring about the realization of the right.

7. Alan Gewirth (1982, 1996) may be a contemporary exception that proves this rule. I am aware of no pre–twentieth century exceptions.

8. Thus Dworkin (1977: 171–72) distinguishes between goal-based, right(s)-based, and duty-based political theories.

(Habermas 1993, 1996, 1998) and recognition (e.g., Gutmann and Thompson 1996; Thompson 2006). Human rights may provide a focal point for forging such a consensus or for negotiating mutual recognition. Certainly there is no other substantive ideal that has come even close to such widespread international endorsement by both governments and movements of political opposition across the globe.[9]

Therefore, in the remainder of this chapter, and in most of the rest of this book, I will be concerned with the political, rather than moral, theory of human rights. Internationally recognized human rights today provide a standard of political legitimacy. In the contemporary world—the world in which there is an overlapping consensus on the Universal Declaration model—states are legitimate largely to the extent that they respect, protect, and implement the rights of their citizens.

4. Equal Concern and Respect

What is the political conception of justice around which this overlapping consensus has formed? I want to suggest that it is something very much like Ronald Dworkin's idea that the state is required to treat each citizen with equal concern and respect.

A. Equality and Autonomy

> Government must treat those whom it governs with concern, that is, as human beings who are capable of suffering and frustration, and with respect, that is as human beings who are capable of forming and acting on intelligent conceptions of how their lives should be lived. Government must not only treat people with concern and respect, but with equal concern and respect. It must not distribute goods or opportunities unequally on the ground that some citizens are entitled to more because they are worthy of more concern. It must not constrain liberty on the ground that one citizen's conception of the good life is nobler or superior to another's (Dworkin 1977: 272–73).

The state must treat all persons as moral and political equals. Inequalities in goods or opportunities that arise directly or indirectly from political decisions

9. This is only a modest exaggeration. "Peace" and "development" are probably more widely endorsed, but neither—at least in their common senses of absence of war and sustainable economic growth—provides anything like the attractive comprehensive standard of political legitimacy offered by human rights. "Justice" may also be more widely endorsed, but only in a very abstract form. When we get to the level of detail of the Universal Declaration, the differences in conceptions of justice become striking.

must be compatible with a political conception of justice founded on equal concern and respect.

This understanding of the equality of all human beings leads "naturally" to a political emphasis on autonomy. Personal liberty, especially the liberty to choose and pursue one's own life, clearly is entailed by the idea of equal respect. For the state to interfere in matters of personal morality would be to treat the life plans and values of some as superior to others. A certain amount of economic liberty is also required, at least to the extent that decisions concerning consumption, investment, and risk reflect free decisions based on personal values that arise from autonomously chosen conceptions of the good life.

Liberty alone, however, cannot serve as the overriding value of social life or the sole end of political association. Unless checked by a fairly expansive, positive conception of the persons in relation to whom it is exercised, individual liberty readily degenerates into license and social atomization. If liberty is to foster dignity it must be not merely equal liberty for all, but liberty exercised within the constraints of a principle such as equal concern and respect.

Autonomy (liberty) and equality are less a pair of guiding principles— let alone competing principles—than different manifestations of the central commitment to the equal worth and dignity of each and every person, whatever her social utility. To justify denying or severely restricting individual autonomy almost necessarily involves an appeal to inequality.[10] Equal and autonomous rights-bearing individuals are entitled to make fundamental choices about what constitutes the good life (for them), and with whom they associate, how. They have no right to force on one another ideas of what is right and proper, because to do so would treat those others as less than equal moral agents. Regardless of who they are or where they stand, individuals have an inherent dignity and worth for which the state must demonstrate an active and equal concern. And everyone is *entitled* to this equal concern and respect (with the political consequences discussed in section 1.1).

The constructivist theory sketched in chapter 1 is thus beginning to acquire some substance. Human rights simultaneously constitute individuals as equal and autonomous citizens and states as polities fit to govern such rights-bearing citizens.

B. The Universal Declaration and Equal Concern and Respect

It is a relatively simple matter to derive the full list of rights in the Universal Declaration from the political principle of equal concern and respect. Other lists of rights can also be derived from this principle. Other political

---

10. The obvious exception is the protection of the equal autonomy of others.

conceptions of justice may be compatible with the Universal Declaration model. I would suggest, however, that the close overlap is much more than a coincidence.

In order to treat someone with concern and respect, she must first be recognized as a moral and legal person. This requires certain basic personal rights. Rights to recognition before the law and to nationality (Universal Declaration, Articles 6, 15) are political prerequisites. In a different vein, the right to life, as well as rights to protection against slavery, torture, and other inhuman or degrading treatment (Articles 3, 4, 5), are essential to recognition and respect as a person.

Rights such as freedom of speech, conscience, religion, and association (Articles 18, 19) protect a sphere of personal autonomy. The right to privacy (Article 12) even more explicitly aims to guarantee the capacity to realize personal visions of a life worthy of a human being. Personal autonomy also requires economic and social rights, such as the right to education (Article 26), which makes available the intellectual resources for informed autonomous choices and the skills needed to act on them, and the right to participate in the cultural life of the community (Article 27), which recognizes the social and cultural dimensions of personal development. In its political dimension, equal respect also implies democratic control of the state and therefore rights to political participation and to freedoms of (political) speech, press, assembly, and association (Articles 19, 20, 21).

Equal concern and respect also require that the government intervene to reduce certain social and economic inequalities. The state must protect those who, as a result of natural or voluntary membership in an unpopular group, are subject to social, political, or economic discrimination that limits their access to a fair share of social resources or opportunities. Such rights as equal protection of the laws and protection against discrimination on such bases as race, color, sex, language, religion, opinion, origin, property, birth, or status (Articles 2, 7) are essential to assure that all people are treated as fully and equally human.

In the economic sphere, an attachment to a market-based system of production both fosters efficiency (and thus aggregate prosperity) and places minimal restraints on economic liberty, thus augmenting personal autonomy. Market distribution, however, tends to be grossly unequal (see section 13.7). Inequality is not necessarily objectionable. Equal concern and respect, however, imply an economic floor, and degrading inequalities cannot be permitted (compare Shue 1980: 19–23). In human rights terms this implies, for example, rights to food, health care, and social insurance (Articles 22, 25).

Efforts to alleviate degrading or disrespectful misery and deprivation do not exhaust the scope of the economic demands of the principle of equal concern and respect. The right to work (Article 23), which is essentially a right to economic participation, is of special importance. Work has considerable intrinsic value, as an element of a life of dignity, as well as instrumental value in satisfying basic material needs and providing an economic foundation for personal autonomy. A (limited) right to property (Article 17) can be justified in similar terms.

Finally, the special threat to personal autonomy and equality presented by the modern state requires a set of legal rights, such as the presumption of innocence and rights to due process, fair and public hearings before an independent tribunal, and protection from arbitrary arrest, detention, or exile (Articles 8–11). More broadly, the special threat to dignity posed by the state is reflected in the fact that all human rights are held particularly against the state. Moreover, they hold against all types of states, democratic as much as any other (compare section 13.3). If one's government treats one as less than fully human, it matters little how that government came to power. The individual does have social duties (Article 29), but the discharge of social obligations is not a precondition for having or exercising human rights.

The substantive attractions of this particular "realistic utopia" (Rawls 1999: 11), I would suggest, go a long way toward explaining the hegemonic power of the Universal Declaration model. This, I believe, largely accounts for the overlapping international consensus on the rights of the Universal Declaration.

5. Toward a Liberal Theory of Human Rights

Equal concern and respect, understood as a political conception of justice, can be endorsed by a variety of comprehensive doctrines. I turn now to one, liberalism. The chapter thus moves from relatively descriptive to largely prescriptive argument. I argue that a particular type of liberalism provides a strong and attractive normative foundation for the Universal Declaration model—although, as the idea of overlapping consensus indicates, many other foundations are also possible.

A. Defining Liberalism

"Liberalism" is a complex and contested set of orientations and values. It is *relatively* uncontroversial, however, to say that it is rooted in a commitment to liberty, freedom, or, in the formulation I prefer, autonomy. More precisely, liberals give central political place to *individual* autonomy, rather than the liberty of society, the state, or other corporate actors. Liberals see individuals as entitled to "govern" their lives to make important life choices for themselves, within limits connected primarily with the mutual recognition of equal liberties and opportunities for others.

	Rights-based	**Good-based**
Thick		
Thin		

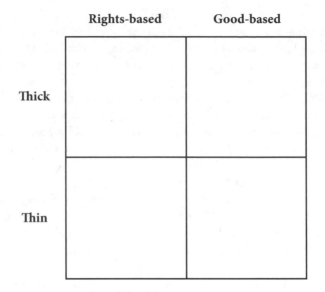

Figure 4.1 A typology of liberal theories

Liberalism also is specially committed to equality[11]—although most liberal (and non-liberal) theories and all liberal (and non-liberal) societies ultimately permit substantial economic, social, or political inequality. Liberty is not a special privilege of the elite but (in principle) available to all. *Equal liberty for all* is at the heart of any liberal political vision.[12]

Not all liberals, though, are friends of rights, let alone human rights, and different liberals cash out the commitment to equal liberty in different ways. Figure 4.1 categorizes liberal theories along two dimensions: the extent to which they emphasize rights or the good (or virtue, or some other value) and the substantive "thickness" of their conceptions of those core values.

Locke is the seminal figure in the strand of liberalism that grounds the commitment to equal liberty on natural (or what we today call human) rights. Its roots go back at least to Leveler and Digger arguments during the English Civil War. Kant, Paine, and Rousseau were leading eighteenth-century proponents. Rawls and Dworkin are prominent recent American representatives.

Liberalism, however, also has a strong historical association, going back at least to Hobbes, with utilitarianism, a good-based theory that makes human

11. Dworkin (1985: chap. 9) offers an especially forceful argument for the centrality of equality to liberalism.
12. There are striking analogies with the motto of the High Commissioner for Human Rights in 1998, the year of the fiftieth anniversary of the Universal Declaration: "All human rights for all."

rights at best a second-order or derivative political principle. (The seminal figure is Bentham, who famously described natural rights as "simple nonsense" and imprescriptible natural rights as "nonsense upon stilts.") This was the dominant vision of liberalism in Britain in the nineteenth century. A microeconomic version underlies contemporary "neoliberal" market-oriented policies.

My purpose here is to advance a rights-based liberal defense of the Universal Declaration model. Although many good-based liberals participate in the overlapping consensus on international human rights, their views will not be considered here. Furthermore, microeconomic, utilitarian "neoliberalism" is fundamentally opposed to the liberal human rights perspective I defend, as we will see in more detail in section 13.7. (Neoliberal equality involves political indifference to competing preferences—unbiased treatment in the marketplace—rather than guaranteed access to essential goods, services, and opportunities.)

Turning to the second dimension of our typology, the range of recognized rights, the end points of the continuum are represented by what I label "social democratic" and "minimalist" (or libertarian) liberalism. A liberalism compatible with the Universal Declaration model must be strongly egalitarian, must actively embrace an extensive system of economic and social rights, and must reflect a robust conception of democratic political control (compare section 13.3).

The European welfare state is the leading practical exemplar. *All* internationally recognized human rights are seen as entitlements of individuals—social and political claims that impose duties on the state and society—rather than mere liberties. Even with recent welfare state retrenchments, all the states of western Europe lie toward the top left of Figure 4.1.

At the bottom left lies a minimalist liberalism that emphasizes individual personal liberties and includes only a short list of economic and social rights. In some circles this is referred to as "classical" liberalism. In the United States it is often called "libertarian."

Minimalist liberalism's truncated list of human rights is substantively incompatible with the Universal Declaration model. Whatever its historical pedigree or philosophical merits,[13] it is best seen as a critique of the substance of the Universal Declaration model, despite the considerable overlap on civil and political rights.[14] For the past half century, *no* Western liberal democratic regime, not even Reagan's America or Thatcher's Britain, has pursued libertarian minimalism (compare section 14.5).

---

13. Section 3.1 criticizes minimalism's characteristic attack on economic and social rights.
14. Most minimalists nonetheless participate in the international overlapping consensus on human rights, subordinating their unease with economic and social rights to their overriding (even defining) commitment to civil and political rights.

A politically important (although perhaps not theoretically coherent) "intermediate" rights-based liberal perspective emphasizes personal and civil liberties, a modest list of economic and social rights provided by a welfare state, and primarily procedural democracy. This "American" vision is much more willing than the libertarian to restrict personal liberties in order to remedy invidious inequalities. It also is somewhat more sympathetic to the idea of state action to assure minimum access to social and economic goods, services, and opportunities. But the American welfare state is much less robust than those of Europe. In the United States this perspective is usually referred to as "liberal," pejoratively by the right. I will treat it as the thinnest plausible liberal conception of the Universal Declaration model.

Both "American" and "social democratic" liberalisms are committed to a democracy that operates only within the substantive requirements of equal human rights for all and to a welfare state that supplements a market system of production with substantial "welfare state" redistribution—in order to assure equal human rights for all. I will use "liberal" without qualification to refer to this shared political ideal based on an underlying vision of equal concern and respect.

B. Equality, Autonomy, Neutrality, and Toleration

Liberals often make exaggerated claims for the neutrality of their principles.[15] Liberalism, however, no less than any other substantive moral or political position, privileges some competing conceptions of the good and marginalizes others. Any list of human rights cannot but make substantive judgments about the range of conceptions of the good life that are considered within the pale of reasonable argument. The real issue is not *whether* certain views are excluded but the *grounds* for inclusion or exclusion. I will defend tolerant, liberal "neutrality" toward a wide range of (but not all) competing visions of the good life.

Liberal neutrality—neutrality bounded by liberal principles—is an expression of the core liberal values of equality and autonomy in a world without indubitable moral and political foundations. If we cannot be certain of the substance of the good life, particularly in its details—more precisely, if our own certainty is not something that is shared by many of those with whom we interact, if we have sufficient respect for them, and if we are committed to the basic moral equality of all human beings—then a stance of at least principled tolerance is required for all conceptions of the good life that respect the equal

---

15. Daniel Bell (1993: 3–4; 1996: 660–62) succinctly but perceptively identifies this shortcoming of many liberal theories.

dignity of all human beings. Commitment to individual autonomy provides additional support for tolerant liberal neutrality: one is entitled to make such determinations for oneself, within the bounds set by the equal autonomy of others.

Looked at from the other side, to impose a particular substantive conception of the good life would be to infringe or deny the equality and autonomy of those on whom it is being imposed. And if one might be wrong, that denial cannot even be justified by paternalistic arguments. Liberal political theory thus seems especially attractive in a world that is skeptical of ostensibly secure, "indubitable" moral foundations (which, conversely, militate against liberal neutrality).

Liberal neutrality, however, is not—cannot be—neutral with respect to claims that some groups of human beings are categorically superior or inferior to others, and thus have different basic rights. Liberals also are not neutral with respect to theories that deny individuals and groups the right to pursue their own conception of the good (so long as they allow exactly the same right to other individuals and groups).

Of course, liberal intolerance toward those who categorically attack equality and autonomy is vulnerable to skeptical external challenge. In practice, however, I do not think that many liberals (or their critics) would be embarrassed to reject out of hand those who claim that some human beings are categorically superior or inferior to others. And I do not believe that liberals (or others) need apologize for rejecting out of hand arguments that some groups are entitled to pursue their conception of the good life at the cost of the good life, thus defined, of others. Quite the contrary, in the contemporary world it is those who challenge the basic moral equality of all human beings and their right to considerable space to choose for themselves the good life, rather than liberals, who are likely to be embarrassed by their own arguments.

Many non-liberals, as well as good-based liberals, are likely to note that most of the real work in the preceding paragraphs is done by the claim of equality. Autonomy provides additional support, but most of the same conclusions can be reached through appeals to equality alone. Therefore, my argument supports, or is at least compatible with, a cluster of positions much broader than liberalism—so long as they are egalitarian and committed to a centrally rights-based political theory. Liberals, in other words, are only one group of participants in the overlapping consensus on the Universal Declaration.

6. Consensus: Overlapping but Bounded

At the risk of some repetition, I want to reemphasize the bounded nature of the consensus on the Universal Declaration model. Bhikhu Parekh may be correct in claiming that "some values are embedded in and underpin all human societies" (1999: 135). That list of values, however, is both short and stated at such a high level of generality as to have little substantive bite. Because most societies have rejected the very notion that all members of *Homo sapiens* are in some important sense equally human beings (compare chapters 8–10), whatever consensus on values does exist will not help us much with human rights.

The overlapping consensus on the Universal Declaration model is *not* a transhistorical, "anthropological" consensus (compare sections 5.1, 5.2). It does not imply that every person, every society, or even every government accepts the Universal Declaration. Rather, the claim is that most leading elements in almost all contemporary societies endorse the idea that every human being has certain equal and inalienable rights and is thus entitled to equal concern and respect from the state—and that what holds this otherwise disparate group together is a fundamental commitment to human equality and autonomy.

Participation in the overlapping consensus on the Universal Declaration model is only possible for those who see "human being" as a fundamental moral category and who see human beings in some important sense as autonomous actors. These "foundational" commitments define the range of views that must be taken into account in cross-cultural and cross-philosophical discussions, to which part 2 of this book is devoted. Those outside the community thus defined should be listened to and perhaps even sought out—because of our own commitment to respect for all human beings and tolerance of diversity, in an effort to change the minds of those who hold such views, or to sharpen our own views by subjecting them to external critique—but proponents of such views are legitimately treated as "unreasonable" in some important sense.

It is not illogical to claim that some members of *Homo sapiens* are born to be slaves or untouchables or subordinated to adult males. It is not necessarily incoherent to claim that members of one racial or ethnic group ought to be subordinated to another. It is, however, almost by definition *morally unreasonable in the contemporary world*. In particular, it is beyond the pale in almost all countries today to advocate social institutions that enforce qualitative differences between groups of human beings, especially when those differences are defined by ascriptive characteristics. Such institutions are not expressions of alternative conceptions of human rights. They fundamentally challenge the idea of human rights.

The core commitment to equality and autonomy underlying the Universal Declaration model suggests the importance of uncoerced consensus. Those same principles, though, also require that the range of substantive positions within that consensus be strictly bounded by a shared commitment to equal autonomy for all.

This is perhaps the essential insight in Rousseau's distinction between the general will and the will of all:[16] there are some individual wills that simply cannot be allowed to be expressed in the general will if it is to maintain its moral character. When Rousseau speaks of forcing people to be free, however,[17] he seems to me (as a liberal) to go too far. Nonetheless, he points toward an important insight. Some forms of behavior cannot be tolerated in a rights-protective society. Some interests must be excluded from the calculation of the public interest, no matter how deeply their proponents are attached to them.

We may be forced to live with or next to those who hold morally and politically loathsome views. Our commitment to equality and autonomy may compel us not to use force against them to try to change those views. We have no obligation, though, to tolerate attempts to impose these views on those who are judged inferior. Quite the contrary, we have (at least) a moral obligation to condemn those who would act to implement, for example, systems of slavery, caste, or racial domination (compare section 12.4), and we would seem to have a national political obligation to resist, with force if necessary, nonverbal behavior that seeks to create institutions of domination and subordination.

A system of equal and inalienable rights cannot be sustained in the face of social practices that deny the possibility of each enjoying his or her rights equally. For example, individual proponents of racial domination have the right to hold, perhaps even to advocate, their views.[18] Efforts to implement them in practice, however, fall outside of the international consensus on human rights and may be—must be—resisted with all vigor.

16. *The Social Contract*, book 1, chapter 3.
17. Ibid., chapter 7.
18. I say "perhaps" because such a liberty is *legally* prohibited by Article 4 of the International Convention on the Elimination of All Forms of Racial Discrimination.

Part II

The Universality and
Relativity of Human Rights

5

A Brief History of Human Rights

Universal human rights have a very particular history. Prior to the second half of the seventeenth century, the idea that all human beings, simply because they are human, have rights that they may exercise against the state and society received no substantial political endorsement anywhere in the world. Although limited applications of the idea were associated with political revolutions in Britain, the United States, and France in the late-seventeenth and eighteenth centuries, an extensive practice of *universal* human rights is largely a twentieth-century creation—and a late-twentieth century creation at that. (For example, the Universal Declaration of Human Rights ignored colonialism, which involved the brutal and systematic denial of most human rights to most Africans, many Asians, and a large number of Latin Americans.)

This chapter very briefly sketches this history, preliminary to a broader discussion of universality and relativity in the following chapters. The first two sections show that the idea and practice of human rights were alien to premodern societies in both the Western and non-Western worlds. The remaining sections explore the "modernity" of human rights and the nature of their relation with "Western" theory and practice.

I. Politics and Justice in the Premodern Non-Western World

It is often argued that human rights have a long history (e.g., Ishay 2004; Lewis 2003). It is also often argued, as we will see in some detail in this section, that human rights have been widely endorsed by many, if not all, of the world's great civilizations. Such claims, however, are demonstrably false— if by "human rights" we mean equal and inalienable rights that all human beings have simply because they are human and that they may exercise against their own state and society, and if by "human beings" we mean, if not nearly all members of *Homo sapiens*, then at least some substantial segment of the species, including prominently many outside of one's own social or cultural group. In this section I briefly canvass arguments that premodern China, Africa, and the Islamic world had practices of human rights. In the next section I develop a parallel argument for the premodern West.

A. Traditional China

It is often argued that "the idea of human rights developed very early in China" (Lo 1949: 186), "as early as 2,000 years ago" (Han 1996: 93). In fact, however, nothing in the mainstream of Chinese political theory or practice prior to the twentieth century supports such contentions.

From the earliest written records, in the Shang dynasty in the second millennium BCE, through to the end of the Qing dynasty in the early twentieth century, hierarchical rule by a king or emperor was the theoretical ideal. For about half of this period, practice more or less conformed with this ideal—and when it did not, the alternative usually was political disintegration characterized by a mix of internal disorder and external invasion that made even law, order, and defense problematic.

"In a broad sense, the concept of human rights concerns the relationship between the individual and the state; it involves the status, claims, and duties of the former in the jurisdiction of the latter. As such, it is a subject as old as politics, and every nation has to grapple with it," writes Tai Hung-Chao (1985: 79). Not all institutionalized relationships between individuals and the state, however, are governed by, related to, or even consistent with human rights. What the state owes to those it rules is indeed a perennial question of politics. Human rights provide but one answer. Divine right monarchy is another. The dictatorship of the proletariat, the principle of utility, aristocracy, theocracy, democracy, and plutocracy are still different answers.

It certainly is true that from at least the Zhou dynasty, in the early first millennium BCE, rule was seen to rest on a Mandate of Heaven, a grant of rule to the emperor contingent on his discharging the duties of his office to assure order, harmony, justice, and prosperity. In the imperial period, if the emperor failed in his obligations, Confucian civil servants, as the authorized representatives of society, were obliged to remonstrate the ruler. If the emperor proved recalcitrant and unusually vicious, popular resistance was authorized, and widespread resistance was evidence that the ruler had lost his mandate. In other words, Chinese rulers were not unaccountable autocrats. Limited government should not, however, be confused with government limited by the human rights of its citizens and irregular political participation in cases of extreme tyranny should not be confused with a human right to political participation.

"The Confucian code of ethics recognized each individual's right to personal dignity and worth, but this right was 'not considered innate within each human soul as in the West, but had to be acquired' by his living up to the code," writes Tai (1985: 88), quoting John Fairbank (1972: 119). Such rights were not *human* rights. They had to be earned. They could be lost. Their ground was not the fact that one was a human being. The dignity and worth in question were not inalienable and inherent.

Many commentators seem uncomfortable with the fact that, as Lo Chung-Sho notes, "there was no open declaration of human rights in China, either by individual thinkers or by political constitutions, until this concept was introduced from the West" (1949: 186). Lo thus continues by arguing that "this of course does not mean that the Chinese never claimed human rights or enjoyed the basic rights of man" (1949: 186). How, though, the Chinese managed to claim human rights without the language to make such claims is certainly a mystery and Lo presents no evidence that they actually asserted or otherwise exercised such rights. Quite the contrary, his examples show only a divinely imposed duty of the ruler to govern for the common good, not rights of the people.

This is not a "different approach to human rights" (Lo 1949: 188). It is an approach to social justice or human well-being that does not rely on human rights. Lo fails to draw the crucial conceptual distinction between having a right and enjoying a benefit (see section 1.1) As a result, he confuses making claims of injustice with claiming human rights. Simply because acts that we would today say involved violations of human rights were considered impermissible does not mean that people were seen as having, let alone that they could claim or enjoy, human rights.

"Different civilizations or societies have different conceptions of human well-being. Hence, they have a different attitude toward human rights issues," writes Lee Manwoo (1985: 131). Even this is significantly misleading. Other societies may have similar or different attitudes toward issues that *we* consider to be matters of human rights. In the absence of the concept of human rights, however, they are unlikely to have *any* attitude toward human rights. To fail to respect this important conceptual distinction is not to show cultural sensitivity, respect, or tolerance but rather to anachronistically impose an alien analytical framework that misrepresents the social and ethical foundations and functioning of a society.

B. Traditional Africa

S. K. B. Asante writes that "the African conception of human rights was an essential aspect of African humanism" (1969: 74). Dunstan Wai concurs: "It is not often remembered that traditional African societies supported and practiced human rights" (1980: 116). As in the Chinese case, such assertions prove to be not only unsupported but actually undercut by the evidence presented on their behalf.

Wai continues: "Traditional African attitudes, beliefs, institutions, and experiences sustained the 'view that certain rights should be upheld against alleged necessities of state'" (1980: 116). This confuses human rights with limited government.[1] There are many other bases on which a government might be limited, including divine commandment, legal rights, and extralegal checks such as a balance of power or the threat of popular revolt. Even a right to limited government may be, for example, legal, traditional, or contractual, rather than a *human* right.

"There is no point in belaboring the concern for rights, democratic institutions, and rule of law in traditional African politics" (Wai 1980: 117). To this we can add only that it is particularly pointless in a discussion of human rights, given the form such concerns traditionally took. Even where Africans had personal rights against their government, those rights were based not on one's humanity but on such criteria as age, sex, lineage, achievement, or community membership.[2]

Asmarom Legesse notes that "many studies . . . suggest that distributive justice, in the economic and political spheres, is the cardinal ethical principle that is shared by most Africans" (1980: 127). Distributive justice and human rights, however, are different concepts. Plato, Burke, and Bentham all had theories of distributive justice. No one, however, would ever think to suggest that they advocated human rights. Although giving each his own—distributive justice—typically involves respecting the rights of others, unless "one's own" is defined in terms of that to which one is entitled simply as a human being, the rights in question will not be human rights. In African societies, rights typically were assigned on the basis of social roles and status within the community.

In a similar vein, Timothy Fernyhough argues that "many precolonial societies were distinguished by their respect for judicial and political procedure" (1993: 61). This is even more obviously irrelevant. The question, of course, is the nature of the procedures, in particular whether they were based on universal rights. They were not.

Rather than a case in which "different societies formulate their conception of human rights in diverse cultural idioms" (Legesse 1980: 124), we

1. "This chapter will argue that authoritarianism in modern Africa is not at all in accord with the spirit and practice of traditional political systems" (Wai 1980: 115). Compare Legesse (1980: 125–27) and Busia (1994: 231). For non-African examples of a similar confusion, see Said (1979: 65), Mangalpus (1978), and Pollis and Schwab (1980: xiv).
2. Fernyhough (1993: 55ff.) offers several examples of personal rights enjoyed in precolonial African societies. See also Mutua (1995: 348–51).

see here fundamental differences of concept and practice. Traditional African societies had concepts and practices of social justice that simply did not involve human rights. It is certainly true that "many African traditional societies did respect many of the basic values that underlie human rights" (Penna and Campbell 1998: 21). The ways in which they were valued, however, and the practices established to implement them were quite different. Recognition of human rights simply was not the way of traditional Africa, with obvious and important consequences for political practice (compare Howard 1986: chap. 2).

C. Islam and Human Rights

"In almost all contemporary Arab literature on this subject [human rights], we find a listing of the basic rights established by modern conventions and declarations, and then a serious attempt to trace them back to Koranic texts," writes Fouad Zakaria (1986: 228). The standard argument in the now quite extensive literature on Islam and human rights is that "Islam has laid down some universal fundamental rights for humanity as a whole, which are to be observed and respected under all circumstances . . . fundamental rights for every man by virtue of his status as a human being" (Mawdudi 1976: 10). Such claims, however, are almost entirely baseless.

For example, Khalid Ishaque argues that "Muslims are enjoined constantly to seek ways and means to assure to each other what in modern parlance we call 'human rights'" (1974: 32). While he admits that "human rights" cannot be translated into the language of the Islamic holy works, he nevertheless claims that they lie at the core of Islamic doctrine. But unless our concepts are independent of language—a highly implausible notion, especially for a social practice such as rights in which language is so central to its functioning—it is hard to see how this claim could even in principle be true. These texts, at most, enjoin functional analogues or different practices to produce similar ends. And in fact the fourteen "human rights" that Ishaque claims are recognized and established by Islam (1974: 32–38) prove to be only duties of rulers and individuals, not rights held by anyone (compare Said 1979: 65–68).

The scriptural passages cited as establishing a "right to protection of life" are in fact divine injunctions not to kill and to consider life inviolable. The "right to justice" proves to be instead a duty of rulers to establish justice. The "right to freedom" is a duty not to enslave unjustly (not even a general duty not to enslave). "Economic rights" turn out to be duties to help to provide for the needy. The purported "right to freedom of expression" is actually an obligation to speak the truth.[3]

3. Compare Khadduri (1946: 77–78), Mawdudi (1976: 17–24), and Moussalli (2001: 126).

Muslims are indeed regularly and forcefully called upon—by scripture, tradition, religious leaders, and ordinary believers—to treat others with respect and dignity. They are enjoined, in the strongest possible terms, to pursue both personal well-being and social justice. These injunctions clearly call to mind the *values* of the Universal Declaration of Human Rights. But they appeal to divine commands that establish duties, not human rights. The *practices* traditionally established to realize these values simply did not include equal and inalienable rights held by all human beings.

Consider Majid Khadduri's claim that "human rights in Islam are the privilege of Allah (God), because authority ultimately belongs to Him" (1946: 78). This is quite literally incoherent: "human rights" that are not rights of human beings but privileges of God. This is not, however, an idiosyncratic conception. Mahmood Monshipouri also argues that "in Islamic traditions human rights are entirely owned by God" (1998: 72). Similarly, Abdul Aziz Said argues that "individuals possess certain obligations towards God, fellow humans and nature, all of which are defined by Shariah. When individuals meet these obligations they acquire certain rights and freedoms which are again prescribed by the Shariah" (1979: 73–74). Such rights are contingent, unequal, earned, and alienable—rather than equal, inalienable, and universal. Being "duty based and interdependent on duties one owes to God and the community" (Ali 2000: 25), these are not human rights.

"Human rights in Islam, as prescribed by the divine law, are the privilege only of persons of full legal status. A person with full legal capacity is a living human being of mature age, free, and of Moslem faith" (Khadduri 1946: 79). These are rights of free Muslim men, not human rights—unless we restrict the category of human beings to free Muslim men, as Sultanhussein Tabendeh does when he claims that the preferential treatment of Muslims in certain criminal cases is "quite free of difficulty" from a human rights perspective, because "people who have not put their reliance in conviction and faith, nor had that basic abiding-place nor believed in the one Invisible God, are reckoned as outside the pale of humanity" (1970: 17). "Human rights" thus are supposed to be based on a conception that sees the majority of the population of the world as "outside of the pale of humanity"[4]—a view to which we will return in chapter 8.

Although most contemporary Muslims reject such views, they represent the historically dominant practice of most Muslim societies—much as most Christian societies throughout most of their histories treated non-Christians as inferior, despite what seems to us today the obviously universalistic egalitarianism of the New Testament. It is certainly true that "the notions of democracy, pluralism, and human rights are . . . in harmony with Islamic

---

4. Compare Ahmad Moussalli's claim that "human rights in Islam are creedal rights" (2001: 126).

thought" (Moussalli 2001: 2)—if by that we mean that Islam (like Christianity) can or ought to be read in this way. Here, however, we are addressing the historical question of how in fact they typically were read and acted upon by "traditional" Muslim societies. Like most other "traditional" societies, rights and duties were largely dependent on community membership. The "community of obligation," to use Helen Fein's apt term (1979: 33), was largely that of all believers[5]—Dar al Islam—not humanity. Even within the community, rights played a relatively minor role, compared to duties, and rights were earned and differed according to social status rather than being inherent and equal.

2. The Premodern West

The idea of human rights was equally foreign to the Western world prior to the mid-seventeenth century—and the practice remained largely foreign long after that. In this section I look briefly at social and political life in classical Greece, medieval Christendom, and early modern Europe.

A. Classical Greece

The Greeks of the classical era (ca. 476–336 BCE) drew a fundamental categorical distinction between Hellenes (the Greek term for "Greeks," the Latin-derived name) and barbarians (non-Greeks), who were considered incapable of self-rule and generally fit to be enslaved. This degradation of the barbarian remained a central feature of ancient political thought and practice right through to the collapse of the Roman Empire. "In the Greco-Roman political tradition the barbarian was the outsider. Rational human order was embodied in Greek or Roman society" (Markus 1988: 87).

Among Hellenes, life revolved around the polis, the independent city-state. During the classical era, citizen self-rule was so central to polis life that some classicists gloss polis not as city-state but citizen-state (Hansen 1993; Runciman 1990: 348; Raaflaub 2001: 75). Although this created a certain formal equality among citizens, sharp categorical distinctions were drawn between citizens and noncitizens. Slavery was universal in the Greek world and central to the Athenian economy.[6] Women were, "of course," politically excluded and socially subordinated. Noncitizen residents enjoyed few rights

---

5. This is both too broad—within the *umma*, the community of believers, there were slaves—and too narrow—Christians and Jews often enjoyed both freedom of religion and limited rights of self-government, despite being treated as legally, politically, socially, and morally inferior to Muslims.

6. Sparta seems to have had few outright slaves, but the Spartiate elite brutally dominated an effectively enserfed helot population that provided their material sustenance and equipment.

beyond some limited property rights and, in some cases, a basic legal personality. Thus even in democratic poleis the vast majority of even adult male residents was excluded from politics and consigned to a reduced and typically degraded social status. In some cities, such as Sparta, only a miniscule minority enjoyed civil and political rights.

Consider in a bit more detail Athens, the iconic "first democracy," the polis "most like us." The Athenians rightly prided themselves on the practice of *isonomia*, equal application of the law to rich and poor alike, and even *isogoria*, the formal right of all to speak in the assembly. Offices were kept to a minimum, filled by lot wherever possible, carefully monitored, and severely constrained in their powers. All important decisions were taken by the assembled people, in frequent, periodic mass meetings requiring a large quorum (of six thousand for important issues in the later fifth and fourth centuries). Furthermore, for the last half of the classical era, attendance at the assemblies and in the law courts was compensated at roughly the wages of a day laborer, making it possible for even poor citizens to play an active political role.

Nonetheless, the requirement that citizen-soldiers arm themselves was an effective bar to full participation by the poor, particularly in the fifth century, when principal reliance was placed on heavy-armored infantry (hoplites). And among citizens, distinctions of birth and wealth remained socially and politically central.

Political leaders were amateurs, in the sense of individuals without professional qualifications or (usually) a formal title. Political success, however, required close to full-time commitment throughout much of one's adult life and brought honor but no financial remuneration, putting it far out of the reach of ordinary citizens. Furthermore, the system of "liturgies" required wealthy private individuals to undertake public functions such as outfitting a ship or sponsoring a chorus in a play in a religious festival. Leaders were also expected to undertake, at their own cost, public functions such as serving on diplomatic missions and hosting visiting dignitaries. Private generosity toward less fortunate citizens was also expected. These various contributions brought one not only status but, if we are to believe the evidence of forensic oratory, special treatment.

Laws against hubris (public disrespect) restrained some of the more degrading demonstrations of elite disdain for the masses. Sumptuary laws considerably restricted some of the more blatant forms of elite display. Such practices, however, only tempered a fundamentally hierarchical system of distinctions between citizens—which rested on top of more fundamental distinctions between citizens and noncitizens and Hellenes and barbarians.

Relatively widespread popular political participation and the practices of *isonomia* and *isogoria* were later looked back upon as important precursors of contemporary ideas of universal human rights. We should not, however, confuse the limited legal and political equality of a privileged elite with contemporary ideas of human rights.

B. Medieval Christendom

In medieval Europe—or, to use the local label, (Western, Roman, or Latin) Christendom—neither being a human being nor being a Christian had significant implications for one's social, economic, or political rights or status. Quite the contrary, society and politics emphasized division and particularity, both in separating Christians from heathens (and heretics) and in the multitude of orders, grades, and statuses of Christians.

Medieval Christians saw themselves as surrounded by dangerous heathens. In the ninth, tenth, and twelfth centuries, Christendom moved significantly north and east. Much Muslim-held territory in Spain and Italy was "reconquered" in the eleventh and twelfth centuries. A largely unsuccessfully series of papally sanctioned Crusades, beginning in 1095, attempted to recover the Holy Land. The crusading form also was applied, with much greater success, to the struggle in the pagan north and east in the thirteenth century. In all of these "missionary" movements, Christians combined contemptuous arrogance with savage violence. Those who resisted the one true faith were treated not as dignified beings who had made a most tragic error but as contemptible, degraded beings undeserving of the least respect or consideration.

Within Christendom, both religious and secular life were hierarchically organized. Emphasis was placed on distinctions between grades of men (and within a particular social stratum, of men over women).

Bishops, who often chafed at assertions of papal authority, aggressively asserted their rank and its privileges over both subordinate clergy and the flocks to which they ministered. Furthermore, religious men were widely perceived to be closer to God than laymen of similar birth, status, and rank.

In the secular domain, the imperial idea retained great ideological appeal. In the German lands, the emperor's claim to superiority typically had considerable practical reality. Further west, kings struggled for power and position with other secular princes. Furthermore, within all polities hierarchy was the reigning principle.

"Feudal" hierarchies were also of central importance for extended periods. Understood narrowly, feudalism is a system based on contractual obligations of vassalage and land holding by fief or fee. More loosely, "feudalism" refers to various types of lordship characteristic of the early second millennium. George Duby (1974 [1973]: 174–77) describes these as "domestic lordship," based on control over the persons of subordinate laborers of varying legal status; "landlordship," based on possession of land and the rents and services it generated from those living on the land; and "banal" lordship, based on the *bannum*, the right of command and the administration of justice. Whatever the details, largely autarkic local communities lived under the (often effectively absolute) rule of local lords, and beneath the lords (*domini* or seigneurs) and their vassals (*vassi* or *homines*)—a class usually demarcated by noble birth and possession of horses and heavy arms—lay the vast bulk of the population, often further divided into slave (and later serf) and free.

Another standard medieval division was between those who fought, those who prayed, and those who worked the land. Those who fought and prayed were seen as morally superior and the ruling element of society. The absolute subordination of the ordinary man was usually emphasized with reference to Paul's Epistle to the Romans: "Let every soul be subject to higher powers: for there is no power but from God: and those that are, are ordained of God" (Rom. 13:1).[7]

Popular protests, often reflecting a millenarian, eschatological vision, were recurrent but almost always relatively easily (and more or less ruthlessly) suppressed. The rise of cities, which often attained considerable freedom from royal or imperial control, resulted in considerable freedom and political power for citizens of Italian communes and the burghers of northern Europe. But they insisted on their rank and status relative to the peasantry and proletariat beneath them no less strenuously than the nobility did with respect to them.

Hierarchy and division, rather than any shared sense of a common humanity or equal rights, dominated political thought and practice. Any moral idea of equal dignity at best referred to the potential of every Christian to be saved in the afterlife. No notion of equal political rights of "men," or even Christians, had any theoretical or practical traction.

C. Early Modern Europe

Early modern Western political practice was as alien to any plausible conception of human rights or human dignity as its ancient and medieval predecessors. Most sixteenth- and seventeenth-century polities were "composite states" (Elliott 1992; Nexon 2009; Trencsényi and Zászkaliczky 2010) created through processes of dynastic agglomeration in which smaller polities were incompletely, in varying degrees, and on varying terms, incorporated into a larger "imperial" polity. Far from revealing the beginnings of democratic

---

7. Tyranny was typically treated as an offense against God, for which the tyrant would be punished in the afterlife. Not only did the people have no right to just rule—let alone a right that they could act on through violent resistance to tyranny—it was typical to cite the passage from Job that described tyranny as divine retribution for the viciousness of a tyrant's subjects. For an extended discussion of these issues in the emblematic theory of Thomas Aquinas, see Donnelly (1980).

politics or popular sovereignty, rule was not merely primarily but increasingly monarchical. For example, it was not until the seventeenth century that the divine right of kings became the ruling orthodoxy of monarchs in France and England.

Appeals to natural rights did begin to be advanced in England with some real political effect, both during the civil wars of the 1640s and in justification of the Glorious Revolution of 1688. At most, though, these arguments brought property a political footing comparable to birth. The vast bulk of even the adult male population remained politically excluded and subordinated. Across Europe, uprisings by the poor were regularly repressed, typically brutally.

Furthermore, most of the early modern period was marked by savage cruelty in the context of national and international religious warfare. Consider just a few highlights.

- The Peasant War of 1524–25, closely associated with what we would today call the "viral" spread of Lutheranism in southwestern Germany, led to the deaths of about one hundred thousand.
- On succeeding to the English throne in 1553, Queen Mary attempted to return the country to Catholicism, by force if necessary, including burning at the stake two to three hundred prominent Protestant leaders. In fairness, though, it must be admitted that "Bloody Mary" did little more than continue the policies of her father, Henry VIII, simply switching the victims from Catholics such as Thomas More to Protestants such as Thomas Cranmer.
- In 1562, an attack on Calvinist worshipers led to a general massacre of Protestants in Vassy in Champagne that plunged France into three and a half decades of sporadically erupting religious warfare.
- The Thirty Years' War combined dynastic and religious rivalry in a particularly brutal form. The population of Germany declined by about a fifth—greater than Soviet losses during World War II—and in some areas, such as Württemberg, more than half of the population was killed.
- In the English Civil War of the 1640s perhaps two hundred thousand people (roughly 4–5 percent of the population) were killed in England and Scotland. In Ireland, a third of the population was killed—more than twice the level of deaths during the potato famine ("the Great Hunger") two hundred years later.
- In 1681, Louis XIV began the forced conversions of French Huguenots, leading to a huge forced emigration. In 1685, he revoked the Edict of Nantes, destroyed Huguenot churches, and closed Protestant schools. The following year, the king boasted of having

removed or converted more than 98 population of the Huguenot population—and promised to deal with the remainder quickly and decisively.

At the end of the seventeenth century, a single state religion, combined with the active persecution of public worship in unapproved forms, remained the European norm. Wealth did begin to compete with birth as the basis for political privilege, but even England at the end of the seventeenth century had managed to achieve little more than some sort of balance between king, lords, and commons—which, it must be remembered, represented only a tiny, propertied elite. On the continent, outside of the few republican enclaves, even that level of "popular" political participation was rare. Any idea of the equal dignity of all men—much less women—or even of all resident men adhering to the state religion, was a fringe idea with little or no political impact.

To this dismal picture we need to add the development of overseas imperialism, often in the most brutal forms, and the revival of slavery (which had largely died out in medieval Europe, primarily for economic and political reasons). If Europeans did not see their civilized Christian neighbors as rights-bearing fellow humans, it is hardly surprising that such an idea seems not even to have crossed the minds of most Westerners when they encountered overseas "barbarians" and "savages."

Dating Western history to the Persian Wars, for its first two millennia the West had neither the idea nor the practice of human rights (understood as equal and inalienable rights that all human beings have and may exercise against society and the state). Athenian democracy, Roman republicanism, and Christian theological egalitarianism could be, and from the late-eighteenth century regularly were, drawn upon to both demand and justify egalitarian rights-based polities. But prior to the late-seventeenth century any such attempts—for example, by early Christian Gnostic sects, radical sixteenth-century Anabaptists, and the millenarian Diggers in the 1640s in England—were ruthlessly (and usually rapidly) repressed. We must not confuse later and earlier appropriations of "the same" cultural resources. Unless we appreciate these differences in social practices—that is, the sharp break with traditional ways implicit in the idea and practice of equal and inalienable rights held by all human beings—we delude ourselves about the past and obscure central elements of the meaning and importance of human rights today.

3. The Modern Invention of Human Rights

What in "modernity" led to the development of human rights? In a gross (but I hope insightful) oversimplification, I want to suggest that modern states and modern markets triggered social processes and struggles that eventually transformed hierarchical polities of rulers and subjects into more egalitarian polities of office holders and citizens.[8]

To reduce three centuries to a few paragraphs, ever more powerful capitalist markets and sovereign, bureaucratic states gradually penetrated first Europe and then the globe. In the process, "traditional" communities, and their systems of mutual support and obligation, were disrupted, destroyed, or radically transformed, typically with traumatic consequences. These changes created the problems that human rights were "designed" to solve: vast numbers of relatively separate families and individuals left to face a growing range of increasingly unbuffered economic and political threats to their interests and dignity.

The absolutist state—increasingly freed from the constraints of cross-cutting feudal obligations, independent religious authorities, and tradition—offered one solution: a society organized around a monarchist hierarchy justified by a state religion. But the newly emergent bourgeoisie, the other principal beneficiary of early modern markets and states, envisioned a society in which the claims of property balanced those of birth. By the late seventeenth century, such claims increasingly were formulated in terms of natural rights.

More or less contemporaneously, the Reformation disrupted the unity of Christendom, with consequences that were often even more violent. By the middle of the seventeenth century, however, states gradually began to stop fighting over religion. Although full religious equality was far off—just as bourgeois calls for "equal" treatment initially fell far short of full political equality even for themselves, let alone for all—religious toleration (at least for some Christians sects) gradually became the European norm.

Add to this the growing possibilities for physical and social mobility—facilitated by the consolidation of states and the expansion of markets—and we have the crucible out of which contemporary human rights ideas and practices were formed. As "modernization" progressed, an ever-widening range of dispossessed groups advanced claims first for relief from legal and political disabilities, then for full and equal inclusion. Such demands took many forms, including appeals to scripture, church, morality, tradition, justice, natural law, order, social utility, and national strength. Claims of equal and inalienable natural or human rights, however, increasingly came to be preferred—and over the past couple decades have become globally hegemonic.

8. If I were to add one more element to this story it would be the development of modern scientific rationality, which both helped to tear down traditional hierarchies and to establish new forms of social, economic, and political organization. The association of modern with scientific rationality has been especially emphasized by the "Stanford School" of "world society theory." See, for example, Meyer et al. (1997), Meyer and Jepperson (2000), and Thomas (2010).

4. The American and French Revolutions

The transformation from "traditional" hierarchical polities to "modern," egalitarian, rights-based polities was neither rapid nor easy. Three centuries separate the Peace of Westphalia from the Universal Declaration of Human Rights, during which prolonged, intense, and often violent political struggles were required to expand both the substance and the subjects of "natural rights." Consider the American and French Revolutions.

These eighteenth-century revolutions were in many ways quite distant from their seventeenth-century English predecessor. This is particularly clear in a comparison between the 1689 English Bill of Rights and the 1776 and 1789 American and French Declarations.

The English Bill begins with "the Lords Spiritual and Temporal and Commons assembled at Westminster" presenting "unto their Majesties . . . a certain declaration in writing." The trappings are much more "medieval" than "modern"—as is the substance of their complaints. The heart of their case is that "the late King James the Second, by the assistance of divers evil counsellors, judges and ministers employed by him, did endeavour to subvert and extirpate the Protestant religion and the laws and liberties of this kingdom." In other words, Parliament acted to replace a bad king with a good one, understanding the badness of the old king in terms of his offenses against the Protestant religion and the traditional laws and liberties of the land.

When they moved on to asserting their rights, they did so "as their ancestors in like case have usually done" and for the purpose of "vindicating and asserting their ancient rights and liberties." In other words, when they appeal to rights it is as Englishmen, not human beings. And they conclude with an oath to "be faithful and bear true allegiance to their Majesties" and to "from my heart abhor, detest and abjure as impious and heretical this damnable doctrine and position, that princes excommunicated or deprived by the Pope or any authority of the see of Rome may be deposed or murdered by their subjects or any other whatsoever. And I do declare that no foreign prince, person, prelate, state or potentate hath or ought to have any jurisdiction, power, superiority, pre-eminence or authority, ecclesiastical or spiritual, within this realm."

The English Bill of Rights, in other words, fits comfortably within the early modern framework of dynastic monarchy and religious warfare. William, who held a title from a small principality in southern France, and had succeeded his father as *stadthouder* of the Dutch Republic, become King of England as a result of his marriage to the daughter of James II, because of dissatisfaction with his wife's father's religion.

Compare the 1776 American Declaration of Independence. The claim of American independence was rooted not in traditional rights and privileges but in "the separate and equal station to which the Laws of Nature and

Nature's God entitle them." The Declaration of Independence is addressed not only to king and country, but no less importantly to "the opinions of mankind" and to "Nature's God." And it states a completely new conception of government.

> We hold these truths to be self-evident, that all men are created equal, that they are endowed by their Creator with certain unalienable Rights, that among these are Life, Liberty and the pursuit of Happiness.— That to secure these rights Governments are instituted among Man, deriving their just powers from the consent of the governed,—That whenever any Form of Government becomes destructive of these ends, it is the Right of the People to alter or abolish it, and to institute new Government, laying its foundation on such principles and organizing its powers in such form, as to them shall seem most likely to effect their Safety and Happiness.

God is still present—but not religion. Rights and liberties remain central—but they are now natural or human rights, not traditional rights. Sovereignty resides not in the king or Parliament but in the people—who are free not just to replace a bad king with a good one but to replace kingship with a republic. Thus, in conclusion, "We . . . by Authority of the good People of these Colonies, solemnly publish and declare [American independence]."

Even more radically, the 1789 French Declaration of the Rights of Man and the Citizen begins by asserting that "ignorance, neglect or contempt of the rights of man are the sole causes of public misfortunes and governmental corruption." Its first three articles assert that "men are born and remain free and equal in rights," that "the purpose of all political association is the preservation of the natural and imprescriptible rights of man," and that "the principle of sovereignty rests essentially in the nation."

By the end of the eighteenth century, the mainstream of Western theory and practice included a new conception of political legitimacy based on a notion of (politically foundational) equal and inalienable rights of man. We should not, however, underestimate either the exceptional nature of these revolutions or their very severe limits.

The rights in question in the American and French Revolutions were indeed the rights of men, not of women, and the men in question were almost exclusively white. The US Constitution of 1787 not only entrenched the institution of slavery within the fundamental law of the new republic but infamously defined slaves as three-fifths of a person for the purposes of electoral apportionment. The French Revolution in its most radical phase did for one year officially abolish slavery. The practice, however, remained essentially unchanged.

Furthermore, property restrictions on the franchise continued to exclude many freeborn white male residents from full or active citizenship, particularly in the Old World. Economic and social rights were restricted largely to the right to property (although in America, where land still could readily be seized from the indigenous populations, this was a less severe limitation than in the Old World). Many basic civil and political rights continued to be deeply contested. For example, the Alien and Sedition Acts of 1798 were intended and used to repress political speech critical of the US government. And it would take most of the rest of Europe until well into the nineteenth century or later to achieve even this level of progress.

5. Approaching the Universal Declaration

In the nineteenth century, the United States continued to expand the depth and range of its rights-based republic—at least for white Christian men—moving in a general direction that can plausibly be described as liberal-democratic. Progress in the Old World was more limited, and more sporadic, especially in the first half of the century. After 1848, though, the tide shifted decisively against the monarchical vision of Europe's future and in the ensuing decades universal suffrage for men became the norm.

Women still remained excluded. In the United States, even after the abolition of slavery, racial discrimination remained systematic, legalized, and extremely harsh. And overseas colonialism was in the midst a new phase of expansion.

Not until after World War II—key symbolic markers are Indian independence in 1947, Ghanaian independence in 1956, and the adoption in 1960 of UN General Assembly Resolution 1514, the Declaration on the Granting of Independence to Colonial Countries and Peoples—did the Western world really came to accept the notion of equal political rights *for all*. More precisely, the West finally came to accept that equal political rights could not be legitimately denied on the basis of "race, colour, sex, language, religion, political or other opinion, national or social origin, property, [or] birth," as the Universal Declaration put it—or colonial status either.

Even this only takes us halfway to the Universal Declaration vision of human rights. The equal importance of economic and social rights in the Western world is largely a phenomenon of the first half of the twentieth century. In the 1920s and 1930s, there was considerable divergence, with Sweden, Denmark, Norway, and the United Kingdom leading and Finland, Switzerland, France, Belgium and Italy lagging (Flora and Alber 1981: 57). By the late 1940s, however, almost all Western states were not merely politically committed to becoming welfare states but well on the way to realizing that commitment. Consider, for example, the flurry of legislation in Britain: the Family

Allowance Act (1945), National Insurance Act (1946), National Insurance (Industrial Injuries) Act (1946), National Health Service Act (1946), Children Act (1948), and National Assistance Act (1948).

The Universal Declaration did not reflect long-held Western ideas and practices. Western states did endorse the Universal Declaration, with considerable enthusiasm—but largely on the basis of what those states had become over the preceding several decades. Roots (as opposed to suggestive intimations) of this conception of human dignity and human rights do not go back much beyond two hundred years before the Universal Declaration and the bulk of the gap between the mainstream of Western practice and the vision of the Universal Declaration was closed in the three or four decades prior to the Declaration.

6. Expanding the Subjects and Substance of Human Rights

The historical development of human rights has involved the interconnected expansions of both the list of human rights and the groups of *Homo sapiens* considered to hold them. Not only does John Locke's list of natural rights to life, liberty, and estates fall significantly short of the Universal Declaration, Locke clearly envisioned them to be held only by propertied white Christian men. Women, "savages," servants, and wage laborers were never imagined to be holders of natural rights at the end of the seventeenth century.

Over the succeeding three centuries, however, racist, bourgeois, Christian patriarchs found the same arguments they used against aristocratic privilege turned against them by members of new social groups seeking full and equal participation in public and private life. In each case, the essential claim was that however different ("other") we—religious dissenters, poor people, women, nonwhites, ethnic minorities—may be, we are, no less than you, human beings, and as such are entitled to the same basic rights. Furthermore, members of disadvantaged or despised groups have used the rights they did enjoy to press for legal recognition of those rights still being denied them. For example, workers used their votes, along with what freedoms of the press and association they were allowed, to press to eliminate legal discrimination based on property.

The substance of human rights thus expanded in tandem with their subjects. For example, the political left argued that unlimited private property rights were incompatible with true liberty, equality, and security for workingmen (and, later, women). Through intense and often violent political struggles this led to regulations on working conditions, the rise of social insurance schemes, and an extended range of recognized economic, social, and cultural rights, culminating in the welfare state societies of late-twentieth-century

Europe. The Universal Declaration codified an evolved shared understanding of the principal systematic public threats to human dignity in the contemporary world (and the rights-based practices necessary to counter them). And, finally, the International Human Rights Covenants, by adding of the right of peoples to self-determination, expanded the subjects of human rights to all human beings everywhere on the globe.

6

The Relative Universality of Human Rights

Universality and relativity are usually presented as opposites defined either dichotomously or as end points of a continuum. The primary sense of "universal," however, as we will see in a moment, is not merely compatible with but necessarily includes an essential element of relativity. The question, then, is not *whether* human rights are universal or relative but *how* human rights are (and are not) universal and how they are (and are not) relative. Exploring these various senses leads to the conclusion that internationally recognized human rights are "relatively universal" in the contemporary world.

I. "Universal" and "Relative"

The first definition of "universal" in the *Oxford English Dictionary* (*OED*) is "extending over, comprehending, or including the whole of something." Universal, in this sense, is "relative" to a particular class or group, the "something" that is encompassed. Universal means "applies across all of a particular domain" (rather than everywhere in the universe). Universality is relative to a *particular* "universe" of application. For example, universal health care, universal primary education, and universal suffrage, involve making health care, primary education, and voting rights available to all citizens, nationals, or residents of a country—not everyone on the globe (let alone anywhere in the universe). A "universal remote control" neither controls all possible entertainment devices nor works everywhere in the universe. It operates only those devices that are "standard" for "us" here and now. Most American "universal remotes" won't even work in Europe.

Universal also is defined as "of or pertaining to the universe in general or all things in it; existing or occurring everywhere or in all things." Little, though, is universal in this sense, other than formal logical systems of propositions, like mathematics, and perhaps some of the laws of physics (or God).

Thus the *OED* describes this sense as "chiefly poetic or rhetorical" (to which we can add philosophical or theological).

The parallel *OED* definitions of "relative" are "arising from, depending on, or determined by, relation to something else or to each other" and "constituted, or existing, only by relation to something else; not absolute or independent." Talk of relativity immediately calls forth the question "Relative to what?" Something cannot be relative in general but must always be relative to (or dependent on) something else in particular. For relativity no less than universality, an adjective that defines a context or type of relativity is essential.

Human rights, as we saw in sections 5.1–2, are definitely not universal in the "occurring everywhere" sense. They are, however, universal in at least three important senses (addressed in the following section). Each of these forms of universality, however, is relative—that is, operates within a particular domain—and additional senses of relativity are the subject of the remaining sections of this chapter.

2. The Universality of Internationally Recognized Human Rights

We have already encountered three ways in which human rights are universal (in the sense of applying across a class). 1) Virtually all states consider internationally recognized human rights to be a firmly established part of international law and politics. 2) Virtually all cultures, regions, and leading worldviews participate in an overlapping consensus on these internationally recognized human rights. 3) This consensus rests on the contemporary universality of the standard threats to human dignity posed by modern markets and modern states. I will call these international legal universality, overlapping consensus universality, and functional universality. Each, however, is associated with a fundamental particularity that also merits emphasis.

A. International Legal Universality

Human rights are universal in the sense that they have been accepted by almost all states as establishing obligations that are binding in international law. As noted in chapter 4, the six core international human rights treaties—the two Covenants plus the conventions on racial discrimination, women's rights, torture, and the rights of the child—in early 2012 had, on average, 172 parties. This 88 percent ratification rate is strikingly high in contemporary international law. Furthermore, there are no systematic patterns of deviation. Although ratification rates are somewhat lower in Asia than in other regions, the substantial majority of states in every regional, religious, or political grouping are parties to most of these treaties.

In other words, despite the cultural, political, regional, and economic diversity of the contemporary world, there is near universal agreement on not only the existence but also the substance of internationally recognized human rights. In the domain of contemporary international law and politics, as the Vienna Declaration of the 1993 World Conference on Human Rights put it in its first operative paragraph, "the universal nature of these rights and freedoms is beyond question." This universality is "beyond question" not in the sense that no one violates, challenges, or denounces these rights. Challenges, however, are typically ruled "out of the question." They simply are not seriously engaged—in much the same way that in most national legal systems challenges to a long-established national constitution are dismissed out of hand, rather than seriously considered, by most political actors.

In the decades immediately following the drafting of the Universal Declaration, international legal universality was rather superficial. Substantial deepening, however, began in the mid-1970s, symbolized by the Helsinki Final Act of 1975, the election of Jimmy Carter as president of the United States in 1976, and the award of the Nobel Peace Prize to Amnesty International in 1977. The 1990s saw another major spurt of development, with the result that today international human rights norms have come to penetrate surprisingly deeply in most regions. Particularly notable is that fact that movements for social justice and of political opposition have increasingly adopted the language of human rights. In addition, growing numbers of new international issues, ranging from migration to global trade and finance, and to access to pharmaceuticals, are being framed as issues of human rights (compare Brysk 2005).

International legal universality, however, is bounded. These rights are binding in international law; that is, states agree that they have obligations with respect to these rights. As we will see in some detail in chapter 11, however, there are no significant international enforcement mechanisms. National, not international, courts provide judicial enforcement and in many countries national legal means of implementation are, to say the least, not very effective.

Nonetheless, international legal universality is of immense theoretical and practical significance. Sovereign territorial states—the designated "universe"—remain by far the most important actors in determining whether people enjoy the human rights that they have. Their formal endorsement of international human rights obligations thus is of immense importance. Local activists, transnational advocates, foreign states, and international organizations can appeal to widely endorsed international norms that in almost all cases the target state has itself repeatedly accepted as binding. This greatly facilitates the work of human rights advocacy and defense. In fact, international legal universality may be the most important *practical* legacy of international action on behalf of human rights.

B. Overlapping Consensus Universality

Law lies at the intersection of power and justice. We thus should expect to find international legal universality both backed by preponderant political power and reflecting deeper ethical, moral, or religious values. It certainly is not coincidental that most of the world's leading military and economic powers strongly support internationally recognized human rights. I will focus here, however, on the cross-cultural ethical foundations of internationally recognized human rights.

As we saw in section 4.2, John Rawls distinguishes "comprehensive religious, philosophical, or moral doctrines," such as Islam, Kantianism, Confucianism, and Marxism, from "political conceptions of justice," which address only the political structure of society, defined (as far as possible) independently of any particular comprehensive doctrine (1996: 31–33, 172–73; 1999: xliii–xlv, 11–15, 174–76). Adherents of very different, and even irreconcilable, comprehensive doctrines may be able to reach an "overlapping consensus" on a political conception of justice (Rawls 1996: 133–72, 385–96). Such a consensus, although partial rather than complete and political rather than moral or religious, is real and important.

This overlapping consensus universality, besides being intrinsically interesting and important, also helps to explain international legal universality. The striking extent of the formal international legal endorsement of human rights reflects the fact that adherents of most leading comprehensive doctrines pretty much across the globe do in fact endorse internationally recognized human rights.

Again, we must carefully specify the limits of this universality. In particular, I am not arguing that all of the comprehensive doctrines that today endorse human rights have done so throughout all or even much of their history. Quite the contrary, they have not, in the Western and the non-Western worlds alike, as we saw in chapter 5.

Nevertheless, the moral equality of all human beings is strongly endorsed by most leading comprehensive doctrines in all regions of the world. This convergence, both within and between civilizations, provides the foundation for a convergence on the rights of the Universal Declaration. In principle, a great variety of social practices other than human rights might provide the basis for realizing foundational egalitarian values. In practice, human rights have become the preferred option.

C. Functional Universality

How can we explain this consensus? Those who focus on culture will find it inexplicable—and thus are likely to appeal to power, imposition, and "cultural imperialism." I want to suggest instead that it rests on near-universal social-structural features of the contemporary world.

As I argued in section 5.3, internationally recognized human rights respond to certain standard threats to human dignity associated with modern markets and modern states, which have penetrated nearly every part of the globe today. This creates what I will call the functional universality of internationally recognized human rights.

Human rights represent the most effective response yet devised to a wide range of standard threats to human dignity that market economies and bureaucratic states have made nearly universal across the globe. Human rights today remain the only proven effective means to assure human dignity in societies dominated by markets and states. Although historically contingent and relative, this functional universality fully merits the label universal—for us, today. Virtually everyone on this planet today lives in a world of modern markets and modern states, which need to be tamed by human rights if those powerful institutions are to be made compatible with a life of dignity for the average person.

Arguments that another state, society, or culture has developed plausible and effective alternative mechanisms for protecting or realizing human dignity in the contemporary world certainly deserve serious attention. Today, however, such claims, when not advanced by repressive elites and their supporters, usually refer to an allegedly possible world that no one yet has had the good fortune to experience. The alleged success stories of the Cold War era, for example, have collapsed in tragic failure, often with dreadful human consequences.

The functional universality of human rights depends on human rights providing attractive remedies for some of the most pressing systemic threats to human dignity. Human rights today do precisely that for a growing number of people of all cultures in all regions. Whatever our other problems, we all must deal with market economies and bureaucratic states. Whatever our other religious, moral, legal, and political resources, we all need equal and inalienable universal human rights to protect us from those threats.

D. The Evolution of Lists of Human Rights

There is also an essential particularity in the specification of universal human rights. A list of rights reflects a contingent response to historically specific conditions. For example, Article 11 of the International Covenant on Civil and Political Rights—"No one shall be imprisoned merely on the ground of inability to fulfill a contractual obligation"—responds to the (historically very unusual) practice of debtor prisons. An authoritative list of human rights emerges out of an ongoing series of political struggles that have changed our understanding of human dignity, the major threats (both old and new) to that dignity, and the institutions, practices, and values necessary to protect it.

In the most general terms, a list of rights reflects a society's understanding of the principal "standard threats" (Shue 1980: 29–34) to human dignity. A human right to excrete, for example, seems silly because there is no serious threat. If preventing excretion, though, were to become a diabolical new tool of torture or repressive social control, recognizing a human right to excrete might make sense.[1] Consider, by contrast, the internationally recognized right to "rest, leisure and reasonable limitation of working hours and periodic holidays with pay." Here we face not the fantasy of a perverse imagination but a common assault on the dignity of workers, from nineteenth-century factories in Manchester, to twentieth-century sweatshops in New York, and to textile and electronics factories across Asia today.

Not every kind of systematic suffering leads to a recognized right. Politics largely determines whether any particular indignity, threat, or right is recognized. Nonetheless, our list of human rights has evolved, and will continue to change, in response to social and technological changes, the emergence of new techniques of repression, changing ideas of human dignity, the rise of new political forces, and even past human rights successes (which allow attention and resources to be shifted to threats that previously were inadequately recognized or insufficiently addressed).

For example, Thomas Jefferson expanded John Locke's "estates" to "the pursuit of happiness," but Jefferson's vision was still primarily agricultural. Economic and social rights as we have come to understand them began to make substantial headway only with the nineteenth-century rise of the urban working class as an effective political force. The resulting political struggles led to new understandings of the meaning of, and conditions necessary for, a life of dignity, rooted in significant measure in the experience of the social and economic devastation of early industrialization. Over the course of more than a century, the right to property gradually was supplemented by, and ultimately largely subordinated to, an extensive set of economic, social, and cultural rights.

Our list of civil and political rights has changed no less dramatically. Today in the West we take the right to a free press largely for granted. Two hundred years ago, however, Tom Paine was prosecuted for sedition because of his pamphleteering and President Adams used the notorious restrictions of the Alien and Sedition Acts against his political adversaries, including Thomas Jefferson. The right to freedom of association has been extended to associations of workers for scarcely more than a century. Genocide was

---

1. This right actually was advanced by Johan Galtung in a paper circulated in the mid-1970s, although I am no longer able to find the reference.

recognized as an international crime only in the aftermath of the Holocaust. "Disappearances" have more recently reshaped our understandings of the rights to life and protection against arbitrary arrest and detention.

Lists of human rights emerge from the concrete sufferings of real human beings and their political struggles to defend or realize their dignity. Internationally recognized human rights reflect a politically driven process of social learning. To take just one more example, Article 2 of the Universal Declaration proclaims, "Everyone is entitled to all the rights and freedoms set forth in this Declaration, without distinction of any kind, such as race, colour, sex, language, religion, political or other opinion, national or social origin, property, birth or other status." Those struggles against discrimination that have been largely successful, at least in theory, are noted explicitly and "other status" points toward future struggles by other excluded groups, such as children, seniors, disabled people, and gays, lesbians, bisexuals, and transgendered persons (to whom we will return in chapter 16).

3. Three Levels of Universality and Particularity

We have already identified at least five senses in which human rights are fundamentally relative.

- Ontological relativity. Human rights are not part of the natural fabric of reality; they do not apply everywhere and at all times.
- Historical or anthropological relativity. Human rights are historically contingent responses to the standard threats posed by modern markets and modern states. They were not present in "traditional" (nonstate and nonmarket) societies, and there is no reason to assume that they will apply in very different types of societies in the future.
- Foundational relativity. Human rights have a considerable number of quite different foundations (which converge on the Universal Declaration in an overlapping consensus).
- Relativity of enjoyment. Human rights, although *held* universally, are implemented nationally, making their enjoyment relative to where one has the good or bad fortune to have been born or to live.
- Relativity in specification. A list of human rights reflects a process of social learning with respect to historically particular and contingent standard threats to human dignity.

Here I want to focus on a different type of relativity—or, perhaps more accurately, particularity. The universality that I have defended exists at a very high level of generality. As our specification of human rights becomes more detailed, the space for legitimate variation across time and space increases.

We can identify three levels of abstraction in the specification of internationally recognized human rights. Basic concepts, I will argue, are largely universal. Particular conceptions or interpretations of those concepts have a significant but limited range of legitimate variation. The particulars of implementation, however, are legitimately matters of considerable local variability.

A. Concepts of Human Rights

The Universal Declaration generally formulates rights at the level of what I will call the *concept*, an abstract, general statement of an orienting value. "Everyone has the right to work, to free choice of employment, to just and favorable conditions of work and to protection against unemployment" (Article 23). At this level of abstraction, human rights are fundamentally universal.

In the contemporary world, it is difficult to imagine serious arguments against recognizing the rights of Articles 3–12, which include life, liberty, and security of the person; the guarantee of legal personality, equality before the law, and privacy; and protections against slavery, arbitrary arrest, detention, or exile, and inhuman or degrading treatment. These are so clearly connected to basic requirements of human dignity, and are stated in sufficiently general terms, that virtually every morally defensible contemporary form of social organization recognizes them (although perhaps not necessarily as inalienable rights). I am even tempted to say that conceptions of human nature or society that are incompatible with such rights are almost by definition indefensible in contemporary international society.

Civil rights such as freedom of conscience, speech, and association may be a bit more relative. Because they assume the existence and positive evaluation of relatively autonomous individuals, they may be of questionable applicability in strong, thriving traditional communities. In such communities, however, they would rarely be at issue. If traditional practices truly are based on and protect culturally accepted conceptions of human dignity, then members of such a community will not have the desire or the need to claim such rights. In the more typical contemporary case, however, in which relatively autonomous individuals face modern states, it is hard for me to imagine a defensible conception of human dignity that did not include (almost all) of these rights. A similar argument can be made for the economic and social rights of the Universal Declaration.

In more than thirty years of working with issues of cultural relativism, I have developed a simple challenge that I pose to skeptical audiences. Which rights in the Universal Declaration does your society or culture reject? Rarely have I had a single full right (other than the right to private property) rejected. Never has it been suggested to me that as many as four should be eliminated.

Typical was the experience I had in Iran in early 2001, where I posed this question to three different audiences. In each case, discussion moved quickly to freedom of religion, and in particular atheism and apostasy by Muslims (which the Universal Declaration permits, as an exercise of the right to freedom of religious, but Iran prohibits).[2] Given the continuing repression of Iranian Baha'is, who the Iranian government views as Muslim apostates, this was quite a sensitive issue. Even here, though, the challenge was not to the principle, or even the right, of freedom of religion (which Muslims support) but to competing "Western" and "Muslim" conceptions of its limits.

Every society places some limits on religious liberty. In the United States, for example, recent court cases have dealt with forced medical treatment for the children of Christian Scientists, live animal sacrifice by practitioners of Santeria, and the rights of Jehovah's Witnesses to evangelize at private residences.[3] The Iranian government draws the limits differently. They may be wrong to draw them where and as they do. But the issue has nothing to do with the concept of freedom of religion. It is about what I will call below competing conceptions of the limits of religious liberty.

I have argued above that in the contemporary world differences at the level of concepts are not especially significant; that there are strong and increasingly deep international legal and overlapping foundational consensuses on internationally recognized human rights. For reasons of space—as well as the fact that negative existential arguments cannot be conclusively established—I leave this claim as a challenge. Critics may refute my argument with several well-chosen examples of substantial cultural variation at the level of concepts. So far, at least, I have not encountered anyone capable of presenting such a pattern of contradictory evidence, except in the case of small and relatively isolated communities.[4]

B. Conceptions or Interpretations

Universality at the level of the concept, however, should not obscure potentially important disagreements concerning definitions and implicit limitations.

2. Gender equality, perhaps surprisingly, did not come up (although these were elite, English-speaking audiences, and Iran has self-consciously made considerable progress on women's rights issues). Even when it does, dispute usually focuses on the meaning of nondiscrimination or on particular practices such as equal rights in marriage.

3. The other example that I have commonly encountered includes some of the details of Article 16, which deals with family rights. Again, though, the basic right to marry and found a family is always strongly endorsed by those who challenge details of the interpretation offered in the Universal Declaration.

4. The general similarity of regional human rights instruments underscores this argument. Even the African Charter on Human and Peoples' Rights, the most heterodox regional treaty, differs largely at the level of interpretation and, in substance or concept, by addition (of peoples' rights) rather than by subtraction.

Consider Article 5 of the Universal Declaration: "No one shall be subjected to torture or to cruel, inhuman or degrading treatment or punishment." The real controversy comes over questions such as what counts as torture or whether particular practices are cruel and inhuman. For example, most European states consider the death penalty to be cruel and inhuman but the United States does not. The Bush administration claimed—with apparent sincerity but little persuasive power—that waterboarding was not torture.

Consider the right to work. Does it mean a guaranteed job, or is it enough to provide compensation to those who are unemployed? Both seem to me plausible interpretations. Some such variations in interpreting rights seem not merely defensible but desirable, even necessary.

Implicit limits on rights also restrict the range of universality. Most of the rights in the Universal Declaration are formulated in categorical terms. For example, Article 19 begins, "Everyone has the right to freedom of opinion and expression." To use the hackneyed American example, this does not mean that one can scream "Fire!" in a crowded theater. All rights have limits. (Logically, there can be at most one absolute right—unless we implausibly assume that rights never conflict with one another.) If these limits differ widely and systematically, the resulting differences in human rights practices might indeed be considerable.

I distinguish two levels of variation: conceptions or interpretations, which may legitimately vary within a range set by overarching concepts, and implementations, which are constrained by interpretations but subject to considerable local variation.

Not all "interpretations," however, are equally plausible or defensible. They are *interpretations*, not free associations or arbitrary, let alone self-interested, stipulations. The meaning of, for example, "the right to political participation" is controversial, but an election in which a people were allowed to choose an absolute dictator for life ("one man, one vote, once") is simply indefensible.

We should also note that the Universal Declaration elaborates some rights at the level of interpretations. For example, the right of free and full consent of intending spouses reflects an interpretation of marriage over which legitimate controversy is possible. Notice, however, that the right (as Section 2 of Article 16) is subordinate to the right to marry and to found a family (over which, at this highest level of generality, there is little international dispute). Furthermore, some traditional customs, such as bride-price, provide alternative protections for women that address at least some of the underlying concerns that gave rise to the norm of free and full consent.

C. Implementation or Form

Just as concepts need to be interpreted, interpretations need to be implemented. For example, taking unemployment compensation as the governing interpretation of the right to work, what rate of compensation should be provided, for how long, in what circumstances? The range of actual and defensible variation here is considerable—although limited by the governing concept and interpretation.

A number of rights in the International Human Rights Covenants clearly involve specifications at the level of form. For example, Article 10(2)(b) of the International Covenant on Civil and Political Rights requires the segregation of juvenile defendants. In many societies the very notion of a juvenile criminal defendant (or a penitentiary system) does not exist. There are good reasons to suggest such rules. To demand them in the face of strong, reasoned opposition, however, seems to me to make little sense—so long as the underlying objectives are realized in some other fashion.

I stress this three-level scheme to avoid a common misconception. My argument is for universality only at the level of the concept. The Universal Declaration insists that all states share a limited but important range of obligations. It is, in its own words, "a common standard of achievement for all peoples and all nations." The ways in which these rights are interpreted and implemented, however, so long as they fall within the range of variation consistent with the overarching concept, are matters of legitimate variation.

This is particularly important because most of the hot-button issues in recent discussions have occurred at the level of implementation. For example, debates about pornography are about the limits—interpretation or implementation—of freedom of expression. Most Western countries permit the graphic depiction of virtually any sex act (so long as it does not involve and is not shown to children). Many others countries punish those who produce, distribute, or consume such material. This dispute, however, does not suggest a rejection of human rights, the idea of personal autonomy, or even the right to freedom of speech.

We should also note that controversy over pornography rages internally within many countries. Every country criminalizes some forms of pornography, and most countries permit some depictions of sexual behavior or the display of erotic images that have within living memory banned as pornographic. Wherever one draws the line, the aim is to leave intact both the basic internationally recognized human right to freedom of speech and the underlying value of personal autonomy.

4. Relative Universality: A Multidimensional Perspective

In the 1970s and 1980s, the dominant tendency was to see universality and relativity as opposites. Over the past two decades, most discussions have tried to move beyond a dichotomous presentation. Most defenders of both universality and relativity today recognize the dangers of an extreme commitment and acknowledge at least some attractions and insights in the positions of their critics and opponents.

Positions typically are arrayed on a spectrum. Thus in the two earlier editions of this book I used the language of strong and weak relativism and universalism, in effect identifying four ranges of views that recognize a mixture of universality and relativity. My own work has been toward the universalist end of this spectrum. Richard Wilson, who argues that ideas of and struggles for human rights "are embedded in local normative orders and yet are caught within webs of power and meaning which extend beyond the local" (1997: 23), is a good example of someone operating toward the relativist end. Andrew Nathan's (2001) conception of "tempered universalism" is perhaps best seen as occupying a position close to the center of the spectrum. (Few if any authors adopt a position of radical or absolute universalism or relativism, which define the ideal-type end points of the spectrum.)

Although such a representation has considerable attractions, my arguments above suggest a different perspective. There are multiple forms of universality and multiple forms of relativity. These forms differ qualitatively, making it fundamentally misleading to talk about relativity and universality in quantitative terms. Different forms of relativity and universality do not add up to any single thing.

Rather than see a two-dimensional space of universality and relativity, I suggest that we think of a multidimensional space of different forms and mixtures of different types of universality and relativity. *All* of this multidimensional space combines elements of universality and relativity. Although pure ideal-type positions define the boundaries of this space, the views of no serious commentators lie at these boundaries. Both relativity and universality are essential to international human rights. The crucial work, then, is to identify the ways in which human rights both are and are not both relative and universal—and to avoid either treating the universal as if it were relative or falsely universalizing the particular.

Human rights empower free people to build for themselves lives of dignity, value, and meaning. To build such lives anywhere in the contemporary world requires internationally recognized universal human rights. One of the central purposes of universal human rights, however, is to protect the free decisions of free people to justify and implement those rights in ways rooted in their own histories, experiences, and cultures.

It is an empirical, not a logical, matter whether the legitimate demands of universality and relativity conflict or coordinate. Perhaps the most striking fact about the universality of human rights in the contemporary world, however, is how infrequently there is a truly fundamental conflict at the level of concepts. Real conflict it is almost always restricted to a particular right or just one part of an internationally recognized human right.

The universality of human rights is relative to the contemporary world. The particularities of their implementation are relative to history, politics, culture, and particular decisions. Nonetheless, at the level of the concept, as specified in the Universal Declaration, human rights are universal. The formulation "relatively universal" is thus particularly apt. Relativity modifies—operates within the boundaries set by—the universality of the body of interdependent and indivisible internationally recognized human rights. But that universality is largely a universality of possession—universalism above all draws attention to the claim that we all have the same internationally recognized human rights—rather than a universality of enjoyment. And universal human rights not only may but should be implemented in different ways at different times and in different places, reflecting the free choices of free peoples to incorporate an essential particularity into universal human rights.

7

Universality in a World of Particularities

Many readers will have been struck by the fact that in the preceding chapter I did not even address, let alone identify as important, *cultural* relativity. That is not accidental. Although appeals to culture are a staple of discussions of relativity and universality, I will argue that human rights are not in any important way culturally relative. The first section of this chapter explores the relationship between culture and human rights. The remainder of the chapter opens out into a broader discussion of the opportunities for and difficulties of pursuing universal human rights in a world of obvious and important cultural, historical, economic, and social particularity.

I. Culture and the Relativity of Human Rights

Cultural diversity is a social fact. Culture, however, explains little of importance about the development of ideas and practices of human rights or what rights we have in the contemporary world—although it is important to advocacy for, and the reception of, internationally recognized human rights.

A. Western Culture and International Human Rights

Human rights as a matter of historical fact developed first in the West. This was not, however, due to any particular features of Western culture. Nothing in classical or medieval culture specially predisposed Europeans to develop human rights ideas. Even early modern Europe, when viewed without the benefit of hindsight, seemed quite an unconducive cultural milieu for human rights. Violent, often brutal, internecine and international religious warfare was the norm. Slavery and overseas imperialism were on the upswing, with "savage" peoples, especially in the Americas and Africa, seen as less than human. Political divisions of birth were the basis of internal social and political organization. The divine right of kings was emerging as the reigning orthodoxy.

What we think of today as Western culture is largely a result, not a cause, of human rights ideas and practices. Cultural resources that in the ancient, medieval, and early modern worlds were appropriated on behalf of a variety of deeply hierarchical social and political systems came to be reappropriated on behalf of natural rights. In the later modern period, however, and especially in the twentieth century, the balance shifted from hierarchical to egalitarian appropriations, fundamentally transforming the basic contours of Western culture.

For example, Christianity, right through the early modern period, was harnessed to support forms of social and political life that were deeply hierarchical and organized people according to divisions—of religion, gender, race, and occupation—rather than drawing any political attention to what bound all human beings or even all Christian men. Today, of course, we are all familiar with Biblical texts that point in a universalistic and egalitarian direction. But mass movements from below inspired by egalitarian readings of Christian ideas were throughout almost all of Christian history effectively (and usually ruthlessly) repressed in the name of Christianity.

Nonetheless, when men and women faced new social conditions— when traditional hierarchies were destroyed and modern ones built—these Christian (and other Western) cultural resources increasingly came to be appropriated by new groups, in new ways, on behalf of the idea of universal human rights. Just as modernity and human rights transformed Western culture, I would argue, so the same transformation not only can take place but is taking place throughout the non-Western world.

If the medieval Christian world of crusades, serfdom, and hereditary aristocracy could become today's world of liberal and social democratic welfare states, then it is hard to imagine a place where a similar transformation would be impossible. For example, Gandhi took Hinduism—on its face perhaps the least likely comprehensive doctrine to support human rights, given its traditional emphasis on qualitative caste differences and its denial of the moral significance of the category human being—and transformed it into a powerful force in support of human rights (compare chapter 10).

No particular culture or comprehensive doctrine is by nature either compatible or incompatible with human rights. It is a matter of what particular people and societies make of and do with their cultural resources. Cultures are immensely malleable, as are the political expressions of comprehensive doctrines. Most cultures—and all the "great civilizations"—have in the past denied human rights, both in theory and in practice. That, however, stops none of them today from not merely endorsing human rights but finding human rights to be a profound expression of their deepest cultural values.

Denying that human rights derive from or are defined by culture implies neither the irrelevance of culture to human rights nor cultural homogenization. Quite the contrary, an overlapping consensus approach (see sections 4.2 and 4.6) emphasizes the importance of people using their own local cultural resources on behalf of their own human rights. Not only is the universality of human rights fully compatible with a world of rich cultural diversity, a central purpose of human rights is to protect the rights of different individuals, groups, and peoples to make those choices of path.

B. The Doctrine of Cultural Relativism: A Critique

Whatever the role of culture in the development of human rights ideas and practices, culture does not provide a plausible *justification* for the practice of human rights. To see this, we must distinguish the fact of cultural relativity—cultures differ, often dramatically, across time and space—from the doctrine of cultural relativism, which imbues culture with overriding prescriptive force.[1]

What we can call methodological cultural relativism—an analytical perspective popular among mid-twentieth-century anthropologists—advocates a radically nonjudgmental analysis of cultures as an antidote to the unconscious, and often even conscious, biases rooted in describing and judging other societies according to modern Western categories and values (see Herskovits 1972). Such arguments lead directly to a recognition of the historical or anthropological relativity of human rights. They say nothing, though, about the criteria for justifying human rights or other social practices.

What we can call substantive cultural relativism is a normative doctrine that roots the legitimacy of social practices in culture. For a substantive cultural relativist, the rights of the Universal Declaration have no normative force in the face of divergent cultural traditions. Practice is to be evaluated entirely by the standards of the culture in question. As the (1947) Statement on Human Rights of the American Anthropological Association (AAA) put it, "man is free only when he lives as his society defines freedom" (1947: 543).[2]

Rhoda Howard-Hassmann (Howard 1993) has aptly described this position as "cultural absolutism": culture provides absolute standards of evaluation; whatever a culture says is right is right (for those in that culture). There are, however, several serious problems with such substantive or absolutist cultural relativism.

1. Tilley (2000) carefully reviews a number of particular conceptions and cites much of the relevant literature from anthropology. Cf. also Renteln (1988).
2. The AAA repudiated this statement in the 1990s and adopted a new "Declaration on Anthropology and Human Rights" (available at http://www.aaanet.org/stmts/humanrts.htm). See Engle (2001). Cf. also Washburn (1987).

The 1947 AAA statement insists that "standards and values are relative to the culture from which they derive so that any attempt to formulate postulates that grow out of the beliefs or moral codes of one culture must to that extent detract from the applicability of any Declaration of Human Rights to mankind as a whole" (1947: 542). The idea that simply because a value or practice emerged in place A makes it, to that extent, inapplicable to B is, at best, a dubious philosophical claim that assumes the impossibility of moral learning or adaptation except within closed cultures. It also dangerously assumes the moral infallibility of culture.

Substantive cultural relativism risks reducing "right" to "traditional," "good" to "old," and "obligatory" to "habitual." Few societies or individuals, however, believe that their values are binding simply or even primarily because they happen to be widely endorsed within their culture.

Cultural absolutism also makes no distinction between intolerant, even genocidal, cultures and tolerant ones. If my culture's values tell me that others are inferior, there is no standard by which to challenge this.

Cultural relativism is particularly problematic when it presents culture as coherent, homogenous, consensual, and static. In fact, though, differences *within* cultures often are as striking and as important as those between them. "The Western tradition," for example, includes both Caligula and Marcus Aurelius, Francis of Assisi and Torquemada, Leopold II of Belgium and Albert Schweitzer, Jesus and Hitler, Don Quixote and Donald Duck, the Arc de Triomphe and the Golden Arches—and just about everything in between. Thus it is problematic even to determine what is to count as evidence for a claim of the form "culture A holds belief *y*."

We must not mistake some particular expressions, however characteristic, for the whole. For example, Christianity and secularism are arguably equally important to modern Western civilization. Nonetheless, the balance between secular and religious forces, values, and orientations varies dramatically with time, place, and issue in "the West."

Such cautions are especially important because culturalist arguments regularly rely on appeals to a distant (and sometimes largely imaginary) past, such as the precolonial African village, Native American tribes, and traditional Islamic societies. The traditional culture advanced to justify cultural relativism far too often no longer exists—if it ever did in the idealized form in which it is typically presented. For example, Roger Ames, in an essay entitled "Continuing the Conversation of Chinese Human Rights," completely ignores the impact of half a century of Communist Party rule, as if it were irrelevant to discussing human rights in contemporary China (1997). Furthermore, there is no obvious reason why we should judge the modern nation-states and contemporary nationalist regimes that have replaced traditional communities and practices by the standards of a bygone era. Culture is not destiny—or, to the extent that it is, that is only because victorious elements in a particular society have used their power to make a particular, contingent destiny.

Finally, cultural relativist arguments usually either ignore politics or confuse it with culture. This point, I think, deserves further elaboration.

C. The Politics of Cultural Relativism

Cultures are not merely diverse but contested. In fact, contemporary anthropologists depict cultures not as things but as sites of contestation; less as "a domain of sharing and commonality" than as "a site of difference and contestation, simultaneously ground and stake of a rich field of cultural-political practices" (Gupta and Ferguson 1997: 5). "Culture" is a repertoire of deeply contested symbols, practices, and meanings over which, and with which, members of a society constantly struggle.[3]

Culture is an ongoing historical and institutional process. "Culture is not a given, but rather a congeries of ways of thinking, believing, and acting that are constantly in the state of being produced; it is contingent and always unstable, especially as the forces of 'modernity' have barreled down upon most people throughout the world over the course of the twentieth century" (Bell, Nathan, and Peleg 2001: 11). The existence of a given custom does not mean that the custom is adaptive, optimal, or consented to by a majority of its adherents. Especially in a rapidly changing environment, cultural practices routinely outlive their usefulness and new practices and values emerge both through internal dialogue within the cultural group and through cross-cultural influences.

"Culture" is constructed through selective appropriations from a diverse and contested past and present. Those appropriations, however, are rarely neutral in process, intent, or consequences. Cultural relativist arguments thus regularly obscure troubling realities of power and politics.

Arguments of cultural relativism are far too often made by (or on behalf of) economic and political elites that have long since left traditional culture behind. Even when this represents an admirable effort to retain or recapture cherished traditional values, it is at least ironic to see "Westernized" elites warning against the values and practices they have adopted. There is also more than a hint of a troubling, even tragic, paternalism. For example, "villagization" in Tanzania in the 1970s, which was supposed to reflect traditional African conceptions, was accomplished only by force, against the strong opposition of much of the population. And even such troubling sincerity is rare. Government officials denounce the corrosive individualism of Western

---

3. For excellent brief applications of this understanding of culture to debates over human rights, see Preis (1996) and Nathan (2001). Cf. Engelhart (2000) and Zechenter (1997).

values—while they line their pockets with the proceeds of massive corruption, drive imported luxury automobiles, and plan European or American vacations. Leaders sing the praises of traditional communities—while they wield arbitrary power antithetical to traditional values, pursue development policies that systematically undermine traditional communities, and replace traditional leaders with corrupt cronies and party hacks.

Relativist arguments become particularly perverse when they support a small elite that has arrogated to itself the "right" to speak for "its" culture or civilization while imposing its own self-interested views and practices on the broader society, invoking cultural relativism abroad while ruthlessly trampling on local customs. In traditional cultures—at least the kinds of traditional cultures that might justify deviations from international human rights standards—people are not victims of the arbitrary decisions of rulers whose principal claim to power is their control of modern instruments of force and administration. Traditional customs and practices usually provide each person with a place in society and a certain amount of dignity and protection. Furthermore, rulers and ruled (and rich and poor) usually are linked by reciprocal bonds. The practices of systematically rights-abusive regimes are as antithetical to such cultural traditions as they are to "Western" human rights conceptions.

D. Explaining the Persistence of Culturalist Arguments

If my arguments are even close to correct, how can we explain the persistence of foundational appeals to culture? At least six possibilities come to mind.

First, it is surprisingly common for even otherwise sophisticated individuals to take the particular institutions associated with the realization of a right in their country or culture to be essential to that right. Americans, in particular, seem to have unusually great difficulty in realizing that the way we do things here is not necessarily what international human rights norms require. This provokes reactive arguments of relativity.

Second, narrow-minded and ham-handed Western (and especially American) international human rights policies and statements exacerbate these confusions. Consider Michael Fay, an American teenager who vandalized hundreds of thousands of dollars of property in Singapore. When he was sentenced to be publicly caned, there was a furor in the United States. President Clinton argued, with apparently genuine indignation, that it was abominable to cane someone but failed to find it even notable that in his own country people were being fried in the electric chair. If this indeed is what universalism means—and I hasten to repeat that it is not—then of course relativism looks far more attractive.

The legacy of colonialism provides a third important explanation for the popularity of relativist arguments. African, Asian, and Muslim (as well as Latin

American) leaders and citizens have vivid, sometimes personal, recollections of their sufferings under colonial masters. Even when the statements and actions of great powers stay within the range of the overlapping consensus on the Universal Declaration and do not involve the threat or use of force, there is understandable sensitivity to external pressure. (Compare the sensitivity of the United States to external criticism even in the absence of such a historical legacy.) When international pressures exceed the bounds of the overlapping consensus, or are deeply coercive, that sensitivity often becomes (justifiably) very intense.

Fourth, culturalist arguments may reflect a misplaced notion of inclusiveness based on the idea that values or practices can be considered universal only if all major groups contributed to their formulation. For example, Asmarom Legesse argues that "any system of ideas that claims to be universal must contain critical elements in its fabric that are avowedly of African, Latin American or Asian derivation" (1980: 123). Such arguments, however, confuse the origins of a practice with its validity, an error that logicians call the genetic fallacy. Human rights are too important to be rejected—or accepted—on the basis of their origins.

Fifth, arguments of relativism are often rooted in a desire to express and foster national, regional, cultural, or civilizational pride. For example, it is no coincidence that the "Asian values" debate took off in the wake of the Asian economic miracle.

Finally, the belief that such arguments have instrumental efficacy in promoting internationally recognized human rights helps to sustain them. For example, Daniel Bell plausibly argues that building human rights implementation strategies on local traditions 1) is "more likely to lead to long term commitment to human rights"; 2) "may shed light on the groups most likely to bring about desirable social and political change"; 3) "allows the human rights activist to draw on the most compelling justifications"; 4) "may shed light on the appropriate attitude to be employed by human rights activists"; and 5) "may also make one more sensitive to the possibility of alternative" mechanisms for protecting rights (1996: 657–59).

This is indeed a powerful argument—if we understand it as a practical argument, not a theoretical one, addressed to the reception rather than the definition or justification of human rights.

2. Advocating Universality in a World of Particularities

Different places at different times will draw on different cultural resources to provide support for (and opposition to) human rights. The different cultural idioms by which human rights are justified and explicated are of immense local importance. Therefore, effective advocacy of human rights requires knowledge of and sensitivity to how human rights fit with local cultures—and histories, and economies, and ecologies, and social structures.

Culture also is often part of the explanation of differences in interpretations and implementations of human rights. Even here, though, striking variations within cultures suggest not attributing too much to culture. Local practices and values certainly are central to both the reception and implementation of human rights. We should be wary, though, of reducing the wide variety of local particularities to "culture."

Human rights advocates typically require judgment more than theory as they encounter and accommodate local particularities. Nonetheless, some general distinctions of value can be drawn and some broad guidelines advanced. The remainder of this chapter focuses on a few issues often encountered by external advocates of universal human rights. Although many internal advocates face similar issues, especially in diverse societies, my focus here is on external advocates, who—if they wish to be successful—cannot avoid coming to grips with the local particularities of advocacy and implementation.

A. Internal versus External Judgments

Respect for autonomous moral communities demands a certain deference by outsiders to a society's internal evaluations of its practices. To commit ourselves to acting on the basis of the moral judgments of others, however, would abrogate our own moral responsibilities. The choice between internal and external evaluations is a moral choice. And whatever choice we make is likely to be problematic.

Where internal and external judgments conflict, assessing the relative importance attached to those judgments may be a reasonable place to start in seeking to resolve them. Figure 7.1 offers a simple typology.

Case 1—morally unimportant both externally and internally—is uninteresting. Whether one maintains one's initial external criticism is of little

		Internal judgement of practice	
		Morally unimportant	Morally very important
External judgement of practice	Morally unimportant	Case 1	Case 2
	Morally very important	Case 3	Case 4

Figure 7.1 *Types of conflicts over culturally relative practices*

significance to anyone. Case 2—externally unimportant, internally very important—is probably best handled with great caution and restraint. To press a negative external judgment that one feels is relatively unimportant when the issue is of great importance internally usually will be, at best, insensitive. Conversely, Case 3—externally very important, internally unimportant—probably presents the best opportunities to press an external judgment (with some tact).

Case 4, in which the practice is of great moral importance to both sides, is the most difficult. Even here, though, we may have good reasons to press a negative external judgment. Our moral precepts are *our* moral precepts. As such, they demand our obedience. To abandon them simply because others reject them is to fail to give proper weight to our own moral beliefs (at least where they involve central moral precepts such as the equality of all human beings and the protection of innocents).

B. Dialogue over Real Differences

Even if I am correct that fundamental differences at the level of concepts are relatively rare, they do exist. Furthermore, differences that are *relatively* minor in the context of the full body of internationally recognized human rights can nonetheless be of considerable importance, especially in day-to-day politics. Questions such as capital and corporal punishment, the limits of religious liberty, and the dimensions of gender equality are issues that merit intensive discussions both within and between states and civilizations.

Should traditional notions of "family values" and gender roles be emphasized in the interest of children and society or should families be conceived in more individualistic and egalitarian terms? What is the proper balance between rewarding individual economic initiative and redistributive taxation in the interest of social harmony and support for disadvantaged individuals and groups? At what point should the words or behaviors of deviant or dissident individuals be forced to give way to the interests or desires of society? Questions such as these, which in my terminology involve conflicting conceptions or interpretations (see section 6.3), are vital issues of political controversy in virtually all societies. In discussing them we must often walk the difficult line between respect for the other and respect for one's own values.

Consider a relatively uncontroversial case—slavery—presented in an unconventional way. Suppose that in contemporary Saudi Arabia a group were to emerge arguing that because slavery was accepted in the early Muslim world it should be reinstituted in contemporary Saudi Arabia. I am certain that most Saudis, from the most learned clerics to the most ordinary citizens, would reject this view. How, though, should this group be dealt with?

So long as these fundamentalists do not attempt to *practice* slavery, dialogue—including harsh criticism by both Saudis and foreigners—seems to me the appropriate route. Those in the majority have, I think, a moral obligation to use the most forceful possible terms. Nonetheless, freedom of belief and speech requires the majority to tolerate these views, in the minimal sense of not imposing legal liabilities on those who hold or express them. Should they attempt to practice slavery, however, it would be entirely appropriate, and probably even demanded, that the force of the law be applied to suppress and punish it.

Suppose, though, that the unthinkable were to occur and the practice of slavery were reintroduced in Saudi Arabia—not, let us imagine, as a matter of law, but rather through the state refusing to prosecute slave-holders. Here we run up against the state system and the fact that international human rights law gives states near total discretion to implement internationally recognized human rights within their own territories. Although one might argue that slavery is legally prohibited as a matter of *jus cogens*, general principles of law, and both customary law and treaties, coercive international enforcement would be, at best, extraordinarily contentious and without much legal precedent. Outsiders, however, remain bound by their own moral principles (as well as by international human rights norms) to condemn such practices in the strongest possible terms and foreign states would be entirely justified in putting whatever pressure short of force they could mobilize on Saudi Arabia to halt the practice.

This hypothetical example illustrates the fact that *some* cultural practices demand our condemnation rather than our respect. It also, however, indicates that some beliefs, although despicable, demand our toleration—because freedom of opinion and belief is an internationally recognized human right. So long as one stays within the limits of internationally recognized human rights, one is entitled to at least a limited and grudging toleration, and the personal space that comes with that.

Many cases, however, are not so "easy," especially where change is substantial or unusually rapid. In much of the global South—and pockets of the developed world as well—we regularly face the problem of "modern" individuals or groups who reject traditional practices. Should we give priority to the idea of community self-determination and permit the enforcement of customary practices against modern "deviants," even if this violates "universal" human rights? Or should individual self-determination prevail, thus sanctioning claims of universal human rights against traditional society?

In discussing women's rights in Africa, Rhoda Howard-Hassmann suggests an attractive and widely applicable strategy (Howard 1984: 66–68). On a combination of practical and moral grounds, she argues against an outright ban on such practices as child betrothal and widow inheritance. She also, however, strongly advocates national legislation that permits women (and the families of female children) to "opt out" of traditional practices. This would permit individuals and families to, in effect, choose the terms on which they participate in the cultures that are of value to their lives.

Sometimes, however, compromise is impossible; conflicting practices are irreconcilable. For example, a right to private ownership of the means of production is incompatible with the maintenance of a village society in which families hold only rights of use to communally owned land. Allowing individuals to opt out and fully own their land would destroy the traditional system. Even such conflicts may sometimes be resolved, though, or at least minimized, by the physical or legal separation of adherents of old and new values, particularly with practices that are not material to the maintenance or integrity of either culture.

C. Judging Divergences from International Human Rights Norms

A choice must sometimes be made, at least by default, between irreconcilable practices. Such cases take us out of the realm in which useful general guidelines are possible. Nonetheless, four criteria can help us to grapple seriously yet sympathetically with claims in support of such deviations. For reasons of space, I simply stipulate these criteria, although I doubt that they are deeply controversial once we have accepted some notion of relative universality.[4]

1) Important differences in threats to human dignity are likely to justify variations even at the level of concepts. Although perhaps the strongest theoretical justification for even fairly substantial deviations from international human rights norms, such arguments rarely are empirically persuasive in the contemporary world. For example, defensible categorical differences between "developed" and "developing" countries, I would argue, involve, at most, differing short-term priorities among particular internationally recognized human rights, not major differences in the list of rights appropriate for individuals in such countries. (Indigenous peoples may be the exception that proves the rule.)

---

4. I am implicitly speaking from the perspective of an engaged participant in international society. A different and more complex subject position may be important "on the ground" where ordinary people have more local and particularistic understandings of their values. I suspect that much of the "talking past each other" in debates on cultural relativism and human rights arises from taking arguments that may be well formulated for a particular setting, be it local or international, and applying them directly in another discursive setting, without the adjustments required to give those arguments resonance and persuasive force in that context. For example, in much of rural China today, direct appeals to internationally recognized human rights are unlikely to be politically efficacious, and often will be positively counterproductive, either for mobilizing peasants or persuading local authorities. Those working directly to improve the day-to-day life of Chinese peasants need to give central place to this fact. I would suggest, though, that it says more about the Chinese state and the enforced isolation and systematic repression of Chinese peasants than about "Asian values."

2) Participants in the overlapping consensus deserve a sympathetic hearing when they present serious reasoned arguments justifying limited deviations from international norms. Disagreements over "details" should be approached differently from systematic deviations or comprehensive attacks. If the resulting set of human rights remains generally consistent with the structure and overarching values of the Universal Declaration, we should be relatively tolerant of particular deviations.

3) A particular conception or implementation that is, for cultural or historical reasons, deeply imbedded and of unusually great significance to some significant group in society deserves, on its face, sympathetic consideration. Even if we do not positively value diversity, the autonomous choices of free people should never be lightly dismissed, especially when they reflect well-established practices based on deeply held beliefs.

4) Tolerance for deviations should decrease as the level of coercion increases. The underlying values of autonomy and equality suggest extreme skepticism toward imposing infringements on internationally recognized human rights through force.

D. Universalism without Imperialism

My account has emphasized the "good" sides of universalism, understood in limited, relative terms. I conclude by considering a few of the political dangers posed by excessive or "false" universalism, especially when a powerful actor (mis)takes its own interests for universal values.

The legacy of colonialism demands that Westerners show special caution and sensitivity when advancing arguments of universalism in the face of clashing cultural values. Westerners must also remember the political, economic, and cultural power that lies behind even their best-intentioned activities. Anything that even hints of imposing Western values is likely to be met with understandable suspicion, even resistance. How arguments of universalism and arguments of relativism are advanced may sometimes be as important as the substance of those arguments.[5]

Care and caution, however, must not be confused with inattention or inaction. As I argued above, our values, and international human rights norms, may demand that we act on them even in the absence of agreement by others—at least when that action does not involve force. Even strongly sanctioned traditions may not deserve our toleration if they are unusually

---

5. I probably would not object to readers who took this as implicit acknowledgment of certain shortcomings in some of my previous work on relativism, although I suspect that we might disagree about the range of applicability of such criticisms.

objectionable. When rights-abusive practices raise issues of great moral significance, tradition and culture are slight defense.

I do not mean to minimize the dangers of cultural and political arrogance, especially when backed by great power. US foreign policy often confuses American interests with universal values. Many Americans do seem to believe that what's good for the United States is good for the world—and if not, then "that's their problem." The dangers of such arrogant and abusive "universalism" are especially striking in international relations, where normative disputes that cannot be resolved by rational persuasion or appeal to agreed-upon international norms tend to be settled by political, economic, and cultural power—of which the United States today has more than anyone else.

Faced with such undoubtedly perverse "unilateral universalism," even some well-meaning critics have been seduced by misguided arguments for the essential relativity of human rights. This, however, in effect accepts the American confusion of human rights with US foreign policy. The proper remedy for "false" universalism is defensible, relative universalism. Functional, overlapping consensus, and international legal universality, in addition to their analytical and substantive virtues, can be valuable resources for resisting many of the excesses of US foreign policy, and perhaps even for redirecting it into more humane channels.

Without authoritative international standards, to what can the United States (or any other great power) be held accountable? If international legal universality has no force, why shouldn't the United States act on its own (often peculiar) understandings of human rights?

International legal universality is one of the great achievements of the international human rights movement, both intrinsically and because it has facilitated a deepening overlapping consensus. Even the United States participates, fitfully and incompletely, in these consensuses. Not just the Clinton and Obama administrations but also both Bush administrations regularly raised human rights concerns in numerous bilateral relationships, usually with a central element of genuine concern. (The real problem with US foreign policy is less where it does raise human rights concerns than where it doesn't, or where it allows them to be subordinated to other concerns.) All of this matters directly to tens or hundreds of thousands of people and indirectly to many hundreds of millions, whose lives have been made better by internationally recognized human rights.

Human rights are not a panacea for the world's problems. They do, however, fully deserve the prominence they have received in recent years. For the foreseeable future, human rights will remain a vital element in national, international, and transnational struggles for social justice and human dignity. The relative universality of those rights is a powerful resource that can be used to help to build more just and humane national and international societies.

Part III

Human Rights
and Human Dignity

8

Dignity: Particularistic and Universalistic Conceptions in the West

I n earlier editions of this book, in the course of discussing the historical particularity of human rights, I suggested that notions of human dignity have underlain the political practices of most societies. I gave no attention, though, to the substance of those ideas. This chapter and the following ones fill that gap—a major gap, given the quasi-foundational appeals to human dignity in international human rights law—arguing that ideas and practices of dignity roughly parallel the political practices discussed in chapter 5.

In the premodern world, dignity was seen not as an inherent feature of all humans but as an attribute of the few. Rather than a universal principle of equality, dignity functioned as a particularistic principle of hierarchy. The following chapters consider Confucian China and Hindu India. This chapter looks at the West. The first three sections present an episodic historical overview, using Rome (and Cicero in particular) and the Jewish and Christian Bibles to illustrate premodern Western conceptions and Kant to illustrate the modern conception. The final two sections step back to look at the concept of dignity and its relation to human rights.

I. *Dignitas*: The Roman Roots of Dignity

The English term dignity derives from the Latin *dignitas*. In classical Latin the noun *dignitas*, the adjective *dignus*, and the verb *dignor* all refer to worth. Lewis and Short's *Latin Dictionary* defines *dignitas* as "being worthy, worth, worthiness, merit, desert," and, used metonymically, "dignity, greatness, grandeur, authority, rank." *Dignus* is similarly defined as "worthy, deserving (in a good or ill sense), of things, suitable, fitting, becoming, proper" and *dignor* as "to deem worthy or deserving." These terms were often used in conjunction with notions such as *amplitudo*—literally, width, size, amplitude, and thus "dignity, grandeur, distinction, consequence"—and *honestas*, meaning "honorableness, reputation, integrity."

Three interrelated features of the Roman conception of dignity are especially relevant us here. First, "dignity" was a term of hierarchical distinction, an attribute of a distinguished few (patricians or "optimates") that marked them off from the vulgar masses. "*Dignitas* was the status that dignitaries had—a quality that demanded reverence from the ordinary common person" (Brennan and Lo 2007: 44). In an English usage that is now largely obsolete, dignity was understood as an attribute of a "worthy," which the *Oxford English Dictionary* defines as "a distinguished or eminent person; a famous or renowned man or woman; esp. a man of courage or of noble character."

Second, "dignity" was a virtue—or the consequence or reward of virtue—in the Aristotelian sense of a learned habit or disposition that realizes human excellence. Some or even all people may have a potential for virtue, which is the proper natural end of humans. What gives one worth and demands respect, however, is the (differential) realization of that potential. And differential virtue provides the ethical basis for social distinction. "Dignity, in Latin usage, refers especially to that aspect of virtue or excellence that makes one worthy of honor—which, as Aristotle put it, accompanies virtue as its crown" (Shell 2003: 53).

Third, "dignity" was specially connected with public appearance. "In Rome the original meaning of *dignitas* referred to an acquired social and political status, generally implying important personal achievements in the public sphere and moral integrity" (England 1999: 1904). Although *dignitas* certainly had an inner basis, it referred particularly to "the outer aspect of a person's social role which evokes respect, and embodies the charisma and the esteem residing in office, rank or personality" (Cancik 2002: 19).[1]

Dignitas, in sum, was a virtue of great people, those meriting special honor or distinction. Practices of dignity involved public recognition and respect—granted by one's peers, the vulgar, society, and the polity—that marked off the dignified as excellent, in the sense of excelling. *Dignitas* was "a manifestation of personal authority, majesty, greatness, magnanimity, gravity, decorum, and moral qualities" (England 1999). The "worth" to which dignity referred was a feature of the few rather than the many (let alone all).

Consider Cicero's *De Officiis* (On Duties), one of the most influential Roman works of ethical theory. The overarching theme is that the highest

---

1. We must thus reject Peter Berger's claim that "dignity, as against honor, always relates to the intrinsic humanity divested of all socially imposed roles or norms. It pertains to the self as such, to the individual regardless of his position in society" (1983 [1970]: 176). This may be true of *contemporary*, and more broadly post-Kantian, ideas of human dignity, but it is simply not the case in the ancient world. This (to us very useful) distinction between honor and dignity simply was not drawn.

human good is a virtuous life in accord with nature and reason. Although there are hints of a shared humanity, the emphasis is on the differential realization of virtue.

Dignitas identifies what is most excellent and worthy of respect in the best humans—rather than what is common to all. In characteristic Stoic fashion, Cicero argues that *dignitas* is to be achieved and preserved by freeing oneself from disturbing emotions, especially desire, fear, pleasure, pain, and anger (1.67–69). *Dignitas* thus clearly refers to the "higher" nature of human beings. But these higher potentials can be made real only by the few. They require a life of considerable leisure, or at least freedom from the burdens of life-sustaining labor—a life of extensive study and meditation, and disciplined self-control.

In one passage Cicero does attribute dignity to humans in general. This is probably the earliest preserved usage in the classical corpus that can be comfortably translated as "human dignity."

> It is essential to every inquiry about duty that we keep before our eyes how far superior man is by nature to cattle and other beasts: they have no thought except for sensual pleasure and this they are impelled by every instinct to seek; but man's mind is nurtured by study and meditation. . . . From this we see that sensual pleasure is quite unworthy of the dignity of man [*dignam hominis*] . . . if we will only bear in mind the superiority and dignity of our nature [*natura excellentia et dignitas*], we shall realize how wrong it is to abandon ourselves to excess and to live in luxury and voluptuousness, and how right it is to live in thrift, self-denial, simplicity, and sobriety. (1.105–6)[2]

Here Cicero draws attention to the categorical distinction between man and beast. There is no suggestion, though, that all human beings possess, or even have a potentiality for, this *dignitas*. Quite the contrary, in an aside elided from the above quotation, Cicero notes that "some people are men only in name, not in fact [*sunt enim quidam homines non re, sed nomine*]" (1.105). Taxonomic and moral "human beings" are very different, and only slightly overlapping, sets.

Our contemporary conceptions of dignity share a core sense of worth that demands respect. Worth, however, in the Roman understanding, was deeply differential—particular and achieved rather than universal and inherent—and the respect it demanded was to be expressed principally in high status and public office not universal rights.

---

2. Translated by Walter Miller, in Cicero (1913 [44 BCE]), available at The Latin Library, http://www.thelatinlibrary.com/cicero/off.shtml.

2. Biblical Conceptions: *Kavod* and *Imago Dei*

Christianity dominated Western thought from the late Roman Empire through much of the modern period. Biblical conceptions of dignity, in their dominant interpretations prior to the twentieth century, likewise emphasized particularistic distinctions that supported inegalitarian social and political practices.

The (old and modern) Hebrew term *kavod* is conventionally translated as "dignity" (as well as "honor," "glory," and "respect"). As I do not read Hebrew, my discussion here must be especially brief. The crucial point for our purposes is that "the combination 'human dignity' (*Kavod Ha'adam*) is in fact not found in the Bible. Although the word Adam (man) can already be found in Genesis (1:26) and the word *Kavod* is widespread throughout the Bible, the term 'human dignity' itself is absent" (Shultziner 2006: 666; compare Cancik 2002: 21). Similarly, "no single expression found in the Rabbinical literature equals the twentieth century concept of human dignity. It would seem that it toys with the idea, but it is not as yet theoretically developed" (Safrai 2002: 104). *Kavod*, instead, is an attribute of God (Lorberbaum 2002: 56; Shultziner 2006: 666–67; compare Kamir 2002).

As in Rome, we are dealing with a certain kind of worth, connected with honor, glory, and (in this case especially) power, that demands respect. Whatever treatment human beings were thought to merit, though, was not a result of their *kavod*.

Genesis also underlies an understanding of dignity that dominated the Western/Christian world for over a millennium and continues to be a powerful presence in contemporary discussions.

> So God created man in his own image, in the image of God created he him; male and female created he them.
>
> And God blessed them, and God said unto them, Be fruitful, and multiply, and replenish the earth, and subdue it: and have dominion over the fish of the sea, and over the fowl of the air, and over every living thing that moveth upon the earth. (Gen. 1.27–28 [KJV])

This placement—below God but above the rest of His creation—gives humans a certain dignity. But "we are honored and loved by God not because we are worthy; we are worthy because we are loved and honored by God" (Englard 1999: 1908). And, in the Christian understanding, "closeness to God still requires redemption" (Kraynak 2003: 83).

Dignity, in this Christian understanding, is inherent and in some important sense universal. It is something "that none of us has by merit, that none of us can receive from others, and that no one can take from us" (Pannenberg

1991: 177). Nonetheless, this traditional Christian conception remained deeply hierarchical.

For example, "Aquinas uses *dignitas* and its cognates 185 times in the *Summa Theologiae* and it tends to mean the value something has proper to its place in the great chain of being; for example, plants have more dignity than rocks; angels more dignity than human beings" (Sulmasy 2007: 11). Furthermore, as we saw in section 5.2.B, Christian society in the medieval and early modern eras was deeply hierarchical. Much as in Cicero's world, the dignities of the well-born and other dignitaries took practical priority over any inherent human dignity.

This understanding was greatly facilitated by another dimension of the Christian tradition that also goes back to Genesis, namely, "the fall of man," original sin. Adam and Eve were created, directly, by God. All later humans, however, were created, as a burdensome punishment for sin, through sexual union. Our nature has been radically degraded. Real men and women have been far removed from their initial, idyllic creation in the image of God.

Debate continues to rage among Christians over the relative importance of man's creation in the image of God and the fall. Augustine gave the problem its classic formulation in the conception of "two cities," the City of God and the City of Man, governed by two loves: heavenly, eternal, and spiritual and earthly, temporal, and physical. Augustine sees both as mixed in each person and in every human group. The tradition usually labeled "Augustinian," however, emphasizes the corruption of original sin—with its associated reduction in human dignity.

In this understanding—which has been politically predominant through most of Christian history—human dignity becomes largely a spiritual potentiality with little earthly social or political significance. Realizing the human potential for a life of dignity depends on divine grace—that is, on the mysterious mercy of God, which cannot be earned and certainly is not owed to all human beings. Furthermore, a life of dignity has relevance principally in the heavenly City of God. As children of God, made in his image, we are *ultimately* good and equal. In this temporal life, however, sin is the predominant fact and inequality is essential if our corrupted, concupiscent nature is to be held in check. Politics is more about repressing evil than perfecting (the best) people. In fact, given the depth of our fall, it is a significant achievement even to create a mildly peaceful space in which the less sinful or more virtuous may have some quiet and protection.

One powerful and historically important expression of this view can be found in the treatise *On the Misery of the Human Condition*, written by the future Pope Innocent III at the end of the twelfth century. It is divided into three books, titled "The Miserable Entrance upon the Human Condition," "The Guilty Progress of the Human Condition," and "The Damnable Exit from the Human Condition." Illustrative of the general approach is the beginning of chapter 2 of book 1:

> "Therefore the Lord God formed man from the slime of the earth," [Gen. 2:7] an element having lesser dignity than others. For God made the planets and stars from fire, the breeze and winds from air, the fishes and birds from water; but He made men and beasts from earth. Thus a man, looking upon sea life, will find himself low; looking upon creatures of the air will know he is lower; and looking upon creatures of fire he will see his is lowest of all. Nor can he equal heavenly things, nor dare put himself above the earthly; for he finds himself on a level with the beasts and knows he is like them. (Innocent III 1969 [c. 1200]: 6)

For most of the history of Christianity, this bleak account of the dignity or worth of the human condition predominated over more optimistic readings that emphasize the likeness of humans to God.

There is a vast distance between "the Judeo-Christian tradition" *as it existed through most of its history* and most late-twentieth- and early-twenty-first century conceptions of "human dignity," including most contemporary Christian and Jewish conceptions. The resources of a religious (or any other) tradition can be extraordinarily malleable, the same foundational texts being put to radically different but equally authentic uses. Taking the reality of a culture, society, or religion seriously, however, requires that we not read contemporary understandings and practices back into a past that was quite dramatically different.

3. Kant

Renaissance humanists toyed with ideas that seem, at least with the benefit of hindsight, precursors of contemporary notions of human dignity (compare Kristeller 1972). Pico de la Mirandola and his compatriots, however, ultimately merely extended—and presented a much less pessimistic account of—the Christian conception that emphasized man's place in the hierarchy of God's creation. There is no notion in Pico or his contemporaries of anything like innate, universal dignity (let alone dignity as the foundation for egalitarian politics).

Only with Immanuel Kant (1724–1804) do we finally find a fully formed account of human dignity that is very similar to that of the Universal Declaration and is placed at the center of moral and political theory. Kant draws on Cicero and the broader Stoic tradition, as well as Samuel Pufendorf (1632–1694), who made significant use of the concept of human dignity (Cancik

2002: 30–35). Kant's conception, however, not only was more comprehensive but has had considerable impact on later ideas—including the Universal Declaration of Human Rights.

It almost certainly is no coincidence that Kant wrote at roughly the same time that early practices of human rights were being implemented through the American and French Revolutions. Kant in effect democratized dignity much as, and at the same time that, the American and French Revolutions democratized politics. Universal rights and universal dignity, in other words, developed in tandem and reinforced one another in the late modern Western world.

Kant's key move was to distinguish two kinds of value, which correspond to two sides of human nature: *dignity* (*Würde*, worth), understood as "an absolute inner worth" (Kant 1991 [1797]: 230 [435]), which is the standard of distinctively human or moral value; and *price*, the standard of value of the material world and man's animal nature. A *human* being is a creature with a worth, a dignity, that is literally priceless, outside of the domain of instrumental value.

"In the system of nature [that is, viewing man in his animal aspect] man (*homo phaenomenon, animal rationale*) is a being of slight importance and shares with the rest of the animals, as offspring of the earth, an ordinary value (*pretium vulgare*)." As a moral creature ("*homo noumenon*"), though, man exists in the realm of dignity (MM 434; compare Kant 1930: 124–25).[3]

"Man regarded as a *person* . . . is exalted above any price; . . . he is not to be valued merely as a means . . . he possesses a *dignity* (absolute inner worth) by which he exacts *respect* for himself from all other rational beings in the world" (MM 434–35; compare MM 462). This in effect restates, in the language of dignity and worth, Kant's famous formulation of the "categorical imperative," the fundamental principle of morality: "Act in such a way that you treat humanity, whether in your own person or in the person of another, always at the same time as an end and never simply as a means" (Kant 1981 [1785]: 36 [429]).

The dignity of humanity in each of us—in ourselves and in others alike—demands respect. Because of this dignity, "every man has a legitimate claim to respect from his fellow men and is *in turn* bound to respect every other" (MM 462). "Humanity in his person is the object of the respect which he can

3. Many of Kant's most important observations on dignity appear in *The Metaphysics of Morals* (1991 [1797]). References here to this text are to MM, with pages from the standard "Academy" edition, which usually are provided in published texts and translations. The *OED* defines "noumenon" as a chiefly philosophical term indicating "an object knowable only by the mind or intellect, not by the senses; *spec.* (in Kantian philosophy) an object of purely intellectual intuition, devoid of all phenomenal attributes." Humans understood as noumenal beings are rational and moral creatures.

demand from every other man" (MM 435). And Kant explicitly links "this duty with reference to the dignity of humanity within us" (MM 436) to rights. In listing a number of maxims that flow from and illustrate this dignity, he begins: "Be no man's lackey. Do not let others tread with impunity on your rights" (MM 436). Human dignity dictates a life of personal autonomy and empowerment.

In politics, this is closely tied to human rights: "Regarded merely as a state of right, the civil state is based *a priori* on the following principles: 1. The *freedom* of every member of society as a *human being*. 2. The *equality* of each member with every other as a *subject*. 3. The *independence* of every member of the commonwealth as a *citizen*" (1983 [1793]: 72 [290]). Kant insists that "this right of freedom comes to him who is a member of the commonwealth as a human being . . . a being who is in general capable of having rights" (1983 [1793]: 73 [291]).

Human dignity, for Kant, is inherent in and possessed by every human being. Their actions also give humans another sort of moral worth. This achieved moral status, however, is independent of inherent worth. And it is the inherent dignity of humanity within each person that lies at the foundation of both personal morality and political right.

The Universal Declaration certainly is compatible with other conceptions of human dignity. (In section 5 I apply the idea of overlapping consensus to human dignity.) The Kantian conception, however, is an historically important source of the idea that human rights rest on the inherent dignity of the human person and was one of the inspirations for the Universal Declaration.

It is illuminating, though, to see in Kant residual elements of older hierarchical conceptions of dignity. Most strikingly, he enumerates the rights of the sovereign executive as the distribution of offices, the distribution of "civil dignities" (i.e., hereditary titles of nobility), and the right to punish (MM 328–29). Kant, however, links this old Roman and medieval sense of the term with a "modern" conception of politics based on equal rights, arguing that the creation of new civil dignities is incompatible with a fully legitimate regime ("the general will"), although it may be prudent to continue to acknowledge and respect already established "dignities" (MM 329).[4]

Particularly interesting for our purposes is Kant's claim that "humanity itself is a dignity" (MM 462). The old notion of dignity as a special status of the nobility (and clergy) is here universalized to all humans. Humanity, which is present in even the lowliest of people, gives each individual a dignity

---

4. Kant also speaks of the dignity of the citizen (MM 329–30). This is a status, though, that may be lost, along with its associated rights, through certain crimes. The dignity of the citizen thus stands in sharp contrast to the inalienable dignity of humanity within each individual.

and status that must be respected by all other individuals, society, and the state. And the details of that respect, especially in its political elements, are specified through human rights.

4. Rights and Dignity in the West

Michael Meyer (2002: 196–97) usefully identifies three senses of dignity:

- "social dignity," associated with positions of high rank;
- "the virtue of dignity," in the sense of "a more or less settled disposition, and attendant attitudes, that over time contributes to the constitution of a good moral or ethical temperament"; and
- "human dignity," understood as "the special moral worth and status had by a human being."

The thrust of the argument above is that notions of "social dignity" and "the virtue of dignity" were hegemonic in ancient, medieval, and early modern Western societies but have given way to ideas and practices of "human dignity" understood in terms of the inherent worth of the human person. In a similar vein, Deryck Beyleveld and Roger Brownsword identify "two seminal notions of human dignity, one the idea that human beings, having intrinsic value, must not be treated simply as a means, the other the idea that dignified conduct is a virtue" (1998: 662). These competing conceptions—which we might label Kantian and Ciceronian—have been dominant, respectively, in the modern and pre-modern Western worlds.

> In the West prior to the Enlightenment, the exercise of the right to a full measure of dignity and self-determination was restricted to upper class and high-status groups: in Ancient Greece, only the male citizen of the polis, not the woman, noncitizen, slave, or non-Hellene; in Rome, male members of the upper orders, not noncitizens, male members of the lower orders, women, or slaves; in medieval Europe, male members of the nobility and highly-placed prelates (and, perhaps, wealthy burghers), not women, serfs, members of the urban lower orders, and non-Christians." (Milton Lewis 2007: 96)

As we have seen, this rejection of ideas of the inherent worth of the human person and of practices of equal rights extended well into the eighteenth century, and beyond.

"The modern notion of dignity drops the hierarchical elements implicit in the meaning of *dignitas*, and uses the term so that all human beings must have equal dignity, regardless of their virtues, merits, actual social and political status, or any other contingent features" (Brennan and Lo 2007: 47). Nonetheless, we must not lose sight of the fact that "the concept of human dignity evolved historically out of the idea of social honor" (Margalit 1996: 43). This involved both incremental extensions of the category of honorable to more and more groups of people and a reorientation of the locus of honor and dignity from ascribed or earned characteristics to an inherent, universal humanity. Associated with these changing conceptions of dignity, Western politics went through a gradual process of largely incremental liberalization that eventually led to full democratization and the granting of the full range of equal rights to all citizens.

5. Dignity and the Foundations of Human Rights

We are finally in a position to be able to speak in a bit more detail about *how* "human dignity" provides a foundation for human rights. Three types of answers dominate the contemporary literature.

"Human dignity" is sometimes presented as a hopelessly vague notion that at best appears to provide some deeper foundation. "The concept of dignity is itself vacuous" (Bagaric and James 2006: 260). "It has different senses and often points us in opposite directions" (Davis 2007: 177). "Dignity is a fuzzy concept, and appeals to dignity are often used to substitute for empirical evidence that is lacking or sound arguments that cannot be mustered" (Chalmers and Ida 2007: 158; quoting Macklin 2002: 212). Where this is true, though, it is an accidental feature of particular usages rather than an essential feature of the concept.

Human dignity is often presented as rooted in some particular characteristic. For example, Alan Gewirth defines human dignity as "a kind of intrinsic worth that belongs equally to all human beings as such, constituted by certain intrinsically valuable aspects of being human" (1992: 12). Following Kant, autonomy and reason are frequently mentioned foundations of human dignity. In contemporary Christian accounts, the notion that human beings are created in the image of God is often appealed to as the substantive foundation of human dignity.

The leading alternative to this "essential attributes" approach is to see human dignity as "foundational, declaratory, and undefined" (Beyleveld and Brownsword 1998: 663), something more like "a sort of axiom in the system . . . a familiar and accepted principle of shared morality" (Harris and Sulston 2004: 797), "a bedrock concept that resists definition in terms of something else" (Weisstub 2002: 2). Such accounts take a variety of particular forms. Klaus Dicke presents human dignity, as it functions in the context of the Universal Declaration, as "a formal, transcendental norm" or "a formal background value" (2002: 118, 120). Joel Feinberg suggests that attributing human dignity involves "expressing an attitude—the attitude of respect—toward the humanity in each man's person" (1973: 94). William Parent argues instead for understanding attributions of human dignity "as essentially ascriptive. Sentences of the form 'I have dignity' and 'she has dignity,' when used to make moral claims, serve to ascribe the fundamental moral right not to be unjustly debased" (Parent 1992: 64). They all, however, share an understanding of human dignity as foundational and yet substantially resistant to analysis.

I want to suggest an understanding that combines these two. Human dignity is not an unanalyzable "Ur-principle" (Witte 2003: 119). Neither, though, is it reducible to one, a few, or any particular set of attributes. It is rather an intermediate concept that links human rights to "comprehensive doctrines." This, I believe, appropriately responds to Paul Kristeller's important injunction that "when we try to make sense out of the idea of human dignity, we should not settle for too cheap and easy a solution" (1972: 21).

Recall the Rawlsian distinction, discussed in section 4.2, between comprehensive doctrines—foundational moral or religious systems of thought or worldviews—and political conceptions of justice. I suggested that human rights should be understood as a political conception of justice around which an international overlapping consensus has formed over the past half century. Now I want to suggest that human dignity is a quasi-foundational notion that lies deeper than human rights but on which there is only an overlapping consensus. Different comprehensive doctrines provide different accounts of human dignity. These accounts are sufficiently convergent, though, that they allow human dignity to serve as an "accepted principle of shared morality" (Harris and Sulston 2004). And for those who for whatever reason do not want to push deeper, it does function as an axiom or Ur-principle.[5]

"Although ambiguous, dignity is a signaling term that goes to the heart of what constitutes the quality of humanness" (Weisstub 2002: 269). That ambiguity, however, arises not from any special lack of clarity or from the absence of deeper substantive foundations. Rather, it arises from the fact that for different people human dignity points to different deeper foundations. These deeper foundations simultaneously provide personal or moral meaning and remove at least some of the ambiguity of meaning from the concept.

This, I believe, helps to explain the fact that "the dignity of the individual is a cliché, yet it retains surprising force" (Tinder 2003: 238). Beneath the

---

5. Compare David Weisstub's suggestion that dignity "has emerged as a convergence point for what is perceived to be a non-ideological humanistic point of departure towards a social liberal ideal" (2002: 263). Dignity, however, is equally a religious conception, as is especially evident in contemporary Catholic social teaching. One of the great attractions of an overlapping consensus account of human rights and human dignity is that it sets aside the controversy between religious and secular/humanistic foundations. Each side can have it its own way, because for the purposes of agreement on human rights and human dignity, this disagreement doesn't matter.

apparently stale and empty cliché lies a wide range of powerful specifications of the meaning of human dignity that despite their differences in detail converge enough to provide a bridge between the body of international human rights law and most of the leading comprehensive doctrines of the contemporary world.[6] Although "the concept of human dignity has become ubiquitous to the point of cliché" (Witte 2003: 121), it is not *simply* a cliché, because of the deeper foundation in comprehensive doctrines.

I thus agree with Jeff Malpas and Norelle Lickiss that "the breadth of the concept, its ubiquity, especially in legal and biomedical contexts, and the difficulty of giving it a clear and unambiguous definition, all point towards its absolutely fundamental character." I also agree with them that "dignity connects up with too many other concepts, and in too many ways, for it to be amenable to any simple rendering" (2007: 1). I want to go further, though, and suggest that the range of the concept is set both by the various foundational doctrines that participate in the overlapping consensus on human rights and by the contemporary substantive consensus on the list of human rights in the Universal Declaration.

Some loosely defined but not empty conceptions of human dignity underlie, and thus help to shape, contemporary conceptions of human rights. Our understandings of human dignity, however, are themselves shaped by the body of established international human rights law and the political practices of states. One can think of human dignity independently of human rights. In practice, however, that is becoming increasingly infrequent. As the prominence of human rights increases, the link between human rights and human dignity is increasingly seen as normative.

Human rights and human dignity mutually co-constitute one another in the contemporary world. Human rights reflect a particular specification of certain minimum preconditions for a life of dignity in the contemporary world. Our detailed understanding of human dignity, however, is shaped by our ideas and practices of human rights and the practice of human rights can be seen as justified, in some ultimate sense, by its production of beings able to live a life of dignity.

---

6. Drawing a distinction between "thin" and "thick" conceptions of dignity (e.g., Shultziner 2004) makes much the same point. My formulation, however, emphasizes the simultaneous presence of multiple converging thick accounts. The *concept* of human dignity, in other words, is inherently thin—at least as it functions in contemporary international human rights discourse. That concept, however, rests on a variety of thick conceptions that converge on the thin account. Still another way to make the point would be to consider human dignity an "essentially contested concept" over which contestation concerning justificatory details does not prevent agreement on its quasi-foundational use in international human rights law.

9

Humanity, Dignity, and Politics in Confucian China

The Confucian tradition begins two and a half millennia ago with Kong Qiu (551–479 BCE), a scholar and teacher born in the state of Lu in eastern China. He was known to his contemporaries as Kongzi, Master Kong, and to later followers as Kong Fuzi, "our Master Kong"—Confucius. What in the West is called Confucianism is more commonly called in China *ruxue*, learning about *ru*, ancient knowledge, or *rujia*, the school of *ru*. Master Kong, the leading *ru* scholar and teacher of his era, practiced at the cusp of the aptly named Warring States period (479–221 BCE), when growing internal and international disorder posed powerful practical and theoretical challenges to the ancient learning. At a pivotal point in history—pivotal in part because of the consequences of his work—Kong Qiu made a heroic effort to preserve and codify the ancient learning and then transmit it, along with his own contributions. The record of some of his sayings, the *Analects* (*Lun Yu*), is one of the central texts of Chinese civilization. The ensuing conversation on his legacy, which continues even today, has helped to define many of the central elements of that civilization.

This chapter begins by considering Confucian cosmology, philosophical anthropology, and social theory, particularly as they relate to ideas of human dignity and political practices that today we consider to be matters of human rights. It then looks briefly at two bodies of Confucian practice, in the Han and Song dynasties. The final sections briefly consider twentieth-century Chinese encounters with rights and the contemporary question of human rights and Asian values.

I. Cosmology and Ethics

"Confucianism" has no fixed doctrine. "Confucians" instead participate in a shared but constantly changing conversation centered around a loosely defined canon. Of special importance are the "Five Classics" (the Books of *Odes, Rites, History* (or *Documents*), and *Changes* (*I Ching*) and the *Spring and Autumn Annals*) and the "Four Books" (the *Analects*, the *Mencius* [a collection of conversations of the fourth-century BCE master Meng Ke, known as Mengzi (Mencius), Master Meng], and *The Great Learning* (*Daxue*) and *The Doctrine [or Practice] of the Mean* (*Zhong-Yong*), chapters of the *Book of Rites* that became separate parts of the canon in the twelfth century. The Confucian tradition has also been deeply engaged with, and often unusually open to, other traditions, including Moism, Legalism, Daoism, Buddhism, and, more recently, Western philosophy—and this only begins to scratch the surface of the diversity of "Confucianism," which is replete with the most serious internal substantive disagreements. Nonetheless, in addition to historical and intertextual connections, there are striking family resemblances across time and otherwise very different authors. What follows identifies themes, concepts, and principles widely acknowledged to be central to Confucian thought that are especially relevant to contemporary issues of human rights and human dignity.

A. Heaven-and-Earth (*tiandi*) and Man

Confucians understand "the world"—nature, the cosmos, the universe—in terms of "heaven-and-earth and the myriad things" (*tian di wan wu*). Special ontological place, though, goes to Heaven (*Tian*), understood both as a space above the earth and, much more importantly, as the source and rule of all reality.

As Roger Ames and Henry Rosemont nicely put it, "*Tian* is both *what* our world is and *how* it is" (1998: 47). Heaven has a Way (*Dao*)—the Way, the Way of Heaven. The world operates according to the Way. Thus *The Mean* begins, "What Heaven has endowed is called the nature. Following the nature is called the Way" (De Bary and Bloom 1999: 334; Chan 1963: 98).[1] "The Way is the basis of Heaven and Earth, and . . . Heaven and Earth are the basis of all things" (Chan 1963: 485 [Shao Yong]. Cf. 570 [Cheng Yi], 614 [Zhu Xi]).

Heaven, although often seen as an active principle, is never anthropomorphized. Furthermore, the language of "divine" is largely inappropriate. Heaven is more a rule rather than a ruler; it is *Dao* (the Way), *Li* (Principle), rather than god. (There is Confucian metaphysics but no Confucian theology.) Much like Western natural law, the Way has essential natural/descriptive and

---

1. Wherever possible, page references are given to the two principal English-language readers, Chan (1963) and De Bary and Bloom (1999), the particular translation used being the first work cited, with the author cited indicated in square brackets.

moral/prescriptive senses, and naturalistic, even rationalistic, understand-ings of Heaven and its Way predominate in the Confucian tradition.

Humans are inescapably a part of "heaven-and-earth" (*tiandi*). "There is no division between Nature and man" (Chan 1963: 538 [Cheng Hao]). "The Way is identical with the nature of man and things and their nature is identi-cal with the Way" (Chan 1963: 614; De Bary and Bloom 1999: 704 [Zhu Xi]). Humans also, however, are qualitatively different from the rest of nature. "Man, living in the world, [i]s more intelligent than the myriad things and more noble than the myriad things" (Chan 1963: 575 [Lu Xiangshan]). "Man occupies the most honored position in the scheme of things" (Chan 1963: 492 [Shao Yong]). "Man is most precious. What makes him more precious is his possession of moral principles and virtue" (Chan 1963: 475 [Zhou Dunyi]). Thus "the world" is often spoken of as Heaven and Earth and Man. "Man and Heaven and Earth coexist as three ultimates" (Chan 1963: 575 [Lu Xiangshan]).

Confucian thought is centrally concerned with understanding the natu-ral principles, rules, and rites of well-ordered human communities. Confu-cius's own central contribution was to put the classics in proper order and thus begin to reveal the models, practices, and principles of a true civilization in harmony with the One, the Ultimate (*Yi, Tai Yi*).

The proper functioning of man and the world is often expressed in terms of *cheng*—integrity, sincerity, equilibrium, centrality, or the mean. "Just as a person of integrity [*cheng*] is someone who holds fast to his or her principles, so too the cosmos is seen as possessing integrity because it keeps to certain principles of action" (Zhang 2002: 140).

> Sincerity [*cheng*] is the Way of Heaven. To think how to be sincere is the way of man. He who is sincere is one who hits upon what is right without effort and apprehends without thinking. He is naturally and easily in harmony with the Way. Such a man is a sage. He who tries to be sincere is one who chooses the good and holds fast to it. (Chan 1963: 107; De Bary and Bloom 1999: 338 [*The Mean*])

> Equilibrium [*cheng*] is the great foundation of the world, and harmony its universal path. When equilibrium and harmony are realized to the highest degree, heaven and earth will attain their proper order and all things will flourish. (Chan 1963: 98; De Bary and Bloom 1999: 334 [*The Mean*])

The Great Learning famously lists the "eight items" that link individuals and families with both nature and society:

> Those in antiquity who wished to illuminate luminous virtue throughout the world would first govern their states; wishing to govern their states, they would first bring order to their families; wishing to bring order to their families, they would first cultivate their own persons; wishing to cultivate their own persons, they would first rectify their minds; wishing to rectify their minds, they would first make their thoughts sincere; wishing to make their thoughts sincere, they would first extend their knowledge. The extension of knowledge lies in the investigation of things. (De Bary and Bloom 1999: 330–31; Chan 1963: 86)

The sequence is then worked back up. "It is only when things are investigated that knowledge is extended; when knowledge is extended that thoughts become sincere; . . . when the state is well governed that peace is brought to the world." Then the final conclusion is drawn: "From the Son of Heaven [the Emperor] to ordinary people, all, without exception, should regard cultivating the person as the root" (De Bary and Bloom 1999: 331; Chan 1963: 87).

B. Humanity [*ren*] and the Exemplary Person [*junzi*]

The Confucian vision of humans and their place in the world revolves around learning and self-cultivation, understood as the key to realizing the Way and achieving earthly harmony and well-being. Self-cultivation is a matter of becoming truly human, *ren*, which "has been translated as 'humanity,' 'benevolence,' 'love,' and, to bring out the sense of relationship, 'co-humanity.' It is also the supreme virtue that encompasses all others and so is rendered 'goodness,' 'perfect virtue'" (Zhang 2002: 285).

The aim of self-cultivation, of becoming *ren*, is to become a *junzi*, which is conventionally translated as "gentleman," in the Victorian sense of that term, but which Ames and Rosemont (1998) felicitously render in English as "exemplary person." Much of Confucian ethics is devoted to understanding how to become an exemplary, fully-realized person. *The Mean* (paragraph 20) gives a particularly clear statement, emphasizing the links between man, society, and nature:

> Men must be active in matters of government, just as the earth is active in making things grow: the government is a growing reed. Therefore, the conduct of government depends on having the man, one obtains the man through one's own person, one cultivates one's own person through the Way, and one cultivates the Way through humaneness [*ren*]. Humaneness [*ren*] is what it means to be human [*ren*], and being affectionate toward one's kin is the greatest part of it. (De Bary and Bloom 1999: 336; Chan 1963: 104)

A patriarchal and paternalistic kinship model of society is distinctively Confucian:

> The universal Way of the world involves five relations, and practicing it involves three virtues. The five are the relations between ruler and minister, between parent and child, between husband and wife, between older and younger brother, and among friends.[2] The three—knowledge, humaneness, and courage—are the universal virtues of the world. And the means by which they are practiced is oneness. (De Bary and Bloom 1999: 336–37; Chan 1963: 105 [*The Mean*])

The core relation, though, is between father and son. Filial piety—a relation available to all people of all stations—is the organizing principle of Confucian ethics.

It is a useful oversimplification to see "classical" (Zhou and Han dynasty) and "Neo-Confucian" (Song, Ming, and Qing dynasty) accounts of ethical behavior. In the classical account, *ren* is but one of the Five Constant Virtues (*wuchang*), along with *yi* (righteousness), *li* (propriety), *zhi* (wisdom), and *xin* (loyalty or integrity), with special emphasis on *li*. *Li*, which is often translated as "rites" or "ritual," also includes notions of etiquette, custom, and the rules of ethical behavior. Its immediate focus is external behavior, which in the Confucian tradition requires special attention to ancient models and formulas (which were believed to conform to the Way). But the true object of *li* is the attitude and understanding underlying ritual performance.[3] *Li* is a matter of conforming both thought and action, including the slightest gesture, to man's true nature and his place in the cosmos.

Neo-Confucian thinkers, beginning in the eleventh century, explicitly shifted the emphasis from particular practices to underlying principles, with an attendant shift in emphasis from the external to the internal. *Ren* came to be understood as a master or summary virtue, encompassing the other four. "*Yi, li, zhi*, and *xin* are all [expressions of] *ren*. [One's duty] is to understand this principle and to preserve *ren* with sincerity and seriousness, that is all" (Chan 1963: 523 [Cheng Hao]. Cf. Chang 1963: 593; De Bary and Bloom 1999: ??? [Zhu Xi]). At a broader metaphysical level, primary attention was

---

2. The *Analects* mentions only three of these five relations (ruler, father, elder) but the *Mencius* (3A:4) notes all five. "From the Han dynasty onward, when most philosophical works mention human relations they generally have in mind the Mencian set of five" (Zhang 2002: 325).

3. "The Master said, 'In referring time and again to observing ritual propriety *(li)*, how could I just be talking about gifts of jade and silk?'" Conversely, "The Master said, 'What could I see in a person who in holding a position of influence is not tolerant, who in observing ritual propriety *(li)* is not respectful, and who in overseeing the mourning rites does not grieve?'" *Analects* 17.1, 3.26. Cf. 3.3, 8.4, 9.3 and *Mencius* 7A:46.

focused on "Principle," the central neo-Confucian concept—which also is transliterated as *li*, but is a different Chinese character.

Ren and *yi* (righteousness), though, however they are to be achieved, represent the core of the Way (*dao*) for human beings in their interactions. As Han Yu, one of the founders of the Neo-Confucian movement, put it, "What I call the Way (*dao*) and Power (*de*, virtue) means combining humaneness (*ren*) and righteousness (*yi*). This is the definition accepted by all under Heaven" (quoted in Kuhn 2009: 100). "To practice [*ren*] in the proper manner is called *yi*. To proceed according to these is called the Way" (Chan 1963: 454 [Han Yu]). "*Ren* is the human heart and *yi* is the human path" (*Mencius* 6A:11).

Taken together, the ideas of *ren*, *yi*, *li* and the *junzi* provide the equivalent of a Confucian account of human dignity. For our purposes here, three points bear special emphasis.

First, although every human being has an innate potential for becoming *ren*, it is the achievement of very few. *Ren* "is an aesthetic project, an accomplishment, something done. The human *being* is not something we are; it is something that we do, and become. Perhaps 'human *becoming*' might thus be a more appropriate term to capture the processional and emergent nature of what it means to become human. It is not an essential endowed potential, but what one is able to make of oneself" (Ames and Rosemont 1998: 49). As a result, "human dignity" was understood as the achievement of a small elite.

Second, humanity is to be achieved in this world. Full human self-realization, which is to be achieved in the here and now, requires knowledge of heaven-and-earth and the Way but does not involve leaving this world for "Heaven" or forsaking the mundane for the "divine." The Indian notion of withdrawal from the world is utterly foreign to the Confucian understanding—as are the Hindu and Buddhist notions of the fundamental unreality of this earthly existence.

Third, humanity is to be achieved in and through society. Although the individual person is the object of cultivation, he is inescapably embedded in society, particularly the family and the polity. The Confucian sage is, ideally, a ruler. The Confucian scholar is, ideally, a minister or civil servant. The exemplary Confucian man is, for all his life, a householder. The ethical and the political, the personal and the social, are not only inseparable but governed by a single Way that applies to all under heaven.

The above account is incomplete and not entirely balanced. Metaphysical strands have been subordinated and the rationalist emphasis on the control over desire, strikingly similar to Western Stoicism, has been largely ignored. The central ethical concept of the Mean has been addressed only in passing and Confucian statecraft has been slighted. Nonetheless, for our topic of human rights and human dignity, the above covers most of the essentials of Confucian cosmology and philosophical anthropology—allowing us to turn now to practice.

2. Confucians and the Early Empires

Confucianism in the early Warring States period was only one of many competing schools—and by no means obviously the most promising. The creation of a truly imperial polity, in the Qin (221–206 BCE) and Han (206 BCE—220 CE) dynasties, did not immediately improve its prospects. Quite the contrary, Qin and early Han theory and practice were much closer to the "Legalist" tradition in China, which has striking similarities with Western notions of Realpolitik. Confucians thus were marginalized, even actively repressed. The first emperor of Qin went so far as to remove all copies of the Five Classics and related works from private hands (which led to scholarly disaster when the imperial library was burned by invaders in 206 BCE). During the course of Han rule, however, Confucianism emerged as a state ideology.

Imperial rule changed China from a world of competing feudal states to a single polity. By 154 BCE, all of the old states had been effectively suppressed. "The old justification through military power faded. Instead, the state increasingly claimed to rule as the patron of a Chinese civilization embodied in the canon, the imperial academy, and the classical virtues" (Mark Edward Lewis 2007: 67). The emperor and the Confucian scholars of the ancient learning now had a common cause—although an awkward and contested relationship.

Han rulers revived the idea of the Mandate of Heaven (*Tian ming*), created by the early rulers of the Zhou dynasty (c. 1050–221 BCE) to justify their replacement of the Shang (Yin) dynasty. The right to rule, the Zhou argued, rested on neither fate or predestination nor the arbitrary or inexplicable choice of the gods. Rather, it was lost by the vice of rulers[4] and could only be gained and maintained by demonstrated virtue.[5] In the case of the Zhou, "God on High in the fields of Zhou observed King Wen's virtue, and so it centered the great mandate in his person."[6] Heaven's appointment thus was as much a charge to be obeyed as a grant of authority—and in fact charge and mandate are both standard translations of the Chinese *ming*.

Even more striking is the fact that the welfare of the people is the measure of royal virtue and vice. "Heaven sees as my people see; Heaven hears as

---

4. "Men lose [Heaven's] favouring appointment because they cannot pursue and carry out the reverence and brilliant virtue of their forefathers" (*Documents, 44 [21] Jun Shi* [Prince Shi]). Cf. *40 [17] Shao gao* [Announcement to Shao]), *38 [15], Jiu gao* [Announcement about drunkenness]. Citations to the *Book of Documents* and *Book of Songs*, the original Zhou sources for the theory of the mandate of heaven, are by document or song number in the standard collation and title.
5. *Documents, 44 [21] Jun Shi* [Prince Shi], *40 [17] Shao gao* [Announcement of Shao], *37 [14] Kang gao* [Announcement to Kang]. *Mencius* (4A:3) explicitly links the mandate to *ren*: "The three Dynasties got the world through being *ren*. They lost the world through not being *ren*."
6. *Documents, 44 [21] Jun Shi* [Prince Shi]. Cf. *56 [26] Wen Hou zhi ming* [Charge to Marquis Wen], *Songs, 241 Huang yi* [Sovereign Might].

my people hear."[7] Maintaining the mandate requires being "respectful [both] upwards and downwards."[8] The ruler is the agent of Heaven. But he has been charged by Heaven to act for the benefit of his people.

We should be careful, however, not to overstate the universalism of heaven's mandate. In the case of the Zhou, it was transferred from one kingly lineage to a new one. It was revived by the Han emperors and adopted by many of their successors as well. And although the doctrine of the Mandate could easily be put to both conservative or authoritarian and progressive or reformist uses (much like the Christian idea that all power is from God), in practice its principal use (as in the Christian case) was to justify incumbent power (although the Chinese never went so far as to present tyrants as divine retribution for an evil people).

Even more important, we should not confuse universalism with egalitarianism. The heavenly standards of justice applied to all rulers. Chinese politics and society, however, were deeply hierarchical. Kingly rule was unquestioned. (Citizen self-rule had never been an historical reality.) And when the Chinese looked back to the depths of their very ancient history for an idealized vision of the good society it was always of a harmonious regime under the rule of a wise and virtuous king.

The emperor—*huangdi*, "celestial magnificence"—was presented as standing at the intersection of Heaven and Earth and functioning as the point of mediation between Man and Heaven. The blessings of heaven flowed from him, or at least through him, to his people, whose well-being was seen as largely dependent on the ability of the emperor and his court to inculcate and realize virtue. The Confucian conception of the five relations, understood paternalistically in terms of filial piety, obviously were attractive to China's new rulers.

The Mandate of Heaven simply was not, as Y. P. Mei claims, an "expression of the democratic ideal" (1967: 155). The people were not entitled to rule themselves. Quite the contrary, the *Book of Documents* explicitly argues that "Heaven gives birth to the people with (such) desires that without a ruler they must fall into all disorders" and that "the minds of the people cannot attain to the right mean (of duty); they must be guided by your [the king] attaining to it."[9]

---

7. *Documents, 28 Da Shi* [Great Declaration]. Cf. *Documents, 50 [24] Gu ming* [Testamentary charge], *35 [13] Da Gao* [Great Announcement], *38 [15] Jiu gao* [Announcement about Drunkenness], *40 [17] Shao gao* [Announcement of Shao].
8. *Documents, 44 [21], Jun Shi* [Prince Shi]. Cf. *Songs 249 Jia le* [All Happiness].
9. *Documents, 11 Zhong Hui zhi gao* [Announcement of Zhong Hui], *53 Jiong Ya* [Lord Ya]. Cf. *16 Taijia* [Taijia], *27 Da Shi* [Great Declaration] ("Heaven, for the help of the inferior people, made for them rulers, and made for them instructors"). For comparable Confucian views, see *Analects* 8.9, 16.2, 16.8 and *Mencius* 2B:2, 3A:3, 3A:4.

In particular, the people had no political rights, either individually or collectively. They were not *entitled* to justice (or even survival). Rather than empowered political agents they were the passive third-party beneficiaries of the cosmic obligations of their rulers. And during the transition between regimes, the people were forced to suffer grievously for the sins of their rulers—until Heaven saw fit to give them good rulers once again.

There were potentials for opposition and reform in the reciprocal nature of the five relations. Parents were entitled to respect from their children, but children had legitimate claims against their parents as well. Likewise, subjects could expect proper treatment from their rulers—although in practice demanding it was rarely an option, at least before the situation deteriorated to the point of peasant rebellions. The closest typical approximation was for virtuous government officials to remonstrate their superiors, even the emperor himself, reminding them of their duties. In practice, though, even this often was met by loss of office and banishment from court, or worse.

Broader egalitarian tendencies in the Confucian sources should also be noted. The Mencian idea that all humans are born good (*Mencius* 6A:6) combined with the hierarchical responsibility of rulers, could be used to criticize emperors, their ministers, and the court for the shortcomings of the people. Confucian prejudices against trade and landlordism and in favor of small peasant production regularly generated sincere proposals for political and financial reform. The classical model of the "well fields" system of small peasant plots laid out on a grid was regularly mobilized for locally egalitarian purposes. The central government could be a source of protection against local social and economic hierarchy—although in practice it often was instead a source of ruinous taxation. Furthermore, the general emphasis on education, wisdom, and virtue as a potential check on hierarchical abuses of power should not be overlooked—or overemphasized.

In all of this, though, there is no idea of the dignity of the ordinary person. Confucian ideals counseled decent and humane treatment for those at the bottom of the social scale. That, though, was the vast majority of the population, who were seen as essentially uncultivated, and thus at best potentially human.

The Han adopted a similar attitude toward the nomadic peoples on their borders. Their "peace and kinship" (*he qin*) policy sent Chinese goods and princesses north in return for "peace," or at least periodic cessations of conflict. The ideological context for this, though, was a division of the world between civilized Chinese and barbarian non-Chinese. "It posited the fundamental unity of a single Chinese civilization defined by what was not nomadic, and it reduced regional divisions to secondary status. China first emerged as a unity through the invention of a Chinese/nomadic dichotomy, and this bipolar concept remained central to Chinese civilization" (Lewis 2007: 135–36).

Attitudes and practices of Chinese superiority waxed and waned, as did Chinese power to act on them. A sharp categorical distinction between civilized and barbarian, however, remained essentially unquestioned for two millennia. That distinction, it should be emphasized, was based on culture not birth. Nonetheless, civilization for the barbarian, like cultivation for the peasant, was an abstract theoretical possibility—and usually nothing more.

3. "Neo-Confucianism" and Song Imperial Rule

The tenth-century transition from the Tang to the Song dynasty marks a decisive rupture in Chinese history.

> The "old world" of the northern hereditary aristocratic families, with genealogies going back hundreds of years, finally vanished in the turmoil and civil wars between 880 and 960. . . . A newly emerging class of scholar-officials, trained in Confucian doctrine and graduated in a competitive civil service examination system, was willing and well-prepared to take on responsibility for reshaping Chinese tradition. . . . a new self-consciousness and self-esteem took shape among the people who identified themselves as descendants of the Han Chinese. The social system they invented during the Song empire became the paradigm for what Chinese and Westerners of the twentieth century would refer to as "traditional China." (Kuhn 2009: 1–2)

Confucian ideas provided an imperial ideology and Confucian scholar-bureaucrats made up most of the administrative cadre of the Song state, especially at the higher echelons. Confucian doctrine, scholars, and bureaucrats were often leading forces for reform, at both the central and local levels. Nonetheless—and of central importance for our purposes here—even the most humane and progressive proposals for reform had no relation to ideas of human rights or human dignity.

"Reform is the keyword for understanding the Song politics of the eleventh century" (Kuhn 2009: 49). With some serious oversimplification, three main groups can be identified. Conservatives, symbolized by Sima Guang (1019–1086), favored modest incremental reforms at home and a pacifist policy with China's neighbors (feeling unable to recover lost lands or assert traditional imperial ideas of universal overlordship). Advocates of reform fell into two groups. A powerful faction in the bureaucracy, led by Wang Anshi (1021–1086), favored an aggressive, state-led program of economic, military, financial, and educational reforms. Another faction favored extensive reforms but with a more Confucian focus on education and individuals. Although not well represented in the top bureaucracy in the eleventh century, by the second half of the twelfth century these new Confucians came to dominate Chinese intellectual life and control the state bureaucracy. Their understanding of the ancient learning and its place in modern politics became the basis for the civil service exam for the remainder of the Chinese empire.

Indicative of the general Neo-Confucian orientation is the so-called Western Inscription of Zhang Zai (1020–1077):

> Heaven is my father and Earth is my mother, and even such a small creature as I finds an intimate place in their midst.
>
> Therefore that which fills the universe I regard as my body and that which directs the universe I consider my nature.
>
> All people are my brothers and sisters, and all things are my companions.
>
> The great ruler (the emperor) is the eldest son of my parents (Heaven and Earth), and the great ministers are his stewards. Respect the aged—this is the way to treat them as elders should be treated. Show deep love towards the orphaned and the weak—this is the way to treat them as the young should be treated. The sage identifies his character with that of Heaven and Earth, and the worthy [*junzi*] is the most outstanding man. (Chan 1963: 497)

Here we see the characteristic Confucian fusion of the cosmic and the human and a strong expression of a universalistic ethical concern for all human beings. We also, however, see the strong Confucian sense of social differentiation and hierarchy. These elements ended up predominating in Song practice. Song emperors, in no small part due to Confucian influences, did attempt to improve the lot of ordinary peasants, for both intrinsic and instrumental reasons. Nonetheless, in Song China, like its Han predecessor, we can find no serious notion of political freedom or equality, even among radical reformers.

Daoism and especially Buddhism—which had become so popular during the Tang dynasty that it threatened to overtake Confucianism—held out the hope of personal salvation. But as Neo-Confucians liked to complain, with some justice, visions of personal salvation were not matched by programs of political reform (e.g., Chan 1963: 554-555, 564 [Cheng Yi]). By contrast, Neo-Confucians were very much concerned with social action here and now in the world. That action, however, was within an unquestioned system of hierarchy and imperial rule.

The most that people could reasonably hope for was protection from external invasion and local oppression, efficient administration, a somewhat reduced taxation burden, and food in time of need. All of this was to be asked for humbly, as a matter of *ren*, *yi*, or justice, not demanded as a matter of right. When one's "elders" and "betters" failed to discharge their obligations of support, the only option, as in the medieval West, was to wait for divine assistance—or, as in the West, rise up in a desperate rebellion that was almost certain to be crushed, the only question being when and with what severity.

4. Twentieth-Century Encounters with "Rights"

Let us jump now to the late nineteenth century. China, although still under imperial rule, was increasingly burdened by an increasingly oppressive and demeaning series of "unequal treaties" that restricted (but did not extinguish) Chinese sovereignty and granted punishing economic, military, political, and religious privileges to the Western powers. The state was nearing collapse. Chinese officials, intellectuals, and citizens largely across the political spectrum were grappling with the meaning of this degradation of China and a wide variety of possible remedies.

One powerful strand of reformist thought traced Chinese decline to the backward-looking rigidities of Confucianism. (Scholar-bureaucrats trained primarily in the classics still dominated the civil service.) In the eyes of these modernists, the sufferings of China were ample evidence of the shortcomings of the doctrines and policies. They thus began to look to the West—whose power could not be denied—for remedies.

Some saw science and technology as the way forward for China, posing in effect a challenge to the traditional Confucian view of nature and the relation of humans to it. For our purposes here, a more interesting challenge was posed by those who took on traditional Confucian statecraft, with its emphasis on the virtue of the emperor and the civil service and its reliance on order and progress from above. Western ideas of political rights thus became of considerable interest.

Marina Svensson, in *Debating Human Rights in China* (2003), tells a nuanced story of the Chinese engagement with ideas of rights. For our purposes here, I want to stress the idea of engagement. Chinese *came* to Western ideas of rights, rather than had them imposed upon them, and they came to those ideas largely as a result of their dissatisfaction with the sufferings of China at the hands of Western state power and the global economy. "The concept of human rights was embraced by Chinese writers as useful in their struggle to save China" (Svensson 2003: 73).

As Svensson emphasizes, "national survival rather than the freedom of the individual from an oppressive state was the main preoccupation" of early-twentieth-century Chinese advocates of rights (2003: 98). Ancient ways, these critics argued, had turned Chinese men and women into weak, slavish beings and brought forth foreign domination. Rights to freedom of thought, speech, and publication, which were a central concern of these critics, were to be used to make the Chinese people, and thus China, strong and dignified again. "This justification of rights was based on the premise that individuals enjoying rights would promote national rights and national salvation" (Svensson 2003: 115).

The relationship between these new ideas and Confucianism, however, was complex. For example, Svensson notes the creation of the term *renge* to translate the Western notion of personality. The traditional notion of *ren*, humanness, was thus reconceptualized, creating

> a semantic field in which personality and enjoyment of rights are used to characterize citizens in contrast to slaves, who have no personality or rights and are completely at the mercy of their masters. . . . The early twentieth-century discourse shows that the concept of human rights, to some extent, could build on Confucian notions of human dignity and human nature, while at the same time it was explicitly formulated as an attack on other aspects of the Confucian tradition, such as its hierarchical nature and submission of women. (Svensson 2003: 104)

In a similar fashion, Stephen Angle argues that the neologism *quanli*, created to translate the Western idea of rights, "does not represent a radical break with the Confucian tradition" (2002: 175), but rather its appropriation in new circumstances and its extension in new directions in light of those circumstances. As Svensson puts it, "new words and concepts were introduced, domesticated, and contested" (2003: 82). In the process they were made Chinese—in much the same way, I would add, that rights concepts were introduced, domesticated, and contested in the West in the preceding two centuries.

Of course, ideas of rights were hardly the whole story of the Chinese reaction to Western domination. And as the history of post-imperial China indicates, in practice rights fared very poorly under both nationalists and communists. Nonetheless, in addition to Chinese embraces of rights—which have been deep and powerful in recent decades in both Hong Kong and Taiwan—the Confucian tradition is arguably undergoing a major regeneration. For example, Feng Youlan (1895–1990) provided a new synthesis of Confucian thought (see Chan 1963: 751–62). A new generation of self-identified "New Confucians" developed in Hong Kong and Taiwan in the 1960s and 1970s (see Liu Shu-Hsien 2003: ch. 8). An even younger generation is trying today to apply Confucian ideas to contemporary social problems (e.g., Bell and Hahm 2003; Chan 1999, 2002). In a rather different vein, the remarkable economic and political success of Singapore is attributed by its architect, Lee Kwan Yew, to a creative synthesis of Western and Chinese, especially Confucian, ideas and practices.

I have neither the expertise nor the desire to speculate on the success or likely consequences of such efforts. I do, however, want to suggest that they suggest a very particular perspective on debates over "Asian values."

5. Human Rights and Asian Values

Asian values are not frozen in an ancient past. They are no less dynamic than Western values—or values anywhere else in the modern world. We must be particularly careful not to confuse what people can be forced to acquiesce to with what they value.

It is possible that forms of politics that differ substantially from Western liberal democracy will be chosen freely by Asian peoples. I am skeptical, and certainly we have seen nothing like that yet. Singapore, which has evolved into a surprisingly liberal semi-democracy, is perhaps closest to a stable viable alternative, but the gap between Singaporean and Western practices is rather rapidly declining. Japan, South Korea, Taiwan, and Hong Kong strongly suggest that where Asians are freely given the choice, they choose human rights no less than those in other parts of the world.

That does not mean that the details will not have distinctive Asian features. (Recall the discussion in sections 6.3 and 7.2 of universality in human rights concepts but substantial particularity in their implementation.) For example, Confucian housing and welfare policy might have quite distinctive characteristics and Asian notions of public propriety might lead to systematically different patterns in the exercise of freedom of speech. However, fundamental concepts of human rights, it seems to me, are and ought to be largely the same in East and West.

As we saw in chapters 5 and 8, human rights did not come to the West easily, let alone naturally, and they came only very late. But Westerners have learned to reshape their values and practices around new ideas of human rights and human dignity. Indians have as well, as we will see in the next chapter. The same argument can be made for Africans and, especially, Latin Americans. I would make it for the Muslim world as well. It also seems to me that East and Southeast Asians, in Confucianism, Daoism, Buddhism, Islam, and traditions of more local provenance, have more than enough indigenous resources to draw on in coming to embrace human rights as they grapple with building lives of dignity in the face of the distinctive opportunities and threats posed by modern states and modern markets.

10

Humans and Society in Hindu South Asia

Hinduism counts close to one billion adherents, approximately 90 percent of whom live in its birthplace, India. Its foundational revealed texts (*śruti*), the Vedas, took shape in the centuries around 1000 BCE, although they draw on sources and traditions that reach back much further. The Puranas, sacred texts that claim an ancestry even prior to the Vedas, were put in written form in the last half of the first millennium of the Christian era. These scriptures are supplemented by a vast store of oral traditions and texts (*smrti*), including the great epics (*itihasa*, history) the *Mahabharata* and the *Ramayana*, which took their canonical form in the several centuries on either side of the zero date in the Christian calendar. More popular *bhakti* (devotional) songs and poems in vernacular (non-Sanskrit) languages also are important. In addition, sacred law books, the most important of which is that attributed to Manu (*Manava Dharmaśastra*, *Manusmrti*), were especially relevant to social life and issues that today are addressed in terms of human rights.

Hindus recognize no central doctrinal or clerical authority. Quite the contrary, the Hindu tradition has been and remains unusually open. It is not uncommon for an individual Hindu to adopt beliefs or practices of "another religion" and yet remain, in her own eyes and those of her community, a Hindu. Furthermore, dominant understandings and practices have repeatedly been transformed, both through internal movements of revival and reform and through encounters with others, especially Islamic invaders from Persia and Central Asia and Christian colonizers from Europe. Nonetheless, a readily identifiable Hindu community continues to share in a three-millennium-old tradition loosely defined by reference to a common body of sacred texts and more-or-less widely shared local and trans-local beliefs, traditions, and rites.

1. Cosmology

Hinduism presents itself as a comprehensive theory of all of reality, which is understood to be composed of three basic *gunas*, "substances": *sattva* ("purity," residing in the mind and providing true knowledge of reality); *rajas* ("virility," residing in life and associated with egoism, selfishness, and violence); and *tamas* ("dullness," residing in the body and giving rise to ignorance). Everything—deities, human beings, demons, animals, plants, objects—is composed of these three substances, but in different proportions. *Sattva* predominates in deities, *rajas* predominates in demons and animals, and *tamas* predominates in plants and objects. Much as in the Western idea of the great chain of being, all of reality is seen as hierarchically ordered, with rank defined largely in terms of ontological distance from *Brahman*, the divine.

For sentient beings, every individual "self" or "soul," *atman*, is enjoined to acquire knowledge of reality in order to prepare for (re-)union with the divinely infused cosmos. One's separate self is, although a very real physical and social reality, a metaphysical illusion. True knowledge of "self" is recognition of the insignificance of the separate self. The meaning of life is, ultimately, recognition of self-estrangement—and through this recognition, an overcoming that reunites the person with all of nature (or, to say the same thing in different terms, the divine).

Three paths to liberation (*trimarga*) have predominated in Hindu practice. *Karmamarga*, the path of works, focuses on achieving purity and merit through ritual practice. *Inanamarga*, the path of knowledge, stresses preparation for liberation through the study of sacred texts and philosophy. *Bhaktimarga*, the path of devotion, emphasizes personal, emotional, loving connection with god. There are, however, seemingly infinite variations rooted in particular times and places.

Likewise, the end, *Brahman*, "God"/nature/reality is variously conceived: in pantheistic terms (as encompassing all of reality); in personalistic, generally monotheistic, terms (although that one god is variously represented); and even in atheistic terms (as something more like a natural principle of right order). In most traditions, though, Hindus represent the divine through a wide array of personalized "gods" that appear in various guises (avatars).

2. Social Philosophy

The Hindu theory of the universe identifies four ends, goals, or interests that are particularly relevant to social life: *dharma*, *artha*, *kama*, and *moksa* (Mittal and Thursby 2004: part 4; Sharma 2003: 10–16, 20–22).

"In Hindu traditions *dharma* is an encompassing category that incorporates and at the same time transcends the distinctions among religion, ritual, law, and ethics that are generally posited in Western traditions" (Holdrege 2004: 213). *Dharma* regulates what in Western categories are the religio-moral dimensions of human life, combining the Thomistic categories of divine law and natural law. *Dharma* provides "a comprehensive concept of social regulation in relation to patterns of ethics in the Hindu tradition" (Creel 1972: 155). *Dharma* also links this ethical life with cosmic order and it identifies the pursuit of "duty" as a prime driver of human life.

Artha ("polity"), which refers more directly to the political and economic domain, identifies the pursuit of worldly goods as the second principal driving force in human life. *Kama*, or bodily desire, is no less central to the comprehensive Hindu vision of humans' place in the cosmos. The highest goal, however, is *moksa*, liberation from the distractions and delusions of "this" world. This is the ultimate end of the three paths identified above.

Hindu ethics and social theory, looked at somewhat more narrowly, revolve around the closely interrelated concepts of *dharma* ("duty") and *karma* ("divine justice") that generate *samsara*, the cycle of birth, death, and rebirth. Each type of creature has duties appropriate to its place in the hierarchy of nature. Individuals move their way up and down the chain of being through right and wrong behavior over a vast succession of lives. Each *atman* (self/soul) occupies a particular station that has been determined by compliance or noncompliance with duty (*dharma*) in previous lives. One's place in the order of nature—from king to cockroach—is a reflection and expression of *karma*, the merit or demerit one has achieved through the practice of one's prior lives.

Any particular birth, however, is but the start of a transitory phase in a long progression toward the divine. All of the particular paths to enlightenment and liberation aim to lead the practitioner ultimately to escape from the cycle of rebirth. The resulting state of *moksa*, "release," "liberation," "consciousness of unity," is very much like what Buddhists identify as nirvana.

As in the other "great civilizations," gender and age hierarchies have been historically central to Hindu society. Hindu society has also been stratified by "class." But "class" stratification takes a particularly rigid form that is typically described as "caste," the division of society into sharply distinguished and largely encapsulated hereditary groups, associated with a particular station and way of life. Caste identity is the most important identity in traditional Hindu society.

The most ancient traditional formula recognizes four *varnas* ("castes"): *Brahmana* or Brahmin (priest), *Ksatriya* (warrior/ruler), *Vaiśya* (landowner and merchant), and *Śudra* (servant). In addition, beneath this formal caste system reside *Chandalas*, "untouchables"—outcastes, in the sense of outside of the caste system, and thus social outcasts. They practiced professions such as sanitation, butchering, and leatherwork that were socially necessary but ritually impure.

In the Hindu worldview, caste rests on natural distinctions not social convention; its justification is not functional but ontological and metaphysical, a matter of the fabric of natural reality and being. "In a just and stable society a correspondence was presumed between a person's qualities and his social position" (Béteille 1983: 10). One's station has its duties (*dharma*), which are held to be suited to one's nature, and the discharge of those duties gives one a place in society and a certain personal dignity. "The various varnas or classes are part of a natural order, and social justice consists in there being a place for everything, and in everything being in its place" (Sharma 2005: 146). Both the *Bhagavad-Gita* (3.35) and the *Laws of Manu* (10.97) emphasize that it is better to perform one's own duties poorly, even to die doing so, than to perform another's well. And the proper discharge of the duties of one's station will be rewarded in the next life. Caste hierarchy is thus "the expression of a secret justice" (Bouglé 1971 [1908]: 76).

3. Caste

Caste is in many ways simply the social expression of the central Hindu belief that the "cosmos is ordered by a premise of ranked inequalities" (Davis 1976: 8–9). The caste system (*varnadharma*), however, is so central to Hindu society, and to the relationship between Hinduism and human rights, that it merits extended consideration. "Whatever one's judgment may be, there is no doubt that caste has shaped Indian society throughout the last several thousands of years and that it is still of large practical significance" (Klostermaier 2007: 288).

A. The Priority of the Particular

The caste system divides society in three principal ways: "*separation* in matters of marriage and contact, whether direct or indirect (food); *division* of labor, each group having, in theory or by tradition, a profession from which their members can depart only within certain limits; and finally *hierarchy*, which ranks the groups as relatively superior or inferior to one another" (Dumont 1980: 21). Separation, division, and hierarchy are common elements of most societies. In Hindu South Asia, however, they have combined in extreme forms to create the traditional caste system.

Whether the classic *varnas* were ever more than an ideal-type representation is a matter of continuing controversy among historians. By the third or fourth century CE, however, "caste" was associated primarily with the *jati*, an endogamous descent group linked to a particular occupation. What we typically call "the caste system" can be understood as the fusion of the social system of *jati* divisions and a religious/ideological justification in terms of *varna*, *karma*, and *dharma*.

There are literally thousands of such "caste" divisions; three thousand is a commonly cited number. Where medieval texts identify just ten divisions among Brahmins, five in the north and five in the south, by the nineteenth century there are hundreds of separately named Brahmin *jatis* alone. In a single Tamilnadu village in the mid-twentieth century André Béteille found twelve distinct endogamous divisions within a Brahmin community of 92 households, plus twenty-four major and many more minor subdivisions among 168 non-Brahmin caste households (Béteille 1965: 73, 80ff., and table 3).

Boundaries between castes were traditionally maintained by exquisitely detailed rules of ritual purity. Among the institutions for preserving purity, endogamy (marriage only within the group) was central. In traditional Hindu doctrine, marriage across caste divisions is unnatural, a type of (almost literally) unholy alliance. Such miscegenation was believed to lead only to miscreants, or at best offspring less pure than their fathers. For example, one traditional account places the origin of *Chandalas* (untouchables) in the offspring of Brahmin women and *Śudra* men. Hereditary occupational segregation, rules of commensality, and restricted access to temples and sacred texts were other important mechanisms for maintaining and reproducing caste hierarchy. Contact with, in some instances even the sight of, lower castes was viewed as polluting.

"Scruples concerning purity are the keystone, or better the foundation stone, of all Hindu construction . . . the parts are only ordered and kept in place by sentiments of pious respect and sacred horror" (Bouglé 1971 [1908]: 125). "Only" is clearly an idealizing exaggeration. Power and wealth certainly interact with purity in maintaining hierarchy. Nonetheless, purity was an important, independent, and ideologically central claim to social status. The doctrine of *varnas* separates ritual, political, and economic power in a way that has allowed Brahmins' claims of birth and purity (and knowledge) to achieve high social status even when substantially detached from political power and economic wealth. Even in the contemporary Hindu world, which recognizes and often values social mobility, traditional ideas of caste division that preserve some idea of hierarchical purity retain considerable social force.

The proliferation of *jatis*, however, indicates a certain historical flexibility in Hindu society. Furthermore, with intense but locally variable fissionings of society needing to be integrated into a single hierarchy, rankings differ locally even when a single overarching principle of order is accepted. Furthermore, over time adjustments regularly are made, especially because caste status (*karma*) is a consequence of both birth and action.

Downward mobility is a very real possibility. Even for those born (relatively) pure, pollution can arise from both one's own acts and violation by others. Over time that pollution can be cumulative. For example, there are *jatis* of "degraded Brahmins" who are shunned by most other castes.

Upward mobility is more problematic. Special individual merit, through particularly dedicated performance of the duties of one's station or by becoming a religious ascetic, will be rewarded by a higher rebirth. In a single lifetime, though, there was almost no way for an individual to move to a higher caste. Collectively, however, a *jati* might move up in the hierarchy. Over time, with the right combination of skill, luck, and resources, a *jati* might reasonably aspire to mobilize its material wealth to create new (social, economic, and ritual) alliances and patronage relations, a new origin myth, and ultimately gain acceptance for its children in higher-status marriage networks (Mandelbaum 1970: chapters 23–25).

Such changes, however, involve only relatively minor and local rearrangements of the parts; they leave the caste *system* untouched. Traditional Hindu society could be remarkably flexible about particulars. It was exceedingly unyielding, though, about basic structures.

B. Dignity and Social Solidarity

Although the "inherited defilement" (Kolenda 1978: 65) of membership in the lower castes has historically been the central social fact, caste theoretically assures that each person is treated according to his or her dessert. The person, however, is conceptualized as the temporary shell within which a particular soul lives out one cycle of mortal life in a multigenerational history of progress toward and falling away from the divine.

Caste membership also gives to each person a defined place in society. Inequality and group repulsion thus may be partially mitigated by the fact that all are bound together into an intricately articulated social and natural order. Over time, one has the opportunity to, as it were, earn one's way up—however closed and predefined one's opportunities in any particular incarnation in the cycle of *samsara*.

The caste system also permits each person to achieve a certain kind of dignity, in the core sense of worth that commands respect. That dignity is differential, not equal; it is defined by and within the parameters of each person's place and status. For both untouchables and those otherwise outside the caste system (e.g., various "tribal" peoples), even this is not possible. Furthermore, such dignity is not restricted to humans but famously extends to other creatures, with the result that cows are seen as having a dignity higher than many humans. (As we saw above, though, such differential conceptions of dignity were equally central to the premodern Western world, even if the details differed.)

The Hindu caste system represents an extreme form of what sociologists, following Emile Durkheim, call organic solidarity—i.e., social solidarity based on integrating qualitatively different social groups. Much as *Brahman*, the divine unity of all existence, provides a metaphysical point of reference toward which all reality aspires (to the extent that it is self-aware), the Brahmin caste provides not merely a social point of reference but the point toward which all social structures are directed and ultimately converge. Caste hierarchy provides membership for all within a coherent and integrated cosmic order.

A sense of solidarity through caste is especially important for those relatively privileged groups that fit into the classical *varna* scheme. This is true not only for high-caste groups but for low-caste groups that occupy a privileged position above "untouchable" outcastes. A subordinate place in society, if relatively secure and stable and a source of differential but still real (station-based) status and respect, can be a powerful social glue—especially in a world in which there are many who have no real place at all. Even for those at the very bottom of the hierarchy, caste can be seen as a mechanism of solidarity to the extent that that hierarchy is perceived as both naturally just and open, over the fullness of time, to the claims of merit—although in contemporary India "acceptance" of one's place at the bottom typically owes more to poverty, discrimination, and violence than a strong sense of social solidarity.

4. Hindu Universalism

So far I have emphasized the particularistic elements of Hinduism's hierarchical conception of reality, which not only on its face but especially in the practice of the caste system seems deeply incompatible with human rights. The Hindu tradition, however, also includes universalistic dimensions that bring it into a closer relationship with contemporary human rights ideas. And these elements have become increasingly important over the past two centuries, especially since the 1930s.

A certain universalism can be found even in the ancient texts. For example, the *Laws of Manu*, the most revered—and most conservative and "Brahminic"—of the ancient legal texts, identifies five virtues that apply to all four *varnas*: abstention from injuring others, truthfulness, abstention from anger or theft, purity, and control over the organs (10.63). A somewhat more extended list of shared virtues is also specified (6.91–92) for the three highest castes.

Admittedly, most of Manu's other 2,600 verses focus on particular duties, but similar formulations appear throughout the Hindu tradition. For example, the *Yoga Sutras* of Patanjali identifies five *yamas* (2.30)—nonviolence (*ahimsa*), truthfulness (*satya*), abstention from stealing (*asteya*), self-restraint, especially with respect to sex (*brahmacharya*), and non-possessiveness (*aparigraha*)—that are "universal and are not restricted by any consideration of the nature of the kind of living being to whom one is related, nor in any place, time or situation" (2.31).

The *bhakti* or devotional tradition offers a very different kind of universalism—namely, the promise of salvation through devotion alone. For example, in the *Bhagavad-Gita* (9.32–33), Krishna offers liberation through devotional discipline to members of low and high caste alike and even to women, who are largely excluded from traditional Brahminic religious practice. By downplaying caste differences at the most fundamental spiritual level, this lays a certain foundation for movement toward a social egalitarianism more compatible with modern ideas of human rights.

At the broadest cosmological level, the oneness of all reality is also a powerful support for universalism. Consider this account of the *varnas* from the *Brhadaranyaka Upanishad* (1.4.11–15).

11. In the beginning this [universe] was Brahman—One only. Being One only, he had not the power to develop. By a supreme effort he brought forth a form of the Good, princely power [*ksatra*]. . .

12. He had no power to develop further. He brought forth the common people [*viś*]. . .

13. He had no power to develop further. He brought forth the class of serfs [*Śudra*]. . .

14. He had no power to develop further. By a supreme effort he brought forth a form of the Good—dharma . . . Right and law [*dharma*] are the same as truth. . . .

15. This Brahman [One divine being], [then], is [at the same time] the princely power and class, the common people, and the serfs.

The sense of a single order under one all-encompassing *dharma* is striking. This presentation of caste is also striking for minimizing rather than emphasizing differences. (An alternative, more particularizing and elitist account, near the end of the *Rig Veda* (10.90), presents the *varnas* as arising from the severed parts of a universal body, corresponding to the mouth, arms, thighs, and feet of this primordial cosmic body.)

5. Opposition to Caste Discrimination

The universalistic elements of Hinduism have been most prominent in opposition to caste discrimination, which has a history of over 2,500 years in the Hindu world. Perhaps the best-known reform movements originated with two sixth-century BCE rulers, Gautama Buddha and Vardhaman Mahavira, who rebelled against the existing system of Brahminic-Vedic dominance and its rigidly elitist conception of caste. Abandoning their lives of power and privilege for a solitary ascetic existence, they developed traditions of teaching and practice that became Buddhism and Jainism. Although in some senses "new religions," they can also be seen as reformist variants of the Hindu tradition, since both emphasize abandoning desire and the material world and practicing a life of nonviolence (*ahimsa*). For example, Jainism's five basic principles of *ahimsa*, *satya* (truth), *asteya* (not stealing), *brahmacharya* (celibacy/self-restraint), and *aparigrha* (non-possessiveness) are the same cardinal virtues noted by Manu and Patanjali, and it has been common for Hindus to adopt some of the beliefs and practices of their Jain and Buddhist neighbors.

Bhakti (devotional or spiritualist) movements, which began in the middle of the first millennium CE and continue to be a powerful presence in popular Hindu practice, have been another powerful source of internal opposition to caste discrimination. Internal reform movements have also been generated in response to Muslim and Western invasions throughout most of the second millennium CE. The combined impact of foreign domination and mass conversions proved a powerful stimulus to both popular and elite efforts at reform, especially because of the *religious* egalitarianism of Islam and Christianity (whatever the realities of foreign domination and the tolerance of the conquerors for maintaining traditional social structures and rules within dominated Hindu communities).

The conjunction of internal and external forces is particularly striking in what is often called the Hindu Renaissance of the nineteenth and early twentieth centuries. One conventional starting point is the reforming efforts of Raj Rom Mohan Roy (1775–1833), who is best known for his efforts to abolish the practice of *sati* (*suttee*), the ritual sacrifice of widows on the funeral pyres of their husbands. In the following decades, a great variety of movements of social, political, and religious reform gave a striking new vitality to Hindu society—and in Bengal in particular provoked a powerful artistic revival. As Arvind Sharma notes, "almost every major Hindu religious figure of modern Hinduism turned his attention to the conditions of the lower classes and attacked untouchability" (2005: 38).

Just as one should not overemphasize the rigidity or particularity of the caste system, though, one should not overemphasize reformist movements. Even religious movements that began as hostile to dominant Brahminic interpretations typically have fallen victim to reabsorption. David Mandelbaum (1970: chapter 28) discusses one common pattern: a charismatic leader teaching ideas of personal purity largely distinct from notions of caste and ritual becomes the leader of a social movement, which then is reabsorbed into the dominant society as a new caste. This pattern is so common that a standard complaint about *bhakti* movements is that "in historical retrospect, their function appears to have been to reinforce the existing social order by channeling discontent into a negative form, rather than bring about structural change" (Ishwaran 1980: 74).

Once again, though, the picture is not all that different from the premodern West, where social movements from below have typically been either repressed or co-opted. The Hindu world, like the Western world, has throughout most of its history been dominated by social, religious, economic, and political hierarchies that have emphasized the differences, and distances, between men (and between men and women). Both traditions, however, also provide resources for resistance against particularistic domination. In the right conditions—the conditions of modernity—these alternative strands of the tradition have moved to the fore.

6. Hinduism and Human Rights in Contemporary India

During the movement for independence, leaders such as Mohandas Gandhi and B. R. Ambedkar placed opposition to untouchability at the center of the struggle. Opposition to caste more generally, however, was a minority view that was largely sidelined. At independence, the Indian government consciously chose to target untouchability in particular rather than caste in general. Thus the Indian Constitution, adopted in 1949, abolishes untouchability (as well as human trafficking and forced labor) but merely prohibits state discrimination on the basis of caste (as well as religion, race, sex, or place of birth) and assures equality before the law and nondiscriminatory access to public places and facilities and public employment.

In the succeeding decades, the Indian federal government, and many state governments as well, have enacted and sought to implement increasingly aggressive remedial programs on behalf of former untouchables—who typically today self-identify as Dalits—and "tribal" peoples (who were similarly outside of the traditional caste system). These groups together make up about a quarter of India's population. The 1955 Untouchability Practices Act (amended and renamed as the 1976 Protection of Civil Liberties Act) and the 1989 Scheduled Castes and Scheduled Tribes (Prevention of Atrocities) Act provide the framework for a comprehensive system of not just protection but, in American terms, affirmative action, including reserved school places and public jobs.

Such measures certainly have reduced the level of suffering of many of those at the bottom of the Indian social hierarchy. They have also created historically unprecedented opportunities for upward mobility. No less importantly, *jatis* have been transformed by the same processes of occupational, educational, and geographical mobility that have undermined traditional social inequalities in other regions of the world. Nonetheless, both official and unofficial discrimination remain a serious problem, especially in relatively backward rural areas. Many Indians, both inside and outside the Dalit community, have attributed such persisting discrimination to Hinduism.

In the modern sector of society and the economy, however, although caste still influences, it typically does not determine, and often does not even fundamentally shape, one's life opportunities—at least not much more than class shapes life opportunities in contemporary Britain or the United States. Perhaps a better analogy is with race in the contemporary United States. Indians typically know the caste of most of those that they deal with regularly and often suspect that they know something about the caste background of even many strangers. This knowledge is by no means socially neutral. Caste, however, is not a formal barrier in any domain of life and for those with "good" education or income (or both) it is usually only an informal impediment that many manage to overcome.

This transformation of legal, political, and social practices has been accompanied by and associated with parallel changes in dominant understandings of Hinduism. The universalistic strands noted above have moved increasingly to the fore and caste discrimination has increasingly come to be seen as an historical perversion of the essence of Hinduism.

Hinduism, however, in recent decades has also come to be mobilized in ways incompatible with human rights. Continued repression of Dalits is often justified (or at least rationalized) by appeals to Hindu scripture and tradition and Hinduism has been mobilized by right wing nationalists, under the label of *Hindutva* ("Hinduness"), exacerbating the recurrently violent "communal" struggles between "Muslims" and "Hindus."

From a human rights perspective, we should be wary of arguments that this does not represent the "true" nature of Hinduism. Setting aside the problem of who is to decide what "true" Hinduism is—a problem that is especially severe in the absence of clerical authority—such an attitude falsely separates "religion" (or "values" or "culture") from broader and related social and political realities. Hinduism, at least as a social reality, "is" what Hindus make it—just as Christianity is what Christians make it and Islam is what Muslims make it. Different Hindus, like different Christians and different Muslims, have made many very different things of it.

In contemporary India, the home of the vast majority of the world's Hindus, Hinduism functions as both a support for and an impediment to the exercise and enjoyment of internationally recognized human rights. The same, however, is true, for example, of Christianity in the contemporary

United States: leading proponents of human rights do so from within various Christian denominations but some of the leading defenses of racism and sexism also root themselves in the Bible.

The Hindu tradition has proven no impediment to independent India's sustained and vibrant, if deeply imperfect, tradition of democratic political rule. Caste continues to be mobilized by the privileged to perpetuate their privilege. *Hindutva* has become a powerful support for discrimination and communal conflict. The universalist elements of Hinduism, however—a single *dharma* governing an integrated and everywhere-divinely-infused reality and regulating a universal struggle toward liberation—have not only provided a powerful critique of deeply entrenched inequalities but become an important indigenous support for internationally recognized human rights.

Part IV

Human Rights
and International Action

11

International Human Rights Regimes

e have seen the central and vital role of international action in the creation of international human rights norms. We have also seen, though, that international human rights law creates a system of national implementation of international human rights. Nonetheless, extensive and significant international action is a regular part of the politics of human rights. Furthermore, human rights has become a standard topic in contemporary international relations. This chapter looks at the principal multilateral mechanisms. The next chapter looks at bilateral foreign policy action.

1. The Global Human Rights Regime

Students of international relations often speak of "international regimes," systems of norms and decision-making procedures accepted by states and other international actors as binding in a particular issue area.[1] Regime norms, standards, or rules (I use the terms interchangeably here) may run from fully international to entirely national. Decision-making procedures can be roughly grouped into enforcement, implementation, and promotional activities. Enforcement involves binding international decision making (and perhaps also very strong forms of international monitoring of national compliance with international norms). Implementation includes monitoring procedures and policy coordination, in which states make regular use of an international forum to coordinate policies that ultimately remain under national control. Promotion involves information exchange and efforts to encourage or assist the national implementation of international norms.

1. The standard introductory discussion is Krasner (1982). See also Rittberger and Mayer (1993), and Hasenclever, Mayer, and Rittberger (1997, 2000).

These types of activities provide a convenient scheme for classifying regimes as promotional, implementation, and enforcement regimes, each of which can be further classified as relatively strong or weak. To this we can add the class of declaratory regimes, which involve international norms but no international decision making (except in the creation of norms). Table 11.2 in section 6 applies this typology to the major international and regional human rights regimes.

The Universal Declaration and the International Human Rights Covenants provide the norms of the global human rights regime, a system of rules and implementation procedures centered on the United Nations.[2] Its principal actors are the UN Human Rights Council, the "treaty bodies" established under the leading international human rights treaties, and the UN High Commissioner for Human Rights.[3]

A. The Human Rights Council

The Human Rights Council (UNHRC) was established in 2006 as a replacement for the Commission on Human Rights.[4] Its members are states, elected by the UN General Assembly largely without regard to their human rights record. For example, Bahrain, China, Cuba, Gabon, Kyrgyzstan, Libya, Mauritania, Qatar, Russia, and Saudi Arabia—all countries with poor to dismal human rights records—were members of the council in 2010–2011.

Given this membership, perhaps the most notable fact about the Human Rights Council is that it regularly does work of real value. It is a largely impartial forum for the consensual development of new international human rights norms. (For example, the Council did the concluding work on the conventions on persons with disabilities and on disappearances, and its resolutions on a variety of subjects are part of the global process of promoting the adoption of international human rights norms.)

The Council also engages in valuable efforts to promote the implementation of internationally recognized human rights as well as limited multilateral monitoring. These efforts are somewhat less impartial, in the sense that some countries, for political reasons, receive more attention than their human rights record would suggest while others receive less—Israel and China, respectively, are often presented as examples—but those countries that are considered generally receive impartial treatment on the basis of well-documented violations.

2. For an excellent recent overview, see Alston (2011).
3. For broad overview of the human rights activities of the UN system, see http://www.un.org/en/rights/.
4. Comprehensive information on activities of the UN Human Rights Council is available at www2.ohchr.org/english/bodies/hrcouncil.

The Council has created a new system of "universal period review," under which the human rights record of every state is subject to public discussion every four years.[5] The process generates a lot of predictable political posturing. Nonetheless, in some instances a frank and open discussion of some value does occur. There are no sanctions, however, other than publicity and because the review covers the full range of human rights practices, it tends to elicit scattered observations that are all over the map.

Of much more value are the special procedures and mechanisms originally developed by the Commission on Human Rights in the 1980s. These bodies are staffed by independent experts, not state representatives.[6] Because of their greater impartiality and their narrower focus, their investigations typically are more penetrating and their efforts more aggressive than those of the Council itself—which, after all, is a political organ of the United Nations.

In 2011 there were thirty-three active "thematic" special rapporteurs or working groups dealing with a range of issues from arbitrary detention, torture, and freedom of religion to the rights to food, adequate housing, and education, as well as topics such as protecting human rights defenders, the use of mercenaries, and toxic and dangerous products and wastes. In addition, nine independent "country" experts or special rapporteurs addressed the human rights situations in Cambodia, Cote D'Ivoire, North Korea, Haiti, Iran, Myanmar (Burma), the occupied Palestinian territories, Somalia, and Sudan. (Cote D'Ivoire and Iran were added to the list in 2011 and the mandate on Burundi was allowed to expire.) These bodies often have well-established records of improving the conditions of individual victims. The offices of the rapporteurs on torture, arbitrary executions, and violence against women are especially well known and respected.

The stature of the mandate-holder also can be used to increase the impact of these special procedures. For example, Juan Mendez (from Argentina), the current special rapporteur on torture, is the former head of Human Rights Watch and the International Center for Transnational Justice. John Ruggie (from the United States), the special representative of the secretary general on human rights and transnational corporations and other business enterprises, is one of the world's leading scholars of international relations (teaching at Harvard and having previously been a dean at Columbia), a former assistant secretary general of the United Nations, and the founder of the Global

---

5. The official website for the Universal Periodic Review is http://www.ohchr.org/EN/HRBodies/UPR/Pages/UPRMain.aspx. For a broader range of information on the process, see UPR Info, http://www.upr-info.org/.

6. See Special Procedures of the Human Rights Council, http://www2.ohchr.org/english/bodies/chr/special/index.htm.

Compact (a leading international actor in the area of corporate responsibility regarding human rights, labor, environment, and corruption).

The immediate impact of these bodies is ultimately a matter of the willingness of governments to engage in conversations with them, allow them to visit their countries, and listen to their concerns and advice. Particularly when either the body or the mandate-holder has a prominent international reputation, many states are willing to make improvements in the treatment of particular individuals. Some of the reports by these experts are also important sources of authoritative information about abuses that is used by national and transnational advocates.

The Council has also inherited and revised older Commission on Human Rights procedures for considering complaints about violations in particular countries. When originally established, back in the 1960s and 1970s, there was considerable hope for these procedures. In practice, though, they have been much less significant than the work of thematic and country experts. These procedures are simply too adversarial to elicit cooperation from governments with the sorts of gross and persistent violations that are required to have a case raised under these mechanisms.

In addition, the Council has regularly exercised its right to convene special sessions. Through 2011 there had been eighteen such sessions, addressing the occupied Palestinian territories, Lebanon, Sudan (Darfur), Myanmar (Burma), Democratic Republic of the Congo, Sri Lanka, Haiti, Cote d'Ivoire, Libya, and Syria, as well as international food prices and the global economic and financial crisis. These have brought additional international attention to these situations and in some cases have provoked a slightly more cooperative response from rights-abusive states. Especially notable are the three special sessions held on Syria in 2011. These reflect the dramatic changes in the region and perhaps even suggest somewhat more aggressive monitoring by the Council in the future.

B. Treaty Bodies

Nine human rights treaties establish a committee of experts to monitor implementation.[7] These so-called treaty bodies, taken collectively, make up the second major focus on multilateral implementation activity on behalf of internationally recognized human rights. Table 11.1 provides basic information about these bodies.

---

7. For comprehensive information on these committees, see Human Rights Bodies, http://www.ohchr.org/EN/HRBodies/Pages/HumanRightsBodies.aspx. The standard work on treaty monitoring is Alston and Crawford (2000). Tyagi (2011) is an up-to-date and thorough review of the work of the Human Rights Committee, the most active and significant of the treaty bodies.

TABLE 11.1 TREATY BODIES

Committee (treaty supervised)	Parties to treaty	Established	Weeks in session each year	Individual communications (first year received)
Human Rights Committee (ICCPR)	167	1976	9	Yes (1976)
Committee on Economic, Social and Cultural Rights (ICESCR)	160	1985	6	Not yet*
Committee on the Elimination of Racial Discrimination (ICERD)	175	1969	6	Yes (1982)
Committee on the Elimination of Discrimination against Women (CEDAW)	187	1981	9	Yes (2003)
Committee against Torture (CAT)	149	1987	6	Yes (1987)
Committee on the Rights of the Child (CRC)	193	1990	9	Not yet*
Committee on Migrant Workers (ICRMW)	45	2004	3	Not yet*
Committee on the Rights of Persons with Disabilities (ICRPD)	107	2009	2	Not yet*
Committee on Enforced Disappearances (ICED)	30	2011	2	Not yet*

* The required number of parties has not yet been reached to put the process into practice. Data dates from the second half of 2011.

Reporting

The principal and most important activity of the treaty bodies is the review of periodic reports on compliance that parties are required to submit. Based on the report and additional information gathered by the committee, questions are prepared and submitted to the state in writing. A state representative participates in the committee's public discussion of the report. A follow-up written exchange often ensues. The process concludes when the committee publishes its comments.

The reporting process thus is essentially an exchange of information that provides limited, noncoercive monitoring. The extent of state participation, beyond submitting its report, ranges from active cooperation to largely non-responsive presence. There are no sanctions of any sort associated with the reporting procedure, even if the country refuses to submit its report (as a few do).

Complaints about the "weakness" of reporting systems, however, assume that the goal is coercive enforcement. In fact, though, the aim is to encourage and facilitate compliance. Judged in these terms, reporting often has a significant positive effect.

The most constructive part of the process is the preparation of the report. Periodic reviews of national practice, if undertaken with any degree of conscientiousness, require states, agencies, and officials to step back from their day-to-day work and reflect on their processes, procedures, and institutions. The external stimulus and oversight of treaty reporting often makes such reviews more frequent and more thorough.

Reporting is especially valuable in countries with an active civil society. NGOs sometimes are directly involved in the process of preparing the national report. Often they lobby the officials in charge of preparing the report. NGOs can use preparation of the report and its public review by the treaty body as occasions for campaigning. They may participate indirectly in the committee review through contacts with individual members and the public hearing and comments by the committee often provide an occasion for amplified publicity.

Two major limits on the impact of reporting systems, however, deserve note. First, the positive effects of reporting depend ultimately on the willingness of the state to change—either because of an active, positive desire to improve or because of an openness or vulnerability to criticism (which all but the most repressive of regimes possess to some degree). Second, the changes produced by such mechanisms are likely to be limited and incremental rather than systematic.

States typically engage in massive violations only when they feel something of great importance is at stake. The national and international political costs of negative publicity and advocacy campaigns are almost never sufficient to overcome the political incentives to continue gross and persistent systematic violations. Where the violations are relatively minor or narrowly circumscribed, however—for example, particular rules on the treatment of prisoners, activities of a single part of the government bureaucracy, particular nondiscrimination policies, or the treatment of a single individual—all but the worst governments may be willing to consider improvements.

Such modest improvements are not insignificant and over time they may accumulate. This is especially true as the process is repeated in multiple treaty bodies—and as the reporting process interacts with other kinds of national, transnational, bilateral, and multilateral mechanisms.

General Comments

The treaty bodies also issue "general comments." This practice, first developed and most effectively employed by the Human Rights Committee, attempts not only to improve the reporting process but also to influence the progressive development of international human rights law by offering quasi-authoritative interpretations of the nature of obligations under the treaty.

Consider a more or less arbitrarily chosen example, General Comment 20 of the Human Rights Committee, adopted in 1992. It interprets Article 7 of the ICCPR, which states (in its entirety), "No one shall be subjected to torture or to cruel, inhuman or degrading treatment or punishment. In particular, no one shall be subjected without his free consent to medical or scientific experimentation." This pithy statement certainly could benefit from some elaboration, which General Comment 20 seeks to provide.

Paragraph 2 states that the aim of the article "is to protect both the dignity and the physical and mental integrity of the individual"—offering a relatively expansive reading that links the provision to the foundational claim in the preamble of the ICCPR that "these rights derive from the inherent dignity of the human person." Paragraph 2 also explicitly links this article to the provision in Article 10 that "all persons deprived of their liberty shall be treated with humanity and with respect for the inherent dignity of the human person," and it explicitly applies these obligations not just to agents of the state acting in their official capacity but also when operating "outside their official capacity or in a private capacity." (Paragraph 8 goes further and claims that the state obligation is not simply to legislatively prohibit such actions but to take positive steps of protection, some of which are specified in paragraphs 10–13.)

Paragraph 3 draws attention to the fact that no exceptions are permitted in times of emergency. (Along similar lines, paragraph 15 expresses concern over amnesties for torturers that have been granted by some states.) In holding that "no justification or extenuating circumstances may be invoked to excuse a violation of article 7 for any reasons, including those based on an order from a superior officer or public authority," the Human Rights Committee in effect applies the provisions of the 1984 Convention against Torture (CAT) to the interpretation of the ICCPR. (The prohibition of the use of evidence obtained by torture, advanced in paragraph 12, does much the same thing.)

Paragraph 4 holds that it is neither necessary nor productive to draw up a list of prohibited acts. Nonetheless, paragraph 5 emphasizes that mental suffering falls within the acts prohibited by Article 7 and that its protections extend to certain forms of corporal punishment, including protection of "children, pupils and patients in teaching and medical institutions." Paragraph 6 explicitly places prolonged solitary confinement within the coverage of Article 7.

Such observations are not formally binding. They do, however, have considerable informal authority. This makes general comments of some use to national and international human rights advocates. General comments thus have become a modest yet significant device for the progressive development of international human rights jurisprudence.

Complaint Procedures

The six core treaties, with the exception of the Convention on the Rights of the Child, also allow individual "communications." Four of these procedures are operative and the fifth (for economic and social rights) should begin soon.

Participation in these procedures, however, is voluntary. (Depending on the treaty, between a third and two-thirds of the parties do not allow individual complaints.) Not surprisingly, some of the worst violators choose not to allow such complaints to be considered. In addition, the number of cases considered is tiny. (The Human Rights Committee, by far the most active body, has registered just over two thousand cases in more than three decades of work and reached a substantive conclusion on less than eight hundred, having found slightly more than that number inadmissible.) In the end, complaint procedures are not even binding in international law. Nonetheless, they are a mechanism of some interest. They have aided many individuals and there may be long-term potential for growth in their usage and impact.

Typically, communications from individuals are screened by professional staff in the Office of the High Commissioner for Human Rights. Those that show potential merit are registered. Registered complaints are then screened further for admissibility. (The principal requirements are that the alleged violations fall under the scope of the treaty and that local remedies have been exhausted).

Once the procedural hurdles have been scaled, the committee corresponds with the government in question, and sometimes with the petitioner or her representative. It also often carries out inquiries into public records and independent sources of information. It then states its views as to whether there has been a violation of the treaty and makes suggestions and recommendations as to remedies.

These findings are, explicitly, merely the views of the committee. They are not binding even in international law (let alone national law). In fact, the state has no obligation even to respond to the committee's views. Nonetheless, many states, especially those with an active civil society, do take the findings seriously. Individuals often receive remedy as a result of their complaints. In some cases—prominent examples include complaints of discrimination on the basis of sexual orientation in Australia and against indigenous women in Canada—national legislation has been changed in response to the recommendations of the committee.

C. The High Commissioner for Human Rights

The Office of the High Commissioner for Human Rights (OHCHR) was created in 1993, following the Vienna World Conference on Human Rights. It plays a central role in disseminating information about the human rights activities of the United Nations—through its excellent website http://www.ohchr.org—and provides vital administrative and research support for the treaty bodies and the UN Human Rights Council. In addition, the high commissioner has emerged as a prominent global advocate for human rights.

The first high commissioner, José Ayala-Lasso of Ecuador, who held the position from 1994 to 1997, was a low-profile figure. His successor, however, Mary Robinson, the former president of Ireland, turned the office into a major force. The quality of the secretarial support work was brought to a high level, the budget increased substantially, and Robinson became a well-known public figure across the globe, as a result of her difficult-to-resist combination of intellectual brilliance, moral commitment, and hard work, combined with an unusual mix of diplomatic skill and a constant willingness to push the bounds of what her targets were willing to tolerate from an international public servant.

Robinson left her successor, Sérgio Vieira de Mello of Brazil, a completely transformed organization when she moved on to other work in 2002. Sadly, he was among the victims of the bombing of the UN offices in Baghdad in August 2003. The acting high commissioner, Bertrand Ramcharan of Guyana, a career UN official and a noted scholar of international human rights law, was succeeded in 2004 by Louise Arbour of Canada, another high-profile high commissioner—she was previously the chief prosecutor for the international criminal tribunals for the former Yugoslavia and for Rwanda—who exercised her mandate aggressively on behalf of human rights and victims of violations. She was succeeded in 2008 by Navanethem Pillay of South Africa, a former judge of the International Criminal Court and former president of the International Criminal Tribunal for Rwanda.

Although the public activities of the high commissioner draw the most attention, the significance of the behind-the-scenes work of the office should not be underestimated. The OHCHR website is a model of clarity and comprehensive coverage that is of great value to activists, scholars, ordinary citizens, and victims. In addition to direct administrative support for the UN Human Rights Council and the treaty bodies, the OHCHR engages in original research, with special attention to the Vienna Programme of Action and the right to development, and provides capacity-building and advisory services to governments seeking to improve their national human rights practices.

Compared to the resources devoted to development assistance, such efforts are very modest. Nonetheless, they represent an immense expansion of activities over the past decade. They also illustrate the possibilities for progressive cooperative action with governments that have some degree of openness to a combination of pressure and assistance from the outside world, especially when it comes through the politically neutral mechanism of multilateral organizations.

2. Political Foundations of the Global Regime

The global human rights regime is a relatively strong promotional regime comprising widely accepted substantive norms, authoritative multilateral standard-setting procedures, and some promotional activity but very limited international implementation that rarely goes beyond information exchange and voluntarily accepted international assistance for the national implementation of international norms. There is no international enforcement.

Such normative strength and procedural weakness is not accidental but the result of conscious political decisions. Regimes are political creations set up to overcome perceived problems arising from inadequately regulated or insufficiently coordinated national action. Robert Keohane (1982) offers a useful market analogy: regimes arise when sufficient international "demand" is met by a state or group of states willing and able to "supply" international norms and decision-making procedures. In each issue area there are makers, breakers, and takers of (potential) international regimes. Understanding the structure of a regime (or its absence) requires that we know who has played which roles, when and why, and what agreements they reached.

The 1945 defeat of Nazi Germany ushered in the global human rights regime. Revulsion at the array of human rights abuses that came to be summarized in the term "Nazi," combined with general postwar optimism, made it *relatively* easy to reach general agreement on a set of international principles against gross and persistent systematic violations of basic rights—namely, the Universal Declaration and the Convention on Genocide (which was even more clearly a direct legacy of Hitler). It is perhaps surprising that this moral "demand" should have produced even this much in a world in which more material national interests usually prevail. Immediately following World War II, however, there were willing and able makers, numerous takers, and no breakers of the regime. The moral and emotional demands ran both wide and deep. Prior to the emergence of the Cold War, countervailing concerns and interests were largely subordinated.

A cynic might suggest that these postwar "achievements" simply reflect the minimal international constraints and very low costs of a declaratory regime: decision making under the Universal Declaration remained entirely national and it would be nearly thirty years before even the rudimentary promotion and monitoring procedures of the International Human Rights Covenants came into effect. Before the war, though, even a declaratory regime had rarely been contemplated.

Moving much beyond a declaratory regime, however, has proved difficult. It is in this relative constancy of the regime (critics and frustrated optimists are likely to say "stagnation") that the weakness of the demand is most evident. A strong global human rights regime simply does not reflect the perceived interests of a group of states willing and able to supply it.

States typically participate in an international regime only to achieve national objectives in an environment of perceived international interdependence. Even then they typically participate only when independent national action has failed and when participation appears "safe," all things considered—a very serious constraint, given states' notorious jealousy of their sovereign prerogatives. A stronger global human rights regime simply does not present a safe prospect of obtaining otherwise unattainable national benefits.

Moral interests such as human rights are no less "real" than material interests. They are, however, less tangible, and national policy, for better or worse, tends to be made in response to relatively tangible national objectives.

In addition, the extreme sensitivity of human rights practices makes the very subject intensely threatening to many states. National human rights practices often would be a matter for considerable embarrassment should they be subject to full international scrutiny. In a number of cases, such as North Korea, Zimbabwe, and Cuba, compliance with international human rights standards would mean removal of those in power.

Finally, human rights—at least in the Universal Declaration model—are ultimately a profoundly national, not international, issue. As I will argue in section 12.6, international action usually can be, at best, an impetus toward and support for national action on behalf of human rights.

If international regimes arise primarily because of international interdependence—the inability to achieve important national objectives by independent national action—how can we account for the creation, and even modest growth, of the global human rights regime? First and foremost, the "moral" concerns that brought it into being in the first place have a persisting relevance and force. Butchers such as Pol Pot and the *genocidaires* of Rwanda still shock the popular conscience and provoke a desire to reject them as not merely reprehensible but also prohibited by clear, public, authoritative international norms. Even governments with dismal human rights records seem to feel compelled to join in condemning the abuses of such rulers.

Although cynics might interpret such condemnations as craven abuse of the rhetoric of human rights, they are just as easily seen as implicit, submerged, or deflected expressions of a sense of *moral* interdependence. States—and frequently citizens as well—often are unwilling to translate this perceived moral interdependence into action, let alone into an international regime with strong decision-making powers. They also, however, are unwilling (or at least politically unable) to return to treating national human rights practices as properly beyond international scrutiny and evaluation.

A weak global human rights regime also may contribute, in a way acceptable to states, to improved national practice. For example, new governments with a commitment to human rights may find it helpful to be able to draw on and point to the constraints of authoritative international standards. We can see this in the case of the Alfonsin government, which took power after the Dirty War in Argentina, and in many of the successor governments in the former Soviet bloc. Likewise, established regimes may find the additional check provided by an international regime a salutary supplement to national efforts, as seems to be the case for many smaller Western powers. Most states, even if only for considerations of image and prestige, are likely to be willing to accept regime norms and procedures that do not appear immediately threatening.

An international regime reflects states' collective vision of a problem, its solutions, and their willingness to "fund" those solutions. In the area of human rights, this vision does not extend much beyond a politically weak moral interdependence. States are willing to "pay" very little in diminished national sovereignty to realize the benefits of cooperation. The result is a regime with extensive, coherent, and widely accepted norms but extremely limited international decision-making powers—that is, a strong promotional regime.

3. Regional Human Rights Regimes

Adopting a metaphor from Vinod Aggarwal, Keohane notes that international regimes "are 'nested' within more comprehensive agreements . . . that constitute a complex and interlinked pattern of relations" (1982: 334). Although "nesting" may imply too neat and hierarchical an arrangement, some regional and single-issue human rights regimes can usefully be seen as autonomous but relatively coherently nested international human rights (sub)regimes. This section considers regional regimes.[8] The following section takes up single-issue human rights regimes.

A. The European Regional Regime

The forty-seven-member Council of Europe operates a strong system of regional human rights enforcement.[9] Its normative core is the [European] Convention for the Protection of Human Rights and Fundamental Freedoms, which covers mostly civil and political rights, and the European Social Charter, which addresses economic and social rights in considerable detail. The most notable element of the system, though, is the European Court of Human Rights (ECHR), which exercises binding jurisdiction and whose decisions create binding legal obligations for states.[10] (The European Social Charter is not subject to judicial enforcement.)

Since the reorganization of the ECHR in 1998, individuals in any member country have direct access, subject to minimal procedural restrictions (most notably the requirement that local remedies have been exhausted). The court is organized into five sections, each with nine or ten judges. A grand chamber hears cases of special interest or importance.

The ECHR has issued more than ten thousand judgments.[11] Some decisions have led to significant changes in national law. Most, when in favor of the petitioner (as is the case about two-thirds of the time), have brought relief, including monetary damages, to victims. The system, however, has become a victim of its own success, with a huge backlog of unprocessed petitions and lengthy delays in the conclusion of cases.

One of the most important and innovative features of the court has been its use of the principle of "evolutive interpretation." Treaty provisions are interpreted not according to the understandings at the time of drafting but in light of current understandings and practices. The ECHR thus serves as an important mechanism for the progressive evolution of regional human rights obligations. This provides a striking institutionalization of the idea, raised in section 2.8, that human rights standards constantly demand more, even of the highest performers.

The Council of Europe system also includes other important human rights mechanisms. The Council of Europe Commissioner for Human Rights

---

8. Shelton (2008) is a good general survey of regional human rights regimes.
9. Useful recent overviews include Council of Europe (2010), Christoffersen and Madsen (2011), and Hammarberg (2011).
10. See European Court of Human Rights, http://www.echr.coe.int/echr/Homepage_EN.
11. Ibid. The case law and jurisprudence of the European system can be searched through the powerful HUDOC database at http://www.hudoc.echr.coe.int/.

(currently Thomas Hammarberg, a Swedish diplomat and human rights activist) has extensive powers to investigate and publicize human rights issues on either a thematic or a country basis.[12] Special procedures exist in the case of torture, including the right of the European Committee for the Prevention of Torture to visit all places of detention in any member state.

Important European regional mechanisms also exist under the Organization for Security and Cooperation in Europe (OSCE), a group of fifty-six states from Europe, Central Asia, and North America.[13] Its work on minority rights has been especially important, with its High Commissioner on National Minorities being a leading regional actor on this topic of immense historic and contemporary importance. Additional programs support elections and rule of law (through the Office for Democratic Institutions and Human Rights), media freedom (OSCE Representative on Freedom of the Media), and gender equality and to combat human trafficking (through the Office of the Special Representative and Coordinator for Combating Trafficking in Human Beings).

The activities of the twenty-seven-member European Union (EU), especially those dealing with social policy, also have an important human rights dimension.[14] The Court of Justice of the European Communities, the supreme judicial organ of the EU, has been particularly forceful in its insistence that fundamental human rights, especially principles of nondiscrimination, are an essential part of EU law.[15]

Citizens of Europe thus have a considerable array of regional multilateral mechanisms available to them not just to encourage their governments to implement their obligations but in many instances to make legally binding findings of violations that, given the context of extensive and intensive regional cooperation, usually are in fact complied with by states.

B. The Inter-American System

The American Declaration of the Rights and Duties of Man was adopted by the General Assembly of the Organization of American States (OAS) in April 1948. Like the Universal Declaration, it is not technically binding. The 1969 American Convention on Human Rights, which is a legally binding

12. See Council of Europe, Commissioner of Human Rights, http://www.coe.int/t/commissioner/default_en.asp.
13. See Organization for Security and Co-operation in Europe, http://www.osce.org/.
14. See European Union, http://europa.eu/. On human rights in particular, see http://europa.eu/pol/rights/index_en.htm.
15. See Court of Justice of the European Union, http://europa.eu/institutions/inst/justice/index_en.htm.

instrument, came into force in 1978. As of late 2010 it had been ratified by twenty-four of the thirty-five OAS members, including all Latin American states (but not the United States, Canada, and a number of English-speaking Caribbean states). The other major normative instrument of the system is the 2001 Inter-American Democratic Charter, which today is arguably as important as the American declaration and convention.

The Inter-American Commission of Human Rights (IACHR) was established in 1959.[16] Much like its UN counterpart, it operates independently, in this case as an autonomous organization within the OAS (whose thirty-five members include all the independent states of the Western Hemisphere). Its seven members are elected by secret ballot by the OAS General Assembly and serve in their personal capacity.

The IACHR conducts country studies and examines thematic issues of regional concern. During the 1970s and 1980s, the commission was particularly aggressive in using its independent authority to pressure repressive governments. Its reporting on Chile under military rule was particularly important to both internal and international human rights advocates. As the overall regional human rights situation has improved in the post–Cold War world, the reports of the commission have become less prominent but they remain significant. For example, the commission issued two reports on Bolivia in 2005 and reports on Honduras in 2009 and 2010 that helped to draw attention to serious problems in these countries, and at the end of 2009 it issued an important report on citizen security and human rights.

The commission also publicizes prominent individual cases. For example, while I was writing this section, it issued a public condemnation of the murder of human rights defender Marisela Escovedo in Mexico. The presence of such an aggressive, independent regional monitoring agency is of real value.

The IACHR also plays a central role in the processing of individual petitions, of which more than a thousand are received every year. After an initial procedural screening, the commission conducts its own fact-finding and typically attempts to facilitate a friendly settlement between the petitioner and her government. If this is not successful, it issues a report, indicating its findings and recommendations. If the state does not accept those recommendations, the commission may refer the case to the Inter-American Court of Human Rights, if the state has accepted the court's jurisdiction. (Currently,

16. See Organization of American States, Inter-American Commission on Human Rights, http://www.cidh.oas.org/DefaultE.htm. I am aware of no good book-length study of the Inter-American Commission. Goldman (2009) offers an article-length survey of its first fifty years of work.

twenty-one states have recognized the jurisdiction of the court.) In practice, the commission usually forwards the case to the court when that is the wish of the petitioner.

The Inter-American Court sits in San José, Costa Rica.[17] Its seven members are elected by "states parties" to the American convention (although nationals of any OAS member state may serve, even if their state is not a party). Individuals do not, however, have direct access to the court. Only the commission and parties to the convention can submit cases. Through November 2010, the court had issued 220 judgments.[18] One of the most interesting and innovative procedures of the court is the use of interim measures to attempt to protect persons in danger of irreparable harm or death.

As noted above, the democracy norm has become especially important in the Inter-American system. In July 2009, the OAS General Assembly suspended Honduras after its elected government was deposed by a military coup. The regional democracy norm seems also to have played an important role in the United States deciding in 2002 not to support the coup against Hugo Chavez in Venezuela, despite its strong opposition to Chavez's policies at home and abroad.

As in Europe, a number of other mechanisms operate within the Inter-American regime. The Protocol of San Salvador addresses economic and social rights. (The American convention deals almost exclusively with civil and political rights.) There are regional conventions on torture, violence against women, disappearances, and discrimination against persons with disabilities, and the OAS has adopted resolutions and declarations on a variety of topics, including freedom of expression, indigenous peoples, and racism and discrimination.

The disappointingly small number of cases heard by the court indicates the relative weakness of the Inter-American regime compared to its European counterpart, but we should be careful not to confuse cause and effect. As I will discuss further below, strong multilateral measures are largely a consequence, not a cause, of a high level of national practice throughout the region. (Even the European system did not allow individuals direct access to its court until 1998, operating until then through a two-stage commission-court process, on which the Inter-American system was modeled.) States agree to, utilize, and comply with strong measures out of a strong sense of national commitment. Thus the growing use of the Inter-American court—it issued judgments in seventeen cases in 2008 and eighteen cases in 2009 in contrast to one case in

---

17. See http://www.corteidh.or.cr/index.cfm?&CFID=666614&CFTOKEN=69520161. Burgourge-Larsen and Úbeda de Torres (2011) is a thorough recent review of the court's practice.
18. See Corte Americana de Derechos Humanos, http://www.corteidh.or.cr/.

1988 and six in 1989—reflects the general improvement in the region since the end of the Cold War. If the trend continues, we should expect a stronger and more effective regional system in the future.

C. The African Regional Regime

A regional human rights regime also operates in Africa, based on the 1981 African Charter on Human and Peoples' Rights. It is substantively much weaker than its European and American counterparts. Nonetheless, it is of great regional symbolic significance and has provided considerable encouragement and support to national activists.

The norms in the African Charter are riddled with "clawback clauses" that weaken the protections. For example, Article 6 states, "No one may be deprived of his freedom except for reasons and conditions previously laid down by law." In other words, so long as a government bothers to pass a law first it can deprive people of their freedom for pretty much any reason it chooses. In addition—and quite oddly for a human rights instrument— the African charter gives considerable emphasis to individual duties. More positively, the charter also attempts to advance the idea of collective peoples' rights, although in practice this seems to have had no discernible impact.

The institutions for monitoring and enforcement are extremely weak. The African Commission on Human and Peoples' Rights is elected by the Assembly of Heads of States and Government of the African Union, from nominees proposed by states.[19] The members thus are much less independent than their European and American counterparts. The reporting system is plagued by poor reports—a reflection of both lack of resources in most states and lack of interest by many—and by underfunding of the commission. As for the investigation of complaints, few states cooperate and the decisions of the commission have been criticized for their vagueness with respect to suggested remedies.

The African Court resembles its American counterpart in that its jurisdiction is optional—twenty-five states had accepted its jurisdiction through 2010—and only states and the commission (not individuals) may submit cases.[20] It first met in July 2006 and issued its first judgment in December 2009, although, in a sad irony, it rejected the case (against Senegal) for lack of jurisdiction. (The case involved an effort by a Chadian national residing in Switzerland to stop proceedings in Senegal against Hissein Habré, the former

19. See African Commission on Human and Peoples' Rights, http://www.achpr.org/. Evans and Murray (2008) is the standard academic account of the African system.
20. See http://www.african-court.org/en/.

head of state of Chad. That the commission allowed the court's first case to be one that was highly politicized, had an obscure relationship to the charter, and came from an applicant who did not even reply to Senegal's response to his initial application, suggests questionable judgment that does not bode well for the short-term future of the court.)

Despite all these limitations, the African Commission is a leading regional voice for human rights. Its meetings provide the occasion for valuable networking by NGOs from across the continent. Its activities have helped to socialize African states to the idea that their human rights practices are legitimately subject to regional scrutiny—a not insignificant achievement given the radical notions of sovereignty and nonintervention that dominated the continent in the 1970s and 1980s. And, whatever the current shortcoming, there is an infrastructure in place that African states can build on in the future.

D. The Arab World and Asia

Regional human rights machinery in Asia and the Middle East has until recently been almost nonexistent—although in the past couple years some important first steps seem to have been taken, especially in the Arab world.

The League of Arab States created a Permanent Arab Commission on Human Rights in 1968, largely in response to the 1967 occupation of Palestinian territory in the West Bank and Gaza. That has remained its principal focus ever since.

The 2004 Arab Charter of Human Rights, which entered into force in 2008, creates an Arab Human Rights Committee.[21] It is still too early to judge its activities. They are, however, formally restricted to the review of state reports and there is nothing to suggest that such reviews are likely to be in any way penetrating, given that most if not all current members hold government positions.

Nonetheless, even the most toothless of instruments represents rather substantial progress in a region where the mean and median levels of performance are probably most charitably labeled poor. This is the flip side of the observation concerning Europe that the character of regional mechanisms is a consequence, rather than a cause, of the regional pattern of human rights performance. Thus the relatively aggressive role that the Arab League played in the spring of 2012 in pressuring the Assad regime in Syria is an extremely hopeful sign—and an indication that the Arab Spring may have a lasting regional legacy.

---

21. See "League of Arab States, Arab Charter on Human Rights, May 22, 2004," University of Minnesota Human Rights Library, http://www1.umn.edu/humanrts/instree/loas2005.html. Rishmawi (2010) provides an introductory overview.

In Asia there is no regional mechanism of any sort. Part of the reason is that Asia is largely a geographical entity, not a true cultural, economic, or political region. Even at the subregional level, though, "regional organizations" that might have a human rights dimension are rare. Southeast Asia is the only region comparable to Europe, the Americas, Africa, and the Arab world as understood above, in that only the Association of Southeast Asian Nations (ASEAN) includes as members all the countries of the geographical region and has a long tradition of collective multilateral consultation.[22]

ASEAN is notorious for its extreme deference to state sovereignty understood in almost absolutist terms. Nonetheless, in 2008—building on more than a decade of work by the Working Group for an ASEAN Human Rights Mechanism—the ASEAN foreign ministers created the High Level Panel to draft terms of reference for an ASEAN human rights organ. In 2009 the ASEAN Intergovernmental Commission on Human Rights (AICHR) was created.[23]

As an intergovernmental body, not much can be hoped for in terms of independent action. As in the Arab case, though, any formal entity within the organization represents a genuine step forward. If democratic states in the region, especially Indonesia, become more assertive in their interest in addressing human rights issues regionally, some further modest progress in the medium term is likely.

4. Single-Issue Human Rights Regimes

A different type of "nested" human rights (sub)regime is represented by universal membership organizations with a limited functional competence and by single-issue regimes that are less institution-bound. Single-issue regimes establish a place for themselves in the network of interdependence by restricting their activities to a limited range of issues—for example, workers' or women's rights—to induce widespread participation in a single area of mutual interest.

We have already encountered some of these regimes in the discussion of treaty bodies. The presentation here is roughly chronological.

---

22. SAARC (South Asian Association for Regional Cooperation) includes all states in the region. The rivalry between India and Pakistan, however, has made it a largely ineffective organization. Although particular human rights issues are addressed regionally (especially child welfare), there is no authoritative regional declaration. In fact, the 1991 Colombo Declaration, which outlines the priorities of the organization, has no section on human rights and explicitly subordinates democracy, human rights, and the rule of law to development initiatives.
23. See the official website of the Association of Southeast Asian Nations, http://www.aseansec. org/22769.htm. Munro (2011) and Tan (2011) provide interesting accounts of the history and politics behind the creation of the body.

A. Minority Rights

Minority rights issues have been handled internationally since the mid-seventeenth century. The Peace of Westphalia (1648) provided limited protections to certain Catholic, Lutheran, and Calvinist minorities in Central Europe. The Congress of Vienna (1815) gingerly addressed some issues of national minorities, especially Poles (in the context of their ratification of the partition of Poland). With the disintegration of the Ottoman Empire's European holdings, minority protections were imposed on the new states of Greece in 1830 and Serbia, Montenegro, and Romania in the 1870s. The League of Nations established a system of minority rights monitoring for states defeated in or created after World War I.[24] In all of these instances, however, minority protection was limited to postwar territorial settlements.[25] No general principal of minority protection was established.

The United Nations proved rather reluctant, though, to build on or universalize this earlier experience. Minority rights thus receded from the leading edge of what today we would call human rights activity to an increasingly marginal topic. *Racial* discrimination received extensive emphasis but the more general problem of ethnic discrimination largely languished. It was not until 1992 that the General Assembly finally adopted a Declaration on the Rights of Persons Belonging to National or Ethnic, Religious and Linguistic Minorities. There still is not treaty on the topic—although now it at least receives regular attention in the work of the UN Human Rights Council.

At the European regional level there has been extensive activity and considerable progress.[26] As noted above, the OSCE High Commissioner for National Minorities supervises a considerable program of monitoring and support for national and regional initiatives.[27] The Council of Europe has a National Minorities and Antidiscrimination Division that operates under the general guidance of the Framework Convention for the Protection of National Minorities.[28] There are also special minority-related provisions in the Inter-American system and work is under way to prepare a Draft Inter-American Convention against Racism and All Forms of Discrimination and Intolerance.

---

24. The standard study is Macartney (1934). See also Claude (1955), which takes the story into the early years of the United Nations.
25. Liebich (2008) tells this history well.
26. Jackson Preece (1998) provides an excellent overview of activities through the mid-1990s. See also Thornberry and Estebanez (2004) and Council of Europe and OSCE (2007).
27. For an official overview, see "Minority Rights," Organization for Security and Co-operation in Europe, http://www.osce.org/what/minority-rights and http://www.osce.org/hcnm.
28. See "Framework Convention for the Protection of National Minorities," Council of Europe, http://www.coe.int/t/dghl/monitoring/minorities/default_en.asp.

B. The Slave Trade and Slavery

International action on the slave trade and slavery goes back to the early nineteenth century (although significant private international action by what we would today call NGOs goes back at least a century further). In 1807, Britain abolished the slave trade within its empire and began efforts to forcibly suppress the international slave trade. In 1833, slavery was abolished in the British Empire, which led to a redoubling of British efforts at suppressing the slave trade (which by the 1840s were also supported by the French, American, and Portuguese navies). Attempting to address the supply of new slaves, rather than slavery itself, though, was something of a half-hearted measure—and one destined to at best limited success, given the continuation of the demand. Furthermore, these efforts were largely unilateral and frequently challenged, not implausibly, as illegal. There was not yet any clearly established international legal norm.

The 1890 Brussels Conference announced a general intention to put an end to the slave trade. A treaty had to wait until 1926, however, when the Convention to Suppress the Slave Trade and Slavery was opened for signature. International Labour Organization (ILO) Convention 29, Concerning Forced or Compulsory Labor, adopted in 1930, focused attention on all forms of forced labor, which were addressed in the 1926 convention only to the extent that they were precursors to or likely to degenerate into slavery. This extension was fully codified in the 1956 Supplementary Convention that covered "institutions and practices similar to slavery."

Although formal chattel slavery is practiced openly nowhere in the world—and covertly in a relatively small number of countries—slavery like practices persist, and a new movement to address "modern slavery" has achieved considerable momentum over the past decade.[29] Certainly more than ten million people, and quite possibly significantly more than twenty million, live in slave-like conditions. Most are bonded laborers, primarily in South Asia, but there is a thriving trade in human beings, primarily directed at women and children in the sex industries.

The United Nations Global Initiative to Fight Human Trafficking was launched in 2007.[30] Interpol has an extensive program as does the Council of Europe.[31] And the International Labour Organization continues to pursue its work on bonded labor, the most extensive and seemingly intractable form of slavery-like practices in the modern world.

---

29. Kevin Bales has done the most to bring this issue to the intersection of scholarly and popular attention. See, for example, Bales (2012) and Bales, Trodd, and Williamson (2009).
30. See Global Initiative to Fight Human Trafficking, http://www.ungift.org/knowledgehub/.
31. See "Action against Trafficking in Human Beings," Council of Europe, http://www.coe.int/t/dghl/monitoring/trafficking/default_en.asp.

C. Workers' Rights

The first international human rights regime of any sort was the functional regime of the International Labour Organization (ILO), established by the Treaty of Versailles.[32] Most of the regime's substantive norms were developed after World War II, including important conventions on freedom of association, the right to organize and bargain collectively, discrimination in employment, equality of remuneration, forced labor, migrant workers, workers' representatives, and basic aims and standards of social policy. Although developed autonomously, these rules supplement and extend parallel substantive norms of the global regime.

Because regime norms are formulated in conventions and recommendations that states adopt or not as they see fit, there is neither universality nor uniformity of coverage. Nevertheless, states are required to submit all conventions and recommendations to competent national authorities to be considered for adoption. They also may be required to submit reports on their practice even with respect to conventions they have not ratified. Most important, periodic reports are required on compliance with ratified conventions.[33] The highly professional Committee of Experts on the Application of Conventions and Recommendations reviews reports. Although it may only make "observations," the committee does so with vigor and considerable impartiality, and its observations have often induced changes in national practice.

Much of the success of this reporting-monitoring system lies in the ILO's "tripartite" structure, in which workers' and employers' delegates from each member state are voting members of the organization, along with government representatives. Because "victims" are represented by national trade union representatives, it is relatively difficult for states to cover up their failure to discharge their obligations, especially if some national workers' representatives adopt an internationalist perspective and question practices in countries where labor has less freedom to organize and bargain collectively.

The issue of workers' rights has also been important to the strength and success of the ILO regime, providing a reasonable degree of ideological homogeneity across a universal membership. During the Cold War, Western, Soviet bloc, and "socialist" Third World regimes certainly had different interpretations of the meaning of "freedom of association" and other relevant norms, but all faced serious internal and ideological constraints on overt noncompliance.

---

32. The classic study of human rights in the ILO is Haas (1970). See also Bartolomei de la Cruz, Potobsky, and Swepson (1996) and Rodgers et al. (2009).

33. There is a procedure for interstate complaints, but it is rarely used. Of more importance is the special complaint procedure for freedom of association cases arising under Conventions 87 and 98, which works through national and international trade union complaints, reviewed by the ILO Governing Body's Standing Committee on Freedom of Association.

In a reversal of the usual pattern, however, post–Cold War changes have not been favorable for workers' rights. Globalization and neoliberal structural adjustment have not been kind to organized labor and its advocates. Furthermore, the Cold War era's warm ideological embrace of workers pretty much across the mainstream of the political spectrum has turned tepid, and in some cases downright chilly.

D. Genocide and Crimes against Humanity

The 1948 Convention on the Prevention and Punishment of the Crime of Genocide was a central part of the first wave of post–World War II international human rights action.[34] It was the most direct international response to the Holocaust, which played a decisive role in moving human rights onto international agendas. In the ensuing decades, however, the genocide regime remained purely declaratory and of little or no practical effect. Furthermore, genocide was legally considered largely outside the framework of internationally recognized human rights. It is mentioned in neither the Universal Declaration nor the International Human Rights Covenants but was instead treated as a sui generis international crime.

One of the major changes in the post–Cold War politics of international human rights has been the development of a practice of multilateral armed intervention against genocide (see chapter 15). At the same time, and through closely related political processes, a system of individual criminal responsibility has been established through ad hoc tribunals for Rwanda and the former Yugoslavia and the creation of the International Criminal Court (ICC).

The interesting, although very odd, result has been the development of a regime with real powers of international judicial punishment and even the capacity to intervene with military force despite the lack of a clear institutional focus or any multilateral supervisory mechanism. Furthermore, international efforts remain largely focused on punishing violators rather than on the promotional and preventive activities characteristic of most other international human rights regimes.

The ICC, which was created in 2002, is a permanent tribunal that provides individual criminal liability for genocide, crimes against humanity, and war crimes. The symbolic significance of individual accountability for particularly egregious, systematic violations of human rights is undoubtedly great. Virtually all violations of internationally recognized human rights, however, lie outside of the jurisdiction of the ICC (which addresses human rights

---

34. The standard international legal discussion is Schabas (2009). On the rather tortured relationship of the United States to the Genocide Convention, see LeBlanc (1991) and Ronayne (2001).

violations only indirectly as they arise in genocide, war crimes, or crimes against humanity) and the ICC can only deal with a very small number of situations and cases.

In 2011 the ICC dealt with situations in the Democratic Republic of the Congo (involving four cases against five individuals), the Central African Republic (one case against one individual), Uganda (one case against four individuals), the Darfur region of Sudan (four cases against six individuals, including the sitting president of the country), Kenya (one case against three individuals), Libya (one case against two individuals), and Cote D'Ivoire (one case against the former president). This is a reasonable sampling of major cases in recent years and the fact that national leaders have been charged is of considerable significance.

The record of the UN Security Council has been somewhat more problematic. Its action in Bosnia and elsewhere in the former Yugoslavia in the early 1990s was late and limited, although in many ways path-breaking. Its failure to act decisively in Rwanda in 1994 was tragic—almost certainly hundreds of thousands of people could have been saved by even moderately forceful international action—but transforming. In 1999, when the Security Council failed to act in Kosovo, NATO took matters into its own hands militarily. Later that year, however, the Security Council authorized action against Indonesian genocide in occupied East Timor that not only stopped the violence but led to independence for East Timor. For all the shortcomings of the international response to Sudanese genocide in Darfur, the Security Council has been actively involved, both independently and in support of action by the African Union. (These cases, especially Kosovo and Darfur, are addressed in more depth in chapter 15.)

E. Racial Discrimination

The 1965 International Convention on the Elimination of All Forms of Racial Discrimination (CERD) provides a clear and powerful extension and elaboration of the global regime's norms against racial discrimination, but its implementation provisions are fairly weak. The Committee on the Elimination of Racial Discrimination, a body of experts established under the convention, has very narrowly interpreted its powers to "make suggestions and general recommendations based on the examination of the reports and information received from the States Parties" (Article 9.2). The interstate complaint procedure has never been utilized and less than fifty individual communications have been considered. Even the information-exchange elements of the reporting procedure are not without flaws; the public examination of reports, although sometimes critical, often is less penetrating than in the Human Rights Committee. All in all, despite the near universal condemnation of racial discrimination, this is probably the weakest of all the major international regimes.

F. Torture

The 1984 Convention against Torture and Other Cruel, Inhuman or Degrading Treatment or Punishment contains a strong elaboration of norms against torture. "No exceptional circumstances whatsoever, whether a state of war or threat of war, internal political instability or any other public emergency, may be invoked as a justification of torture" (Article 2.2). Orders from superiors are explicitly excluded as a defense. Special obligations are established for training law enforcement personnel and reviewing interrogation regulations and methods. To reduce incentives for torture, statements obtained through torture must be made inadmissible in all legal proceedings. The convention also requires that wherever the alleged torture occurred, and whatever the nationality of the torturer or victim, parties must either prosecute alleged torturers or extradite them to a country that will. This system of "universal jurisdiction" has been put to effect in a number of countries, perhaps most aggressively in Spain.

The Committee against Torture receives and reviews periodic reports from "states parties" every four years. The convention also contains optional provisions that allow the committee to receive communications about general situations, as well as interstate complaints and individual communications. The committee uses these powers aggressively—as suggested by the fact that it has the lowest level of ratifications of any of the major treaties—and with some impact. It has registered more than four hundred individual communications and its review of state reports is generally of a very high quality.

Although the Convention against Torture and the Committee against Torture stand at the core of the international regime against torture, other actors are important participants. The UN special rapporteur on torture has played a prominent role. The very strong European regional regime against torture has unprecedented on-site investigatory powers.[35] The weaker 1985 Inter-American Convention to Prevent and Punish Torture is also of some note, especially in the context of the history of the region.

Ongoing promotional activities include, for example, the UN Voluntary Fund for Victims of Torture, established in 1982, which makes grants to

---

35. See "The Prevention of Torture and Ill-Treatment in Europe," Council of Europe, http://www.coe.int/web/coe-portal/what-we-do/human-rights/prevention-of-torture, and European Committee for the Prevention of Torture and Inhuman or Degrading Treatment or Punishment, http://www.cpt.coe.int/en/default.htm. Evans and Morgan (1998) and Morgan and Evans (1999) are standard scholarly works, although they are becoming a bit dated.

groups throughout the world. Contributions peaked at nearly $12 million in 2008, dipped below $10 million in 2010, and appear to be set to stay at about that level.

Finally, the NGO dimension is particularly significant in the area of torture (as well as in women's rights, considered immediately below).[36] The campaigns of Amnesty International contributed greatly to the creation of both the Convention against Torture and the office of the UN special rapporteur and have been extremely important in continuing to publicize the issue, thus increasing the impact of the regime. In a very different vein, Copenhagen is the home of an international Rehabilitation and Research Center for Torture Victims, a location that reflects the leading role of Denmark in international action against torture. Similar centers operate in Canada, Norway, the United States, and other countries.

G. Women's Rights

The issue of women's rights was until recently something of a stepchild in the field of human rights. Although racial discrimination is considered in the UN Commission on Human Rights and throughout the UN-centered regime, gender discrimination was largely segregated in the UN Commission on the Status of Women. The slogan "women's rights are human rights," popularized at the 1995 Beijing World Conference on Women, was seen by many at the time as a radical claim. In past two decades, though, there has been a substantial normative and procedural evolution of the women's rights regime. In recent years, the language of "women's human rights"—as opposed to classic "women's rights"—has entered the mainstream of discussions.[37]

The Commission on the Status of Women, a subsidiary body of the UN Economic and Social Council (ECOSOC) established in 1947, has played a role in norm creation very similar to that played by the Commission on Human Rights, having drafted a variety of specialized treaties, such as the 1952 Convention on the Political Rights of Women, as well as the major general treaty in this area, the 1979 Convention on the Elimination of All Forms of Discrimination against Women. The Commission on the Status of Women has also undertaken various promotional activities, and studied individual communications between 1984 and 2000.

The Optional Protocol to the Convention, which entered into force at the end of 2000, has moved the consideration of communications to the

36. For a good introduction to the role of NGOs in UN treaty bodies, see Bayefsky (2000: Part IV) and especially Grant (2000).
37. For a useful discussion of these linguistic issues and some of their implications, see Peach (2001). For good recent overviews, see Ross (2008) and Reilly (2009).

Committee on the Elimination of Discrimination against Women (CEDAW). CEDAW, which meets annually, has examined reports of "states parties" since its inception in 1982. It now has an array of powers roughly comparable to that of the Human Rights Committee. Although the symbolism of this change was very important to a number of activists, it seems to have had little impact on the functioning of the regime.[38]

The strengthening of the women's rights regime can be traced primarily to the changing international awareness of women's issues centered around the designation of 1975 as International Women's Year and the associated world conference in Mexico City. In conjunction with political and "consciousness-raising" activities of national women's movements, a major international constituency for women's rights was created. A growing set of regime makers and takers emerged, while potential breakers were deterred from active opposition either by domestic ideological stands or by the emerging international normative consensus. Follow-up conferences in Nairobi in 1985 and Beijing in 1995 have helped to solidify and deepen this international consensus. They have also provided striking illustrations of the important role of NGOs, and their dramatic proliferation, especially in the non-Western world.

H. Children

Children are perhaps the only group with more universal appeal than victims of racial or gender discrimination and torture.[39] Nonetheless, the speed with which the 1989 Convention on the Rights of the Child came into force was stunning: it took less than a year to obtain the twenty required parties (in contrast to two and a half years for the Convention against Torture) and barely more than two years to reach one hundred parties. In 2012 it had 193 parties, the most of any international human rights treaty. In contrast to many other international human rights topics, however, there does not appear to be much urgency to the issue (except for particular questions, such as child soldiers and sexual abuse) and the Committee on the Rights of the Child has not become a significant international actor.

38. For a thoughtful assessment of the opportunities and constraints facing CEDAW, see Bustelo (2000).
39. Alston, Parker, and Seymour (1992), Asquith and Hill (1994), Wallace (1997: chap. 5), Van Beuren (1998), Fottrell (2000), and Detrick (1999) provide good general overviews of the children's rights regime. For a more philosophical approach, see Freeman (1997). On the Convention on the Rights of the Child in particular, see Detrick, Doek, and Cantwell (1992) and LeBlanc (1995). The important issue of integrating international standards with traditional values and practices, which provides an interesting context for exploring some of the issues we considered in part 2, is considered in Alston and Gilmour-Walsh (1996) and Douglas and Sebba (1998).

I. Disabled People

The most recent major single-issue regime concerns the rights of disabled people. In contrast to racial discrimination, women's rights, torture, and children, the 2006 Convention on the Rights of Persons with Disabilities adds to, rather than elaborates on, rights recognized in the Universal Declaration and the International Human Rights Covenants. It reflects a fundamental change in attitudes from the 1940s, 1950s, and 1960s, when international human rights norms were established. Officially, at the international level, disabled persons are now recognized as fully human.

It is far too early to determine how and with what effects this single-issue regime will function.[40] It is clear, though, that is poses problems that, if not qualitatively different than other single-issue regimes, are at least more pronounced than in many other single-issue regimes. Issues of cost are likely to be of considerable significance in all but the richest countries. Furthermore, especially sharp divergence between elite attitudes, which have been generally supportive of international protection of the rights of disabled peoples, and popular attitudes towards disability are likely to pose serious problems even for less costly measures to end discrimination.

Nonetheless, it seems clear that the international impetus from the convention will be great. In fact, this may arguably be a case in which the impact of international norms will prove to be usually significant. For all its diffuseness, the regime should serve as a significant impetus to both normative and policy transformation in countries across the globe.

J. Indigenous Peoples

The United Nations Declaration on the Rights of Indigenous Peoples was adopted by the UN General Assembly in 2007.[41] This is the current culmination of a long and often tortured process of norm creation that goes back at least to the creation in 1972 of a UN Working Group on Indigenous Peoples.

Conceptually, there have long been questions as to whether the rights of indigenous peoples are a sui generis class of rights or international human rights. The trend began to turn toward incorporation within a human rights framework with the 1989 ILO Convention on Tribal and Indigenous Peoples (No. 169). Even today, though, the international community seems unclear as to how to think of the place of indigenous rights. The UN Economic and Social Council has a Permanent Forum on Indigenous Issues, created in

---

40. For initial scholarly assessments of the process of implementation, see Arnardóttir and Quinn (2009) and especially Flynn (2011).
41. The four countries that voted against the declaration (Australia, Canada, New Zealand, and the United States) have all since indicated that they support it.

2002, that has a mandate largely outside the domain of human rights. The Human Rights Council, however, created an Expert Mechanism on the Rights of Indigenous Peoples, in conjunction with the adoption of the declaration, to provide advice through studies and research. And a Special Rapporteur on the Rights of Indigenous Peoples (since 2008, James Anaya of the United States, a noted human rights scholar and activist) operates within the program of thematic mechanisms discussed above.

The rights of indigenous peoples are distinctive in the context of human rights for at least four reasons.[42] First, although there are about a third of a billion indigenous peoples in approximately seventy countries, more than three fifths of all states have no indigenous peoples in their territories. Nearly all other internationally recognized human rights present real issues of domestic policy in nearly all states.[43] This significantly alters the politics of indigenous rights.

Second, protecting the rights of indigenous peoples typically requires creating special mechanisms to comply with or respect traditional practices. It also often requires rather significant restrictions on certain rights of members of the mainstream community. Perhaps most important, instituting private property in land where indigenous peoples reside would destroy their traditional way of life. More generally, a separate legal regime will often be required to protect the rights and practices of indigenous communities and their members.

Third, the rights of indigenous peoples are held principally by the group as a whole, not its individual members. This creates not only conflicts between different rights, which exist for all internationally recognized human rights, but conflicts between different right-holders. And as the preceding and following points suggest, these conflicts often will be not only extensive but intense.

Fourth, the potential economic costs of many indigenous rights claims are potentially astronomical. In countries like the United States and Canada, where indigenous peoples have been largely dispossessed and restricted to economically unpromising and socially destructive ghetto communities ("reservations"), restoring indigenous communities to their lands would be staggeringly expensive and disruptive. Even providing fair-market-value compensation would be extraordinarily expensive (even setting aside issues

42. The best current discussion of indigenous rights and international human rights is Anaya (2009).
43. This does not mean that the rights of indigenous peoples are somehow not universal. All peoples who fit the definition living anywhere have all the rights identified in the declaration. It just happens that the right-holders of these rights are not as geographically dispersed as the holders of other internationally recognized human rights.

of political controversy). In countries like Brazil and India, where indigenous peoples still possess at least some of their lands, the conflict between development of the national economy and the rights of indigenous peoples is often stark and politically incendiary.

For all of these reasons, it is unlikely that we will see a rapid move from the declaration to an international convention on the rights of indigenous peoples. And even if that does come in the near future, there is little reason to expect that it will receive wide endorsement. (ILO Convention 169 has received only twenty ratifications in more than twenty years.) The regime is likely to remain a very weak declaratory regime for the foreseeable future. Nonetheless, the fact that there is even a declaration creates normative constraints and pressures that are likely to be of some valuable to indigenous activists.

5. Assessing Multilateral Human Rights Mechanisms

How do we assess the welter of multilateral institutions considered above? I will focus on differences in regimes that arise from the source of their authority (based on a treaty or rooted in a wider international organization), their range or focus, and the character of their powers. Each type of mechanism has its own strengths and weaknesses.

Human rights institutions based in international and regional organizations can draw on the prestige and influence of the broader organization. This is one of the greatest resources of the Office of the High Commissioner for Human Rights and the Human Rights Council. Organization-based institutions may also benefit from internal political linkages. The other objectives states are pursuing within the organization may constrain them from resisting the organization's human rights initiatives. In addition, the decisions of international organizations represent the collective activities of states, with their associated power resources.

Politicization, however, is the price often paid for the political power of multilateral organizations. For example, in the United Nations during the Cold War, countries were singled out for scrutiny largely on the basis of their lack of international political support. Even though serious violations were addressed, the procedures were corrupted by the taint of political partisanship.

Committees of independent experts have been relatively nonpartisan. Even during the Cold War, the Human Rights Committee, for example, was far less politicized than even the UN Commission on Human Rights, let alone the General Assembly. Given the heavy reliance on publicity and persuasion, a reputation for integrity and fairness can be a powerful tool.

Combining these two lines of argument suggests that an international human rights institution can maximize its impact if it is backed by a broader organization while avoiding the taint of politicization. This assessment is confirmed by the record of the UN Human Rights Council and Commission, the Inter-American Commission, and the European Court. The Inter-American Commission was far more aggressive, and effective, than the highly politicized OAS General Assembly. The UN Commission, especially in the 1980s and early 1990s, was able to draw on the combination of a reputation for relative impartiality and the prestige of the broader organization. This enabled, for example, improved access for special rapporteurs in closed countries such as Iran and Burma. Likewise, the widespread voluntary compliance with the decisions of the European regime rests on a combination of the prestige and influence of the Council of Europe and the unparalleled reputation for neutrality of its human rights machinery. This line of argument also helps to explain the emergence of the UN high commissioner as a major international actor.

Single-issue and country-specific initiatives have largely complementary strengths and weaknesses. Because thematic or single-issue mechanisms avoid singling out individual countries, even when they do address particular state practices, the inquiry is likely to be somewhat less threatening. Thematic and single-issue initiatives also may appear less threatening because they do not address the full range of human rights issues. Although initiatives on single issues may appear timid and almost beside the point in countries guilty of gross violations, significant incremental improvements in particular areas may result from single-issue mechanisms even where systematic violations persist. Whether the initiatives are countrywide or issue-specific, the concrete achievements usually are, at best, incremental improvements in limited areas, such as the release of prominent political prisoners or the modification of particular laws, decrees, or administrative practices.

In examining particular implementation mechanisms, we again see a picture of complementary strengths and weaknesses. The strengths and weaknesses of reporting were considered in section 1.B above. Here I focus on investigations and communications.

The individual petition system in Europe often appears to be the ideal mechanism. From an individual victim's point of view, the near-universal compliance with the decisions of the European Court are undoubtedly preferable to the uncertainties of reporting and investigatory-diplomatic methods. The Inter-American system, however, suggests that it is not so much the formal availability of individual petitions that is crucial but the commitment of states not simply to abide by the resulting quasi-judicial proceedings but to do the tough domestic legal and political work of implementing regional decisions.

Regional or global petition systems thus are best seen as modest supplementary elements in an effective system of enforcing human rights. This is particularly true where, as with the Human Rights Committee and the Inter-American Court, the procedure is optional—presenting a striking example of the typical trade-off between the scope and the strength of international procedures. Even the European regime is an example of the strongest procedures applying only to a relatively small group of states with relatively good human rights records.

The other obvious drawback of individual complaint mechanisms is the small number of cases they can address. Even the thousands of cases handled by the European Court, the Inter-American Commission, and the Human Rights Committee are but the tiniest drop in the sea of human rights violations.

Nonetheless, the focus on individual cases gives these procedures a valuable specificity and concreteness. Because violations are personalized and detailed evidence of individual violations is provided, it is more difficult for states to deny responsibility.

Individual petitions, like the other kinds of procedures, occupy a special niche. They are particularly desirable where violations are either narrow or sporadic. Investigation and reporting mechanisms will continue to be needed for a very long time. I am even tempted to argue that they are the heart of multilateral human rights activity. In a world still organized around sovereign states, the international contribution to implementing human rights rests on persuasive diplomacy, which itself rests considerably on the power of shame that lies at the heart of investigatory and reporting mechanisms.

If this is true, the key to change in state practices probably lies not in any one type of forum or activity but in the mobilization of multiple, complementary channels of influence—which leads us to consider human rights in bilateral foreign policy, the subject of the next chapter.

6. The Evolution of Human Rights Regimes

What, if anything, can we say in general about the nature, creation, and evolution of international human rights regimes? Table 11.2 presents a summary overview of the regimes discussed in this chapter, viewed periodically since 1945. The most striking pattern is the near-complete absence of international human rights regimes in 1945, in contrast to the presence of several in all the later periods. We can also note the gradual strengthening of most international human rights regimes over the last thirty years. Even today, though, promotional regimes remain the rule.

Once states accept norms stronger than nonbinding guidelines, declaratory regimes readily evolve into promotional regimes. If the regime's norms are important or appealing enough for states to commit themselves to them,

TABLE 11.2 CHANGE IN INTERNATIONAL HUMAN RIGHTS REGIMES, 1945–2010

Global regime	1945	1960	1975	1990	2000	2010
	—	Declaratory	Promotional	Strong promotional	Strong promotional	Strong promotional
REGIONAL REGIMES						
European	—	Implementation	Enforcement	Enforcement	Enforcement	Enforcement
Inter-American	—	Declaratory	Promotional	Promotional/enforcement	Promotional/enforcement	Promotional/enforcement
African	—	—	—	Declaratory	Declaratory/promotional	Declaratory/Promotional
Arab/Middle Eastern	—	—	—	—	—	Weak declaratory
Asian	—	—	—	—	—	—*
SINGLE-ISSUE REGIMES						
Minority rights	Weak declaratory	Weak declaratory	Weak dedaratory	Weak declaratory	Declaratory	Declaratory
Slavery	Declaratory	Declaratory	Declaratory	Declaratory	Declaratory	Declaratory/promotional
Workers' rights	Promotional	Promotional/implementation	Promotional/implementation	Promotional/implementation	Promotional/implementation	Promotional/implementation
Racial discrimination	—	—	Strong promotional	Strong promotional	Strong promotional	Strong promotional
Women's rights	—	Declaratory/promotional	Declaratory/promotional	Strong promotional	Strong promotional	Strong promotional
Torture	—	—	Weak dedaratory	Promotional/implementation	Implementation	Implementation
Genocide	—	Declaratory	Declaratory	Declaratory	Implementation/enforcement	Implementation/enforcement
Disabled	—	—	—	Weak declaratory	Weak declaratory	Promotional
Indigenous peoples	—	—	—	Weak declaratory	Weak declaratory	Declaratory

* Weak declaratory regime in Southeast Asian (ASEAN) sub-region

then it is difficult to argue against promoting their further spread and implementation. The move to implementation or enforcement, however, involves a major qualitative jump that most states resist, with considerable vigor when necessary, and usually with success.[44]

Regime evolution may be gradual and largely incremental within declaratory and promotional regimes (and perhaps within implementation and enforcement regimes as well), but there seems to be a profound discontinuity in the emergence of implementation and enforcement activities. Promotional regimes require a relatively low level of commitment. The move to an implementation or enforcement regime requires a major qualitative increase in the commitment of states that rarely is forthcoming. Most of the growth in international human rights regimes has therefore been "easy" growth that does not naturally lead to further expansion. This would seem to explain the merely incremental growth of almost all international human rights regimes in the post–Cold War era, despite the substantially improved international human rights climate.

We have already considered some of the central factors that explain this pattern of limited growth, emphasizing both awareness and power, which usually are created or mobilized by conceptual changes in response to domestic political action (e.g., women's rights) or international moral shock (e.g., the global regime or torture). Such awareness and power typically function by galvanizing support for the creation or growth of a regime and delegitimizing opposition, which may make moral interdependence more difficult for states to resist. National commitment, cultural community, and hegemony are of significant importance.

National commitment is the single most important contributor to a strong regime; it usually is the source of the oft-mentioned "political will" that underlies strong regimes. If a state has a good human rights record, then not only will a strong regime appear relatively unthreatening but also the additional support it provides for national efforts is likely to be welcomed. The European regime's unprecedented strength provides the most striking example of the power of national commitment.

The importance of cultural community is suggested by the fact that the only enforcement regimes are regional (or involve the narrow and unique issue of genocide). In the absence of sociocultural and ideological consensus, strong procedures are likely to appear too subject to partisan use or abuse to be accepted even by states with good records and strong national

---

44. For an interesting attempt to theorize the national adoption of international human rights norms, based on carefully designed and executed case studies, see Risse, Ropp, and Sikkink (1999).

commitments.[45] For example, opponents of stronger procedures in the global human rights regime and in most single-issue regimes include major countries from all regions, with good, mediocre, and poor national human rights records alike. The very scope of all but the regional regimes undercuts the relative homogeneity that seems almost necessary for movement beyond a promotional regime.

Finally, I must stress the importance of dominant power and hegemony, which should be kept analytically distinct. Beyond mere dominant power, hegemonic leadership requires substantial ideological resources, a crucial element in the acceptance of, or at least acquiescence in, the authority of the hegemon. The effective exercise of even hegemonic power usually requires not merely dominating material and organizational resources but also an ideological justification sufficiently powerful to win at least acquiescence from non-hegemonic powers.

Leaders require followers; regime makers need takers. The reasons for taking a regime may be largely accidental or external to the issue. Sometimes, though, the reasons for taking a regime are connected with the ideological hegemony of the proposed project. The seemingly inescapable normative appeal of human rights over the past half-century, even during the ideological rivalry of the Cold War, thus is an important element in the rise of international human rights regimes. Power, in the sense that the term traditionally has had in the study of international politics, still is important, but true hegemony often is based on ideological power as well. We might even argue that the ideological hegemony of human rights is more important than dominant material power.

A hegemonic idea such as human rights may actually draw power to itself. Power may coalesce around, rather than create, hegemonic ideas, such as human rights and the regimes that emerge from them. For example, the overriding ideological appeal of the idea of workers' rights has been crucial to the success of the ILO. In Europe, the "hegemonic" power behind the very strong European regime came not from any single dominant state but from a coalition built around the ideological dominance of the idea of human rights. The ideological hegemony of human rights is essential to explaining the creation of an African human rights regime in the face of the notorious respect of the Organisation for African Unity (OAU) for even the tiniest trappings of sovereignty. The emergence of the global human rights regime cannot be understood without taking account of this impulse, discussed earlier in terms of perceived moral interdependence.

---

45. The United States presents an exaggerated version of such fears, most strikingly in the US Senate's extended resistance to, for example, the Genocide Convention and the International Covenant on Civil and Political Rights, with which US law and practice have already conformed in almost all particulars. These fears, in a less extreme form, are common and widespread.

Hegemonic power, however, does ultimately require material power, and even hegemonic ideas have a limited ability to attract such power. Hegemonic ideas can be expected to draw acquiescence to relatively weak regimes, but beyond promotional activities (that is, once significant sacrifices of sovereignty are required) something more is needed. In other words, hegemony too points to the pattern of limited growth noted earlier.

The evolution toward strong promotional procedures can be expected to continue but we should expect states to resist, usually successfully, efforts to cross over to implementation and enforcement. In the second edition of this book, I wrote that we had little reason to expect that the 2010 column of the summary table would show many significant changes from 2000, other than the solidification of emerging regimes on the rights of the disabled and of indigenous peoples. That has been largely the case. And we should expect similarly constrained incremental change over the next decade.

We must not forget how far we have come since 1945. But we should not forget the severe limits of multilateral action in the global human rights regime.

12

Human Rights and Foreign Policy

Much international action on behalf of human rights takes place in the multilateral forums discussed in the preceding chapter. Human rights have also become an increasingly important (although typically fairly modest) part of the bilateral foreign policies of many states. This chapter draws attention to both the reality and the limits of states' concern with international human rights.

1. Human Rights and the National Interest

When I first began working on human rights, in the mid-1970s, discussion of human rights and foreign policy usually centered on whether states ought to have an international human rights policy. The answer given to that question was as often no as yes. I address arguments against pursuing human rights in foreign policy in an appendix to this chapter, because they are of largely historical interest. Today it has become completely normal for states to pursue human rights objectives in their bilateral and multilateral foreign policies. Especially in liberal democratic countries, the questions have become what should be included in a country's human rights foreign policy, where should it be pursued, and how aggressively. Such a change reflects a fundamental redefinition of the national interest.

Despite arguments of advocates of Realpolitik (political realism, power politics) that the national interest is or should be defined in terms of power—an argument that makes human rights a merely moral concern that must be rigorously subordinated to vital material national interests—the national interest in fact is whatever states and their citizens are interested in. If states feel that it is in their interest to expend some of their foreign policy resources and attention on the rights of foreigners, there is no compelling reason why they should not. Furthermore, the grounds for doing so need not be instrumental (for example, the idea that rights-protective regimes are more peaceful or better trading partners). An intrinsic interest in living in a more just world fully justifies including international human rights in a country's definition of its national interest. In fact, many countries have done precisely that.

The United States was the first to adopt an assertive international human rights policy, beginning with President Jimmy Carter (who took office in 1977). In the preceding years, the United States had addressed particular human rights issues in its foreign policy, especially human rights violations in the Soviet bloc. Congress had mandated a limited linkage of foreign aid to the human rights practices of recipient states. Only with Carter, though, did international human rights in general become part of US foreign policy.

This decision was, at that time, highly controversial. Carter's successor, Ronald Reagan, campaigned against Carter's human rights policy (arguing that it harmed US interests by inappropriately prioritizing human rights over anticommunism in relations with several "friendly" countries, especially military and civilian dictatorships in Latin America). Pressure from the American public and Congress, however, eventually helped to convince even the Reagan administration to embrace a comprehensive international human rights policy in its second term. Since the late 1980s human rights has been a largely uncontroversial and bipartisan element of US foreign policy.

Although countries like the Netherlands and Canada had by the early 1980s made international human rights an explicit and increasingly emphasized part of their foreign policies, most Western countries did not have important international human rights policies until the later 1980s or early 1990s. In most of the rest of the world, human rights became a matter of bilateral foreign policy only after the end of the Cold War. Today, however, most democratic countries in all regions of the world have more or less ambitious international human rights objectives in their bilateral foreign policies. (Most nondemocratic regimes, by contrast, although they at least tolerate the multilateral mechanisms discussed in the preceding chapter, do not extend their international human rights policies to bilateral relations.)

The rise of human rights on the foreign policy agendas of democratic states has both internal and international dimensions. Democracies tend to identify themselves internally with the pursuit of human rights. Carrying this pursuit over into their foreign policies thus seems "natural." It also gives expression to a sort of universal solidarity based on a common humanity (without challenging the system of national implementation of international human rights).

Democratic regimes, though, long predate international human rights norms. Bilateral human rights policies arose only with the maturing of the global human rights regime. (It is not a coincidence that Carter was elected in the same year that the International Human Rights Covenants came into force and took office in the same year that Amnesty International won the Nobel Peace Prize.) The expression of a "natural" internal inclination to pursue human rights in foreign policy was in fact greatly facilitated, and in some senses even created, by changes in international norms.

Foreign policy involves how a state sees itself, the world around it, and its place in that world. The global human rights regime has created a world in which a government's commitment to human rights is seen as essential to full national and international legitimacy. That has not only enabled the expression of existing tendencies to address human rights in national foreign policies but also created additional support for such policies. The transformation of the national interest represented by the rise of bilateral human rights policies is thus both a cause and a consequence of both the domestic preferences of states and the global human rights regime, mutually interacting to push policy in a particular direction.

2. International Human Rights and National Identity

States choose to pursue human rights in their foreign policy for a variety of reasons. Often, though, a significant reason is that human rights are important to national identity. This is particularly clear in the case of the United States, where a combination of moral, historical, political, and national interest concerns have led to a relatively strong and assertive international human rights policy. Historian Arthur Schlesinger Jr. writes, "The United States was founded on the proclamation of 'unalienable' rights, and human rights ever since have had a peculiar resonance in the American tradition. Nor was the application of this idea to foreign policy an innovation of the Carter Administration. Americans have agreed since 1776 that the United States must be a beacon of human rights to an unregenerate world. The question has always been how America is to execute this mission" (1979: 505).

William F. Buckley Jr. is, typically, more acerbic in noting America's "cyclical romances with the notion of responsibility for the rights of extranationals" (1980: 776). This responsibility has been expressed in two principal forms, implying very different international human rights strategies. On the one hand, America has been seen as a beacon, the proverbial city on the hill, whose human rights mission was to set an example for a corrupt world. This strand of the American tradition can be traced back at least to Washington's Farewell Address (Gilbert 1961). In its extreme forms this leads to neutralism and isolationism. On the other hand, the American mission has been seen to require positive action abroad. The United States must teach not simply by its domestic example but by active international involvement on behalf of human rights. This equally venerable strand of the American tradition has been predominant in the contemporary revival of concern for human rights.

The United States is hardly unique, however, in its identification with human rights. Human rights were also part of the founding self-image of the states of Central and South America, when they threw off Spanish and Portuguese colonial rule. The tortured fate of human rights in most of Latin America since independence, however, makes India a much more interesting case. Indian independence in 1947 gave considerable additional impetus to the post-World War II surge of decolonization, and India's identification with the human rights values of self-determination and racial equality was (along with its relatively great power) central to its leadership efforts in the Third World during the Cold War era.

Countries without human rights in their founding myths have in recent decades increasingly incorporated human rights into their national self-conceptions. In South Africa, for example, human rights became a central part of the national self-image through a revolutionary (although not especially violent) political transformation that brought the end of apartheid. The United Kingdom and the Netherlands illustrate the path of evolutionary transformation. By the end of World War II, both countries had come to identify themselves with the cause of universal human rights—at home. Once they had dismantled their colonial empires, in part through the influence of human rights ideas (in both metropolitan and colonized political communities), human rights emerged as an increasingly prominent part of both national identity and foreign policy.

Immediately after World War II, the Netherlands fought to maintain colonial rule over Indonesia. In the 1960s, massive Indonesian human rights violations were met by little more than muted verbal condemnation. By the early 1990s, however, the Netherlands was willing to accept modest but real economic and political costs, and face the stinging charge of neocolonialism, to press concerns over Indonesian human rights violations (Baehr 2000: 71–72).

In these cases, and many others, national and international ideas and values interacted dynamically. The international dimension has been perhaps most striking in cases of revolutionary transformation, going back at least to Tom Paine's pamphleteering on behalf of the American and French revolutions. In India, Gandhi learned from his earlier South African experiences and, like many later nationalist leaders in Asia and Africa, effectively used the "Western" language of self-determination and equal rights against colonialism. The struggle against apartheid in South Africa had an important international dimension that ultimately changed the foreign policies of most Western countries. In the Soviet bloc, the Helsinki Final Act and the follow-up meetings of the Commission on Security and Cooperation in Europe (CSCE) provided important support for human rights activists, especially in Russia and Czechoslovakia, and contributed subtly but significantly to the delegitimation of totalitarian rule (Thomas 2001).

In most of western Europe, participation in the Council of Europe's regional human rights regime has placed national rights in a broader international perspective that has facilitated their incorporation into foreign policy. Britain's decision in 1997 to incorporate the European Convention directly into British law is a striking example of the interpenetration of national and international rights conceptions. A very different kind of international impetus was provided by Jimmy Carter's 1977 decision to make human rights an explicit priority in US foreign policy. It is no coincidence, for example, that the seminal 1979 Dutch White Paper followed closely on the US example.

3. Means and Mechanisms of Bilateral Action

Having considered briefly why states pursue human rights in their foreign policies, we can now turn to how they do this. Like other foreign policy objectives, human rights may in principle be legitimately pursued with all the means of foreign policy short of the threat or use of force, which contemporary international law reserves for self-defense and action against genocide.

Evan Luard provides a fairly broad list of means that have been used in the pursuit of human rights objectives: confidential representations, joint representations with other governments, public statements, support for calls for international investigation, initiation of calls for investigation, cancellation or postponement of ministerial visits, restrictions on cultural and sporting contacts, embargoes on arms sales, reductions in aid, withdrawal of ambassadors, cessation of aid, breaking diplomatic relations, and trade sanctions (Luard 1981: 26–27). To this list we should add support for civil society groups, aiding legal opposition groups, aiding illegal nonviolent opposition movements, aiding armed opposition movements, and invasion. Only when faced with genocide or severe humanitarian emergencies, though, have states used force to pursue international human rights objectives.

We can divide these varied means into two broad groups: diplomacy, understood as the use of discursive means of action, and sanctions, understood as the use of material means. We can also divide the mechanisms of foreign policy into persuasive and coercive means, conceptualized as a continuum. (These two distinctions overlap only partially. Although diplomatic measures tend to be persuasive they sometimes have a coercive dimension. Sanctions tend to be relatively coercive. When they involve carrots rather than sticks, though, they are fundamentally persuasive.)

A. Diplomacy

Human rights diplomacy tends to have three principal targets: the treatment of particular individuals (usually dissidents and political prisoners), particular policies, and the character of the regime (with a focus on patterns of gross and systematic violations of internationally recognized human rights). These objectives are pursued through both public and private means.

Although most attention is rightly focused on public human rights diplomacy, private diplomatic initiatives—"quiet diplomacy"—can be important, especially when dealing with individual victims or attempting to change particular laws, policies, or practices. For example, privacy can facilitate negotiation. It may also allow the target to save some face. Nonetheless, private action alone, without at least the plausible threat of public action, rarely helps even in the most limited cases. When gross and systematic violations are at issue, quiet diplomacy is almost certainly an inadequate response.

Public human rights diplomacy has at least three important dimensions: gathering and disseminating information, communicating opposing views, and mobilizing pressure. Although mobilizing pressure certainly is of central importance, we should not underestimate the importance of information gathering and the diplomatic exchange of views.

The international politics of human rights is largely a matter of mobilizing shame. Reliable information about national human rights practices thus is essential to human rights advocacy of any sort. Professional diplomats are well positioned to develop and disseminate such information, both through their own direct inquiries and through contacts with human rights advocates.

The United States in particular has made a major contribution through its annual Country Reports on Human Rights Practices.[1] These have, especially since the end of the Cold War, become a major source of information about national human rights practices and are used not only by foreign policy decision makers in numerous countries but also by national and transnational human rights advocates across the globe.

The private and public exchange of views, especially among friendly countries, is often overlooked as a means of exerting influence. This may be a particularly effective means of influence in countries that have fair to good human rights records and where foreign policy initiatives support the work of local activists. Knowing that one's international allies—especially powerful friends—are watching and will raise an issue sometimes influences a government's actions. This is rarely the case when addressing gross and systematic violations, but when dealing with particular individuals or particular

---

1. See "Human Rights Reports," U.S. Department of State, http://www.state.gov/g/drl/rls/hrrpt/.

practices it can be of considerable help. Especially when undertaken in concert with other national, international, and transnational action, persuasive diplomacy not only often can make a difference, it occasionally may even prove the decisive, final element that tips the balance.

Discursive policy, however, can be, and often needs to be, coercive, not merely persuasive. Rarely will the privately expressed views of other countries, or even polite public disagreements among friends, be sufficient to improve even very specific human rights practices. Diplomatic discretion often leads states to rely on other actors, both national and transnational, to bear the burden of vocal public criticism. Such criticism, however,— or at least its threat—is almost always necessary to win even incremental improvements in human rights practices. And when confronting severe and systematic violations, anything less than public criticism may appear to be complicity.

B. Sanctions

Although words are the principal tool of bilateral human rights policy, states typically have more material means at their disposal that can be utilized on behalf of internationally recognized human rights than most multilateral human rights actors (and transnational human rights NGOs).

Foreign aid has often been linked to the human rights practices of recipients. Many countries have reduced aid in response to human rights violations (and, to a somewhat lesser extent, increased aid to reward improved human rights performance). Some countries, however, including Canada, the Netherlands, and Norway, have gone further, choosing aid recipients in significant measure on the basis of good or improving human rights records.

States also have a variety of other relations that they can manipulate in order to support their bilateral human rights policies. At the lowest level, which shades into diplomacy, states may engage in symbolic gestures, such as recalling an ambassador for consultations or delaying the nomination of a new appointee to a vacant ambassadorial post. Cultural contacts can be expanded or curtailed, as can joint military or political actions. Trade relations have occasionally been curtailed. Very rarely, diplomatic relations may be broken.

The use of material means of persuasion and coercion, however, are often problematic. As a result, there has been a general move away from most sanctions over the past two decades.

Cutting development assistance, assuming that that assistance had previously been effectively employed, perversely punishes people for being oppressed by their government. Major economic sanctions, although relatively rare, have also had such perverse results, perhaps most dramatically in Iraq in the 1990s where at least tens of thousands of children died because of the impact of sanctions on health care and sanitation. (South Africa under apartheid is the one clear exception, in part because there was considerable support from the majority of the South African population for the sanctions but also because they proved, in the end, not to be particularly punishing.)

There has thus been a move to "targeted sanctions." For example, rather than block investment in a country, the overseas bank accounts of rights-abusive foreign leaders and officials are targeted. In rare cases, though, such as Myanmar and North Korea, where a brutal government has insinuated itself in all areas of the economy and society, suspending all but the most narrowly defined humanitarian aid may prove the right course, all things considered.

The coercive power of sanctions, however, is limited, especially in cases of severe violations (which are, ironically, typically the only cases where sufficient support for sanctions can be mobilized to implement them). Where human rights violations are so severe and systematic that comprehensive material sanctions seem appropriate, perhaps even demanded, they are unlikely to have much effect. Rulers in North Korea and, until recently, Myanmar, need little from the outside world—because they are willing to make their people suffer the consequences of being denied access to external resources. Comprehensive sanctions thus are likely to have little direct or immediate impact.

Nonetheless, to most human rights advocates sanctions still seem appropriate even when they have little prospect of altering the behavior of the target government. This raises the question of what we expect international human rights policies to achieve.

4. The Aims of Human Rights Policy

The most obvious aim of international human rights policies and initiatives is to improve the human rights practices of the targeted government. This is indeed an important objective, but it is not the only aim. Sometimes it is not even the principal purpose.

International human rights policies that do not eliminate or even reduce the violations being immediately addressed may nonetheless reduce or prevent further deterioration. They may also deter future violations of a comparable type. States may be reluctant to appear to be bowing to external pressure. That pressure, though, may be factored into calculations in the future, especially if there is a reasonable prospect that it will be repeated. The deterrent effect may also operate on countries other than the direct target of action.

International human rights policies may have punitive effects even where they have no remedial effect. Making the lives of human rights violators less pleasant is a good thing, even if it does not improve the lives of their present or future victims.

Even where there is no discernible direct impact—immediately or in the future, remedial or punitive, in the direct target or in other countries engaging in similar violations—there may be a diffuse impact. International human rights policies reinforce and help to further disseminate international human rights norms. Over time this may subtly but significantly change the context of national or international action. In the most optimistic scenario, new generations of leaders and citizens may, as a result of regular and aggressive international human rights policies, internalize human rights norms to a much greater extent than their predecessors.

Finally, even if we have reason to believe that our policies will have no discernible impact on the world, they may nonetheless be appropriately undertaken simply because they are right. Our values demand that we act on them simply because they are our values. Taking a stand is something that we owe ourselves, and those who share our values.

5. Foreign Policy and Human Rights Policy

Issues of tradeoffs and (in)consistency are regularly raised in discussions of international human rights policies. Some human rights advocates are uncomfortable with—even critical of—balancing human rights against competing foreign policy objectives. Human rights advocates also are often critical of "inconsistent" policies that treat comparable human rights violations in different countries differently.

Such criticisms, however, typically fail to distinguish international human rights policy from national foreign policy; that is, they fail to take seriously the idea that human rights are but one of many interests pursued in foreign policy. Human rights interests *should* be balanced against other national interests—which sometimes appropriately take priority—and states in their foreign policy should aim for *foreign policy* consistency, even if that means treating similar human rights violations differently.

Moralists may see the demands of human rights as categorical. Foreign policy decision makers, though, are not independent moral actors. Their job is not to realize personal, national, or global moral values but to pursue the national interest of their country. They are office holders, with professional and ethical responsibilities to discharge the particular duties of their office. There certainly are moral and legal constraints on the pursuit of the national interest, but the principal aim of national foreign policy is the national interest, which includes many objectives, and those varied interests regularly conflict and thus must be balanced against one another.

As we saw above, many countries today include fostering the international realization of human rights in their definition of the national interest, but the national interest—and thus the goals of foreign policy—are not reducible to human rights. The issue then is not whether human rights are appropriately balanced against other objectives of foreign policy—if they are national interests there is no reasonable alternative to such balancing—but what weights should be assigned to the values being balanced.

The foreign policies of most states can, in a highly stylized fashion, be said to include security, economic, and other goals. Most states tend to rank these classes of goals in roughly this order, but there are also gradations within each category. High-order security interests usually take priority over all other objectives of foreign policy, including human rights, and there is nothing wrong with that *as a matter of national foreign policy*. Low-level security interests, however, often are appropriately sacrificed to major economic or other concerns, including human rights, and this too is entirely appropriate.

Setting priorities among various national interests is an essential part of the process of defining the national interest. International human rights law does not oblige states to include human rights among their foreign policy objectives, but states are free to use the full range of foreign policy instruments short of force on behalf of international human rights. For those states that have included international human rights in their foreign policies we can reasonably demand that human rights actually enter into calculations balancing competing interests, with a weight that roughly matches their stated place in the hierarchy of national interests.

Two tests are particularly revealing. Are human rights objectives pursued with "friends" as well as "enemies"? Do human rights policies sometimes cause problems in other areas? If so, there is at least prima facie evidence that human rights really are being taken seriously in a country's foreign policy.

People may reasonably disagree over whether a state has appropriately ranked its international human rights objectives or is doing enough on their behalf. At minimum, though, we should insist that pursuing human rights objectives should sometimes be inconvenient, even costly—as the pursuit of security and economic objectives regularly are. Otherwise, human rights are not really a part of foreign policy, but a moral add-on after the "real" foreign policy decisions have been made—which was the typical situation before the transformation of foreign policies noted above that took place in the 1970s, 1980s, and 1990s.

There *is* something morally disquieting about subordinating international human rights objectives to national security objectives—let alone economic objectives. Often, though, this is the right thing to do, all things considered, *as a matter of national foreign policy*. Critics may reasonably argue for moving international human rights objectives up on the list of national foreign policy priorities. In the foreseeable future, though, there is no prospect that they will reach the pinnacle, let alone occupy that pinnacle alone. The national interest and the "human interest" represented by universal human rights cannot be expected to coincide—although we can reasonably work to bring them closer together.

We should thus not bemoan tradeoffs of human rights to other foreign policy interests—any more than we bemoan the sacrifice of economic interests to human rights interests—so long as these tradeoffs properly reflect reasonable assessments of the value of the interests at stake. We should also not criticize as inconsistent treating comparable human rights violations differently—any more than we bemoan pursuing comparable international economic interests more aggressively in some countries than in others—so long as the differences reflect a reasonable balancing of the full range of national interests at stake in the particular cases.

Hypocrisy, however, is a completely different matter. When there is not a reasoned justification for the subordination of international human rights objectives, in terms of previously established foreign policy priorities, we have not a defensible foreign policy tradeoff but an unjustifiable sacrifice of human rights interests. If human rights almost always lose out in a contest with almost any other foreign policy objective, we have concrete evidence that a country's international human rights objectives have been assigned a very low priority. In such a case, though, the problem is not inconsistency but the inadequate weight or attention given to international human rights objectives.

I have admittedly drawn the distinction between morality and foreign policy overly sharply. In countries with international human rights policies, human rights are matters of both moral and national interest. Moral inconsistency thus does pose problems for foreign policy. Although the inconsistent pursuit of material interests does not damage those interests, the inconsistent pursuit of moral interests may. Being inconsistently self-interested is not a problem. Being inconsistently moral often is.

Again, though, hypocrisy seems to get at the problem better than "inconsistency." Professions of commitment to human rights values that are not backed up by actions that regularly have at least modest foreign policy costs suggest the sort of hypocrisy that undermines human rights as both a moral interest and a national interest. These must be avoided. A policy that carefully balances human rights against other national interests, however, is unlikely to undermine either the moral character or instrumental value of human rights.

Many states have made substantial progress toward a serious and substantial incorporation of human rights into their foreign policy. Most if not all, though, have more that they can do. We cannot be satisfied with the fact that compared to thirty years ago most democratic states today have more aggressive and more effective international human rights policies. The moral demands of human rights continue to push for a deeper penetration of human rights into national foreign policy and a greater willingness to take full advantage of the space available for the pursuit of international human rights objectives.

6. The Limits of International Action

Part 4 of this book has focused on multilateral and bilateral human rights action. Human rights, however, are ultimately a profoundly *national*, not international, issue. In an international system where government is national rather than global, human rights are by definition principally a national matter. States are the principal violators of human rights and the principal actors governed by international norms. They are also the principal protectors of human rights. Thus the probable impact of international action is limited.

The likelihood of international implementation and enforcement is also reduced because international action on behalf of human rights rests on perceived moral (rather than material) interdependence. Other states are not directly harmed by a government's failure to respect human rights; the immediate victims are that government's own citizens. Therefore, the self-interested incentives of other states to retaliate are low, or at least intangible.

In addition, "retaliation" is difficult. The only leverage available, beyond moral suasion, must be imported from other issue areas, such as trade or aid. This makes retaliation relatively costly and increases the risk of escalation. In addition, because the means of retaliation are not clearly and directly tied to the violations, its legitimacy is likely to be seen as more questionable.

Even in the best of circumstances, respecting human rights is extremely inconvenient for a government—and the less pure the motives of those in power, the more irksome human rights appear. Who is to prevent a government from succumbing to the temptations and arrogance of position and power? Who can force a government to respect human rights? The only plausible candidate is the people whose rights are at stake.

Foreign pressure may help to remove a repressive government. With luck and skill, foreign actors may even be able to place good people in charge of finely crafted institutions based on the best of principles. They may provide tutelage, supervision, and monitoring; moral and material support; and protection against enemies. All this is extremely unlikely. Even if we do attribute such unrealistically pure motives and unbelievable skill and dedication to external powers, though, a regime's ultimate success—its persistence in respecting, implementing, and enforcing human rights—will depend principally on *internal* political factors.

A government that respects human rights is almost always the legacy of persistent national political struggles against human rights violations. Most governments that respect human rights have been created not from the top down but from the bottom up. Paternalism, whether national or international, is unlikely to produce respect for human rights.

The struggle for international human rights is, in the end, a series of national struggles. International action can support these struggles, or it can frustrate and sometimes even prevent them. International action is thus an important factor in the fate of human rights. Although it is almost never the most important factor, this does not suggest giving up on international action. Quite the contrary, few states press at the limits of the possibilities of international action in either their bilateral relations or their activities in international organizations.

Furthermore, there is a paradox at the heart of international action: precisely where it is most needed it is least likely to be effective. When human rights violations are gross, systematic, and severe the target regime usually must put itself out of business in order to remedy the human rights abuses. Survival, in other words, is at stake. The resources of international actors, however, although hardly trivial, are almost never anywhere close to adequate to either compel or induce regime change. Cases of genocide may be an exception, discussed in chapter 15. (The other notable exception is providing safe haven for a dictator who sees the writing on the wall and chooses to flee rather than continue to fight. Examples include the shah of Iran, Idi Amin, and Ferdinand and Imelda Marcos.) The most likely targets for immediate success in altering the practices of targeted governments thus involve small or modest changes, especially in countries with fair to relatively good general human rights records. In such cases—which involve convenience rather than survival—the inconveniences of international pressure (or positive inducements) may be enough to induce the regime to alter particular human rights practices.

I also emphasize the limits of international action because the academic study of human rights has been, and still remains, dominated by students of international law and politics. In addition, policy-oriented discussions of human rights in North America, and to a lesser extent in Europe, have focused predominantly on human rights practices abroad and on the ability of Western governments to influence them. If my arguments above are correct, such scholarly efforts have been misdirected, at least in part.

I do not suggest that the international dimensions of human rights have been studied too much. It is clear, however, that the national dimensions have been woefully insufficiently studied. We should not stop studying the international dimensions of human rights, let alone give up pursuing human rights goals in national foreign policies and through international and regional regimes. We must not forget, though, that international mechanisms are, at best, supplemental to national endeavors. Furthermore, even specialists in international relations cannot successfully carry out studies of human rights independent of the work of students of national or comparative politics. We must also pay greater attention to the interaction of national and international factors in the success or failure of international initiatives.

The principal target of international action on behalf of human rights, no less than national action, is national governments. International factors are a significant but subsidiary part of the picture of implementing and enforcing international human rights.

Part 4 thus ends, appropriately, by once more emphasizing the interaction between the universality and the particularity of human rights. The moral universality of human rights, which has been codified in a strong set of authoritative international norms, must be in the end realized through the particularities of national action.

Appendix: Arguments against International Human Rights Policies

As R. J. Vincent put it at the outset of *Foreign Policy and Human Rights*, "there is no obvious connection between human rights and foreign policy" (1986: 1). In fact, there are at least three standard arguments against making the connection. The realist rejects a concern for international human rights because foreign policy ought to be about the national interest defined in terms of power. The statist (or legalist) considers an active concern for the human rights practices of other states inconsistent with the fundamental principle of state sovereignty. The relativist (or pluralist) views international human rights policies as moral imperialism.

These arguments point to problems in overemphasizing human rights in foreign policy. They do not, however, establish that the human rights practices of other states are or ought to be an illegitimate concern of foreign policy. The practice of contemporary states clearly demonstrates that it is possible to pursue substantial, strong, and at least sometimes effective international human rights policies.

A. The Realist Argument

Realists see international politics as a struggle between self-aggrandizing states in an environment of anarchy. Faced with a world of potential or real enemies and no government to turn to for protection, a concern for power must override just about everything else. To act in any other way—for example, to pursue justice or act out of compassion—would leave oneself open to, even invite, attack. Foreign policy, to use Hans Morgenthau's famous formulation, is (must be) about the "[national] interest defined in terms of power" (1954: 5). An intrinsic concern for human rights in foreign policy, as opposed to using human rights instrumentally to further the national interest, would be a dangerous mistake.

Realists argue that state leaders, because of the nature of their office and the realities of international politics, cannot afford to act on the basis of moral considerations. Morality is appropriate to individual relations but not to the relations of states.[2] Thus Reinhold Niebuhr's *Moral Man and Immoral Society* (1932) emphasizes the disjunction between the individual world of moral relations and the world of collective action, which is dominated by power. The tragic necessity of amorality, even immorality, is for the realist an enduring, almost a defining, fact of international relations.

Power, however, is at most only the cardinal, not the exclusive, concern of foreign policy. Furthermore, it is an empirical question whether the pursuit of other concerns is in fact compatible with the pursuit of power. Realism, if true, reveals the danger of overemphasizing human rights, but that is quite a different matter from excluding them altogether on principle.

Morgenthau argues that "the principle of the defense of human rights cannot be consistently applied in foreign policy because it can and must come in conflict with other interests that may be more important than the defense of human rights in a particular circumstance" (1979: 7). Although this is true of most objectives of foreign policy, realists (rightly) do not rail against pursuing economic interests, friendly diplomatic relations, cultural contacts, or the principle of *pacta sunt servanda* (agreements must be kept) because they sometimes conflict with the pursuit of power. We should not accept such arguments with respect to human rights.

In certain contingent circumstances it may be unwise to pursue human rights. That, however, must be determined empirically, case by case. Realists simply are not entitled to categorically exclude human rights (or any other concern) as a legitimate goal of foreign policy.

B. The Statist (Legalist) Argument

The practice of international relations is structured around the principle of sovereignty, which grants a state exclusive jurisdiction over its own territory and resources, including its population. Sovereignty in turn implies nonintervention in the internal affairs of other states. The statist or legalist argues that human rights must be excluded from foreign policy because what a state does with respect to its own nationals on its own territory—which is what we usually are concerned with when we discuss human rights violations—is

---

2. "I stick to the fundamental principle that lying is immoral. But I realize that when you are dealing in the context of foreign policy, lying is inevitable. In private affairs, however, you do not deceive others, especially friends" (Morgenthau 1979: 10–11).

on its face an archetypal matter of sovereign national jurisdiction and thus of no legitimate concern to other states.

Where the realist is concerned with the realities of power in an environment of anarchy, the statist stresses the most important and most widely accepted limits on the pursuit of power, namely, sovereignty and the traditional body of international law that flows from it. Where the realist argues that it is unwise to pursue human rights in foreign policy, the statist argues that it contravenes the fundamental structural and normative principles of international politics.

Statists, like realists, begin from an important insight. For all the talk of globalization, states remain the primary actors in contemporary international relations. However much we may talk of world public order, international law is at its core a law of sovereignty, and virtually all states in every region regularly insist on the primacy of sovereignty, especially when their own sovereign rights are at stake.

Sovereignty, however, is the starting point of international law, not its end point. In fact, international law can be seen as the body of restrictions on sovereignty that have been accepted by states through the mechanisms of custom and treaty. Over the past half-century an extensive body of international human rights law has been developed. Human rights thus have become a legitimate subject in international relations even from a strict legalist position—because sovereign states have chosen to make them so.

The weakness of existing international implementation and enforcement mechanisms might allow the statist to argue that incorporating human rights into foreign policy still contravenes the fundamental principle of nonintervention. In practice, many states whose human rights practices are called into question make precisely such an argument, even when they are willing to raise human rights issues elsewhere. But most instrumentalities of foreign policy—for example, diplomatic representations and granting (or withdrawing) preferential trade agreements—do not involve intervention. Such means may be used on behalf of human rights as legitimately as they may be used on behalf of other goals of foreign policy. Illegitimate intervention occurs only when influence is exercised through strongly coercive, essentially dictatorial means, usually involving the use or threat of force. So long as such means are avoided, statism provides no ground for excluding human rights concerns from foreign policy.

C. The Relativist (Pluralist) Argument

Viewed as a way to protect one's own state from outside interference, statism fits nicely with realism. Many proponents of a strong principle of nonintervention, however, advance a relativist argument that emphasizes the principle of self-determination or a commitment to international pluralism. A country's social and political order, it is argued, should be, on its face, entirely a matter of domestic jurisdiction. In human rights terms, it reflects (or at least ought to reflect) the exercise of basic human rights such as the right to political participation.

Pluralists argue that each society, acting collectively and independent of external coercion, ought to be allowed to choose its own form of government. Within a certain range of freedom, the autonomous choices of a free people should be respected. A similar conclusion can be reached by stressing the positive value of cultural diversity or respect for the values of other peoples and cultures.

Realists often make similar relativist arguments. For example, Morgenthau speaks of "the issue of what is now called human rights—that is, to what extent is a nation entitled and obliged to impose its moral principles upon other nations?" (1979: 4). Kennan argues that "there are no internationally accepted standards of morality to which the U.S. government could appeal if it wished to act in the name of moral principles" (1985/86: 207). But this simply is not true in the case of human rights.

Virtually all states regularly and explicitly proclaim their commitment to the human rights enumerated in the Universal Declaration and the International Human Rights Covenants. To act on behalf of internationally recognized human rights is not to impose one's own values on other countries. It involves an effort to bring the practice of other governments more into line with their own professed values (which we share).

There *are* authoritative international human rights norms. So long as human rights policy is based on these norms, it does not reflect moral imperialism. In fact, failure to insist on compliance with internationally recognized human rights norms perversely risks reverse racism or elitism. The standards of internationally recognized human rights are minimal standards of decency, not luxuries of the West. Given their extensive formal and informal endorsement, as expressed in international legal and overlapping consensus universality (see section 6.2), pursuing international human rights objectives in foreign policy is completely appropriate.

Part V

Contemporary Issues

13

Human Rights, Democracy, and Development

Human rights has become a hegemonic political idea in contemporary international society, a widely accepted standard of international political legitimacy (see section 4.1). Development and democracy also have a comparable status in the contemporary world. Regimes that do not at least claim to pursue rapid and sustained economic growth ("development"), popular political participation ("democracy"), and respect for the rights of their citizens ("human rights") place their national and international legitimacy at risk.[1]

The relationship between these goals, however, is complex. This chapter challenges the comfortable contemporary assumption that, as the Declaration and Programme of Action of the 1993 Vienna World Conference on Human Rights put it, "democracy, development and respect for human rights and fundamental freedoms are interdependent and mutually reinforcing." Without disparaging the important practical and theoretical linkages, and without denying that they *may be made* interdependent, I focus on tensions between the logics of human rights, democracy, and development.[2]

The consequences of development for human rights, and of human rights for development, are in large measure political and they vary considerably with time, place, and policy. The same is true of democracy and human rights. Unless democracy and development are understood and pursued in very particular ways, they may place human rights at risk.

1. Exceptions such as North Korea or Taliban Afghanistan typically advocate an ostensibly counter-hegemonic revolutionary ideal and are (self-consciously) isolated from an international society that tends to ostracize them.
2. I do not pursue relations between democracy and development for reasons of space, interest, and the focus of this book.

I. The Contemporary Language of Legitimacy

The link between legitimacy and prosperity (which today we regularly speak of in terms of development) is close to a universal, cross-cultural political law. Whatever a ruling regime's sociological and ideological bases, sustained or severe inability to deliver prosperity, however that may be understood locally, typically leads to serious political challenge.

Democracy has much less regularly been a ground for legitimacy. Most polities throughout history have rested authority on a divine grant, natural order, or tradition that has legitimated hierarchical rule by those with superior "virtue" (defined by birth, age, gender, wealth, skill, or power). For the past half-century, however, most regimes have appealed to bottom-up authorization from "the people" rather than a "higher" source.

Human rights began to make claims for a similar status following World War II. Since the end of the Cold War human rights has joined democracy and development to complete a legitimating triumvirate.

Democracy, development, and human rights do have important conceptual and practical affinities. Most obviously, international human rights norms require democratic government. As Article 21 of the Universal Declaration puts it, "The will of the people shall be the basis of the authority of government." Democracy, although not necessary for development (especially in the short and medium run) may restrict predatory misrule that undermines development. Civil and political rights provide accountability and transparency that can help to channel economic growth into national development rather than private enrichment. The redistributions required by economic and social rights similarly seek to assure that prosperity is diffused throughout society. Conversely, those living on the economic edge, or with no realistic prospect of a better life for their children, are less likely to be willing to accommodate the interests of others or respect their rights.

Realizing such affinities, however, depends on context, institutional design, and political practice. For example, people often want to do extremely nasty things to some of their "fellow" citizens. Vast inequalities in countries such as Brazil and the United States underscore the central role of politics in translating "development" (aggregate national prosperity) into the enjoyment of internationally recognized economic and social rights. South Korea and Taiwan, as well as western Europe in the nineteenth century, show that development can be sustained for decades despite systematic denials of civil and political rights. During the Cold War, numerous states justified systematic sacrifices by appeals to the "higher" imperatives of development and democracy.

Although appeals to alleged development imperatives that override human rights still are a feature of contemporary international discussions, arguments of interdependence have become the norm since the end of the Cold War. The power of this new vision of international legitimacy is evident in the surprisingly rapid demise of most of the standard regime types of the Cold War era. Peoples' democracies—which sacrificed the rights of class enemies to a greater (party-specified) collective good—passed rapidly from the scene wherever the people were offered a choice. National security states—which sacrificed whatever and whomever they deemed necessary in the struggle against communism—have also become discredited. So have paternalistic regimes, which once were a fairly popular postcolonial form of government.

We should not overemphasize the power of the idea of human rights. Economic failure has been central to the collapse of most alternatives. Popular demands for democracy and human rights have often been naive. Official policy statements are often disingenuous. Appeals to cultural relativism and national particularities have hardly disappeared from discussions of human rights. Nonetheless, the strong endorsement of the universality of internationally recognized human rights at the World Conference on Human Rights in Vienna in 1993, despite the substantial efforts of China and its allies on behalf of a strong cultural relativism, illustrates the dramatic change in dominant international attitudes.[3] Even "the war on terror" has not led to a systematic subordination of human rights (or democracy or development). Whatever the gap between theory and practice, most states today prominently feature appeals to human rights, democracy, and development in their efforts to establish national and international legitimacy.

As a practical matter, much of the appeal of this vision rests on the success of Western liberal democratic (and social democratic) welfare states. Economically, they are very well off—yet remain deeply committed to an extensive, redistributive welfare state. Politically, they enjoy vigorous and open competitive electoral systems—along with an unusually strong consensus on basic political values and structures. And nowhere else has so much progress been made in assuring that close to the full population enjoys most internationally recognized civil, political, economic, and social rights. This particular fusion of development, democracy, and human rights, however, also reflects a distinctive and contingent balancing of markets (development), elections (democracy), and individual human rights.

3. The Vienna Declaration asserts that "the universal nature of these rights and freedoms is beyond question." "All human rights are universal, indivisible and interdependent and interrelated. The international community must treat human rights globally in a fair and equal manner, on the same footing, and with the same emphasis. . . . it is the duty of States, regardless of their political, economic and cultural systems, to promote and protect all human rights and fundamental freedoms."

2. Defining Democracy

"Democracy is based on the freely expressed will of the people to determine their own political, economic, social and cultural systems and their full participation in all aspects of their lives." This statement from the Vienna Declaration is as good a place as any to begin. Like all plausible definitions, it is rooted in the etymology of the term, the Greek *demokratia*, literally, rule or power (*kratos*) of the people (*demos*).

In ancient Greece, however, the *demos* was not the whole population, but rather a particular social class, the masses: *hoi polloi*—literally "the many," with the same social connotations as the transliterated term in Victorian England. Athenian democracy, even in its "Golden Age," was class rule by ordinary citizens, a class (of free males) that typically saw their interests as opposed to their aristocratic, oligarchic, or plutocratic "betters." Throughout most of its history, the theory and practice of democracy has focused on opposing claims to authority by competing social classes. Thus David Held begins *Models of Democracy* by defining democracy as "a form of government in which, in contradistinction to monarchies and aristocracies, the people rule" (1987: 2).

Democracy therefore has had, until relatively recently, a bad name—consider, for example, the negative connotations even today of "demagogue," a leader of (speaker for) the people—and not just because democrats until the late eighteenth century almost always lost in the struggle with their "betters." Unless we assume, as few societies have, that reason or virtue are more or less randomly distributed among citizens or subjects, the claims of ordinary citizens to rule rest on "mere numbers." Thus from Plato and Aristotle through Kant and Hegel, democracy was disparaged as incompatible with good government. Even advocates of mixed or "republican" regimes—from Aristotle to Machiavelli, Madison, and Kant—counterbalanced the interests and claims of the many by the claims of the few to superior wisdom or virtue.[4] Only over the past two centuries—and especially the past sixty or seventy years—have liberal, socialist, and anticolonial struggles transformed dominant conceptions of "the people," and thus delegitimated nondemocratic rule.[5]

---

4. Even the American Revolution was more "republican" than "democratic": the leading political parties in the early republic styled themselves Republicans and Federalists; "Democrats" did not become a major force for forty years. Likewise, the strong democrats of the French Revolution were largely defeated. The term "democracy" did not gain widespread political currency in France until 1848. Rosanvallon (1995: 140).

5. Democracy has also been advocated on instrumental grounds: for example, as a device to limit abuses of power or to balance competing class interests. I am interested here, however, only in arguments for democracy as an intrinsically desirable form of rule.

What, though, does it mean for the people to rule? Held offers a partial list of common meanings:

1. That all should govern, in the sense that all should be involved in legislating, in deciding on general policy, in applying laws and in governmental administration.
2. That all should be personally involved in crucial decision making, that is to say in deciding general laws and matters of general policy.
3. That rulers should be accountable to the ruled; they should, in other words, be obliged to justify their actions to the ruled and be removable by the ruled.
4. That rulers should be accountable to the representatives of the ruled.
5. That rulers should be chosen by the ruled.
6. That rulers should be chosen by the representatives of the ruled.
7. That rulers should act in the interests of the ruled. (1987: 3)

The last of these senses, although often encountered, is not a defensible conception of democracy. Chinese emperors, Bourbon kings, and Ottoman sultans all (contentiously yet plausibly) claimed to rule in the interests of the people. Government *for* the people may or may not be democratic. Democracy, if that term is to mean more than the absence of systematic misrule by a narrow segment of society, must be government *of* or *by* the people. Beyond benefiting from good governance, the people in a democracy must, at minimum, be the source of the government's authority to rule. More plausibly, they must also have at least a central role in the activity of rule.[6]

Held's six other senses, however, encompass an immense variety of political forms that can plausibly be called democratic. Furthermore, there is considerable room for variation within each sense. What does it mean to "be involved" in decision making? What are the mechanisms and measures of "accountable" government? How should the ruled "choose" their rulers? To return to the Vienna formulation, the trick is to determine "the freely expressed will of the people."

Democratic theories often are distinguished by their reliance on either substantive or procedural tests. Rousseau provides a good illustration of the difference. The will of the people might be determined by consulting them, directly or through representatives. Rousseau, however, disparages this (procedural) "will of all," which often expresses only particular individual and group interests. Instead he advocates following "the general will," the reflective, rational

---

6. There is an interesting parallel here with the distinction between having a right and being a rights-less beneficiary of someone else's obligation.

interest of the whole people—which frequently is *not* the same as (and sometimes not even close to) the aggregated preferences of individuals and groups.[7]

Substantive conceptions, however, tend to lose the link to the idea of the people *ruling*, rather than just benefiting. "Democratic" thus easily slides into a superfluous synonym for "egalitarian." Substantive conceptions are also subject to a variety of practical problems and abuses, ranging from naive overestimates of the goodness of real people to a paternalism that sees the people as needing to be directed by those with the virtue or insight needed to know their "true" interests.

The tendency in recent discussions to stress procedural democracy thus is, in my view, generally justified. Although popular and policy discussions, especially in the United States, often overemphasize multiparty elections, leading procedural conceptions in the theoretical literature also stress mechanisms to assure an open and unfettered electoral process. For example, Robert Dahl's "polyarchy," a common reference point in scholarly discussions, requires not only free and fair elections based on an inclusive franchise but also extensive political freedom to assure truly open elections, including the right of all to run for office, freedom of expression, access to alternative sources of information, and freedom of association (1971, 1989).

Elections, however, no matter how free and open, are merely mechanisms for ascertaining the will of the people. Pure procedural democracy can degenerate into empty formalism. Substantive conceptions rightly insist that we not lose sight of the core values of popular authority and *effective* control over government.

Rather than extend this discussion of forms and types of democracy,[8] I want to bring it to a close by noting the important role of adjectives—e.g., subtantive, procedural, electoral, direct, representative, liberal, guided, people's—in most discussions of democracy. I will argue that the human rights work of most contemporary democracies is rooted in substantive adjectives such as the term liberal. And electoral democracy, even in a broad, polyarchic sense of the term, falls far short of the demands of internationally recognized human rights.

3. Democracy and Human Rights

Democracy and human rights share a commitment to the ideal of equal political dignity for all. Furthermore, international human rights norms, as we

---

7. *Social Contract*, book 2, chapter 3. Rousseau even argues that "while it is not impossible for a private will to be in accord on some point with the general will, it is impossible at least for this accord to be durable and constant. For by its nature the private will tends toward having preferences, and the general will tends toward equality" (book 2, chapter 1).

8. Those interested in pursuing the diversity of definitions should begin with Collier and Levitsky (1997), which is close to exhaustive with respect to recent procedural accounts.

have already noted, require democratic government. The link, however, need not run in the other direction. Democracy contributes only contingently to the realization of most human rights. Even where democracy and human rights are not in direct conflict, they often point in significantly different directions.

A. Empowerment: Of Whom? For What?

Democracy aims to empower the people collectively to assure that they, rather than some other group in society, rule. Democracy allocates sovereign authority to the people who, because they are sovereign, are free, as the Vienna Declaration put it, "to determine their own political, economic, social and cultural systems."

Human rights, by contrast, aim to empower individuals—and thus *limit* the sovereign people and their government. The acceptable range of political, economic, social, and cultural systems and practices is severely restricted by the requirement that every person receive certain goods, services, and opportunities. Beyond who ought to rule—which is indeed given a democratic answer—human rights are concerned with what rulers do, with how the people (or any other group) rules.

Democracies have a significantly better *average* human rights record than nondemocratic regimes. Some nondemocratic states, however, perform better on many rights than some democratic states. Furthermore, human rights practices among democracies vary dramatically.

Democracy contributes to realizing human rights *only* if a sovereign people wills respect for human rights, and thus constrains its own interests and actions. In practice, however, the will of the people, no matter how it is ascertained, often diverges from the rights of individual citizens.[9] Electoral democracies often serve the particular interests of key constituencies. Direct democracy, as ancient Athens dramatically illustrates, can be remarkably intolerant.

Marxist "peoples' democracies" provide a striking example of the differences in the political projects implied by "All human rights for all" and "All power to the people." The dictatorship of the proletariat, whatever the practical problems of real-world Stalinist regimes, was rooted in the classical democratic ideal, updated with a deeply egalitarian vision of the proletariat as a universal class.[10] Those claiming human rights who insisted on pursuing class (or other selfish) interests inconsistent with the interests of the people (proletariat) were, in the name of democracy, to be coerced into compliance

---

9. One may stipulate that the people don't *really* will anything inconsistent with internationally recognized human rights. For example, Rousseau claims that the general will is always perfect and incorruptible (*Social Contract*, book 1, chapter 3). In such a case, however, either democracy or human rights becomes superfluous.

10. For a defense of Marx's democratic credentials, see Miller (1986).

with the good of all. Any other alternative would be, in an important sense, antidemocratic.

Human rights advocates would respond, "So much the worse for democracy." In fact, human rights are in an important sense profoundly antidemocratic. The US Supreme Court is often criticized as antidemocratic, because it regularly frustrates the will of the people. It is. And that is a very good thing indeed. A central purpose of constitutional review is to assure that the people, through their elected representatives, do not exercise their sovereignty in ways that violate basic rights.

At this point, if not earlier, a frustrated reader might respond that people today have in mind not ancient Greece or theorists like Kant and Madison, let alone Marx. History and etymology inform but do not determine contemporary conceptions of democracy, which have as their standard referent governments like those of Britain, France, Germany, India, Japan, and the United States.

Fair enough. But exactly what form of government is this?

B. Liberal versus Electoral Democracy

The standard answer from comparative politics is "liberal democracy," a very specific kind of government in which the morally and politically prior rights of citizens (and the requirement of the rule of law) limit the range of democratic decision making.[11] Democracy and human rights are mutually reinforcing in contemporary liberal democracies because the competing claims of democracy and human rights are resolved in favor of human rights.

In liberal democracies, some rights-abusive choices are denied to the people ("Congress shall make no law . . .") and some rights-protective choices are mandated ("Everyone has the right . . ."). Democratic or popular rule operates only within the constraints set by individual human rights. The liberal commitment to individual rights more than the democratic commitment to popular empowerment makes contemporary liberal democracies rights-protective. The adjective "liberal" rather than the noun "democracy" does most of the human rights work.[12] The struggle for liberal democracy is a struggle for human rights only because human rights have been built into the definition through the adjective. In fact, I would suggest that a more descriptive term would be "democratic liberalism" because in "liberal democracies" the

11. There is no necessary connection, however, between democracy and the rule of law. The people may choose to rule through standing, neutral laws or through some other mechanism. Conversely, nondemocratic regimes in principle may (although in practice rarely do) respect the rule of law.
12. As elsewhere in this volume, I use "liberal" to refer to theories and supporters of rights-based political systems (pretty much across the conventional left–right spectrum).

democratic logic of empowering the people is subordinated to a logic that limits what the people or their representatives may legitimately do.

The link between electoral democracy (or democracy without adjectives) and human rights, however, is tenuous. Although electoral democracy may remove old sources of violations, it need not take us very far toward implementing or enforcing many human rights. Establishing secure electoral democracy in, say, Libya, will only be a small (if valuable) step toward establishing a rights-protective regime.

The "democratic revolutions" of the 1980s and 1990s undoubtedly benefited human rights. But even where antidemocratic forces have not reasserted themselves, numerous internationally recognized human rights continue to be violated systematically in a number of new but illiberal democracies. Those not part of the group that exercises the power of the people still need the protection of human rights against democratic governments.

This is *not* a matter of "immature" (electoral) versus "mature" (liberal) democracies. Liberal democracy is tempered or constrained, not matured (fully developed), electoral democracy. Similar difficulties beset efforts to talk about liberal democracy as thick, full, or robust, in contrast to a thin electoral democracy. The differences are qualitative not quantitative. Rather than completing or realizing the full logic of popular rule, liberal democracy puts popular rule in its proper place: subordinate to human rights.

Such distinctions are of more than theoretical interest. The struggle for human rights can be subtly yet significantly eroded if merely electoral democracies are treated, even implicitly, as reasonable approximations, or a step toward the more or less automatic achievement, of liberal democracy. This is an especially important caution for US foreign policy, which grossly overemphasizes the mechanism of elections.

4. Defining Development

Definitions of development are almost as diverse as, and perhaps even more contentious than, definitions of democracy.[13] I will distinguish between conceptions that emphasize either *economic* development, understood largely in terms of growth in national productive capabilities, and those that stress *human* development, often very broadly understood.

Defining development as substantial, sustainable growth in per capita gross domestic product (GDP), along with an associated structural transformation

13. A good standard textbook introduction can be found in Todaro (1994: chapter 3). Dickson (1997: part 1), although a basic introductory undergraduate text, is useful. See also Weiner (1987). Much more heterodox are Escobar (1995) and Sachs (1992). See also Grillo and Stirrat (1997); Marglin and Marglin (1990); and Hobart (1993).

of the economy, despite decades of criticism, continues to dominate the economic, political, and popular mainstreams.[14] The renaissance of market-oriented economic strategies in the past three decades has increased the grip of growth conceptions of development: markets are social institutions tuned to maximize growth (aggregate output).

The most forceful and influential critics of the 1970s and early 1980s emphasized "dependency," conceptualizing underdevelopment as the result of mal-development (rather than a natural, pre-industrial state).[15] Although theoretically moribund today, the dependency perspective usefully focused attention on the dark distributional underside of standard growth strategies. Partly in response, mainstream perspectives now emphasize long-term or sustainable growth. (In addition to a broader time frame, sustainable development perspectives give attention to environmental and other "externalities" excluded from neoclassical accounts.) Nonetheless, this richer and more holistic understanding of economic processes still sees the capacity for autonomous increases in productive capability, and thus per capita GDP, as what is to be sustained.

More radical alternatives to growth-based understandings of development have emphasized equity or social justice rather than narrowly "economic" processes. The United Nations Development Programme (UNDP) vision of "sustainable human development" provides the current culmination of this movement:

> We define human development as expanding the choices for all people in society. . . . There are five aspects to sustainable human development—all affecting the lives of the poor and vulnerable:
>
> Empowerment—The expansion of men and women's capabilities and choices increases their ability to exercise those choices free of hunger, want and deprivation. It also increases their opportunity to participate in, or endorse, decision-making affecting their lives.
>
> Co-operation—With a sense of belonging important for personal fulfillment, well-being and a sense of purpose and meaning, human development is concerned with the ways in which people work together and interact.
>
> Equity—The expansion of capabilities and opportunities means more than income—it also means equity, such as an educational system to which everybody should have access.
>
> Sustainability—The needs of this generation must be met without compromising the right of future generations to be free of poverty

14. Classic examples include Rostow (1960) and Chenery and Syrquin (1975).
15. Cardoso and Faletto (1979) is often considered to be the most subtle and powerful statement of the perspective. The best brief analytical overview remains Palma (1977).

and deprivation and to exercise their basic capabilities.

Security—Particularly the security of livelihood. People need to be freed from threats, such as disease or repression and from sudden harmful disruptions in their lives. (1997: chapter 1; compare Anand and Sen 1996)

Although I have considerable sympathy with the motives behind such efforts, I reject them *for my purposes here* on analytic grounds. "Human rights and sustainable human development are inextricably linked" (UNDP 1998) only by definitional legerdemain. "Sustainable human development" simply redefines human rights, along with democracy, peace, and justice, as subsets of development. Aside from the fact that few ordinary people or governments use the term in this way, such a definition leaves unaddressed the relationship between human rights and *economic* development, an important domain of contemporary social action and aspiration. Real tensions between these objectives cannot be evaded by stipulative definitions.

Less radical equity-oriented conceptions face similar problems.[16] For example, "redistribution with growth" is indeed a desirable objective, but it involves two processes, redistribution and growth, that sometimes support and sometimes conflict with each another. As with liberal democracy, two fundamentally different social and political logics are combined. Although I endorse this combination no less heartily than I endorse liberal democracy, there are analytical and political reasons to draw attention to the differences between the logics of growth and redistribution. Thus by "development" I will mean sustainable growth of per capita GDP.[17]

5. Development-Rights Tradeoffs

The contemporary tendency to conflate all good things—reflected not only in discussions of sustainable human development but in some of the more extravagant recent accounts of human security (see section 15.5)—stands in sharp contrast to the conventional wisdom of the Cold War era. Human rights

16. For example, UNDP's annual *Human Development Report* uses a measure that combines per capita GDP with life expectancy and literacy. Although better than GDP alone, it fails to address the relationship between the social and economic indicators of "human development," which reflect very different political logics. Adding life expectancy and literacy does not get us all that much closer to human rights.

17. One final definitional issue should be noted. The 1986 Declaration on the Right to Development (General Assembly resolution 41/128) rests on a conception of development that is as broad as "sustainable human development," and poses similar analytical drawbacks. Elsewhere (Donnelly 1985, 1993) I have argued at length against the moral, political, legal, and analytical wisdom of recognizing such a human right. Here I simply note that the human right to development fails to address the relationship between *economic* development and the human rights specified in the Universal Declaration and the international Human Rights Covenants.

advocates then regularly faced the argument, advanced with considerable vigor from both ends of the political spectrum, that "the necessity of development . . . supersedes all other legitimate claims and prior rights" (Ruffin 1982: 122); that "impressive economic performance . . . in the modern period has depended upon massive poverty and political repression, and it would not have been possible under democratic governments pursuing egalitarian economic policies" (Hewlett 1980: 4); and that "the tough political systems associated with successes (in satisfying basic needs) . . . have not so far had a good record in terms of liberal virtues. . . . a more liberal political system may be incapable of producing and sustaining the reorientation in the economy necessary for these types of success" (Stewart 1985: 212). Development was regularly held to conflict with human rights, at least in the short- and medium-term time frames within which politicians and development planners operate.

Such arguments have not disappeared from national and international discussions. For example, they remain a staple in the self-justifications of rights-abusive Asian regimes. They are also an implicit element of the standard IMF-imposed structural adjustment package. Tradeoff arguments therefore continue to deserve (critical) attention, which I offer in this section.

Three tradeoffs have been widely advocated.

The needs tradeoff.[18] Rather than devote scarce resources to social programs to satisfy basic human needs (and associated human rights to, for example, food and health care), relatively high levels of absolute poverty (need deprivation) must be accepted in order to maximize investment. This forgone consumption, however, will be returned with interest in the additional production purchased, thereby minimizing the total economic and human cost of overcoming mass poverty. A "strong" needs tradeoff attempts to constrain and control consumption in order to capture the largest possible share of total resources for investment. A "weak" needs tradeoff simply excludes consumption-oriented human rights from development planning.

The equality tradeoff.[19] A "weak" equality tradeoff is based on the so-called Kuznets (1955) or (inverted) U hypothesis. Both average incomes and income inequality tend to be lower in the "traditional" sector than in the "modern" sector. Therefore, during the transition to a modern economy, inequality in the size distribution of income will first increase, then be maintained at a high

18. "An autonomous reduction in consumption . . . is the human price that must be paid for a rapidly growing domestic national product" (Enke 1963: 181). "A conscious effort must be made to increase savings, either from existing incomes or by capturing a major share of the rising incomes that result from inducing greater effort and productivity" (Morris 1967: 306).
19. "Equality, in other words, is a luxury of rich countries. If a poor society is to achieve anything at all it must develop a high degree of inequality—the small economic surplus must be concentrated in a few hands if any high-level achievements are to be made" (Boulding 1958: 94). "There is likely to be a conflict between rapid growth and an equitable distribution of income; and a poor country anxious to develop would probably be well advised not to worry too much about the distribution of income" (Johnson 1962: 153).

level, and finally recede at moderately high levels of national income, thus producing a U-shaped curve when inequality is plotted against the per capita gross national product (GNP).

A "strong" equality tradeoff sees inequality as a contributor to, not just an unavoidable consequence of, development. Because only the relatively well to do can afford to save and invest, and because investment is the key to rapid growth, inequality is often held to be in the long-term best interest of the poor. Inequality is also often justified as an incentive or reward for superior economic performance.

The liberty tradeoff.[20] The exercise of civil and political rights may disrupt or threaten to destroy even the best-laid development plan. Elected officials may feel pressured to select policies based on short-term political expediency rather than insist on economically essential but politically unpopular sacrifices. Freedoms of speech, press, and assembly may be exercised so as to create or inflame social division, which an already fragile polity may be unable to endure. Free trade unions may merely seek additional special benefits for a labor aristocracy. Elaborate and punctilious legal systems on the Western model may seem to be extravagant anachronisms. Civil and political liberties, it is therefore argued, must be temporarily suspended.

All three tradeoffs have been widely held to be not only necessary but also temporary and self-correcting. The trickle-down theory of growth is a theory of eventual automatic returns to the poor. The U hypothesis envisions an automatic return to greater equality. Growth and development have been widely held to be crucial to establishing, maintaining, and expanding liberty in the Third World. So long as rapid growth was achieved it was expected that everything else would take care of itself. Each of these tradeoffs thus implies "growth first" development strategies.

Such arguments, however, are tragically misguided. Particular sacrifices of human rights *may* contribute to development. Categorical tradeoffs, however, are almost always unnecessary and often positively harmful. Human rights tradeoffs, except perhaps at the very early stages of the move from a "traditional" to a "modern" economy,[21] are not development imperatives but policy choices undertaken for largely political, not technical economic, reasons.

It is relatively easy to make such an argument in the case of the needs and equality tradeoffs on the basis of the so-called East Asian model of development.[22] Countries such as South Korea and Taiwan—which, it must

20. See, e.g., Lipset (1959), Bayley (1964), Bhagwati (1966), Huntington (1968), and Huntington and Nelson (1976).
21. I canvassed such an argument, not entirely unsympathetically, in sections 2 and 3 of chapter 10 of the first edition of this book.
22. Much of chapter 9 of the first edition was devoted to developing just such an argument, in some detail, in the case of South Korea.

be remembered, in the 1950s were generally seen as relatively *un*likely cases for development success—achieved extremely rapid growth and substantial structural transformation of their economies without gross income inequality (as measured by international comparisons) and with steadily improving basic needs satisfaction pretty much across the entire income distribution.[23] There is considerable, often vociferous, debate over the sources and causes of this performance and the extent to which it may be replicable elsewhere. Nonetheless, it is clear that in at least certain circumstances, aggressive policy interventions are able to harmonize the pursuit of growth and economic and social rights.[24]

The liberty tradeoff, however, is more problematic for my argument.

6. Development and Civil and Political Rights

There is a strong historical correlation between repression and the early stages of rapid economic growth and structural economic transformation. It is unclear, however, that the relationship is causal. I think that it is very difficult to argue convincingly that repression has been *necessary* for development, rather than convenient for those in charge of the state and the economy. (Let me immediately add, however, that it is no less difficult to argue convincingly that it is not necessary.)

It would appear to be extremely difficult, perhaps impossible, to avoid some repression. I would suggest, however, that this may be due as much as anything to the fact that peaceful structural change of any sort is difficult (especially when it cannot be buffered by the side payments to disadvantaged groups that a high level of development makes possible). Although often functional for *particular* "development" strategies, most repression, rather an economic necessity, appears to be rooted instead in contingent local political opportunities, problems, and challenges and the particular interests of those doing the repressing.

23. On the East Asian combination of growth, needs satisfaction, and relative income equality, see, for example, Leipziger and Thomas (1997), Campos and Root (1996), Rowen (1998), and Goodman, White, and Kwon (1998).

24. Although these countries followed an outward-looking, export-oriented development strategy that explicitly incorporated certain international market signals into the planning process, internal markets were not even close to "free" and the relationship to international markets was highly managed. Furthermore, the equity benefits were substantially dependent on aggressive policy interventions to redistribute resources to rural areas. It is crucial to recognize "the strategic role of states in directing a process of economic development with distributive as well as growth objectives, resulting in a relatively egalitarian pattern of income distribution compared with other industrializing regions such as Latin America" (White and Goodman 1998: 13).

If this is even close to correct, we need to turn our attention—for the liberty tradeoff no less than the needs and equality tradeoffs—away from general blanket arguments toward detailed empirical studies of the conditions in which human rights and development are and are not competing goals. That, however, is the work for economists and country specialists, not human rights theorists. What I can offer instead is a critique of contemporary mirror-image arguments that suggest a necessarily positive relationship between human rights and development.

Sustainable industrial growth has been achieved by repressive regimes in South Korea, Taiwan, Singapore, and China in recent decades, replicating the earlier experience of western Europe. Most developmental dictatorships, however, have been dismal failures. In sub-Saharan Africa, even short-term growth rarely was achieved. In socialist party-state dictatorships, along with most Latin American and Asian military dictatorships and civilian oligarchies, short- and medium-term growth proved unsustainable. Those forced to sacrifice personal rights and liberties usually have not received development (sustainable growth) in return.

In large measure because of this experience, blanket advocacy of the liberty tradeoff—a staple of the 1960s and 1970s—is rarely encountered today.[25] "Soft" authoritarianism still receives some respect, especially when, as in Singapore, promised economic goods are delivered. The growing tendency, however, is to emphasize compatibilities between civil and political rights and development. For example, international financial institutions over the past quarter century have increasingly emphasized the economic contributions of "good governance."[26]

Even where sustained economic development has been achieved by highly repressive regimes, there is little evidence that repression has been *necessary* for, rather than not incompatible with, development. Therefore, because the liberty tradeoff is intrinsically undesirable, it is entirely appropriate to emphasize, and explore the conditions that allow for or encourage the compatibility between civil and political rights and economic development.

7. Markets and Economic and Social Rights

The relationship between development and economic and social rights is more complex, especially when we consider the role of markets. Markets are social institutions designed to produce economic efficiency. Countries such as Cuba and Sri Lanka, which achieved short- and medium-term success but long-term

25. China is the major exception that proves the rule. When the rhetoric is repeated in places like North Korea, Myanmar, and Belarus, few take it seriously, either inside or outside the country.
26. Perhaps the most important multilateral statement is World Bank (1992). See also Stiefel and Wolfe (1994) and Ginter, Denters, and Waart (1995).

failure under development plans emphasizing state-based redistribution, suggest that a considerable degree of economic efficiency (and thus reliance on markets) is necessary for *sustainable* progress in implementing economic and social rights.

Nonetheless, the often-uncritical contemporary enthusiasm for markets, especially in the United States, is extremely problematic from a human rights perspective. Like pure democracy, free markets are justified by arguments of collective good and aggregate benefit, not individual human rights. Markets foster efficiency, not social equity or the enjoyment of individual rights *for all*. Rather than ensure that people are treated with equal concern and respect, markets systematically disadvantage some individuals to achieve the collective benefits of efficiency.

Markets, *by design*, distribute growth without regard for individual needs and rights (other than property rights). Market distributions reflect economic value added, which varies systematically across social groups (as well as between individuals). The poor tend to be "less efficient"; as a class, they have fewer of the skills valued highly by markets. Their plight is exacerbated when, as is often the case, political disadvantage reinforces a vicious rights-abusive cycle.

Market advocates typically argue that in return for such short-term disadvantages for the few, everyone benefits from the greater supply of goods and services made available through growth. "Everyone," however, does not mean each and every person. The referent instead is the *average* "individual," an abstract collective entity. And even "he" is assured gain only in the future. In the here and now, and well into the future, many human beings and families suffer.

Efficient markets improve the lot of some—ideally even the many—at the cost of (relative and perhaps even absolute) deprivation of others. Furthermore, that suffering is concentrated among society's most vulnerable elements. Even worse, because markets distribute the benefits of growth without regard to short-term deprivations, those who suffer "adjustment costs"—lost jobs, higher food prices, inferior health care—acquire no special claim to a share of the collective benefits of efficient markets. One's "fair share" is measured solely in terms of efficiency (monetary value added). The human value of suffering, the human costs of deprivation, and the claims they justify, are outside the accounting of markets.

All existing liberal democracies use the welfare state to compensate some of those who fare less well in the market. The underlying logic is that individuals who are harmed by the operation of social institutions (markets and private property rights) that benefit the whole are entitled to a fair share of the social product their participation has helped to produce. The collectivity that benefits in the aggregate has an obligation to look after individual members who are disadvantaged in or harmed by markets. The welfare state guarantees *all* individuals certain economic and social goods, services, and opportunities irrespective of the market value of their labor.

Assuaging short-term suffering and assuring long-term recompense—which are matters of justice, rights, and obligations, not efficiency—are the work of the (welfare) state, not the market. They raise issues of individual rights that markets simply cannot address—because they are not designed to.

Free markets are an economic analog to a political system of majority rule without minority rights. Like pure democracy, free markets sacrifice individuals and their rights to a "higher" collective good. The welfare state, from this perspective, is a device to assure that a minority that is disadvantaged in or deprived by markets is treated with minimum economic concern and respect. Because this minority is shifting and indeterminate—much like the minority that would engage in unpopular political speech or be subject to arbitrary arrest—these "minority rights" are defined as individual rights for all.

Human rights are required to civilize both democracy and markets by restricting their operation to a limited, rights-defined domain. Only when the pursuit of prosperity is tamed by economic and social rights—when markets are embedded in a welfare state—does a political economy merit our respect.

8. The Liberal Democratic Welfare State

The liberal democratic welfare states of western Europe, Japan, and North America are attractive models for much of the rest of the world because of the particular balance they strike between the competing demands of democratic participation, market efficiency, and internationally recognized human rights. Democracy and development, however, in the absence of a prior commitment to the full range of internationally recognized human rights, lose much of their attraction.

Democracy is almost always preferable to authoritarian rule.[27] Liberal democracy, however, is preferable to merely electoral democracy. Markets are preferable to command economies. Welfare states, however, are preferable to free markets. In both cases, a logic of universal individual rights constrains an essentially collectivist, utilitarian logic of aggregate benefits in order to

---

27. A free people may reasonably choose an efficient benevolent autocrat over a corrupt incompetent democratic regime. Rarely, however, will such a choice actually be faced (or even available), efficient benevolent autocrats being extraordinarily rare.

assure that the common good or good of all is pursued in ways consistent with the rights of each.

All actual liberal democratic welfare states fall short of realizing all human rights even for all their own nationals. Nonetheless, only such states are systematically committed to the full range of internationally recognized human rights. Only in such states do robust markets and democracies operate within systematic limits set by human rights. And only (or at least primarily) because of such limits are their markets and democracies worthy of emulation.

If the deepest and broadest attractions of the regimes we most admire arise from their commitment and contribution to human rights, we need to keep that in the forefront of the language by which we speak of them. If we are really interested in regimes that protect the full range of internationally recognized human rights—which is what I think most well-meaning Western advocates of "democracy" have in mind—why not just say that? Why take the risk of being misread, or glossing over the crucial qualifying adjectives, by talking about democracy? My argument might then be reformulated as a plea for a focus on the creation of rights-protective regimes, as defined by the Universal Declaration of Human Rights.

Those regimes will be democratic. They are desirable, however, because we think that we have good reason to believe that empowering the people is the best political mechanism we have yet devised to secure all human rights for all. Rights-protective regimes will also pursue economic development. Development, though, is desirable as much for the resources it makes available to provide economic and social rights for members of disadvantaged groups as for the intrinsic value of the goods produced.

Countless people over hundreds of years have struggled and suffered for democracy and development. Usually, though, they have seen them not as ends but as means to a life of dignity. Contemporary international society has in substantial measure defined such a life of dignity in terms of respect for internationally recognized human rights. My plea is to keep human rights, and thus this particular understanding of the substantive commitment to human dignity, explicitly central in our political language. Unless we keep human rights explicitly at the center of the discussion, we will place needless conceptual and practical hurdles in the pursuit of such policies that seek equal concern and respect for all.

14

The West and Economic
and Social Rights

O ver the past three decades, discussions of economic and social human rights have become deeply entwined with controversies over the role of markets in Western democracies and economic liberalization and structural adjustment in the Third World. This political context has supported a widespread perception among human rights scholars and activists that the West is and has been hostile, or at best indifferent, to economic and social rights. Adamantia Pollis, for example, asserts "The Western doctrine of human rights excludes economic and social rights" (Pollis 1996: 318–19), and Chandra Muzaffar writes, "The dominant Western conception of human rights . . . emphasizes only civil and political rights" (Muzaffar 1999: 29).[1]

This story has increasingly come to take a "three generations, three worlds" form: successive generations of civil and political rights, economic, social, and cultural rights, and solidarity or peoples' rights being championed by the West, socialist countries, and the Third World respectively.[2] The international norm of the interdependence and indivisibility of all human rights is presented as a compromise forced upon a resistant West, which with the

---

Parts of this chapter are drawn from an article I originally wrote with Daniel Whelan (Whelan and Donnelly 2007), and much of the material about the drafting of the Universal Declaration and International Human Rights Covenants draws heavily on Whelan (2010: chaps. 3–6).
1. Compare Wright (1979: 19), Hehir (1980: 9), Henry (1996: xix), Felice (2003: 7), and Senarclens (2003: 141).
2. On three generations, see Vasak (1984, 1991), Marks (1981), Flinterman (1990), Mbaye (2002: 47–48), Smith (2003: 46–47), Tomuschat (2003: chap. 3), and Ishay (2004: 10–11, chaps. 2–4). Gros Espiell (1979) and Pollis (1992) are classic statements of the three worlds argument. For an extended general critique of idea of three generations of human rights, see Donnelly (1993: 125–31). To appreciate the utter lack of historical basis of such claims, consider simply the famous triads of Locke, Jefferson, and the French revolution: life, liberty, and property; life, liberty, and the pursuit of happiness; and liberty, equality, fraternity.

coming of globalization has come to pursue an ever more narrowly one-sided emphasis on civil and political rights (Otto 2001: 55; Felice 2003: 7; Evans 2005: 57, 60, 61).

This myth of Western opposition to economic and social rights is patently ludicrous. It is hard to imagine that anyone could look at the welfare states of Europe and claim with a straight face that economic and social rights "are largely dismissed in the West" (Chomsky 1998: 32). Neither in the development of international human rights law nor in national or international practice is there the slightest evidence of Western resistance to economic and social rights. Even in the United States there has not been categorical opposition to economic and social rights but rather an attempt to realize more of them through market rather than state mechanisms. *This* story, I argue, has important implications for the current assault by the political right in the United States on "entitlements."

I. The Universal Declaration of Human Rights

Adherents of the Western opposition thesis typically argue that the Universal Declaration of Human Rights, the foundational document of the global human rights regime, undervalues economic, social, and cultural rights, which were included only in the face of Western opposition. "The UDHR contains primarily civil and political rights (those favored by Western nations) as well as a few economic, social, and cultural rights (those championed by the Third World and the Soviet bloc)" (Renteln 1990: 30). "The insistence on including SE [social and economic] rights as rights of equal status in the UDHR was the result of the demand of the USSR and its bloc of nations" (Gavison 2003: 54n46). "Western states originally resisted including economic and social rights in the Universal Declaration" (Henkin 1995: 191). "The West proposed proclaiming at the world level *only the civil and political rights.* . . . It was only in a second stage, given the hostility of the Socialist countries and under strong pressure from the Latin Americans . . . that the West agreed to incorporate into the Universal Declaration a number of economic and social rights as well" (Cassesse 1990: 35; compare Mbaye 2002: 45).

As Bard-Anders Andreassen delicately puts it, "this theory is not verified . . . by the records of the meetings of the Commission. Right from the beginning of the Commission's work the drafts included rights to social and economic goods and benefits" (1992: 333; compare Morsink 1999: 222–30). None of the passages quoted in the previous paragraph advances even a single supporting source—because the record, which is clear and unambiguous, points in almost exactly the opposite direction.

The Atlantic Charter of August 14, 1941 committed Britain and the United States to "securing, for all, improved labor standards, economic advancement and social security" and the goal "that all the men in all lands may live out their lives in freedom from fear and want." This Atlantic Charter had nothing to do with the Soviet Union or its concerns.

Economic and social rights were included in the initial draft of an international declaration of human rights prepared in the US State Department in the fall of 1942. As Secretary of State Cordell Hull put it in a radio address in July 1942, "Liberty is more than a matter of political rights, indispensable as those rights are. In our own country we have learned from bitter experience that to be truly free, men must have, as well, economic freedom and economic security" (quoted in Whelan 2010: 41).

At the United Nations, "the inclusion of social and economic rights was an uncontroversial decision, tacitly agreed to beforehand. . . . From the very beginning of the drafting process, it was agreed to include these rights in the Declaration" (Samnoy 1999: 11; compare Eide 1995: 28–29; Eide and Eide 1999: 528). In opening the first meeting of the Commission on Human Rights— which, we should recall, was created as a subsidiary body of the Economic and Social Council—Assistant Secretary-General for Social Affairs Henri Laugier, a Belgian, charged the delegates with "showing . . . that today . . . the declaration of the rights of man must be extended to the economic and social fields" (UN document E/HR/6: 2).

The story of the drafting of the Declaration has already been told, most notably by Johannes Morsink (1999) and Ashlid Samnoy (1993). Economic and social rights were central in the original Secretariat Outline (prepared by a Canadian). They remained central when that draft was revised by René Cassin, a Frenchman with a long interest in and involvement with economic and social rights (Agi 1998: 255–62, 358–65). The American delegate and chair of the commission, Eleanor Roosevelt, supported economic and social rights throughout the drafting process. And so forth.

It simply is not true that several Western delegates "had some difficult accepting these new rights as human rights" (Mbaye 2002: 41 [my translation]). Not a single Western state pressed for a Declaration without economic and social rights. Quite the contrary, almost all insisted that economic and social rights were an essential element of the Declaration. The Universal Declaration was drafted precisely at the time of the flowering of the Western welfare state and was seen by most Western states as part of the process of consolidating an understanding of human rights that prominently features economic and social rights. Even Tony Evans, who argues powerfully against the hegemonic Western bias of the global human rights regime, allows that "western states did not reject the idea that economic, social and cultural rights had a proper and appropriate place in any twentieth century declaration" (1996: 77). Western opposition to and Soviet responsibility for including economic and social rights in the Universal Declaration is, as Ashlid Samnoy puts it, "a myth" largely attributable to "later political developments" (1999: 11; compare Craven 1995: 8–9, 16).

2. Domestic Western Practice

The Western opposition thesis becomes patently ludicrous if we look at what Western states were doing at home while drafting the Declaration. I will look briefly at Britain and the United States, the two leading Western powers during and after the war and two of the Western countries usually presented as least sympathetic to economic and social rights.

A. Making the British Welfare State

Britain, the classic home of nineteenth-century laissez faire liberalism, was in the first half of the twentieth century transformed into a comprehensive welfare state, with strong support from all three major parties. "An old system of social provision was finally put aside and a new one . . . took its place." "The social rights of citizens . . . [replaced] the alms and doles of earlier periods" (Bruce 1961: 2, 15).

England's "poor laws," which date to the late sixteenth century, were until well into the nineteenth century "not only outstanding but unique" (Bruce 1961: viii) in accepting ultimate state responsibility for true unfortunates. By the early 1830s, about a fifth of total government expenditure went to poor relief (Bruce 1961: 76). But the desire to keep down poor rates, in the context of massive class bias in the distribution of political rights and a growing moral contempt for the poor, led to chronically inadequate funding that fatally undermined whatever good intentions may have been present. The system was harshly punitive and intentionally so unappealing that only the desperately destitute would accept assistance.

Throughout the nineteenth century, beginning with the Health and Morals of Apprentices Act of 1802 (which covered pauper apprentices in cotton mills), piecemeal legislation addressed a variety of workplace safety, housing, and sanitation issues, as well as maximum hours of work. The period 1905–1911, however, saw a flurry of social legislation that, at least with the benefit of hindsight, began to point toward a welfare state. The 1905 Unemployed Workman Act, for all its inadequacies, clearly established the principle of national responsibility. Lloyd George's Peoples' Budget of 1909 transformed the parameters of British political debate. The 1911 National Insurance Act was the first big step toward the post–World War II welfare state.

Steady incremental progress continued in the interwar period, largely irrespective of the party in power, and World War II facilitated a fundamental change in the British vision of the social compact. In 1940, supplementary pensions were introduced. Just a week after the defeat at Dunkirk, a national milk plan, with the government as the payer of last resort, was introduced. In 1941, the means test was eliminated, marking a decisive move toward universal provision. The Beveridge Report of 1942 set what soon became the almost universally agreed upon framework for the postwar British welfare state, with a focus on full employment, a national health system, and family allowances. 1944 saw major white papers on social insurance and employment policy and the creation of a new Ministry of National Insurance. The end of the war brought the Family Allowance Act (1945), National Insurance Act (1946), National Insurance (Industrial Injuries) Act (1946), National Health Service Act (1946), Children Act (1948), and National Assistance Act (1948).

Including economic and social rights in the Universal Declaration was simply an international expression of the new social compact. Neither domestically nor internationally was there any serious British resistance to incorporating economic and social rights into the dominant system of legal norms and political practices. Quite the contrary, there was immense enthusiasm for that project pretty much across the political spectrum.

The British case thus decisively refutes the common claim that liberals rejected economic and social rights, which were championed instead by socialists.[3] Quite the contrary, liberal leadership was central. In the early years of the twentieth century, as the first elements of the welfare state were being established, "most working men were Liberals, but there were many Conservatives. . . . Socialists were rare and the trade unions mainly concerned with limited practical aims" (Bruce 1961: 139–40). After 1911,

> all major parties [agreed] on expanding social welfare rights: advances were made in the 1920s and 1930s with pensions, expansion of the scope of national insurance, non-contributory national assistance, slum clearance and planning for housing. Harold MacMillan's influential 1933 plea for a national policy on reconstruction and his *The Middle Way* (1938), arguing the necessity for abolition of poverty, need remembering. The Atlantic Charter reference to social security, the joint work of Churchill, Attlee and Bevin, was relied on by Beveridge in his Report, the main thrust of which was accepted by both parties and which would have been implemented in broadly similar fashion by Churchill, had he won the 1944 election. . . . Churchill's 1906 remark that 'we want to draw a line below which we will not allow

3. Ishay (2004: chap. 3) offers a lively, although ultimately indefensible, version of this argument. For a useful brief summary of the eclectic origins of economic and social rights, see Siegel (1985: 260–65).

persons to live and labour' reflects the policy of all United Kingdom parties. (Palley 1991: 58–59)

B. Roosevelt's American Welfare State

The welfare state came to the United States later, more slowly, and with greater reliance on market regulation relative to direct state provision. This certainly had and still has consequences for the nature of the American welfare state (Goodin et al. 1999). Roosevelt and the other architects of the New Deal, however, insisted that an industrial market economy required reconceptualizing traditional American liberties, and economic and social rights were and are no less central to the functioning and legitimacy of the state in the United States than in Europe.

Responding to the profound loss of personal security and freedom caused by the Depression, Roosevelt, in a 1932 campaign speech, called for "an economic declaration of rights" (quoted in Sunstein 2004: 65). The 1936 platform of the Democratic Party proclaimed "We hold these truths to be self-evident—that government in a modern civilization has certain inescapable obligations to its citizens, among which are: (1) Protection of the family and the home; (2) Establishment of a democracy of opportunity of all the people; (3) Aid to those overtaken by disaster" (quoted in Sunstein 2004: 75). In his acceptance speech, Roosevelt explicitly tied these "principles of 1936" to those of 1776: "The rush of modern civilization itself has raised for us new difficulties, new problems which must be solved if we are to preserve to the United States the political and economic freedom for which Washington and Jefferson planned and fought" (Roosevelt 1938: 231).

The most comprehensive statement of this vision came in the 1944 State of the Union Address. Echoing the "four freedoms" speech of three years earlier, Roosevelt suggested that in addition to the rights and freedoms protected by the original Bill of Rights, the nation had already begun to accept a number of self-evident *economic* truths: "true individual freedom cannot exist without economic security and independence. 'Necessitous men are not free men.' People who are hungry and out of a job are the stuff of which dictatorships are made" (Roosevelt 1950: 41).

In transmitting the 1943 report of the National Resources Planning Board to Congress, Roosevelt wrote, "We can all agree on our objectives and in our common determination that work, fair pay and social security after the war is won must be firmly established for the people of the United States of America" (United States National Resources Planning Board 1943). Whatever the disagreements over the details, this was an accurate statement of the changes that had been wrought in American ideas of rights under the dual pressures of the Depression and the war.

Such plans reflected a fundamental rethinking of the relations between state and market, based on the understanding that *unregulated* capitalism posed a profound threat to individual economic security. In a 1932 speech, Roosevelt framed unemployment as a loss of personal security and called for a new understanding of economic and social guarantees as "rights." "Private economic power is, to enlarge an old phrase, a public trust as well." If private industry did not adequately discharge this trust, "the Government must be swift to enter and protect the public interest" (Roosevelt 1938: 753, 755). Likewise, the "right to life" needed to be understood expansively to include "the right to make a comfortable living," an opportunity to acquire a share of the national plenty "sufficient for his needs, through his own work" (Roosevelt 1938: 754). Similar guarantees were required for children, the elderly, the infirm, and others unable to work (Roosevelt 1938: 754).

As in Britain, the internationalization of these domestic principles in the Universal Declaration was "natural" and "organic," pointing toward what Borgwardt (2005) calls "A New Deal for the World."

3. The International Human Rights Covenants

On first sight, the International Human Rights Covenants appear to support the view that "Western states viewed economic, social, and cultural rights with suspicion" (Puta-Chekwe and Flood 2001: 41). The initially envisioned single treaty was divided, largely through Western influence, in order to define less stringent obligations with respect to economic, social, and cultural rights. This, however, simply was not a reflection of the fact that "socialist and capitalist cultures pursued human rights attributes of their political ideologies, one by emphasizing social and economic rights, the other by giving priority to political and civil rights" (Stacy 2004).

The crucial passages appear in Article 2. The International Covenant on Civil and Political Rights (ICCPR) requires parties "to respect and to ensure" the enumerated rights and to provide "an effective remedy . . . [and] to develop the possibilities of judicial remedy." The International Covenant on Economic, Social and Cultural Rights (ICESCR), requires instead that each party "undertakes to take steps, individually and through international assistance and co-operation . . . to the maximum of its available resources, with a view to achieving progressively the full realization of the rights recognized in the present Covenant by all appropriate means, including particularly the adoption of legislative measures."

The clear implication is that civil and political rights can and should be made justiciable in national law. Economic, social, and cultural rights, however, are treated less as individual legal claims than solemn statements of important public policy goals. For economic and social rights, states are obliged (only) to do what resources allow toward progressive realization.

Although these are important differences, nothing in either covenant questions the paramount substantive importance of economic, social, and cultural rights. The implicit logic instead is that most states have the immediate capability to create subjective civil and political rights (Hohfeldian claim rights) in national law for all individuals. Few states, however, have the resources to provide comparable legal guarantees for most economic and social rights. And there was nothing distinctively Western about this view. As the Indian delegate put it during the drafting, referring to developing countries, "their resources and state of economic development did not permit them to implement the economic and social rights at one stroke of the pen" (UN document E/CN.4/SR.248: 6).

Furthermore, in the years following World War II, the implications of making most civil and political rights justiciable were relatively clear. The jurisprudence of most economic and social rights, by contrast, was limited or nonexistent. (The principal exception was workers' rights, which, not coincidentally, are formulated in Articles 6–8 of the ICESCR in much more readily justiciable terms.) In addition, international human rights norms were being established precisely as welfare states were dramatically expanding. Western states thus were profoundly unsure about the practical implications of justiciability—and thus unwilling to accept potentially open-ended obligations. The diversity of national practices also made negotiating detailed justiciable obligations extremely difficult. Add dramatic differences in resource bases, especially across regions, and it was almost impossible to imagine global recognition of anything more than a severely truncated list of seriously justiciable economic and social rights.

Only a tiny minority of commentators, and not a single Western state, seriously resisted international legal recognition of economic and social rights—so long as they were formulated in the "proper" terms of progressive realization. No Western state voted against the ICESCR in either the UN General Assembly or its Third Committee (Social, Humanitarian, and Cultural Affairs). All Western states except the United States have ratified both the ICCPR and the ICESCR.

Finally, understanding economic and social rights as goals of state policy rather than justiciable individual rights is *not* distinctively Western. Quite the contrary, it was shared by virtually all states. *No* state, Western or non-Western, seriously proposed—in the sense of being willing to adopt as a matter of enforceable national law—treating economic, social, and cultural rights as matters of immediate rather than progressive realization.

Consider the actual treatment of economic and social rights in communist states, where, András Sajó writes, "certain social welfare services were indeed provided to a very great number of citizens . . . although they were not provided in terms of rights, i.e. the respective claims were not enforceable in an independent court. These services were administered on a more or less reliable and egalitarian basis as in-kind additional compensation to one's salary. The state had no duties in this respect; it provided its services on a discretionary basis and in exchange for loyalty in everyday life" (Sajó 1996: 141–42). The Soviets, for all their talk about economic and social rights, treated them exactly as the ICESCR does—namely, as important goals of social policy rather than individual rights enforceable in national courts. This is how most economic and social rights have been treated in most of the Third World as well. Ironically (at least from the perspective of the Western opposition thesis), only in the West has substantial general progress been achieved in making a wide range of economic and social rights justiciable.

As for a presence of an individual complaint mechanism for civil and political rights but not economic, social, and cultural rights, this flows directly from the differences in the obligations in the two covenants. Without nationally justiciable obligations to respect and assure economic, social, and cultural rights for all individuals, a quasi-judicial supranational complaint procedure makes little sense (compare Tomuschat 2003: 92).[4]

4. Functional and Regional Organizations

A similar picture is evident when we turn to functional regimes for finance, trade, and workers' rights and the European regional human rights regime. In each case, once again, we find Western states strongly supporting, not resisting or opposing, economic and social rights.

A. Remaking the Global Economy

Full employment was essential to the emerging Western vision of "social citizenship" (Marshall 1950, 1981). The welfare states then coming into being "embodied a notion of citizenship centred on labour market participation," with many of their particular programs and policies shaped by "the fact that

---

4. The initial absence of a Committee on Economic, Social, and Cultural Rights, by contrast, certainly was unjustifiable, but there is no evidence that it seriously bothered the Soviet bloc and Third World, let alone that their sustained efforts to create a committee were blocked by the West. In fact, Alston (1992: 478, citing A/C.3/L.1360) notes that in the final stages of negotiation the United States proposed creating a committee of experts, but this proposal drew little support. Even more problematic is the name "Human Rights Committee" for a body that deals only with civil and political rights. This is indeed an affront to economic, social, and cultural rights. But we cannot put the blame on the West. It appears to be an artifact of an earlier draft of a single covenant that no one on any side of the debate thought to correct.

the vast majority of the population were directly or indirectly dependent on wages for subsistence" (Deakin 2005: 35). A citizen, in this newly hegemonic vision, is entitled not only to legal security and civic and political participation but also to economic and social security and participation.

Therefore, during World War II, Western planners and leaders, haunted by the memory of sustained mass unemployment during the 1930s, stressed the sense of dignity, autonomy, and full and equal participation in society that a job provided.[5] This vision was clearly expressed at the Bretton Woods Conference, which in the summer of 1944 concluded two years of Anglo-American negotiations over the architecture of the postwar international economic order.

Particularly important was agreement on an International Monetary Fund (IMF). Although the IMF is today widely reviled by supporters of economic and social rights, the picture in the 1940s was radically different. Consider the second paragraph of Article 1 of the Articles of Agreement, which set out the purposes of the IMF: "To facilitate the expansion and balanced growth of international trade, and to contribute thereby to the promotion and maintenance of high levels of employment and real income and to the development of the productive resources of all members as primary objectives of economic policy." This passage was not merely unsurprising to contemporaries but "natural" and "necessary." As Dag Hammarskjold put it while he was still permanent secretary to the Ministry of Finance of Sweden, "the aim of economic policy contemplated in the expression 'full employment' has been universally accepted" (1945: 19).

This was no last minute addition to pretty up, or even obscure, cruder material interests. Similar language appears in the 1944 joint statement issued by American and British monetary experts: "To facilitate the expansion and balanced growth of international trade and to contribute in this way to the maintenance of a high level of employment and real income . . . must be a primary objective of economic policy" (Horsefield 1969: 131). That language in turn can be traced back to drafts of what became the Bretton Woods agreement from October and May 1943 (Moggridge 1980: 380; Horsefield 1969: 85–86). The same vision can be seen in Keynes's earliest memos on postwar monetary reform, written in September 1941: "If we fail, our best hopes of finally abolishing economic want and of providing continuous good employment at a high standard of life will be lost to us. A vast disappointment, social disorders and finally a repudiation of our ill-judged commitments will be the result" (Moggridge 1980: 27). At Bretton Woods, Keynes presented the IMF as an essential mechanism for "raising the standard of life and the conditions of

---

5. For a powerful expression of this attitude, see Beveridge's *Full Employment in a Free Society* (1945).

labour everywhere, to make the resources of the world more fully available to all mankind" (quoted in George and Sabelli 1994: 30).

Turning from money to trade, there was "a remarkable degree of unanimity . . . on the interdependence of trade and employment policy" (Gardner 1956: 109). The parallel to Bretton Woods was the October 1946 London International Conference on Trade and Employment. "The separate and equal status of the employment provisions indicated the importance which the subject was accorded in the Anglo-American negotiations" (Gardner 1956: 146). Although an International Trade Organization was ultimately stillborn, the fatal disagreements were about implementation and means, not the centrality of employment and the welfare state. In trade no less than money, the goal was "a relatively open and multilateral system . . . that would reconcile openness and trade expansion with the commitment of national governments to full employment and economic stabilization" (Ikenberry 1992: 290).

The "classical" liberalism of laissez faire trade and the gold standard was replaced by an "embedded liberal" order, to use the phrase coined by John Ruggie (1982: 392–93), designed around the goal of full employment. A new vision of the role of the state with respect to the market was extended, partially, to the international economy in the 1940s and 1950s, both reflecting and attempting to solidify "the shared legitimacy of a set of social objectives to which the [Western] industrial world had moved, unevenly but 'as a single entity'" (Ruggie 1982: 398). Embedded liberalism reflected the deeply rooted intentions and extensive hard work of Anglo-American politicians, planners, and negotiators, as well as their Canadian, French, and other Western colleagues. The Soviet role was less than negligible and the non-Western contribution was insignificant.

B. Workers' Rights

The work of the International Labor Organization (ILO) was briefly discussed in section 11.3.G. Like most of the League of Nations system, the ILO moved toward hibernation in the late 1930s. It sprang to life again, though, at the ILO's 26th General Conference in 1944. This historic meeting adopted, with the enthusiastic support of the United States and Britain, the Declaration of Philadelphia, which is suffused with a vision of international cooperation to realize social citizenship. Article 1 insists that "labor is not a commodity" and that "the war against want requires to be carried on with unrelenting vigor within each nation, and by continuous and concerted international effort." Article 2 asserts that "all national and international policies and measures, in particular those of an economic and financial character, should be judged in this light and accepted only in so far as they may be held to promote and not to hinder the achievement of this fundamental objective," namely, that "all human beings, irrespective of race, creed or sex, have the right to pursue both their material well-being and their spiritual development in conditions of freedom and dignity, of economic security and equal opportunity."

This promise of a new beginning was pursued aggressively in the early years of the peace. Conventions 87 (1948) on freedom of association and 98 (1949) on collective bargaining created a relatively strong system of international supervision that applied even to states that had not ratified those conventions (Haas 1970; Bartolomei de la Cruz, Potobsky, and Swepson 1996: chapters 20–23). Comparable coverage has yet to be achieved in any other area of human rights. Over the following two decades the ILO continued to push forward, adopting important new conventions on social security, equal treatment, and social benefits. These initiatives both reflected the emerging Western welfare states and served as a multilateral mechanism to foster their spread and deepening.

Even today, the area of workers' rights remains the domain of internationally recognized human rights where standards are most fully developed and multilateral monitoring is most advanced. This was not, however, forced on reluctant Western powers. Quite the contrary, they actively supported the formation of the ILO, were the driving force behind its revitalization in the 1940s and 1950s, and have remained (with the exception of the United States) leading supporters.

C. The European Regional Regime

The European regional regime, discussed in section 11.3.A, shows a similar picture. As with the International Human Rights Covenants, civil and political rights are justiciable but economic and social rights are not. These differences, however, have nothing to do with any reticence toward economic and social rights. Rather, they reflect a particular conception of the appropriate nature of regional legal obligations.

As the Parliamentary Assembly of the Council of Europe put it in Recommendation 838 (1978), "in order to be incorporated in the Convention, any right must be fundamental and enjoy general recognition, and be capable of sufficiently precise definition to lay legal obligations on a State, rather than simply constitute a general rule" (quoted in Berenstein 1982: 265). Thus the list of civil and political rights in the European Convention on Human Rights is significantly narrower than in the Universal Declaration, lacking rights to recognition as a person before the law, nationality, freedom of movement, asylum, to take part in government, and to periodic genuine elections. As the Committee of Experts explained in its 1984 report introducing Protocol No. 7, it included "only such rights as could be stated in sufficiently specific terms to be guaranteed within the framework of the system of control instituted by the Convention" (quoted in van Dijk and van Hoof 1998: 681).

Consider also Protocol No. 1, adopted in 1952. In addition to the right to political participation, it also adds the right to property, an economic right, and the right to education, a social or cultural right. These rights are fundamental, generally recognized, and justiciable. The fact that they are economic, social, and cultural rights not only did not preclude their inclusion it seems not to have been a significant consideration at all.[6]

Furthermore, we should disparage neither the substance nor the implementation procedures of the European Social Charter. Its part 1 goes well beyond the ICESCR, with nineteen rights and principles (expanded to thirty-one in the 1996 revised Social Charter) that must be accepted "as a declaration of the aims which it will pursue by all appropriate means." In addition, states must adopt five of seven core articles in part 2 and a total of no less than forty-five numbered paragraphs (increased to six of nine core articles and sixty-three of ninety-eight numbered paragraphs in the 1996 revision). These rights typically are defined in detailed and demanding terms. For example, Article 12 of the Social Charter requires parties to assure that their systems of social security meet, in the 1961 Charter, the requirements of International Labour Convention No. 102 (Concerning Minimum Standards of Social Security), or, in the revised Social Charter, the European Code of Social Security, which includes several pages of detailed standards for benefits for medical care, sickness, unemployment, old age, work accident and disease, family, maternity, disability, and survivors.

Although the Social Charter is not subject to judicial enforcement, the European Committee of Social Rights (ECSR) subjects periodic state reports to fairly rigorous scrutiny, with explicit, paragraph-by-paragraph judgments of conformity or nonconformity. For example, the committee's conclusions for Norway, hardly a laggard in the area of economic and social rights, cover over eighty pages for 2004–2005. Conclusions of noncompliance are further reviewed by the Council of Europe Governmental Committee. Selected regional and national employers and workers organizations and NGOs have since 1998 been authorized to file complaints and are also involved in the work of the Governmental Committee. This is far more rigorous review than under either the ICESCR or the ICCPR.

Could more be done for economic, social, and cultural rights in the European regional regime? Of course. Does the European regional regime disparage economic and social rights? Not at all. Quite the contrary, the European Social Charter provides a substantively more demanding list of rights and a

---

6. The European Convention also includes the right to marry and found a family. Although this right appears in the ICCPR, it is probably best classified as a social right.

significantly stronger review process than the ICESCR or any other regional system.

5. Further Evidence of Western Support

If we take the story from the foundations of the global human rights regime up to the present, we find much the same story of extensive and enthusiastic Western support for economic and social rights.

One standard measure of support is acceptance of international legal obligations. Defining "the West" to include Australia, Austria, Belgium, Canada, Denmark, Germany, Finland, France, Greece, Iceland, Ireland, Italy, Luxembourg, the Netherlands, New Zealand, Norway, Portugal, Spain, Sweden, Switzerland, the United Kingdom, and the United States, twenty-one of these twenty-two countries are parties to both the ICESCR and the ICCPR (the United States is party only to the ICCPR). Nineteen of those twenty-one states became parties to both on the same day (Australia and Greece became parties to the ICESCR five and twelve years, respectively, before becoming parties to the ICCPR). At the broadest normative level, then, the West has expressed not only unusually strong support for economic and social rights—a 95 percent ratification rate compared to an 80 percent rate for other countries—but also equal support for the interdependence of civil and political rights and economic and social rights.

Words, however, are relatively cheap. Domestic action is what really matters. The best single measure of such action is money: the willingness of governments and societies to put their money where their mouths are.

The best series of social spending data, from the Organisation for Economic Co-operation and Development, goes back only to 1980. To avoid distortion from the effects of the global recession, I will stop the story at 2005.

On average, social spending as a percentage of GDP increased by more than a fifth between 1980 and 2005, rising from 18 percent to 22 percent (although the 2005 figure of 22.1 percent is slightly below the 1995 figure of 22.8 percent). As a percentage of government expenditures, social spending rose by 30 percent, from 39 percent in 1980 to 51 percent in 2005, with an unbroken upward trend. In other words, the typical Western government today spends about half of its resources and a fifth of the nation's domestic economic output on social insurance broadly understood: that is, economic and social rights.[7] Measured by government budget outlays, the *primary* business of Western states is economic and social rights.

This data admittedly measures effort rather than outcomes. There are often considerable inefficiencies in transforming social spending into effective

---

7. Computed from OECD.Stat Extracts, http://stats.oecd.org/.

enjoyment of the targeted rights. Quality and coverage also are not addressed in social spending data. Neither are values such as equality and autonomy. In addition, rising overall costs may force retrenchments in particular areas, a particularly serious issue as the ratio of workers to nonworkers declines. Nonetheless, social spending is the single best general measure of societal and governmental effort on behalf of economic and social rights. That evidence shows strong, consistent, and modestly rising Western support for economic and social rights—at least prior to the Great Recession.

Data for the decades immediately following World War II are less consistent and less comparable. The general picture, however, is of steady growth in the range, depth, and coverage of welfare programs during the decades that are often referred to, with good reason, as the "golden age" of the Western welfare state.

For example, for fourteen Western countries, social transfers as a percentage of GDP on average more than doubled from 1950 to 1975, from 7.2 percent to 15.3 percent.[8] Public expenditures as a percentage of GDP in the same period increased by almost 60 percent, from an average of 27.1 percent to 43.1 percent. (Most, although not all, of this increase was due to rising social spending.)

For seventeen Western countries, social welfare spending (principally on pensions, unemployment, health care, family allowances, and income support) as a percent of GDP rose, on average, from 11.2 percent in 1960 to 15.4 percent in 1973 to 21.5 percent in 1982.[9] (Note that variations in definitions and data do not permit comparisons across these sets of figures.)

Coverage is no less important than expenditure. Peter Flora and Jens Alber show that "the period from 1945 to 1960 stands out as the phase of major extension" in the coverage of Western welfare states (1981: 57). For example, pension coverage in eleven Western counties rose from 75 percent in 1945 to 97 percent in 1975 while health coverage rates increased from 69 percent to 92 percent (Ferrera 2005: Table 2.3).

The earnings of workers are one very rough, but ready, indicator of the impact of social welfare policies in industrial societies. In a sample of eleven Western countries, employee compensation as a percentage of national income rose in every country from 1950 to 1970, by an average of 18 percent.[10]

8. Computed from Kohl (1981: Tables 9.1 and 9.4). The countries included are Austria, Belgium, Canada, Denmark, Finland, France, Germany, Italy, the Netherlands, Norway, Sweden, Switzerland, the United Kingdom, and the United States.
9. Computed from Hicks and Misra (1993: Table 2). The countries included are Australia, Austria, Belgium, Canada, Denmark, Finland, France, Germany, Ireland, Italy, the Netherlands, New Zealand, Norway, Sweden, Switzerland, the United Kingdom, and the United States.
10. Computed from Kraus (1981: Table 6.3). The countries included are Austria, Belgium, Denmark, Finland, Germany, Italy, Netherlands, Norway, Sweden, Switzerland, and the United Kingdom.

TABLE 14.1 MEASURES OF WELFARE EQUALITY

	Germany	Netherlands	United States
Pre-government Gini			
1985–1989	0.390	0.349	0.396
1990–1994	0.395	0.360	0.415
Post-government Gini†			
1985–1989	0.235	0.204	0.328
1990–1994	0.250	0.231	0.354
Post-government 90/10 ratio*			
1985–1989	2.9	2.4	4.8
1990–1994	3.1	2.7	5.2

† Income plus transfers minus taxes
* Income of top decile divided by income of bottom decile
Source: Goodin et al. (1999: Appendix Table A3)

Increasing equality, and in particular reducing degrading inequalities, is an important aim of most social welfare systems. Theoretical, data, and measurement issues abound. Goodin et al. (1999), however, provide some useful measures for Germany, the Netherlands, and the United States, which represent the three principal types of Western welfare regimes.[11] Although covering only the period 1985–1994, the data in Table 14.1 is extremely suggestive.[12]

In all three cases, state intervention significantly decreases inequality—by more than a third in the European cases and by a sixth in the United States—as measured by comparing the Gini coefficient of market incomes ("pre-government") with net incomes after transfer payments and taxes.

However one looks at the data, at whatever time in the postwar era, there is a clear and consistent pattern of Western domestic support for economic and social rights.

6. Understanding the Sources of the Myth

In addition to the Western reluctance to create justiciable claims subject to quasi-judicial international monitoring, three additional kernels of truth lie behind the myth of Western opposition—although that myth systematically misrepresents their meaning and significance.

---

11. A threefold division has been standard in the welfare-state literature since Esping-Andersen (1990). See also Huber and Stephens (2001), who add a fourth category for Australia and New Zealand.
12. Pre- and post-government Gini data for Germany for 1973–1993 (Hauser and Becker 2000: Table 2) and 1985–2005 (Sachweh 2008: Figure 1a) paint a similar picture. The same is true for the United States across the 1980s and 1990s (Kelly 2004: Figure 2; Hungerford 2008: Figure 1).

First, in the nineteenth century most Western governments and elites did indeed oppose economic and social rights other than the right to property. By the time of the Universal Declaration, however, *no* Western state had any serious theoretical or practical opposition, domestically or internationally, to economic and social rights.

Second, the aggressive advocacy of markets that began with Thatcher and Reagan provoked exaggerated hopes and fears about the demise of state provision of economic and social rights. In practice, however, neither the Thatcher nor the Reagan government seriously threatened economic and social rights *in general* or even tried to dismantle the welfare state,[13] and few other Western countries have shown even this much enthusiasm for cutbacks in state provision of economic and social rights. Throughout the West we have instead seen selective, largely incremental, retrenchments that have usually been undertaken only reluctantly and regrettably. In the context of day-to-day politics, these retrenchments certainly merit heavy emphasis and attention. From a broad historical perspective, though, this has been minor tinkering at the edges of the welfare state that the myth of Western opposition has misrepresented as full-scale opposition to economic and social rights.

Third, when human rights were reintroduced into international relations in the 1970s—at Helsinki, by the US Congress and the Carter administration, and by a growing range of human rights NGOs—primary attention *in the international politics of human rights* was given to civil and political rights. Legitimate and important critiques of Western and especially US foreign policies, however, spilled over to support a fundamentally inaccurate picture of the Western attitude toward economic and social rights.

Furthermore, the Western neglect of economic and social rights in foreign policy was, and remains, frequently exaggerated. The United States, especially under Carter, included modest attention to basic human needs and subsistence rights. Some Western states, most notably the Netherlands, Norway, and Canada, integrated economic and social rights into their human rights and development assistance policies from the early 1980s on. Since the end of the Cold War, human rights and development policies in the most Western donor countries have begun to come into fruitful interaction. Human rights NGOs have also given more attention to economic and social rights. (Of course, none of this says anything about domestic Western practice, which certainly provides better evidence of Western values.)

---

13. For example, government spending as a percentage of GDP increased in the United Kingdom from 38.8 to 42.3 percent from 1970 to 1995. During this same period, social security transfers increased from 8.3 to 15.4 percent of GDP, and from 1980 to 1995, social expenditure increased from 18.3 to 22.5 percent of GDP. Comparable figures for the United States are 31.6 to 34.3; 7.6 to 13.2; and 13.4 to 15.8 (Burgoon 2001: 530, Table 2).

The second and third of these reasons refer to practices and debates of the 1970s and 1980s. This may seem odd, given the focus here on the years following World War II. I have been able to find no work on the global human rights regime from the 1950s, or even 1960s, however, that adopts the myth. What seems to have occurred is that during the international revival of human rights in the mid- and late-1970s, current debates pitting West against East and North against South (especially in the context of demands for a new international economic order) were unthinkingly projected back into the past, thus facilitating the development and spread of the myth.

Part of the explanation certainly lies in partisan Cold War politics. The myth, however, also reflects a willingness of many in the West to accept uncritically the self-representation of socialist bloc and Third World regimes. The reasons for this were many, including hope and optimism, respect for diversity, and postcolonial guilt. As a result, however, an absurdly charitable reading of the non-Western world was contrasted to a not merely uncharitable but deeply inaccurate caricature of the West.

Economic and social rights are, like civil and political rights, *universal* rights. They are an essential part of any plausible conception of human dignity in the contemporary world, irrespective of region, culture, or worldview. Whatever the (often substantial) shortcomings of Western governments, both at home and especially abroad, the West is the region of the world where the interdependence and indivisibility of all internationally recognized human rights have received their most forceful endorsement and their most consistent and effective application in practice.

7. Why Does It Matter?

Why does it matter what we think about how Western states approached economic and social rights during and after World War II? Beyond any intrinsic value in setting the record straight, the issues have important contemporary practical implications. Especially if we adopt Robert Cox's dictum that theory, and more broadly knowledge, "is always *for* someone and *for* some purpose" (1996: 87), understanding the social forces behind historical representations becomes particularly important. How we construct or choose to remember history has implications for how we act, now and in the future.

The myth of Western opposition impedes rather than contributes to contemporary struggles to defend the welfare state as we have come to know it or to construct humane alternatives (rather than simply return economic and social provision to markets, families, and societies). Ceding the past to far-right free-marketers, as the myth of Western opposition in effect does, is as politically counterproductive as it is historically inaccurate. The Hayeks, Friedmans, and Thatchers ought to be represented as what they are, namely, critics of the mainstream of twentieth-century Western social and political theory and practice. They represent a deviant (although in recent years increasingly influential) strand of theory—a theology of markets—that has in practice been decisively rejected in *every* Western country for more than half a century.

We need to remind both defenders and critics of global markets that what made "the Western model" the envy of much of the rest of the world was not just civil and political rights but also the unprecedented achievements in providing economic and social rights—that is, a profound practical commitment to the interdependence and indivisibility of civil and political and economic, social, and cultural rights. This holds internationally no less than nationally.

As capital and markets increasingly escape state regulation, we must return to the central insight of the liberal democratic welfare state, the UN Charter, the Universal Declaration of Human Rights, and the original Bretton Woods system. Markets are to be valued only for their contribution to human welfare, which requires that markets be tempered by, and embedded within a deeper commitment to, minimal distributional equity, as expressed in internationally recognized economic and social rights.

Franklin Roosevelt, Winston Churchill, Eleanor Roosevelt, John Maynard Keynes, John Humphrey, René Cassin, and a host of less-well-known architects of the postwar international order understood the vital importance of economic and social rights to the welfare of their compatriots, the legitimacy of their own states, and prospects for a just and humane world order. Western publics and elites, for their own good reasons, enthusiastically supported the efforts of their leaders and governments on behalf of economic and social rights. Getting *that* record straight—discursively resituating Western states where they in fact have always been, namely, in fundamental harmony with the basic thrust and demands of the full range of internationally recognized human rights—just may contribute to efforts to protect the liberal democratic welfare state, and the vision of interdependent and indivisible human rights that underlies it, from the host of challenges its faces in the early twenty-first century.

15

Humanitarian Intervention against Genocide

The 1990s produced a "prodigious" stream of humanitarian interventions (Kritsiotis 1998: 1007) running from Somalia, through Bosnia and Rwanda, to Kosovo and East Timor.[1] This body of practice created, remarkably rapidly, a right of humanitarian intervention against genocide that, despite the shortcomings of the international responses to genocide in Darfur, remains an important feature of the international human rights landscape.[2] This chapter examines the legal, moral, and political dimensions of humanitarian intervention—which, as we will see, regularly conflict. I argue that when faced with massive suffering, both intervening and not intervening often seem both demanded and prohibited—especially when, as is usually the case, the UN Security Council is unwilling to take decisive action. This ambivalence, however, is clear evidence of progress from earlier eras when moral outrage at genocide, unless accompanied by major immediate selfish interests, was almost always subordinated to a strong principle of nonintervention.

I. Intervention and International Law

Intervention is ordinarily defined as coercive foreign involvement in the internal affairs of a state; violation, short of war, of a state's sovereign rights;

---

1. For an overview of these cases, see, for example, Tatum (2010). For the Cold War era and pre–World War II practice, see Wheeler (2000) and Carmichael (2009).
2. In a technical international legal sense, genocide is not a human rights violation. Genocide is not mentioned in either the Universal Declaration or the International Human Rights Covenants. It is a unique international crime. In common parlance, however, genocide is a violation of human rights (beyond the violations of internationally recognized human rights involved in genocidal acts). As this is not a technical treatise in international law, I will follow this broader usage here. See also section 6 below.

imposition that impairs a state's policy independence. "Intervene" also has broader senses, as when we speak of intervening in a discussion, but to count even diplomatic expressions of concern as intervention, as many governments have in response to human rights criticism, renders the concept of little interest.

Foreign policy usually aims to influence the behavior of other states, thus "interfering" with their decision making. Persuasive diplomatic "interference," however, stands in sharp contrast to intervention, which coercively seeks to impose one's will. Although nonviolent coercion is possible—an economic boycott may remain entirely peaceful yet be sufficiently punishing to be more coercive than persuasive—I will be concerned here only with armed humanitarian intervention.

Thus defined, intervention is, on its face, illegal. Nonintervention is the duty correlative to the rights of sovereignty. As Article 2.7 of the UN Charter puts it, "Nothing contained in the present Charter shall authorize the United Nations to intervene in matters which are essentially within the domestic jurisdiction of any state." This is reinforced by Article 2.4: "All members shall refrain in their international relations from the threat or use of force against the territorial integrity or political independence of any state."

The legal presumption against intervention, however, can be overcome. For example, Article 2.7 concludes with the proviso that "this principle shall not prejudice the application of enforcement measures under Chapter VII." Furthermore, what is considered to be "essentially within the domestic jurisdiction of any state" may change over time.

2. Humanitarian Intervention and International Law

An intervention is typically called humanitarian if undertaken to halt, prevent, or punish "genocide," understood as gross and systematic and severe human rights violations involving extensive political killing, or in response to humanitarian crises such as famines or massive refugee flows.[3] The nationality of those aided is also relevant. Rescue missions to save one's own nationals, although sometimes called humanitarian interventions, are more accurately seen as self-defense or self-help: they rest on the special bond between states and their nationals, as is underscored by the fact that rescuing states typically fail to assist local citizens facing similar suffering. Humanitarian interventions, to borrow the title of Nick Wheeler's book (2000), are about saving strangers.

Is there a humanitarian exception to the general international legal prohibition of intervention? Prior to the end of the Cold War there clearly

---

3. Murphy (1996: 8–20) provides a good overview of definitional issues.

was not.[4] Although enterprising international lawyers tried to find precedents in the behavior of the European Great Powers in the Ottoman and Chinese Empires in the mid-nineteenth and early-twentieth centuries (e.g., Stowell 1921: 154–59), even a casual student of history must be amused—or shocked—by this notion. These interventions usually were restricted to protecting co-nationals or coreligionists. Many sought not even to alleviate suffering or eliminate discrimination but rather to impose preferential treatment for Westerners or Christians.[5]

During the Cold War, hundreds of regimes were guilty of gross, systematic, and persistent violations of internationally recognized human rights. We can count on our fingers, though—with digits to spare—the interventions with a central humanitarian intent.[6] The regular practice of states when faced with grossly repressive regimes was *not* to intervene. And this was almost universally seen as a matter of obligation. As UN General Assembly Resolution 2625 (XXV) put it, "no state or group of states has the right to intervene, directly or indirectly, for any reason whatever, in the internal or external affairs of any other state." The Security Council, reflecting this understanding, undertook no humanitarian interventions during the Cold War.

Contemporary international human rights law, as we saw above (section 2.6.A and chapter 11) has left implementation of the extensive body of international human rights obligations largely to individual states, typically with only modest supervision by international committees of experts lacking coercive enforcement powers. A very limited humanitarian exception, however, emerged in the 1990s that I will argue represents a desirable development.

First, though, we must consider the moral and political dimensions of humanitarian intervention. Although there is considerable artificiality in the separation of law, morality, and politics, it is a convenient shorthand device to emphasize that considerations of (moral) rectitude, (legal) authority, and (political) self-interest interact in decisions to intervene and in judgments of the legitimacy of intervention. I thus overdraw the distinctions in order to emphasize the interaction of these different types of considerations.

4. Franck and Rodley (1973) provides a classic statement (and defense) of this standard interpretation. See also Brownlie (1973, 1974).
5. For a generally critical but slightly less jaundiced reading of pre–UN Charter practice, see Murphy (1996: 49–64).
6. There are only three prominent candidates: India's intervention in East Pakistan, Tanzania's intervention in Uganda, and Vietnam's intervention in Cambodia. In each case, humanitarian concerns were a secondary or even tertiary consideration. Wheeler (2000: chaps. 2–4) provides useful descriptions and thoughtful evaluations.

3. The Moral Standing of the State

Does the state have a moral standing or are its foundations purely political and legal? Michael Walzer (1977, 1980) presents a social contract justification of sovereign states, based on self-determination, that I find largely persuasive, perhaps because it fits so nicely with the general approach to human rights I have adopted in this volume.[7]

A. Self-Determination and Nonintervention

Drawing heavily on John Stuart Mill's "A Few Words on Non-Intervention," Walzer argues that the sovereign rights of states "derive ultimately from the rights of individuals" (1977: 53). A sovereign state expresses the right of citizens collectively to choose their form of government.

Self-determination, Walzer argues (quoting Mill), is only "the right of a people 'to become free by their own efforts' if they can, and nonintervention is the principle guaranteeing that their success will not be impeded or their failure prevented by the intrusions of an alien power. It has to be stressed that there is no right to be protected against the consequences of domestic failure, even against a bloody repression" (Walzer 1977: 88). Our obligation is to respect the autonomous choices of other political communities. "A state is self-determining even if its citizens struggle and fail to establish free institutions, but it has been deprived of self-determination if such [free] institutions are established by an intrusive neighbor" (Walzer 1977: 87).

States that systematically infringe the human rights of their citizens violate both their international legal obligations and their moral and legal obligations to their citizens. These offenses, however, do not authorize foreign states or international organizations to intervene. "As with individuals, so with sovereign states: there are things that we cannot do to them, even for their own ostensible good" (Walzer 1977: 89). Citizens have no right to good government, or (ordinarily) even to protection against bad government, and foreign states (and nationals) have neither a right nor an obligation to save citizens from their own government.

In grappling with the competing moral demands of human rights and self-determination, Walzer emphasizes respect for autonomy. His critics give priority to the universality of the moral claims of the victims of suffering.[8] This dispute reflects competing conceptions of "the international

7. See, however, Nardin (2002), which contrasts more statist defenses such as Walzer's with an alternative tradition that makes direct appeals to substantive principles of natural law and justice.
8. See especially Beitz (1979, 1980), Doppelt (1978, 1980), Luban (1980a, 1980b), and Slater and Nardin (1986).

community." Walzer's critics give priority to the cosmopolitan moral community to which all individual human beings belong, without the mediation of states. Walzer, however, focuses on the society of states, the ethical as well as political community of sovereign states, which has its own body of ethical norms.

We thus have a dispute over the relative weights to be given to competing ethical principles and obligations. Even Walzer accepts humanitarian intervention in response to genocidal massacres. In fact, some humanitarian interventions *must* be morally permissible if the moral standing of the state rests on self-determination, respect for autonomy, or respect for the rights of citizens. Conversely, even strong cosmopolitans grant some moral standing to at least some states.

B. Pluralism, Paternalism, and Political Community

Robert Jackson offers the closest thing that we have in the recent literature to a principled blanket denial of the legitimacy of humanitarian intervention, based on the values of normative pluralism and anti-paternalism. "Sovereignty is no guarantee of domestic well-being; it is merely a framework of independence within which the good life can be pursued and hopefully realized" (2000: 308). A people has no right to be rescued from misrule, and international society has no right to come between a people and its government, even a brutal, tyrannical government.

Although I have considerable sympathy with the general thrust of this argument, Jackson clearly goes too far. Whatever the political or legal reasons to deny a humanitarian exception to a strong principle of nonintervention, such a position is ethically untenable—at least in a world of universal human rights.

We value pluralism not so much for itself but in so far as it reflects the autonomous choices of free moral agents. Furthermore, not all choices deserve even our toleration, let alone our respect. The spread of international human rights values has substantially reduced the range of defensible appeals to normative pluralism. Unusually severe human rights violations thus may overcome even a strong pluralist presumption against intervention.

Pluralism can also be seen as a rejection of paternalism because it denies autonomous agency. But unusually severe and heinous human rights violations, such as genocide and slavery, are such profound denials of individual autonomy that even a strong presumption against paternalism must give way.

As Walzer puts it, "When a government turns savagely upon its own people, we must doubt the very existence of a political community to which the idea of self-determination might apply" (1977: 101). When human rights violations are "so terrible that it makes talk of community or self-determination . . . seem cynical and irrelevant" (Walzer 1977: 90), the moral presumption against intervention may be overcome. Human rights violations that "shock the moral conscience of mankind" (Walzer 1977: 107) conclusively demonstrate that there are no moral bonds between a state and its citizens that demand the respect of outsiders.

One could argue that from a purely moral point of view, this has always been the case. What has changed is that in the post–Cold War era such violations, especially genocide, are increasingly seen as offenses not simply against cosmopolitan moral values but also against the ethical norms of the society of states. (I will return to this point in the final section below.)

4. Politics, Partisanship, and International Order

States (and international organizations), in addition to being moral and legal agents, are political actors. Therefore, they should be evaluated by political standards. This includes not only the national interests of particular states but also the interests that states and international society have in international order—and in its character.

Political leaders are required, by their office, to give central place in their actions to the interests of their own states. They are also, however, in varying degrees at liberty, expected, or required to take into consideration law, morality, and humanity. (That all of these standards are relevant is a matter of no real controversy, however intense the debate over the relative weights to be assigned to these various concerns.) In addition, the society of states has interests as well as values of its own that its members (states) may also appropriately take into consideration. As a result, states may have good, even sufficient, reasons for not intervening when they are morally and legally authorized.

Even successful, purely humanitarian interventions may threaten international order. The exclusive spheres of domestic jurisdiction provided by territorial sovereignty dramatically reduce the occasions for interstate conflict. Humanitarian intervention reintroduces human rights violations and humanitarian crises as legitimate subjects of violent international conflict. Even if desirable, all things considered, this is not without cost.[9]

I want to focus here, however, on the political problem of partisan abuse. Moral principles alone rarely determine political behavior. International legal precepts regularly are interpreted and applied with an eye to power. Adequately evaluating either individual interventions or proposals for a general

---

9. Bull (1977: chap. 4) provides a classic discussion of the tension between order and justice in international society.

authorizing rule thus requires political knowledge of how doctrines and precedents are likely to be used by those with the power to intervene.[10]

Throughout the Cold War era both the United States and the Soviet Union appealed to "humanitarian" concerns and principles such as "democracy" largely as masks for geopolitical, economic, and ideological interests. The problem then was less too little intervention of the right kind than too much of the wrong kind. A pattern of superpower *anti*-humanitarian intervention, in places such as Guatemala, Hungary, Czechoslovakia, and Nicaragua, was well established.

Therefore, both during the Cold War and in the immediate post–Cold War years I argued strongly against a humanitarian exception to the principle of nonintervention (1984; 1993). Despite the strong moral case, the political and legal environments were so unpromising that giving priority to the danger of partisan abuse seemed the best course. There was a clear international normative consensus, across the First, Second, and Third Worlds, that humanitarian intervention was legally prohibited, and genuinely humanitarian intervention was politically unlikely, not only because of likely veto in the Security Council but because neither superpower had much of an inclination to intervene for reasons that were centrally, let alone primarily, humanitarian.

Today, however, the international environment does not suggest such a blanket rejection. Partisanship remains a serious problem that is likely to increase when bipolar or multipolar political rivalry reasserts itself. (Iraq is the obvious example, even though humanitarianism was not central to the American rationale for intervention.) Interventions not authorized by the Security Council may undermine respect for international law and order even if they have genuinely humanitarian motivations and consequences. And the United Nations has proved no humanitarian panacea, as Rwanda and, only a bit less tragically, Sudan illustrate. Nonetheless, changing conceptions of security and sovereignty—which are closely connected to the growing penetration of international human rights norms into the political thinking of ruling elites, political opposition movements, and ordinary citizens around the globe—have (in my view appropriately) moved international society to accept an anti-genocide exception to the prohibition of intervention.

---

10. For arguments that even in the post–Cold War era the language of humanitarianism remains a mask for great power domination, see Mutua (2001), Hadjor (1998), and, with special reference to Kosovo, Nambiar (2000). Mutua, for example, argues that universal human rights claims are a symptom of "a seemingly incurable virus" that leads the West to assert its "cultural and conceptual dominance" (2001: 210).

5. Changing Conceptions of Security and Sovereignty

The classic referent of "security" in international relations is national or state security, defined primarily in military and secondarily in economic terms. Thus understood, there is no necessary or even obvious connection between security and human rights. In fact, ruling regimes have frequently viewed national security and human rights as competing concerns. Consider, for example, the national security states of Latin America in the 1970s, the states of the Soviet bloc during the Cold War, and the United States during the McCarthy era.

This began to change with the 1975 Helsinki Final Act of the Conference on Security and Cooperation in Europe (CSCE).[11] The states of Europe, plus the United States and Canada, met primarily to ratify the European borders established after World War II and to lay the foundations for a more stable policy of détente. The most important elements of the Helsinki process, however, proved to be its human rights provisions (Thomas 2001).

Human rights were not merely addressed in a major security agreement between the superpowers, they were treated as a security issue. Although the central concern for national security was not supplanted, it was supplemented by a conception of personal security. In a series of CSCE follow-up conferences, Western states emphasized the security of individuals and drew attention to the threats to that security, defined in terms of internationally recognized human rights, posed by Soviet bloc states. In the 1990s, talk of "human security" became all the rage (although in practice we saw, at best, a modest increase in the non-national dimensions of security in the foreign policies of most states).

The Helsinki process, however, did not challenge reigning conceptions of sovereignty. Other than public shaming, foreign states had no direct role in implementing human rights. Challenges to a rigid, legal positivist conception of sovereignty emerged from a more general diffusion of human rights values.

Sovereignty is typically defined as supreme authority: to be sovereign is to be subject to no higher authority. States often present their sovereignty as a natural right or an inescapable logical feature of their existence. In fact, however, it is a matter of mutual recognition: sovereigns are those who are recognized as sovereign by other sovereigns. Furthermore, that recognition never

---

11. The UN Charter, especially in the preamble and Article 1, explicitly links human rights to international peace and security. These statements of moral and political aspirations, however, did not solidify into legal and political norms—let alone practice—in the following decades.

has been unconditional. At minimum, states are required to control their territory and be willing to participate in the system of international law. Historically, other tests have been applied as well.

In the nineteenth century, full sovereign rights were extended only to states that met minimum standards of "civilization" (Gong 1984; Schwarzenberger 1955). Even during the height of nineteenth-century imperialism, Western states recognized (rather than denied or extinguished) the sovereignty of China, Japan, the Ottoman Empire, and Siam. The sovereignty of these "uncivilized" states, however, was treated as impaired. The Chinese description of this period as the era of unequal treaties nicely captures the situation: treaties were between sovereigns but not equals.[12] I would suggest that human rights—or, more precisely, avoidance of genocide—has over the past half-century emerged as something like a new standard of civilization.[13]

Aggression provides another model for understanding changing conceptions of sovereignty. States guilty of aggression forfeit their right to nonintervention, as Iraq after the invasion of Kuwait so dramatically illustrates. Although they remain sovereign, their aggression authorizes international action that infringes their territorial integrity and political independence. States guilty of, or about to embark on, genocide may likewise forfeit the protections of the principle of nonintervention.

We might also think of individuals—or at least large groups of victims of violence—acquiring some sort of international legal standing. Even under classical positivist conceptions of sovereignty, massacring *foreign* nationals in one's own territory was prohibited (as an offense against the state of which they were nationals). A comparable right for one's own nationals seems to have emerged. International society is in effect asserting a legitimate interest in the rights of all human beings threatened by genocide. Genocide has come to be seen as an offense against international society, not just those directly attacked.

The Kosovo intervention, along with Bosnia, East Timor, the strong international reaction against inaction in Rwanda, and the considerable (if inadequate) international response to Sudanese depredations in Darfur, suggest

12. Although this practice reflected crude Western self-interest, it was not simply hypocritical. Japan provides the classic example of a country "graduating" to full status after having made the changes necessary to meet Western standards of "civilization" (Gong 1984: chap. 6; Suganami 1984).

13. I develop such an argument in "Human Rights: A New Standard of Civilization?" (Donnelly 1998). The uncomfortable overtones of abusive paternalism in this language underscore the potential for partisan abuse. Past abuse, however, is no reason to avoid doing the right thing in the future—although it does demand careful, skeptical scrutiny of allegedly principled behavior.

that much of the international community, including some leading powers, is no longer willing to accept continued national authority for implementing the internationally recognized human right to protection against genocide. Law and politics seem to be converging toward the moral view that genocide can be tolerated by neither civilized states nor international society.

6. Justifying the Anti-genocide Norm

The 1948 Convention on the Prevention and Punishment of the Crime of Genocide defines genocide as "acts committed with intent to destroy, in whole or in part, a national, ethnical, racial or religious group, as such" (Article 1). Many mass killings do not meet this authoritative international legal definition. For example, most of the victims of the Khmer Rouge were targeted for political reasons (although certain minority ethnic groups, such as the Cham, were singled out for special attacks that probably did meet the treaty definition). In at least some humanitarian crises—perhaps Somalia in 1992 or eastern Zaire in 1996—suffering has been largely unintended.

I will use "genocide," however, in a looser sense to refer to any killing of large numbers of people in a particular place in a short time. Although international law and many national legal systems provide greater protection against racial and ethnic discrimination than against political discrimination, the trend in recent discussions seems to be toward treating mass killing as mass killing ("genocide"), whatever the reason or modality. (The technically more correct term "politicide" has not caught on outside of a narrow group of scholars.)

The moral case for intervention against "genocide" is relatively unproblematic. The nature of the crime even allows us to use an overlapping consensus argument (see section 4.2) to circumvent the notorious incommensurability of competing moral theories. Whatever one's moral theory—at least across most of today's leading theories and principles—*this* kind of suffering cannot be morally tolerated.

We should not, however, underestimate the problematic character of a narrow genocide exception to a strong principle of nonintervention. If all human rights are interdependent and indivisible, and human rights are about a life of dignity not mere life, then acting forcefully *only* against genocide is highly problematic. We place ourselves in the morally paradoxical position of not only failing to respond to other human rights violations but of failing to respond to comparable or even greater suffering so long as it remains geographically or temporally diffuse. Nonetheless, this seems to me the least indefensible option when we take into account the full range of moral, legal, and political claims in contemporary international society. In the absence of a clear overlapping consensus—which I think exists today only for genocide—the moral hurdle of respect for the autonomy of political communities seems to me insurmountable.

7. Changing Legal Practices

The Genocide Convention (Article 6) specifies enforcement through trial before "a competent tribunal of the State in the territory of which the act was committed, or by such international penal tribunal as may have jurisdiction"— of which there were none until the 1990s. Nuremberg set a precedent for international judicial action, not for armed intervention. Furthermore, as we have seen, prior to the 1990s there was no evidence of a customary right to intervene against genocide.

Today, however, we have both ad hoc and permanent international criminal tribunals. In addition, an emerging body of state practice supports an argument for the existence of an international legal right of humanitarian intervention. Debate in the legal literature thus increasingly addresses not whether humanitarian intervention is ever legally permissible but who has a right to intervene against genocide, when.

"Collective humanitarian intervention, when undertaken or authorized by the U.N., now meets with little controversy" (Nanda, Muther, and Eckert 1998: 862). This may have been a considerable exaggeration at the time, before the politically decisive 1999 interventions in Kosovo and East Timor. Over the ensuing decade, though, it has become quite accurate. (Controversy today is about whether the UN Security Council should or will intervene, not whether it has the authority to do so.)

What, though, about actions not authorized by the Security Council? These still are generally considered illegal. Louis Henkin spoke for most commentators when he wrote, following the Kosovo intervention, that "the law is, and ought to be, that unilateral intervention by military force by a state or group of states is unlawful unless authorized by the Security Council" (Henkin 1999: 826). Little has changed in the ensuing decade.

The *moral* arguments for humanitarian intervention, however, should not be ignored. A world of lawyer kings would not be all that much more attractive than one of philosopher kings. If we are to confront seriously the problems posed by humanitarian intervention, we must weigh the full range of competing norms and claims against one another. The "justification" of humanitarian intervention needs to be much more subtle and complex than it often has been presented to be, especially in the legal and moral literatures (which, understandably but ultimately unhelpfully, tend to focus on a single set of norms).

Consider Kosovo. Having "learned the lesson of Rwanda," NATO neither waited until the bodies were piled high nor was deterred by the lack of

Security Council authorization. The response was outrage in some circles and substantial unease even among many who accepted the intervention as justified. I would argue that this ambivalence was not merely fully justified but almost perfectly appropriate. The tension was even clearer in the conclusion of the Independent International Commission on Kosovo that the NATO intervention was "illegal but legitimate" (2000: 4).

8. "Justifying" Humanitarian Intervention

The "justification" of a humanitarian intervention (or nonintervention) is, given the multiplicity of standards and the controversies over legal and political standards, an extremely complicated matter.

A humanitarian intervention might be held to be justified only if (fully) *"authorized"* in the sense that it meets the demands of all relevant standards. The force of the moral principle of self-determination and the legal principle of sovereignty gives such a stringent conception considerable appeal. There are, however, other important and relevant senses of "justification."

"Contested" justifications arise when different standards point in different directions.[14] Positive "authorization," as I have defined it, requires that all relevant standards be satisfied; that is, where an action is prohibited by *a* but permitted by *b*, *a* trumps *b*. It is no less plausible, however, to see *a* and *b* as offsetting, making the intervention both "justified" and "unjustified." This seems to me the right way to assess genuinely humanitarian interventions not authorized by the Security Council: they are legally prohibited but morally (and perhaps also politically) authorized.

Two types of contested interventions merit special note. Some interventions are clearly prohibited but nonetheless *"excusable."* Stealing food to feed one's family, for example, is clearly illegal but we are disinclined to say that it is simply, or perhaps even all things considered, unjustified. Even in a court of law (let alone the court of public opinion) the moral obligation to one's family may carry considerable weight, especially at the time of sentencing. Thus the Tanzanian intervention that overthrew Idi Amin in Uganda, although a clear violation of international and regional law, met with only relatively modest verbal condemnation—and received considerable informal and popular support—because it removed a barbarous regime at relatively modest cost (assuming that we need not attribute the atrocities of the second Obote regime to the Tanzanians).

---

14. Almost all interventions are likely to be contested in the sense that someone (other than the target) objects. I distinguish here between interventions that are *relatively* uncontested and those where leading powers or a large number of states plausibly reject or counter a plausibly advanced claim of authorization.

Contrast this with Vietnam's intervention that removed the Khmer Rouge in Cambodia. Read (as I think it can plausibly be seen) as an effort to impose a quasi-imperial regional hegemony, it was, at best, merely *"tolerable."* If excusable interventions intentionally produce desirable outcomes, tolerable interventions produce good results largely unintentionally. Good consequences certainly carry some weight. Intentions, however, are also important to our evaluation.

An excusable act reflects an underlying norm with which we have considerable sympathy. We may even want to commend that norm: you *ought* to steal if that is truly the only way to feed your family. The principle underlying a merely tolerable act, however, cannot be widely endorsed. The positive humanitarian consequences are largely a fortunate accident. However thankful we may be for the results, we should not give much credit to those who produce them.[15]

These varied senses of "justified" reflect the pull of competing norms. The resulting confusion and complexities have led to regular efforts to formulate tests or criteria for permissible humanitarian interventions.[16] Although in many ways helpful, such lists at best identify factors that need to be taken into consideration. They cannot provide necessary and sufficient conditions that define an unambiguous threshold of justifiability. The multiple considerations that need to be balanced against one another are fundamentally incommensurable, causing the metaphor of balancing to break down. There is no simple, mechanical means for resolving the competing moral, legal, and political considerations raised by most humanitarian interventions. "The calculations are tortuous, and the mathematics far from exact" (Weiss 1999: 22). Usually we can only appeal to our best considered judgment and strive for arguments that, although not decisive, have a certain force. (In section 11 below I offer an illustration of such an assessment in the case of Kosovo.)

9. Mixed Motives and Consistency

A different kind of conflict of standards arises when interveners have mixed motives. A growing number of states see preventing, stopping, or punishing genocide as part of their national interest. Such interests, however, rarely

---

15. These references to consequences remind us that a full evaluation of an intervention must take into account how it was carried out. For reasons of simplicity and economy I have focused solely on the decision to intervene, with the implicit proviso that good humanitarian consequences may provide some sort of mitigation in the case of otherwise unjustifiable interventions.

16. See, for example, Lillich (1967: 347–50), Fonteyne (1974: 258–68), Fairley (1980: 60–61), Hassan (1981: 890–900), Nanda (1992), Charney (1999: 838–40), and Farer et al. (2005).

determine foreign policy when soldiers must be put at risk or when interveners face high financial or political costs. Humanitarian interventions thus are likely only when humanitarian motives are supported, or at least not seriously undercut, by more selfish national interests.

Any suggestion that such economic and political interests invalidate humanitarian motives and render an intervention unjustified, however, reflects an absurd moral perfectionism that is dubious even in individual action and is certainly misguided when applied to states. Even when political motives conflict with moral or legal norms—which is not always the case—we need to *balance* the competing motives for and consequences of both action and inaction. The degree of humanitarian motivation certainly should be taken into account when judging an intervention. The presence, even centrality, of non-humanitarian motives, however, does not necessarily reduce its justifiability.

A variant on the theme of mixed motives is the charge of selectivity or inconsistency: because one did not intervene in A, which is in all essential ways similar to B, intervening in B is somehow unjustified. Consistency is desirable, for many political, psychological, and even moral reasons.[17] However, as Peter Baehr nicely puts it, "one act of commission is not invalidated by many acts of omission" (2000: 32n75). The fact that I have acted badly in the past ought not to compel me to act badly in the future.

Faced with multiple conflicting standards, the very notion of consistency becomes problematic. A state that supports genocide when committed by friends but intervenes against it when committed by an enemy may merit disdain, but not for inconsistency. Such behavior shows great political consistency and a consistent lack of central humanitarian motivation. Inconsistency arguments usually prove to be instead arguments that give categorical priority to one set of standards—in the case of humanitarian intervention, usually law or morality—over another (compare section 12.5).

I have argued, by contrast, for an appreciation of the complex and contingent interaction of often-competing moral, legal, and political considerations.[18] We may, all things considered, have good reasons to give priority to concerns of (il)legality or moral purity, but simple answers to the question "Is this humanitarian intervention justified?" rarely are good answers, at least where there are either genuine humanitarian motives or significant humanitarian consequences.

---

17. For a thoughtful discussion of when selective interventions are problematic and why, see Brilmayer (1995).
18. Damrosch (2000) offers a thoughtful discussion and limited defense of "selectivity" in the context of the Kosovo intervention.

10. Politics and the Authority to Intervene

The problem of the authority to intervene can also be reformulated in terms of competing standards of evaluation. The UN Security Council has the legal authority to intervene but has been, and is likely to remain, extremely reluctant to exercise it. Other actors, such as NATO in Kosovo, may have the will and the capabilities to intervene but they lack the legal authority. When faced with a conflict between legal and moral norms, I would argue that political considerations are not a corrupting influence but instead ought to weigh heavily both in decisions to act and in judgments of such actions.

Enforcement action by the Security Council, beyond its legal attractions, has the political virtue of being unlikely in the absence of a central humanitarian aim. Although Council-authorized action may in principle reflect merely the shared selfish interests of the great powers, in practice this is improbable. A similar logic may apply to regional organizations that are not hegemonically dominated. The need to build political coalitions across states reduces the likelihood of partisan abuse.

Great powers acting alone have historically engaged in many more *anti*-humanitarian than humanitarian interventions. Therefore, multilateral rather than unilateral intervention is on its face to be preferred. Nevertheless, unilateral state power may save lives that would be lost while waiting for a more "pure" multilateral intervention that never comes.

Order, security, and even justice in the anarchical society of states cannot be separated from state power—which may be used for good as well as evil. Where intervention rests almost entirely on selfish national interests, with little broader support among other states or in the target country, the "authority" of the intervening state is much like that of the highwayman. Legally unauthorized action, however, may be more that of a policeman when a state or group of states intervenes as a de facto representative of victims or of broader communities. Even a single state may act on behalf of broader moral or political communities—which may offer active or passive support, or the indirect "support" of not opposing the intervention.

How should we handle claims of moral or political authority in the absence of the legal authority of Security Council authorization? The dangers of partisan abuse still seem to me sufficiently great that such interventions usually should be considered only excusable even when genuinely humanitarian motives are central. We must deal with purported humanitarian interventions case by case, as they arise, being especially wary of treating them as precedents. Developing a *doctrine* of humanitarian intervention without Security Council authorization, whatever its moral attractions, seems to me profoundly unwise.

This admittedly leaves regional and unilateral interveners in an awkward position. That, though, seems to me not merely preferable to the alternatives but fundamentally correct; they *should* bear an additional justificatory burden. We should take seriously, but not too seriously, the illegality of humanitarian intervention not authorized by the Security Council.

II. Judging the Kosovo Intervention

With all of these considerations in mind, let us return to the case of Kosovo. To sharpen the argument, let us give the NATO decision to intervene the most favorable possible interpretation. In particular, let us agree that genocide was either imminent or already underway.[19]

Security Council action was blocked by the relatively "principled" objections of Russia and China, as well as Russia's selfish political interests in its relationship with Serbia. The OSCE, the most obvious regional actor, had neither the desire nor the legal authority to use force. A similar combination of legal and political constraints blocked action through the European Union or the Council of Europe. Unilateral action by the United States, however, was unacceptable to almost all states.

Nonetheless, the United States, Britain, and many states of continental western Europe were unwilling to stand by and allow genocide in Kosovo. Faced with a genuine dilemma, the members of NATO decided, not implausibly, that intervention was the lesser of two evils. The decision to intervene can thus be seen as at least tolerable and perhaps even excusable.[20]

Interveners in such cases, however, ought to bear the burden of demonstrating that their illegal behavior is not ultimately culpable. The leading powers were less than clear in their self-justifications, in large part, it seems to me, because of their reticence to appeal centrally to humanitarian concerns. In fact, however, vital national interests, in the realist sense of that term, played a surprisingly peripheral, tenuous, and shifting role in the arguments of both the United States and Britain. Even David Rieff, who has been generally critical of US policy in the region and who specifically attacked the handling of the Kosovo intervention after it was launched, allows that it was "undertaken more in the name of human rights and moral obligation than out of any

---

19. If the reader cannot bring herself to accept this account, what follows can be read as an illustrative discussion of a hypothetical case loosely modeled on "the real" Kosovo.

20. A more complete assessment would require considering the rights of innocents, which were infringed by the excessive reliance on high-altitude bombing, and the obligations of proportionality. The picture, however, is complicated by political realities. Could the intervention have been carried to its conclusion if several NATO pilots had been shot down? If not, did the positive humanitarian consequences that were achieved outweigh the costs to innocent civilians? These seem to me profoundly difficult questions.

traditional conception of national interest" (1999: 1) and it is difficult to discern any material advantage obtained by the interveners.

Furthermore, the United States in this case acted like a leader, claiming normative authority and a collective purpose. The intervention, although "unilateral" in the technical legal sense that it was not authorized by the Security Council, had substantial endorsement and participation by other Western powers, few of whom were coerced into support. A Russian resolution rejecting the NATO intervention was not vetoed but defeated (on March 26, 1999) by a vote of twelve to three. In other words, four-fifths of the Security Council opposed condemning the NATO action.

As a liberal American whose political views were shaped during the Vietnam War, I must admit to being more than a bit uncomfortable with this (limited) defense of the Kosovo intervention. Although I think that it is substantively sound in this particular case, it has considerable potential for partisan abuse—as in some arguments advanced by Russia when it invaded Georgia in 2008—and a very troubling "selectivity." In most of the world there is neither a regional organization nor a dominant actor with the power, legitimacy, and commitment needed to intervene successfully. This has been part of the problem in trying to marshal more effective action in Darfur.

Nevertheless, regionalism, and even ad hoc coalitions (which were given a particularly bad name by the "coalition of the willing" that backed the US invasion of Iraq in 2003), may fill a gap when global institutions are unwilling or unable to aid victims.[21] Regional intervention is likely to increase the role of genuine humanitarian motivations, if only by increasing the number of (potentially competing) national interests that have to be accommodated. Selective humanitarian intervention, for all its problems, may be preferable to no humanitarian intervention at all.

Problems of authority, selectivity, and inequality are likely to recur so long as we retain an international system structured around sovereign states—that is, for the foreseeable future. Perhaps, though, we are finally beginning to grapple with them, rather than leaving complete authority to sovereign states, even if they choose to exercise that authority by practicing genocide. Giving full weight to both the moral limitations of intervening only against genocide and the very real dangers of partisan politics, this still seems to me a small but significant step forward for international human rights.

---

21. Some system of after-the-fact review, by the Security Council or even the General Assembly, might reduce the risks of partisan abuse. Unfortunately, there is no evidence that even an informal practice of review is emerging, and good reason to expect strong, and—in the short term, at least—fatal resistance to any such proposals, especially (but by no means only) from the United States.

12. Darfur and the Future of Humanitarian Intervention

The above has largely focused on the transformation of norms and practices in the 1990s, culminating in the NATO intervention in Kosovo and the Australian intervention, under the authority of the Security Council, in East Timor. This transformation was dramatic. For example, Kofi Annan, secretary-general of the United Nations, an institution that traditionally had treated sovereignty and nonintervention with almost religious reverence, wrote, "When we read the Charter today, we are more than ever conscious that its aim is to protect individual human beings, not to protect those who abuse them" (Annan 1999).

The December 2001 report of the International Commission on Intervention and State Sovereignty was a watershed event in international discussions of humanitarian intervention.[22] It, in effect, attempted to codify a right to humanitarian intervention against genocide and to argue for an even stronger principle, the responsibility to protect. Clearly, neither states nor the Security Council recognize any such responsibility. We have instead a *right* to humanitarian intervention that, like any right, is exercised only at the discretion of the right holder.

That right was soon put to the test in Darfur. In 2003, the largely Arab and Muslim government in Khartoum began to wage war against the largely non-Arab and non-Muslim population of Darfur, both directly and through government-supported militias (*janjaweed*). The parallels to Serbian "ethnic cleansing" in Bosnia and Kosovo are striking. A conscious effort seems to have been made both to limit the killing, which was aimed primarily at causing targeted populations to flee, and to engage diplomatically with critics in order to forestall an effective, full-scale multilateral intervention. Even this "restrained" violence, however, forced more than two and a half million people—40 percent of the prewar population—to flee, and killed perhaps a third of a million people (three quarters of those deaths being from disease among refugees).

Both the genocidal violence and the international constraints on it deserve emphasis. On the one hand, Sudan has been largely undeterred and unpunished. Although the violence has substantially moderated, a peace plan of sorts was agreed to in the summer of 2011, and relatively few new refugees are being created, few of the displaced have returned home and conditions remain generally dismal. On the other hand, there has been considerable regional and international action. The African Union (AU) sent its first 150 peacekeepers in August 2004. In 2005 it increased that number to seven thousand. In 2006

22. See http://responsibilitytoprotect.org/ICISS%20Report.pdf.

the Security Council authorized a peacekeeping force of more than seventeen thousand. Major campaigns by NGOs mobilized considerable publicity and pressure on Western governments. Charges were even brought against leaders behind the violence, including Sudan's President Omar al-Bashir. Given the savagery of Sudanese actions over nearly half a century of internal conflict in southern Sudan, it seems clear that international scrutiny and pressure moderated the violence.

All of this, to be sure, was far short of the international response in Kosovo and East Timor. Those, however, were logistically much easier targets. (Darfur is roughly the size of Spain and almost completely lacking in modern infrastructure.) The United States, when Darfur emerged in 2004 as an international issue, was already bogged down with wars in Afghanistan and Iraq. The AU was no NATO. Russia and China had not only been made wary by Kosovo but also had more at stake in Sudan (especially oil for China). And in the government in Khartoum the world faced a much more recalcitrant and formidable enemy. Given all of this, the level of international response, and the continuing disquiet about its inadequacy, suggests that there has been no backing away from a right to humanitarian intervention—although no movement toward a responsibility to protect.

Precedents are created by later practice that makes the precedent. International responses to Darfur clearly treated Rwanda as a negative precedent. Inaction simply was not an option. International action, although not particularly effective, was not insubstantial. Furthermore, the Sudanese government seemed to believe that they did not have the sort of free hand that they would have had just a decade earlier. One might even suggest that Khartoum engaged in a delicate balancing act to keep the number of direct deaths below what it calculated as the level that would provoke a more forceful international response.

Success in Kosovo and especially East Timor created unrealistic expectations among many. Nonetheless, these cases, representing the culmination of a decade of progress, clearly set a new baseline. States and international organizations today seem unable, and in some cases even unwilling, to turn a blind eye—as they almost universally did during the Cold War and earlier, treating genocide as a purely moral concern rather than an offense against international society. Darfur has raised questions about the level of commitment. In particular, it has reminded us that the relatively low costs of action in Kosovo and East Timor were an important part of the calculus. Politics is still vital to the exercise of the right to humanitarian intervention. Perhaps most troubling, a series of prominent failures still could reverse the progress of the 1990s, which was based equally on normative change and supporting practice.

Nonetheless, in 2012 the general international consensus is that there is a right to humanitarian intervention, especially when authorized by the UN Security Council—in sharp contrast to the dominant view, well supported by practice, just two decades earlier. For all its shortcomings, the genocide regime has been transformed from a purely declaratory regime to the only international human rights regime backed—however fitfully—by the use of armed force. Genocide is the exception to the general rule that only means short of the threat or use of force can be used on behalf of internationally recognized human rights.

16

Nondiscrimination for All: The Case of Sexual Minorities

rticle 1 of the Universal Declaration of Human Rights begins, "All human beings are born free and equal in dignity and rights." The right to protection against discrimination, recognized in Article 2, is an explicit guarantee of equal—and thus all—human rights for every person. In practice, however, international human rights law does not protect all victims of systematic discrimination. This chapter critically examines the exclusion of gay men, lesbians, and members of other sexual or gender minorities from the full protection of international human rights norms. This is an issue of intense controversy in many countries that illustrates some of the limits of international human rights norms and the procedures for their progressive development.

1. The Right to Nondiscrimination

Article 2 of the Universal Declaration proclaims, "Everyone is entitled to all the rights and freedoms set forth in this Declaration, without distinction of any kind, such as race, colour, sex, language, religion, political or other opinion, national or social origin, property, birth or other status." This statement, however, is seriously exaggerated. Everyone cannot be entitled to all human rights without distinction of *any* kind. States are not prohibited from taking into account *any* status differences. We are (at most) entitled only to protection against *invidious* discrimination, discrimination that tends to ill will or causes unjustifiable harm.

Social life is full of legitimate discriminations. Individuals, groups, and even the state often not merely recognize but legitimately act upon differences between groups of people. For example, all societies restrict the rights of children, a distinction based on age or mental capacity. Distinctions of nationality are deeply embedded in international human rights regimes: individuals ordinarily can claim human rights only against the government of which they are nationals (or under whose jurisdiction they fall on the basis of residence). Those incarcerated for criminal behavior have a variety of their human rights legitimately restricted because of their past behavior.

The internationally recognized human right to nondiscrimination prohibits invidious public (or publicly supported or tolerated) discrimination that deprives target groups of the legitimate enjoyment of other rights. Although it may be hateful to choose one's friends on the basis of race, this is not an appropriate subject for regulation through antidiscrimination law. Only when friendships or social contacts systematically influence access to economic, social, or political opportunities do they become a matter of legitimate state regulation. Likewise, discrimination in choice of marriage partners on the basis of family background does not fall within the confines of the right to nondiscrimination—unless that discrimination is publicly supported or required (as, for example, in laws against miscegenation).

Furthermore, human rights address only certain socially recognized egregious or widespread systematic practices, not every affront to human dignity or even every public indignity. The Universal Declaration thus highlights race, color, sex, language, religion, political or other opinion, national or social origin, property, and birth. The notion of suspect classifications in American constitutional jurisprudence nicely captures this idea. Because we know that race, for example, has been the basis for invidious discrimination in the past, practices that use racial categorizations are inherently suspect and thus subject to special judicial scrutiny.

Article 2.2 of the International Covenant on Economic, Social, and Cultural Rights is slightly more subtle: "The States Parties to the present Covenant undertake to guarantee that the rights enunciated in the present Covenant will be exercised without discrimination of any kind as to race, colour, sex, language, religion, political or other opinion, national or social origin, property, birth or other status." "Distinction" of any kind is replaced by "discrimination" of any kind. And rather than present the enumerated grounds as examples of prohibited discrimination—"such as race"—this formulation is exhaustive: "without discrimination . . . as to." (Flexibility is provided through the addition of "other status" at the end.)

In either formulation, though, the practical heart of the right is the list of prohibited grounds of invidious discrimination. Such explicit listing—which, as I suggested in section 6.2.D, reflects extended and difficult, often violent, political struggles—often is essential to strong and unambiguous protection. The list of protected groups provides a record of the successful struggles by excluded and despised groups to force full (or at least formally equal) inclusion in political society.

2. Nondiscrimination and Political Struggle

Protections against discrimination based on birth and social origin take us back to the beginning of the modern Western struggle for human rights against aristocratic privilege. Although most societies have assigned rights in significant measure on the basis of birth, today we require that human rights be equally available to those born high or low on society's scale of social status or origins.

Those who have forced their social "betters" to recognize their equal rights, however, have regularly denied the same rights to members of other social groups. Consider, for example, both Britain and the United States, which, as we saw in chapter 5, after their revolutions effectively extended human rights only to propertied white males of certain Christian sects.

Nonetheless, race, color, sex, language, religion, political or other opinion, national or social origin, and property, which previously were accepted grounds of legal and political discrimination, are today almost universally considered illegitimate bases for differences in the assignment and enjoyment of rights. The state may no longer invidiously take these features into consideration when dealing with citizens and subjects.

Such changing conceptions of the criteria for full and equal membership in society have rested on and interacted with wider social, economic, and political transformations. Consider Locke's link between property and citizenship. The rise of mass literacy seriously undercut arguments that those without property lacked the leisure required to develop their rational capacities sufficiently to participate fully in political society. So did mass electoral politics, which transformed political participation from direct decision making to authorizing and reviewing the actions of representative office holders. The claim that the unpropertied lacked a sufficient "stake" in society to be allowed full political participation fell to changing conceptions of political membership symbolized by the American and French Revolutions, the rise of mass popular armies, and growing nationalist sentiments. Discrimination based on the lack of independence of the unpropertied gave way in the face of the increasingly impersonal relations between workers and employers and the general depersonalization of relations in urban setting. The implicit assumption of the coincidence of wealth and virtue was eroded by general processes of social leveling and mobility. Our expanded list of economic and social rights also reflects a growing appreciation of alternative means for realizing economic security and participation in a world of industrial capitalism.

Likewise, women and nonwhites were until well into this century widely seen as irreparably deficient in their rational or moral capacities, and thus incapable of exercising the full range of human rights. These racial and gender distinctions, however, were in principle subject to moral and empirical counterarguments. Over the past several decades, dominant political ideas and practices in Western and non-Western societies alike have been transformed by national and international movements to end slavery, and later colonialism; to grant women and racial minorities the vote; and to end discriminations based on race, ethnicity, and gender. A similar tale can be told in the case of Jews, nonconformist Christian sects, atheists, and other religious minorities.

In each case, a logic of full and equal humanity has overcome claims of group inferiority, bringing (formal) equal membership in society through explicitly guaranteed protections against discrimination. Signs of difference that previously were seen as marks of moral inferiority and grounds for justifiable subordination have been excluded from the realm of legally and politically legitimate discriminations. Adherents of different, even despised, religions have come to be recognized as nonetheless fully human, and thus entitled to the same rights as other (dominant groups of) human beings. Africans, Arabs, and Asians have come to be recognized as no less human than white Europeans. And so forth.

Such an account emphasizes the progressive development of the right to nondiscrimination—and human rights more generally—through processes of social and political struggle. It also implicitly raises the question of other groups currently subject to discrimination; that is, victims of invidious public discrimination whose suffering remains legally and politically accepted. The remainder of this chapter focuses on those subject to discrimination because of their sexual behavior or orientation.

3. Discrimination against Sexual Minorities

Let us begin with the matter of linguistic conventions. "Homosexual" and "gay" have become relatively neutral and fairly inclusive terms in the American mainstream. Among activists in these communities, the formula of "lesbian, gay, bisexual, and transgendered (LGBT)" has considerable currency at the moment. In addition to being more inclusive, this formulation has the virtue of emphasizing *differences* among those who engage in same-sex erotic behavior or relationships. Also, by explicitly including transgendered persons it undermines conventional links between sex (defined by genitalia or chromosomes), behavior, gender, sexual orientation, and personal identity.

Following the logic laid out in the preceding section, however, I will adopt the language of sexual minorities. This terminology is even more inclusive, being open to any group (previously, now, or in the future) stigmatized or despised as a result of sexual orientation, identity, or behavior. Furthermore, the language of minorities explicitly focuses our attention on the issue of discrimination, and at least the possibility of political action to eliminate it.[1]

Sexual minorities are despised and targeted by "mainstream" society because of their sexuality and, in most cases, for transgressing gender roles. Like victims of racism, sexism, and religious persecution, they are human beings who have been identified by dominant social groups as somehow less than fully human, and thus not entitled to the same rights as "normal" people, "the rest of us."

Discrimination against sexual minorities is widespread and deep in most contemporary societies. In many countries, the intimate behavior and loving relationships of sexual minorities are defined as crimes. They are singled out for official, quasi-official, and private violence. In most countries, sexual minorities suffer under substantial civil disabilities.

In approximately eighty countries sexual relations among adult members of the same sex are legally prohibited.[2] In Iran, Mauritania, Saudi Arabia, Sudan, and Yemen (plus certain states in Nigeria) penalties up to death may be imposed.[3] In Iran, at least three gay men were executed in both 2010 and 2011.[4] (The actual number is almost certainly much higher.) While I was revising this chapter, four more were sentenced to death.[5]

Discrimination and violence against sexual minorities is common and well-documented. For example, a single human rights organization, Human Rights Watch (HRW), over the three year period 2009–2011, issued major reports on Burundi, Cameroon, Honduras, Iran, Iraq, Senegal, and South Africa.[6] In addition, HRW's annual reports covering these years documented

1. The drawback of this language, as Kees Waaldijk has pointed out to me in private conversation, is that by including those engaging in despised sexual practices that are not related to gender roles it moves away from the implicit emphasis on gender in the LGBT formulation. For example, were sadomasochists or rubber fetishists to be targets of systematic discrimination, they would fall under my definition of sexual minorities. I am not convinced, however, that discriminations based on sexual behavior unrelated to gender should not be included. To the extent that "sex" or sexual behavior is part of the issue, as I believe it is, the alternative of "gender minorities," besides its rhetorical shortcomings, has its own conceptual problems. Also, the special association of the language of gender with women's rights raises the likelihood of unintended analytical ambiguities and confusions.
2. For a fairly comprehensive and reasonably up to date overview of the legal status of LGBT rights, see http://en.wikipedia.org/wiki/LGBT_rights_by_country_or_territory.
3. See http://www.ipsnews.net/2011/08/executed-for-being-gay/.
4. See http://www.guardian.co.uk/world/2011/sep/07/iran-executes-men-homosexuality-charges and http://physiciansforhumanrights.org/blog/irans-barbaric-execution-of-three-gay-men-signals-dangerous-direction.html.
5. See http://www.huffingtonpost.com/2012/05/14/iran-gay-men-executed-hanging_n_1515207.html.
6. http://www.hrw.org/reports/2009/07/30/forbidden, http://www.hrw.org/reports/2010/11/04/criminalizing-identities-0, http://www.hrw.org/reports/2009/05/29/not-worth-penny-0, http://www.hrw.org/reports/2010/12/15/we-are-buried-generation, http://www.hrw.org/reports/2009/08/16/they-want-us-exterminated, http://www.hrw.org/en/reports/2010/11/30/fear-life-0, and http://www.hrw.org/reports/2011/12/05/we-ll-show-you-you-re-woman.

discrimination and violence against sexual minorities in Belarus, China, Colombia, Egypt, Gaza, Indonesia, Kenya, Kuwait, Kyrgyzstan, Malaysia, Nepal, Nigeria, Papua New Guinea, Rwanda, Serbia, and Uganda.[7] In other words, violations based on sexual orientation or gender identity were sufficiently prominent to be documented in about a quarter of the countries covered in HRW's annual reports. And this is but the tip of the iceberg.

In some well-known instances, national leaders have engaged in campaigns of vilification that have fueled discrimination and violence. Particularly notorious is President Robert Mugabe of Zimbabwe, who has claimed, repeatedly, over the course of nearly two decades that gays are "worse than dogs and pigs."[8] Uganda has received considerable attention recently for (so far unsuccessful) efforts to increase the legal penalties for homosexuality and an associated upsurge in private and semi-official violence against sexual minorities, most prominently the murder in early 2011 of activist David Kato.[9] In the 1990s, "social cleansing" in Colombia (Ordonez 1994) and Ecuador (Amnesty International 2001b) saw a general climate of official and quasi-official political violence against "disposable" people spill over into death squad attacks on gays, lesbians, and transvestites.

Equally troubling, though, is the pervasive presence of violence against sexual minorities even in countries with good records on LGBT rights. For example, Laurens Buijs, Gert Hekma and Jan Willem Duyvendak (2011) document a serious problem of anti-gay violence in Amsterdam, the most liberal city in one of the most gay-friendly countries in the world. In Brazil we see what Eduardo Gómez (2010) calls a friendly government but a cruel society. Over the past decade, the Brazilian government and courts have instituted major changes in law and policy, as symbolized in the 2004 report *Brazil without Homophobia: The Program to Combat Violence and Discrimination Against GLBT and Promotion of Homosexual Citizenship*. Nonetheless, violence against sexual minorities remains a serious problem. A leading Brazilian advocacy group (Grupo Gay da Bahia) documented 208 murders due to sexual orientation or gender identity in 2009 and 272 in 2011, or roughly one every thirty-six hours.[10]

7. http://www.hrw.org/sites/default/files/reports/wr2010.pdf, http://www.hrw.org/sites/default/files/reports /wr2011.pdf, http://www.hrw.org/sites/default/files/reports /wr2012.pdf.

8. See, for example, Worldwide Queer Info, Queer Resources Directory, http://www.qrd.org/qrd/world/africa/zimbabwe/mugabe.renews.attacks, reprinting from Globe and Mail, August 12, 1995, A8, and http://www.thezimbabwemail.com/zimbabwe/11835-we-re-are-against-homosexuality-chinamasa.html.

9. http://www.nytimes.com/2011/01/28/world/africa/28uganda.html.

10. http://deepbrazil.com/2010/11/23/one-brazilian-gay-killed-every-two-days/, http://www.thedailybeast.com/articles/2012/04/08/brazil-s-surge-in-violence-against-gays-is-just-getting-worse.html. Groupo Gay de Bahia has documented over a hundred anti-gay murders a year since the mid-1980s. See Mott (1996). It is unclear, however, how much of the higher recent numbers are due to better reporting (and thus an improving situation) and how much to a rise in actual violence.

In most countries, sexual orientation is an accepted ground for discrimination in employment, housing, access to public facilities and social services, inheritance, adoption, and social insurance. In the United States, Evan Wolfson nicely summarizes the situation: "Our society forbids gay people to marry, denies us equal pay for equal work, throws us off the job, forbids us from serving our country in the armed forces, refuses us health insurance, forces us into the closet, arrests us in our bedrooms, harasses our daily associations, takes away our children, beats and kills us in the streets and parks, smothers images of ourselves and others like us, and then tells us we are irresponsible, unstable, and aberrant" (1991: 31). Sadly, although twenty years old, this description remains largely accurate.

Discrimination against sexual minorities also has international dimensions (beyond the exclusion of sexual minorities from the protections of international human rights law). Many countries deny entry to homosexuals as threats to public health or morals.[11] Outside the West, it is still relatively rare to recognize sexual orientation or behavior as grounds for asylum, which in international law requires establishing that one has a well-founded fear of persecution back home.[12]

These pervasive violations, and their acceptance by state officials in much of the world, reflects deep currents of social prejudice against sexual minorities. As I argued in part 2, however, the cultural or historical depth of a practice cannot justify systematic denials of human rights. The remainder of this chapter argues that gays, lesbians, and others of "deviant" gender or sexuality are "a stigmatized minority requiring [and deserving] protection" (Kallen 1996: 209).

4. Nature, (Im)morality, and Public Morals

The common charge that homosexuality is "against nature" is hardly worth arguing against here. Sexuality and sexual orientation are constructed sets of social roles.[13] Many societies, including currently homophobic societies, have for extended periods tolerated, or even highly valued, male homoerotic relationships.

11. For example, in 1967 the US Supreme Court upheld deportation of aliens on grounds that homosexuality counted as "afflicted with psychopathic personality" and thus gays and lesbians were excludable. This ruling remained in force until the Immigration Act of 1990. See Foss (1994).

12. In the United States, the first case was a Brazilian, Marcelo Tenorio, who was severely beaten and hospitalized in a gay-bashing incident in Rio de Janeiro in 1989, was refused a US visa, and then entered illegally in 1990 (Grider 1994).

13. The most influential version of this argument is Foucault (1990). Blackwood and Wieringa (1999) provides an interesting selection of contemporary cross-cultural case studies.

In the West, the best-known examples come from ancient Greece,[14] but even the Christian tradition does not seem to have been consistently homophobic during its first millennium.[15] Melanesia, South Asia, and the Muslim Near East also have traditions of male homoerotic relations (Herdt 1984; Ratti 1993; Schmitt and Sofer 1992).

Homoerotic relations in Asia are of special interest because of the prominence of arguments against homosexuality in recent debates over "Asian values." In fact, however, male-male sexual relationships have a traditional basis in both China (Lau and Ng 1989) and Japan (Schalow 1989; Hinsch 1990; Leupp 1995; Pflugfelder, 1999). There even seems to be evidence of same-sex marriage in Ming dynasty (1368–1644) Fujian (Hinsch 1990: 127–34).

Nonetheless, the fact remains that homosexuality is widely considered— by significant segments of society in all countries, and probably still by most people in most countries—to be profoundly immoral. The language of perversion and degeneracy is standard.

Drawing on such attitudes, advocates of discrimination are likely to point to provisions in the International Human Rights Covenants that permit restrictions on a number of recognized rights on the grounds of "public morals."[16] All the groups explicitly recognized as covered by the right to nondiscrimination today, however, were at one time perceived to be a threat to public morals. Consider some more or less randomly selected historical material from my own country concerning discrimination against those of African and Asian descent.

Slavery was explicitly permitted (and racial discrimination was not prohibited) in the US Constitution and its Bill of Rights. Just one year after the founding of the republic, a 1790 law confined naturalization to free white persons.

In the infamous Dred Scott case of 1857 (60 US [19 How.]), Chief Justice Taney held that even emancipated negroes did not "compose a portion of this people" and were not "constituent members of this sovereignty" but rather were a permanently "subordinate and inferior class of beings." From colonial times, Taney argued, "a perpetual and impassable barrier was intended to be erected between the white race and the ones which they had reduced to

---

14. The standard scholarly study is Dover (1986). See also Cantarella (1992) and, with explicit reference to contemporary debates, Nussbaum (1994).

15. See, for example, Boswell (1980), Brooten (1996), Jordan (1997), and Kuefler (2001). More controversial is Boswell (1994).

16. For example, Article 19 of the International Covenant on Civil and Political Rights permits restrictions on the right to freedom of expression that are "provided for by law and are necessary . . . for the protection of . . . public health or morals." Similar limitations are allowed in Articles 12, 14, 18, 21, and 22.

slavery." In fact, he argued, throughout American history blacks had been considered by whites as "below them in the scale of created beings."

More than three-quarters of a century later, Senator James O. Eastland, on the floor of the US Senate, publicly proclaimed, "I believe in white supremacy, and as long as I am in the Senate I expect to fight for white supremacy. . . . The cultural debt of the colored peoples to the white race is such as to make the preservation of the white race a chief aim of the colored, if these latter but understood their indebtedness. That the colored race should seek to 'kill the goose that lays the golden egg' is further proof that their inferiority, demonstrated so clearly in cultural attainments, extends to their reasoning processes in general" (quoted in Kennedy 1959: 32). Making resistance to domination the decisive sign of inferiority is a rhetorical move as brilliant as it is frightening.

When US law was changed in 1870 to permit naturalization of freed blacks, foreign-born Asians continued to be denied the right to American nationality. A provision was proposed at the California Constitutional Convention of 1878–1879 to prevent Chinese immigration in order to protect Californians "from moral and physical infection from abroad" (Ringer 1983: 590). "The Chinese bring with them habits and customs the most vicious and demoralizing. . . . They are, generally, destitute of moral principle. They are incapable of patriotism, and are utterly unfitted for American citizenship. Their existence here, in great numbers, is a perpetual menace to republican institutions, a source of constant irritation and danger to the public peace" (Ringer 1983: 606–7).

In the same year, a California State Senate Special Committee on Chinese Immigration found that "the Chinese seem to be antediluvian men renewed. Their code of morals, their forms of worship, and their maxims of life, are those of the remotest antiquity. In this aspect they stand as a barrier against which the elevating tendency of a higher civilization exerts itself in vain. . . . there can be no hope that any contact with our people, however long continued, will ever conform them to our institutions, enable them to comprehend or appreciate our form of government, or to assume the duties or discharge the functions of citizens" (Ringer 1983: 604).

Almost half a century later, V. S. McClatchy, publisher of the *Sacramento Bee*, the leading paper in California's state capital, delivered a speech in Honolulu where he argued that Japanese migrants were "an alien, unassimilable element." McClatchy even went so far as to appeal to "the biological law which declares that races of widely different characteristics perpetuate through intermarriage, not their good, but their less desirable categories" (McClatchy 1979 [1921]: 5, 10). And during World War II, not just Japanese immigrants but US citizens of Japanese origin were forcibly interned in the American West.

Such examples could be readily multiplied for other groups and other countries. Jews have long been a special target of attack in the Western world. Women were almost universally considered mentally and morally inferior to men until well into the twentieth century—and in many places of the world still are. In all such cases, certain marks of difference came to be constructed as "permissions-to-hate" (Woodward 1966: 81), grounds that authorize treating members of a group as less than fully human. Erik Erikson's notion of "pseudospeciation" nicely captures the dehumanizing logic, which we saw above in Mugabe's (unfavorable) comparison between gays and dogs.

Returning to the case of homosexuals, compare an interim report of a US Senate subcommittee in 1950 investigating "Employment of Homosexuals and Other Sex Perverts in Government." The subcommittee's charge was "to determine the extent of the employment of homosexuals and other sex perverts in Government; to consider reasons why their employment by the Government is undesirable; and to examine into the efficacy of the methods used in dealing with the problem" (Katz 1975: 1). There was no question that these people were perverts who needed to be kept out of government (if they could not be fully purged from society). The only issue was whether enough reasons had been developed to achieve this unquestioned end and whether sufficiently strenuous efforts were being undertaken.[17]

The subcommittee found that employment was inappropriate because "first, they are generally unsuitable, and second, they constitute security risks." "Those who engage in overt acts of perversion lack the emotional stability of normal persons. . . . sex perversion weakens the moral fiber of an individual to a degree that he is not suitable for a position of responsibility." Because homosexuals "frequently attempt to entice normal individuals to engage in perverted practices," and show a strong "tendency to gather other perverts about [them]," they must be rigorously sought out. "One homosexual can pollute a Government office" (Katz 1975: 4). This is the same logic of incorrigible degradation and fear of pollution we saw above with Africans and Asians.

Even accepting, for the purposes of argument, that voluntary sexual relations among adults of the same sex or families headed by same-sex couples are a profound moral outrage, discrimination against sexual minorities cannot be justified from a human rights perspective. "Perverts," "degenerates," and "deviants" have the same human rights as the morally pure and should

---

17. The committee, with a logic strikingly reminiscent of the red scare that was building at the same time, found that the government was insufficiently vigilant. The State Department, as during the McCarthy witch hunt, came in for special attack for allowing "known homosexuals" to resign for "personal reasons" without properly noting their homosexuality in their official personnel files (Katz 1975: 11).

have those rights guaranteed by law.[18] Members of sexual minorities are still human beings, no matter how deeply they are loathed by the rest of society. They are therefore entitled to equal protection of the law and the equal enjoyment of all internationally recognized human rights.

Human rights rest on the idea that *all* human beings have certain basic rights simply because they are human. How one chooses to lead one's life,[19] subject only to minimum and general requirements of law and public order,[20] is a private matter—no matter how publicly one leads that life. Human rights do not need to be earned, and they cannot be lost because one's beliefs or way of life are repugnant to most others in a society. In fact, the real test of human rights comes when a state or society deals with unpopular or despised deviants rather than those comfortably in the mainstream. Likewise, it is those on the social margins—especially when they have been forced to the margins—who have the greatest need and the most important uses for human rights.

Rhoda Howard's (1999) interviews with Canadian civic leaders canvass some of the psychological and sociological barriers to acceptance of this moral position even within relatively "enlightened" or "liberal" groups in a country with a (generally deserved) reputation for tolerance, compassion, and a commitment to human rights. It is disheartening, if historically and sociologically understandable, to see leaders elsewhere, such as Mugabe, who came to power by opposing racist denials of his full humanity, resorting to vicious sexual hate mongering. Such resistance, however widespread, has no more moral force than past and present attitudes of racism, sexism, and religious intolerance. Just as other despised minorities have had to struggle against a dominant oppressive mainstream, ultimately forcing them to renounce their permissions to hate, sexual minorities face just such a struggle today.

Popular attitudes of hatred and contempt are the problem to be overcome, not the solution to anything. Whatever the state of popular moral sentiments, we must remain committed to the overriding objective of all human rights for all. Sexual minorities, however, have to struggle not only against local attitudes and laws. They also face a body of international human rights law that accepts discrimination against them, in clear contradiction to the human rights logic of equality for *all*.

18. I trust it is clear that I use this language not to be inflammatory or because it expresses my own views, but rather to engage some standard moral condemnations of homosexuality.
19. I am implicitly assuming here that sexual orientation is "chosen" and thus more like religion than race—although, of course, racial identity is largely socially constructed. If homosexuality is "genetic," the case for discrimination is even more tenuous.
20. For example, sexual relations with children may be legitimately prohibited so long as both homosexual and heterosexual relations are prohibited.

5. Strategies for Inclusion

The moral and conceptual case for extending nondiscrimination protection to gay men, lesbians, and other sexual minorities is overwhelming. They are human beings exercising their rights of personal autonomy to behave as they choose, and to associate, in public and private, with whom they choose, as they choose. Until the deep social prejudice against "perverts" is broken down, however, they will be subject to continued victimization and there is no chance for explicit inclusion of sexual orientation among internationally prohibited grounds of discrimination.

As in most other areas of human rights, the central battlegrounds are local and national. The international dimension of the human rights movement is, in general, supplementary to and supportive of national struggles. Nonetheless, it will be my focus here. I want to consider briefly some of the tactical and strategic issues involved in bringing sexual minorities under international nondiscrimination protections.

A. Incorporation into International Human Rights Law

The International Human Rights Covenants are largely fixed standards that reflect attitudes of the 1940s, 1950s and early 1960s, when no country had a substantial gay rights movement. In principle it is possible to "amend" the covenants, as has been done with the Second Optional Protocol to the ICCPR (which outlaws the death penalty), but this process is extremely difficult. Even supplementary norm creation, through a separate declaration (as, for example, was done for disappearances and the right to development) is not promising.

As we saw above, the list of those groups explicitly recognized as protected against discrimination reflects the success of particular historical struggles for inclusion. Explicit listing was less a cause of their inclusion than an effect. Only after a tipping point of changes in ideas and practices is explicit recognition a realistic possibility. After that, formal legal recognition provides another useful resource for continuing and completing the struggle for full inclusion. But it is a rather late stage in the process.

In the case of sexual minorities, this implies that for at least the next decade or two, central attention needs to be focused elsewhere. This is especially true because internationally recognized human rights have been developed through a process of genuinely consensual negotiation. Unanimity is not required. If objections are more than a few and scattered, though, objectors may block the process from going forward. In the current international political climate, explicit inclusion of sexual minorities under the general protections of international human rights law simply is not a possibility.

This may be unfortunate for sexual minorities. Consensus, however, has been essential to the authority of international human rights norms. By the time a right is explicitly recognized in international human rights law, it has been accepted—with varying degrees of enthusiasm to be sure, but accepted nonetheless—by virtually all states in all regions and blocs. And that near universal acceptance is essential to the impact that international human rights law has had.

If the text can't be changed directly and explicitly, we need to rely instead on interpretation. Sexual orientation is on its face an obvious case of an "other status" by which human beings are singled out for invidious discrimination. A campaign to emphasize these status disabilities can at least highlight the suffering publicly imposed on sexual minorities. Of course, for those who consider such suffering appropriate, this is likely to have little impact. It is hard to see, though, what sort of political action is likely to be effective against those who consider sexual minorities sufficiently degenerate to merit systematic deprivations of their rights. The only hope would seem to be to mobilize a widespread social attitude of tolerance, or perhaps even sympathy, to force such views in the closet.

This strategy may be particularly promising if some linkage can be established with other struggles. For example, since 1999 the annual resolution adopted by the UN General Assembly on extrajudicial killings has included reference to those killed because of their sexual orientation.[21] The suffering of sexual minorities is through such actions associated with otherwise identical suffering of those targeted for reasons that have already been authoritatively prohibited. Advocates might also emphasize substantive analogies with those subject to discrimination on the basis of, for example, disability, age, or unpopular religious views. The rights of disabled persons are especially interesting because their recognition involves a clear expansion of the range of the right to nondiscrimination. (Disability was not envisioned as an impermissible ground for discrimination by the drafters of the Universal Declaration and the International Human Rights Covenants.) The underlying idea is to emphasize that the list of explicitly prohibited grounds in Article 2 is illustrative, not exhaustive, and that there remain a number of other statuses that are still widely used to justify public discrimination.

A more radical strategy of interpretative incorporation would to be read "sex" in Article 2 to include sexual orientation. This was done by the Human

---

21. In 2010, this reference was removed in committee—although extensive lobbying by human rights NGOs led to the provision being restored in the final version. See http://www.hrw.org/news/2011/02/14/restoring-protection-lgbt-people-against-extrajudicial-executions.

Rights Committee in the Toonen case.[22] Although a clever and provocative move, the Human Rights Committee provided no grounds for such a finding. In its report it simply stated, without further elaboration, "that in its view the reference to 'sex' in articles 2, paragraph 1, and 26 is to be taken as including sexual orientation."[23] This, however, certainly was *not* what was intended at the time the provision was drafted; it is not even a widely held view in legally "advanced" European countries, and it is substantively problematic. Sexual minorities are in many ways no more analogous to women—the initially intended reference of "sex"—than they are to religious minorities. They suffer in systematically, even fundamentally, different ways from women, and those differences deserve to be highlighted rather than obscured.[24]

There are also procedural problems with existing international mechanisms for interpretation. The Human Rights Committee and the Committee on Economic, Social and Cultural Rights are *not* authorized to make authoritative interpretations (let alone act to enforce their understandings of the meaning of the human rights covenants). It is not even clear that these bodies are authorized to use what within the European regime is called "evolutive interpretation," a reading of the meaning of the text based on current understandings rather than on those at the time of drafting.

Finally, such interpretative strategies also run up against the problem of consensus. The constraints on novel interpretations are somewhat less severe than those on the recognition of new rights or new classes of right-holders. Nonetheless, without something close to consensus any such interpretations will lack the normative weight needed for them to be of real practical value.

Clear incorporation into the mainstream of international nondiscrimination law, in other words, will be more a consequence than a cause of changing attitudes and practices. When such incorporation does come, international legal prohibition of discrimination on the basis of sexual orientation or behavior will be a resource for further progress. That recognition will only come, though, once a fundamental normative consensus has been reached—probably decades from now.

In the interim, we are in the stage of international norm creation comparable to what we saw with the rights of disabled persons and indigenous peoples in the 1970s, 1980s, and 1990s. For example, in 2011 the UN Human

22. Human Rights Committee, Communication 488/1992, submitted by Nicholas Toonen against Australia. UN document CCPR/C/50/D/488/1992, April 4, 1994.
23. Ibid., paragraph 8.7.
24. A strong tactical counterargument would advocate pursuing similarities first, taking advantage of the entrenched nature of women's rights in many legal systems, and then moving on later to dealing with differences.

Rights Council adopted a resolution expressing concern over violence against people because of sexual orientation. The vote was only 23-19-3; that is, a bare majority. Even on the limited issue of violence—let alone the more fundamental issue of discrimination—there is nothing even close to an international consensus. Nonetheless, for the first time at the United Nations, sexual orientation has been the subject of a human rights resolution. There is a long way still to go before sexual orientation is clearly included within "other status" in authoritative understandings of the internationally recognized human right to nondiscrimination. The struggle, however, has begun to show early (if still largely symbolic) successes that bode well for the future.

B. National and Regional Mechanisms of Incorporation

The other principal source of interpretation in our decentralized international legal system is national legislatures and courts. These are authoritative—but only nationally. As part of a long-term struggle, precedents set in one national jurisdiction may be drawn on by others, and as more and more national systems are changed, pressure for international changes may increase and resistance may be eroded.

We have already passed the point at which a majority of states no longer criminalize homosexuality. This is a modest but still significant development. As I suggested in section 3.2.A, toleration, in the minimal sense of not imposing formal disabilities on members of despised groups, is an important form of protection in itself and often a wedge for more active and inclusive protections. One might thus use decriminalization as a rough measure of whether a state would be willing to consider seriously endorsing formal international protection for sexual minorities.

At the other end of the spectrum, same-sex marriage has become a major battleground issue in countries with relatively strong records on or commitments to active protection of sexual minorities. It, along with adoption by same-sex couples, has proved an unusually powerfully emotive issue even among many people that strongly support removing other legal disabilities. As I complete the final revisions of this chapter, same-sex marriage is legally recognized and performed in Argentina, Belgium, Canada, Denmark, Iceland, Netherlands, Norway, Portugal, Spain, South Africa, and Sweden, plus some jurisdictions in Mexico and the United States, and recognized but not performed in Israel. In addition, nearly twenty countries recognize some form of domestic partnership for same-sex couples, which provides certain rights, but often far short of the full set characteristic of marriage, and in any case not granting the same status (and thus perpetuating legal disability based on sexual orientation). Thirty years ago, this might have seemed fantastic to all but the most optimistic advocates. Nonetheless, this is still only about one-sixth of the countries of the world.

Regional action suggests an intermediate arena of struggle. With Danish legislative approval of same-sex marriage in June 2012, pressure has increased on Finland, the only remaining Nordic country that denies marriage equality. I would suspect that within the next decade a regional norm will be fairly firmly established in Western Europe—although until that spreads into Eastern Europe, perhaps through the Council of Europe human rights system, it will not have a powerful global impact. Looking a bit further into the future, the Inter-American system seems a promising arena, perhaps twenty years from now, for regional action. And such regional hubs can serve both to press laggards in the region and to push the global struggle to a higher level. This is particularly true if there is substantial diversity of views in other regions, allowing advocates to argue that the more progressive regions reflect the emerging trend of international action.

6. Paths of Incremental Change

One other prominent place for international action should be noted. Article 17 of the International Covenant on Civil and Political Rights includes a right to privacy. Toonen brought his case against a Tasmanian sodomy law criminalizing consensual sex among members of the same sex. The Human Rights Committee found that "it is undisputed that adult consensual sexual activity in private is covered by the concept of 'privacy.'"[25] Although perhaps true in this particular case, where Australia did not deny the private nature of the acts, such an understanding, as we have seen above, is anything but undisputed in many countries of the world. But in such countries, privacy and the decriminalization of same sex relations may represent an important foot in the door.

The limited nature of the progress represented by mere decriminalization needs to be emphasized. It does nothing directly to eliminate civil disabilities, let alone social prejudice. Real *protection* for sexual minorities must involve inclusion within the right to nondiscrimination (and probably also incorporation under the rubric of equal protection of the laws). While struggling for that full protection and inclusion, though, an expanding sphere of privacy and protection against criminal prosecution are valuable resources.

We have thus worked backward from an ultimate aim of explicit recognition as a prohibited ground of discrimination to the very minimal toleration of decriminalization of private same-sex relations. If we think historically and politically, however, rather than conceptually and theoretically, we can reverse the direction of the flow and see an implicit strategy for achieving full inclusion.

---

25. Human Rights Committee, Communication 488/1992, paragraph 8.2.

Kees Waaldijk has found something very much like such a sequence in the recognition of legal rights for homosexuals in European countries: "The law in most countries seems to be moving on a line starting at (0) total ban on homo-sex, then going through the process of (1) the decriminalisation of sex between adults, followed by (2) the equalisation of ages of consent, (3) the introduction of anti-discrimination legislation, and (4) the introduction of legal partnership. A fifth point on the line might be the legal recognition of homosexual parenthood" (Waaldijk 1994: 51–52). The basic logic is one of gradual inclusion, moving through increasingly active measures of nondiscrimination in a wide range of areas of public activity.

Waaldijk identifies ten principal areas of legal change: touching, safety, organizations, leisure, information, nondiscrimination, services, employment, partnerships, and parenthood. Within each domain there is a similar functional logic of progress from minimal toleration through active recognition and support. For example, within the category of homosexual safety he identifies three principal areas of activity, ranging from ending of official repression (e.g., police raids, lack of safety in prisons, official registration), through the application of general laws to crimes against homosexuals, to special provisions to protect lesbians and gays. In the area of lesbian/gay organizations, progress can be measured from permission to organize, through official recognition as legal persons, to support from the authorities (Waaldijk 1994: 69–72).

Waaldijk's concluding advice for national activists bears repeating here:

1. Think of the legal recognition of homosexuality as a number of parallel developments in more than ten different fields.
2. Think of the developments in each field as a series of many small steps.
3. Look at the experiences in other countries to find out what these steps normally are, and what their standard sequence is.
4. Look at the experiences in other foreign countries to find out where, at this moment of time, political pressure for legal reform can be most effectively applied.
5. Do not try too hard to make your legal system jump; be content with it only taking steps. But do keep the system walking. (Waaldijk 1994: 68)

At the international level, similar advice seems warranted. Keep in mind the ideal of full explicit inclusion under international nondiscrimination law, but don't expect miracles. Take advantage of whatever avenues are available to transform international human rights norms in ways that can contribute to lifting the burden imposed on sexual minorities. Remain ready for a long struggle.

As the continuing problems of women, racial and ethnic minorities, and some religious minorities remind us, even after formal protection is granted the struggle for effective enjoyment of rights to nondiscrimination is likely to remain difficult. "All human rights for all" is a goal to which, even in the best of circumstances, we will always be aspiring. While striving to close the gap between ideal and reality, we can never expect practice to conform completely to theory. The case of sexual minorities reminds us that progress in one area—in this case, discrimination against women and racial minorities—often allows, and by example perhaps even encourages, attention to shift to new problems.

References

Agi, Marc. 1998. *René Cassin, Prix Nobel de la Paix (1887–1976):Père de la Déclaration universelle des droits de l'homme.* N.p.: Librairie Académique Perrin.

Alexander, John M. 2004. Capabilities, Human Rights and Moral Pluralism. *International Journal of Human Rights* 8 (4):451–69.

Ali, Shaheen Sardar. 2000. *Gender and Human Rights in Islam and International Law: Equal Before Allah, Unequal Before Man?* Boston: Kluwer Law International.

Alston, Philip, ed. 2011. *The United Nations and Human Rights: A Critical Appraisal.* Oxford: Oxford University Press.

Alston, Philip, and James Crawford, eds. 2000. *The Future of UN Human Rights Treaty Monitoring.* Cambridge: Cambridge University Press.

Alston, Philip, and Bridget Gilmour-Walsh. 1996. *The Best Interests of the Child: Towards a Synthesis of Children's Rights and Cultural Values.* Florence: International Child Development Centre, UNICEF.

Alston, Philip, Stephen Parker, and John Seymour, eds. 1992. *Children, Rights, and the Law.* Oxford: Clarendon Press.

American Anthropological Association, Executive Committee. 1947. Statement on Human Rights Submitted to the Commission on Human Rights, United Nations. *American Anthropologist* 49 (4):539–43.

Ames, Roger. 1997. Continuing the Conversation on Chinese Human Rights. *Ethics and International Affairs* 11:177–205.

Ames, Roger, and Henry Rosemont Jr. 1998. *The Analects of Confucius: A Philosophical Translation.* New York: Ballantine Books.

Amnesty International. 2001. *Ecuador: No to "Social Cleansing of People because of their Sexual Orientation*: AI Index AMR 28/011/2001.

Anand, Sudhir, and Amartya K. Sen. 1996. *Sustainable Human Development: Concepts and Priorities.* New York: United Nations Development Programme, Office of Development Studies.

Anaya, S. James. 2009. *International Human Rights and Indigenous Peoples.* New York: Aspen Publishers.

Andreassen, Bard-Anders. 1992. Article 22. In *The Universal Declaration of Human Rights: A Commentary*, edited by A. Eide, G. Alfredsson, G. Melander, L. A. Rehof, A. Rosas and T. Swinehart. Oslo: Scandinavian University Press.

Angle, Stephen C. 2002. *Human Rights and Chinese Thought: A Cross-Cultural Inquiry*. Cambridge: Cambridge University Press.

Annan, Kofi. 1999. Two Concepts of Sovereignty. *Economist*, September 18, http://www.economist.com/node/324795.

Arkes, Hadley. 1998. The Axioms of Public Policy. In *Natural Law and Contemporary Public Policy*, edited by D. F. Forte. Washington, D.C.: Georgetown University Press.

Arnardóttir, Oddny Mjöll, and Gerard Quinn, eds. 2009. *The United Nations Convention on the Rights of Persons with Disabilities: European and Scandinavian Perspectives*. Leiden: Brill.

Asante, S. K. B. 1969. Nation Building and Human Rights in Emergent Africa. *Cornell International Law Journal* 2:72-107.

Asquith, Stewart, and Malcolm Hill, eds. 1994. *Justice for Children*. Dordrecht: Martinus Nijhoff.

Austin, John. 1954 [1832]. *The Province of Jurisprudence Determined*. New York: Noonday Press.

Baehr, Peter R. 2000. Trials and Errors: The Netherlands and Human Rights. In *Human Rights and Comparative Foreign Policy*, edited by D. P. Forsythe. Tokyo: United Nations University Press.

Bagaric, Mirko and Allan James. 2006. The Vacuous Concept of Dignity. *Journal of Human Rights* 5 (2):257–70.

Bales, Kevin. 2012. *Disposable People: New Slavery in the Global Economy*. Berkeley: University of California Press.

Bales, Kevin, Zoe Trodd, and Alex Kent Williamson. 2009. *Modern Slavery: The Secret World of 27 Million People*. London: Oneworld.

Bartolomei de la Cruz, Hector, Geraldo von Potobsky, and Lee Swepson. 1996. *The International Labor Organization: The International Standards System and Basic Human Rights*. Boulder: Westview Press.

Bay, Christian. 1977. Human Needs and Political Education. In *Human Needs and Politics*, edited by R. Fitzgerald. Rushcutters Bay, Australia: Pergamon Press.

——. 1982. Self-Respect as a Human Right: Thoughts on the Dialectics of Wants and Needs in the Struggle for Human Community. *Human Rights Quarterly* 4 (1):53–75.

Bayefsky, Anne F., ed. 2000. *The UN Human Rights Treaty System in the 21st Century*. The Hague: Kluwer Law International.

Bayley, David. 1964. *Public Liberties in New States*. Chicago: Rand McNally.

Bedau, Hugo Adam. 1979. Human Rights and Foreign Assistance Programs. In *Human Rights and U.S. Foreign Policy*, edited by P. G. Brown and D. Maclean. Lexington: Lexington Books.

Beitz, Charles R. 1979. Human Rights and Social Justice. In *Human Rights and U.S. Foreign Policy*, edited by P. G. Brown and D. Maclean. Lexington: Lexington Books.

——. 1980. Nonintervention and Communal Integrity. *Philosophy and Public Affairs* 9(4):385-391.

Bell, Daniel A. 1993. *Communitarianism and Its Critics*. Oxford: Oxford University Press.

——. 1996. The East Asian Challenge to Human Rights: Reflections on an East-West Dialogue. *Human Rights Quarterly* 18 (3):641–67.

Bell, Daniel A., and Hahm Chaibong, eds. 2003. *Confucianism for the Modern World.* Cambridge: Cambridge University Press.

Bell, Lynda, Andrew J. Nathan, and Ilan Peleg, eds. 2001. *Negotiating Culture and Human Rights.* New York: Columbia University Press.

Benn, Stanley I. 1967. Rights. In *The Encyclopedia of Philosophy.* New York: Macmillan.

Berenstein, Alexandre. 1982. Economic and Social Rights: Their Inclusion in the European Convention on Human Rights. Problems of Formulation and Interpretation. *Human Rights Law Journal* 2 (3–4):257–80.

Berger, Peter. 1983 [1970]. On the Obsolescence of the Concept of Honour. In *Revisions: Changing Perspectives in Moral Philosophy*, edited by S. Hauerwas and A. MacIntyre. Notre Dame: University of Notre Dame Press.

Béteille, André. 1965. *Caste, Class, and Power: Changing Patterns of Stratification in a Tanjore Village.* Berkeley: University of California Press.

——. 1983. *The Idea of Natural Inequality and Other Essays.* Delhi: Oxford.

Beveridge, William H. 1945. *Full Employment in a Free Society.* New York: W. W. Norton.

Beyleveld, Deryck, and Roger Brownsword. 1998. Human Dignity, Human Rights, and Human Genetics. *Modern Law Review* 61 (5):661–80.

——. 2001. *Human Dignity in Bioethics and Biolaw.* Oxford: Oxford University Press.

Bhagwati, Jagdish. 1966. *The Economics of Underdeveloped Countries.* New York: McGraw Hill.

Blackwood, Evelyn, and Saskia E. Wieringa, eds. 1999. *Female Desires: Same-Sex Relations and Transgender Practices across Cultures.* New York: Columbia University Press.

Boaz, David. 1997. *Libertarianism: A Primer.* New York: The Free Press.

Borgwardt, E. 2005. *A New Deal for the World: America's Vision of Human Rights.* Cambridge, Mass.: Harvard University Press.

Boswell, John. 1980. *Christianity, Social Tolerance and Homosexuality: Gay People in Western Europe from the Beginning of the Christian Era to the Fourteenth Century.* Chicago: University of Chicago Press.

——. 1994. *Same-Sex Unions in Premodern Europe.* New York: Villard Books.

Bouglé, Celestin. 1971 [1908]. *Essays on the Caste System.* Cambridge: Cambridge University Press.

Boulding, Kenneth E. 1958. *Principles of Economic Policy.* Englewood Cliffs, N.J.: Prentice-Hall.

Brennan, Andrew, and Y. S. Lo. 2007. Two Conceptions of Human Dignity: Honour and Self-Determination. In *Perspectives on Human Dignity: A Conversation*, edited by J. Malpas and N. Lickiss. Dordrecht: Springer Netherlands.

Brilmayer, Lea. 1995. What's the Matter with Selective Intervention? *Arizona Law Review* 37:955–70.

Brooten, Bernadette J. 1996. *Love Between Women: Early Christian Responses to Female Homoeroticism.* Chicago: University of Chicago Press.

Brown, Chris. 1999. Universal Human Rights: A Critique. In *Human Rights in Global Politics*, edited by T. Dunne and N. J. Wheeler. Cambridge: Cambridge University Press.

Brownlie, Ian. 1973. Thoughts on Kind-Hearted Gunmen. In *Humanitarian Intervention and the United Nations*, edited by R. B. Lillich. Charlottesville: University Press of Virginia.

——. 1974. Humanitarian Intervention. In *Law and Civil War in the Modern World*, edited by J. N. Moore. Baltimore: Johns Hopkins University Press.

Bruce, Maurice. 1961. *The Coming of the Welfare State*. London: B. T. Batsford.

Brysk, Alison. 2005. *Human Rights and Private Wrongs: Constructing Global Civil Society*. New York: Routledge.

Buckley, William F., Jr. 1980. Human Rights and Foreign Policy: A Proposal. *Foreign Affairs* 58:775–96.

Buijs, Laurens, Gert Hekma, and Jan Willem Duyvendak. 2011. 'As Long as They Keep Away from Me': The Paradox of Antigay Violence in a Gay-Friendly Country. *Sexualities* 14(6):632-52.

Bull, Hedley. 1977. *The Anarchical Society: A Study of Order in World Politics*. New York: Columbia University Press.

Burgoon, Brian. 2001. Globalization and Welfare Compensation: Disentangling the Ties that Bind. *International Organization* 55 (3):509–51.

Burgourge-Larsen, Laurence, and Amaya Úbeda de Torres. 2011. *The Inter-American Court of Human Rights: Case Law and Commentary*. Oxford: Oxford University Press.

Busia, Nana Kusi Appea, Jr. 1994. The Status of Human Rights in Pre-Colonial Africa: Implications for Contemporary Practices. In *Africa, Human Rights, and the Global System: The Political Economy of Human Rights in a Changing World*, edited by E. McCarthy-Arnolds, D. R. Penna and D. J. C. Sobrepena. Westport: Greenwood Press.

Campos, Jose Edgardo, and Hilton L. Root. 1996. *The Key to the Asian Miracle: Making Shared Growth Credible*. Washington, D.C.: The Brookings Institution.

Cancik, Hubert. 2002. "Dignity of Man" and "*Persona*" in Stoic Anthropology: Some Remarks on Cicero, *De Officiis I*, 105–7. In *The Concept of Human Dignity in Human Rights Discourse*, edited by D. Kretzmer and E. Klein. The Hague: Kluwer Law International.

Cantarella, Eva. 1987. *Pandora's Daughters: The Role and Status of Women in Greek and Roman Antiquity*. Baltimore: Johns Hopkins University Press.

Cardoso, Fernando Henrique, and Enzo Faletto. 1979. *Dependency and Development in Latin America*. Berkeley: University of California Press.

Carmichael, Cathie. 2009. *Genocide before the Holocaust*. New Haven: Yale University Press.

Cassesse, Antonio. 1990. *Human Rights in a Changing World*. Philadelphia: Temple University Press.

Chalmers, Don, and Ryucichi Ida. 2007. On the International Legal Aspects of Human Dignity. In *Perspectives on Human Dignity: A Conversation*, edited by J. Malpas and N. Lickiss. Dordrecht: Springer Netherlands.

Chan, Joseph. 1999. Confucian Perspective on Human Rights for Contemporary China. In *The East Asian Challenge for Human Rights*, edited by J. Bauer and D. A. Bell. Cambridge: Cambridge University Press.

——. 2002. Moral Autonomy, Civil Liberties, and Confucianism. *Philosophy East and West* 52 (3):281–310.

Chan, Wing-Tsit, ed. 1963. *A Source Book in Chinese Philosophy*. Princeton: Princeton University Press.

Charney, Jonathan I. 1999. Anticipatory Humanitarian Intervention. *American Journal of International Law* 93 (4):834–41.

Chenery, Hollis, and Moises Syrquin. 1975. *Patterns of Development, 1950-1970*. London: Oxford University Press.

Chomsky, Noam. 1998. The United States and the Challenge of Relativity. In *Human Rights Fifty Years On: A Reappraisal*, edited by T. Evans. Manchester: Manchester University Press.

Christoffersen, Jonas, and Mikael Rask Madsen, eds. 2011. *The European Court of Human Rights between Law and Politics* Oxford: Oxford University Press.

Cicero, Marcus Tullius. 1913 [44 BCE]. *De Officiis*. Loeb Classical Library. Cambridge, Mass.: Harvard University Press.

Claude, Inis, Jr. 1955. *National Minorities: An International Problem*. Cambridge, Mass.: Harvard University Press.

Cohen, Joshua. 2004. Minimalism about Human Rights: The Most We Can Hope For? *Journal of Political Philosophy* 12 (2):190–213.

Collier, David, and Steven Levitsky. 1997. Democracy with Adjectives: Conceptual Innovation in Comparative Research. *World Politics* 49:430–51.

Council of Europe. 2010. *The European Court of Human Rights in Facts and Figures*. Strasbourg: Council of Europe.

Council of Europe, and Organization for Security and Cooperation in Europe. 2007. *National Minority Standards: A Compilation of OSCE and Council of Europe Texts*. Strasbourg: Council of Europe.

Cox, Robert W. 1996. *Approaches to World Order*. Cambridge: Cambridge University Press.

Cranston, Maurice. 1964. *What Are Human Rights?* New York: Basic Books.

——. 1973. *What Are Human Rights?* New York: Taplinger.

Craven, Matthew C. R. 1995. *The International Covenant on Economic, Social, and Cultural Rights: A Perspective on its Development*. Oxford: Clarendon Press.

Creel, Austin B. 1972. Dharma as an Ethical Category Relating to Freedom and Responsibility. *Philosophy East and West* 22 (2):155–68.

Dahl, Robert A. 1971. *Polyarchy: Participation and Opposition*. New Haven: Yale University Press.

——. 1989. *Democracy and Its Critics*. New Haven: Yale University Press.

Damrosch, Lori Fisler. 2000. The Inevitability of Selective Response: Principles to Guide Urgent Action. In *Kosovo and the Challenge of Humanitarian Intervention: Selective Indignation, Collective Action, and International Citizenship*, edited by A. Schnabel and R. Thakur. Tokyo: United Nations University Press.

Davis, Julia. 2007. Doing Justice to Dignity in the Criminal Law. In *Perspectives on Human Dignity: A Conversation*, edited by J. Malpas and N. Lickiss. Dordrecht: Springer.

Davis, Marvin. 1976. A Philosophy of Hindu Rank from Rural West Bengal. *Journal of Asian Studies* 36:5–24.

Deakin, Simon. 2005. Social Rights in a Globalized Economy. In *Labour Rights as Human Rights*, edited by P. Alston. Oxford: Oxford University Press.

De Bary, William Theodore, and Irene Bloom, eds. 1999. *Sources of Chinese Tradition: Volume One, from Earliest Times to 1600*. New York: Columbia University Press.

Dicke, Klaus. 2002. The Founding Function of Human Dignity in the Universal Declaration of Human Rights. In *The Concept of Human Dignity in Human Rights Discourse*, edited by D. Kretzmer and E. Klein. The Hague: Kluwer Law International.

Detrick, Sharon. 1999. *A Commentary on the United Nations Convention on the Rights of the Child*. The Hague ; Boston: M. Nijhoff Publishers.

Dickson, Anna F. 1997. *Development and International Relations: A Critical Introduction*. Cambridge: Polity Press.

Donnelly, Jack. 1980. Natural Law and Right in Aquinas' Political Thought. *Western Political Quarterly* 33:520–35.

———. 1985a. *The Concept of Human Rights*. New York: St. Martin's Press; London: Croom Helm.

———. 1985b. In Search of the Unicorn: The Jurisprudence of the Right to Development. *California Western International Law Review* 15:473–509.

———. 1993. Third Generation Rights. In *Peoples and Minorities in International Law*, edited by C. Brolmann, R. Lefeber, and M. Zieck. The Hague: Kluwer.

———. 1998. Human Rights: A New Standard of Civilization? *International Affairs* 74 (1):1–24.

———. 2005. The Virtues of Legalization. In *Legalization and Human Rights*, edited by B. Cali and S. Meckled-Garcia. London: Routledge.

Doppelt, Gerald. 1978. Walzer's Theory of Morality in International Relations. *Philosophy and Public Affairs* 8:3-26.

———. 1980. Statism without Foundations. *Philosophy and Public Affairs* 9(4):398-403.

Douglas, Gillian, and Leslie Sebba, eds. 1998. *Children's Rights and Traditional Values*. Aldershot: Ashgate Dartmouth.

Dover, K. 1986. *Greek Homosexuality*. Second ed. Cambridge: Harvard University Press.

Dreze, Jean, and Amartya Sen. 1990. *Hunger and Public Action*. Oxford: Clarendon Press.

Duby, Georges. 1974 [1973]. *The Early Growth of the European Economy: Warriors and Peasants from the Seventh to the Twelfth Century*. Ithaca: Cornell University Press.

Dumont, Louis. 1980. *Homo Hierarchicus: The Caste System and Its Implications*. Chicago: University of Chicago Press.

Dworkin, Ronald. 1977. *Taking Rights Seriously*. Cambridge, Mass.: Harvard University Press.

———. 1985. *A Matter of Principle*. Cambridge, Mass.: Harvard University Press.

Dyck, Arthur J. 1994. *Rethinking Rights and Responsibilities: The Moral Bonds of Community*. Cleveland: Pilgrim Press.

Economist. 2001. Righting Wrongs. *Economist*: August 18–24.

Eide, Asbjørn. 1995. Economic, Social and Cultural Rights as Human Rights. In *Economic, Social and Cultural Rights: A Textbook*, edited by A. Eide, C. Krause and A. Rosas. Dordrecht: Martinus Nijhoff.

Eide, Asbjørn, Gudmundur Alfredsson, Göran Melander, Lars Adam Rehof, Allan Rosas, and Theresa Swinehart, eds. 1992. *The Universal Declaration of Human Rights: A Commentary*. Oslo: Scandinavian University Press.

Eide, Asbjørn, and Wenche Barth Eide. 1999. Article 25. In *The Universal Declaration of Human Rights: A Common Standard of Achievement*, edited by G. Alfredsson and A. Eide. The Hague: Martinus Nijhoff.

El-Hage, Youssef K. 2004. Human Rights: A Western, Christian Invention? *Theological Review* 25 (2):3–19.

Elliott, J. H. 1992. A Europe of Composite Monarchies. *Past and Present* 137:48–71.

Engelhart, Neil A. 2000. Rights and Culture in the Asian Values Argument: The Rise and Fall of Confucian Ethics in Singapore. *Human Rights Quarterly* 22 (2):548–68.

Englard, Izhak. 1999. Human Dignity: From Antiquity to Modern Israel's Constitutional Framework. *Cardozo Law Review* 21:1903–27.

Engle, Karen. 2001. From Skepticism to Embrace: Human Rights and the American Anthropological Association from 1947–1999. *Human Rights Quarterly* 23 (3):536–59.

Enke, Stephen. 1963. *Economics for Development*. Englewood Cliffs, N.J.: Prentice-Hall.

Escobar, Arturo. 1995. *Encountering Development: The Making and Unmaking of the Third World*. Princeton: Princeton University Press.

Esping-Andersen, Gosta. 1990. *The Three Worlds of Welfare Capitalism*. Princeton: Princeton University Press.

Evans, Malcolm D., and Rod Morgan. 1998. *Preventing Torture: A Study of the European Convention for the Prevention of Torture and Inhuman or Degrading Treatment or Punishment*. New York: Oxford University Press.

Evans, Malcolm, and Rachel Murray, eds. 2008. *The African Charter on Human and Peoples' Rights: The System in Practice, 1986–2006*. Cambridge: Cambridge University Press.

Evans, Tony. 1996. *US Hegemony and the Project of Universal Human Rights*. Houndmills: Macmillan Press.

———. 2005. *The Politics of Human Rights: A Global Perspective*. 2nd ed. London: Pluto Press.

Fairbank, John King. 1972. *The United States and China*. 3rd ed. Cambridge, Mass.: Harvard University Press.

Fairley, H. Scott. 1980. State Actors, Humanitarian Intervention, and International Law: Reopening Pandora's Box. *Georgia Journal of International and Comparative Law* 10:29–63.

Farer, Tom J., Daniele Archibugi, Chris Brown, Neta C. Crawford, Thomas G. Weiss, and Nicholas J. Wheeler. 2005. Roundtable: Humanitarian Intervention After 9/11. *International Relations* 19 (2):211-250.

Fein, Helen. 1979. *Accounting for Genocide: National Responses and Jewish Victimization during the Holocaust*. Chicago: University of Chicago Press.

Feinberg, Joel. 1973. *Social Philosophy*. Englewood Cliffs, N.J.: Prentice-Hall.

———. 1980. *Rights, Justice and the Bounds of Liberty: Essays in Social Philosophy*. Princeton: Princeton University Press.

Felice, William. 2003. *The Global New Deal: Economic and Social Human Rights in World Politics*. Lanham: Rowman and Littlefield.

Femia, Joseph V. 1981. *Gramsci's Political Thought: Hegemony, Consciousness, and the Revolutionary Process*. Oxford: Clarendon Press.

Fernyhough, Timothy. 1993. Human Rights and Precolonial Africa. In *Human Rights and Governance in Africa*, edited by R. Cohen, G. Hyden and W. P. Nagan. Gainesville: University Press of Florida.

Ferrera, Maurizio. 2005. *The Boundaries of Welfare: European Integration and the New Spatial Politics of Social Protection*. Oxford: Oxford University Press.

Finnis, John. 1980. *Natural Law and Natural Rights*. Oxford: Clarendon Press.

Flinterman, Cees. 1990. Three Generations of Human Rights. In *Human Rights in a Pluralist World: Individuals and Collectivities*, edited by J. Berting et al. Westport: Meckler.

Flora, Peter, and Jens Alber. 1981. Modernization, Democratization, and the Development of Welfare States in Western Europe. In *The Development of Welfare States in Europe and America*, edited by P. Flora and A. J. Heidenheimer. New Brunswick, N.J.: Transaction Books.

Flynn, Eilionóir. 2011. *From Rhetoric to Action: Implementing the UN Convention on the Rights of Persons with Disabilities*. Cambridge: Cambridge University Press.

Fonteyne, Jean-Pierre L. 1974. The Customary International Law Doctrine of Humanitarian Intervention: Its Current Validity under the UN Charter. *California Western International Law Review* 4:203–70.

Fortin, Ernest. 1982. The New Rights Theory and the Natural Law. *Review of Politics* 44:590–612.

Fortin, Ernest L., ed. 1996. *Human Rights, Virtue, and the Common Good: Untimely Meditations on Religion and Politics*. Lanham: Rowman and Littlefield.

Foss, Robert J. 1994. The Demise of Homosexual Exclusion: New Possibilities for Gay and Lesbian Immigration. *Harvard Civil Rights—Civil Liberties Law Review* 29:439–475.

Fottrell, Deirdre, ed. 2000. *Revisiting Children's Rights: 10 Years of the UN Convention on the Rights of the Child*. The Hague: Kluwer Law International.

Foucault, Michel. 1990. *The History of Sexuality: Volume I: An Introduction*. New York: Vintage Books.

Franck, Thomas M., and Nigel S. Rodley. 1973. After Bangladesh: The Law of Humanitarian Intervention by Military Force. *American Journal of International Law* 67 (2):275–305.

Freeman, Michael. 1994. The Philosophical Foundations of Human Rights. *Human Rights Quarterly* 16 (3):491–514.

Frost, Mervyn. 1996. *Ethics in International Affairs: A Constitutive Theory*. Cambridge: Cambridge University Press.

Gardner, Richard N. 1956. *Sterling-Dollar Diplomacy: Anglo-American Collaboration in the Reconstruction of Multilateral Trade*. Oxford: Clarendon Press.

Gavison, Ruth. 2003. On the Relationship between Civil and Political Rights, and Social and Economic Rights. In *The Globalization of Human Rights*, edited by J.-M. Coicaud, M. W. Doyle and A.-M. Gardner. Tokyo: United Nations University Press.

George, Susan, and Fabrizio Sabelli. 1994. *Faith and Credit: The World Bank's Secular Empire*. Boulder: Westview Press.

Gewirth, Alan. 1982. *Human Rights: Essays on Justification and Applications*. Chicago: University of Chicago Press.

——. 1992. Human Dignity as the Basis of Rights. In *The Constitution of Rights: Human Dignity and American Values*, edited by M. J. Meyer and W. A. Parent. Ithaca: Cornell University Press.

——. 1996. *The Community of Rights*. Chicago: University of Chicago Press.

Gilbert, Felix. 1961. *To the Farewell Address: Ideas of Early American Foreign Policy*. Princeton: Princeton University Press.

Ginter, Konrad, Erick Denters, and Paul J. I. M. de Waart, eds. 1995. *Sustainable Development and Good Governance*. Dordrecht: Martinus Nijhoff.

Glendon, Mary Ann. 2003. The Forgotten Crucible: The Latin American Influence on the Universal Declaration of Human Rights Idea. *Harvard Human Rights Journal* 16:27–39.

Goldman, Robert K. 2009. History and Action: The Inter-American Human Rights System and the Role of the Inter-American Commission on Human Rights. *Human Rights Quarterly* 31:856–87.

Gómez, Eduardo J. 2010. Friendly Government, Cruel Society: AIDS and the Politics of Homosexual Strategic Mobilization in Brazil. In Javier Corrales and Mario Pecheny, eds., *The Politics of Sexuality in Latin America: A Reader on Lesbian, Gay, Bisexual and Transgendered Rights.* Pittsburgh: University of Pittsburgh Press.

Gong, Gerrit W. 1984. *The Standard of 'Civilisation' in International Society.* Oxford: Clarendon Press.

Goodin, Robert E., Bruce Headley, Ruud Muffels, and Henk-Jan Dirven. 1999. *The Real Worlds of Welfare Capitalism.* Cambridge: Cambridge University Press.

Goodman, Roger, Gordon White, and Huck-ju Kwon, eds. 1998. *The East Asian Welfare Model: Welfare Orientalism and the State.* New York: Routledge.

Gordon, Joy. 1998. The Concept of Human Rights: The History and Meaning of its Politicization. *Brooklyn Journal of International Law* 23:689–791.

Gramsci, Antonio. 1971. *Selections from the Prison Notebooks.* Translated by Q. Hoare and G. N. Smith. New York: International Publishers.

Grant, Stefanie. 2000. The NGO Role: Implementing, Expanding Protection and Monitoring the Monitors. In *The UN Human Rights Treaty System in the 21st Century,* edited by A. F. Bayefsky. The Hague: Kluwer Law International.

Green, Reginald Herbold. 1981. Basic Human Rights/Needs: Some Problems of Categorical Translation and Unification. *Review of the International Commission of Jurists* 27:53–58.

Grider, Stuart. 1994. Sexual Orientation as Grounds for Asylum in the United States. *Harvard International Law Journal* 35:213–24.

Griffin, James. 2008. *On Human Rights.* Oxford: Oxford University Press.

Grillo, R. D., and R. L. Stirrat, eds. 1997. *Discourses of Development: Anthropological Perspectives.* Oxford: Berg.

Gros Espiell, Hector. 1979. The Evolving Concept of Human Rights: Western, Socialist and Third World Approaches. In *Human Rights: Thirty Years after the Universal Declaration,* edited by B. G. Ramcharan. The Hague: Martinus Nijhoff.

Gupta, Akhil, and James Ferguson. 1997. Culture, Power, Place: Ethnography at the End of an Era. In *Culture, Power, Place: Explorations in Critical Anthropology,* edited by A. Gupta and J. Ferguson. Durham: Duke University Press.

Gutmann, Amy, and Dennis Thompson. 1996. *Democracy and Disagreement.* Cambridge: Belknap Press.

Haas, Ernst B. 1970. *Human Rights and International Action: The Case of Freedom of Association.* Stanford: Stanford University Press.

Habermas, Jurgen. 1993. *Justification and Application: Remarks on Discourse Ethics.* Cambridge: MIT Press.

——. 1996. *Between Facts and Norms: Contributions to a Discourse Theory of Law and Democracy.* Translated by W. Rehg. Cambridge, Mass.: MIT Press.

——. 1998. Remarks on Legitimation through Human Rights. *Philosophy and Social Criticism* 24 (2/3):157–71.

Hadjor, Kofi Beunor. 1998. Whose Human Rights? *Journal of Asian and African Studies* 33 (4):359–68.

Hammarberg, Thomas. 2011. *Human Rights in Europe: No Grounds for Complacency: Viewpoints by the Council of Europe Commissioner for Human Rights.* Strasbourg: Council of Europe.

Hammarskjold, Dag. 1945. *From Bretton Woods to Full Employment.* Stockholm: Ivar Haeggstroms Boktryckeri.

Han, Yanlong. 1996. Legal Protection of Human Rights in China. In *Human Rights: Chinese and Dutch Perspectives*, edited by P. R. Baehr, F. van Hoof, N. Liu, Z. Tao and J. Smith. The Hague: Martinus Nijhoff.

Hansen, Mogens Herman. 1993. The *Polis* as a Citizen-State. In *The Ancient Greek City-State*, edited by M. H. Hansen. Copenhagen: Royal Danish Academy of Sciences and Letters.

Harris, John, and John Sulston. 2004. Genetic Equity. *Nature Reviews. Genetics* 5 (10):796–800.

Hartney, Michael. 1995. Some Confusions Concerning Collective Rights. In *The Rights of Minority Cultures*, edited by W. Kymlicka. Oxford: Oxford University Press.

Hasenclever, Andreas, Peter Mayer, and Volker Rittberger, eds. 1997. *Theories of International Regimes*. Cambridge: Cambridge University Press.

———. 2000. Integrating Theories of International Regimes. *Review of International Studies* 26 (1).

Hassan, Farooq. 1981. Realpolitik in International Law: After the Tanzanian-Ugandan Conflict 'Humanitarian Intervention' Revisited. *Willamette Law Review* 17 (Fall).

Hasson, Kevin J. 2003. Religious Liberty and Human Dignity: A Tale of Two Declarations. *Harvard Journal of Law and Public Policy* 27 (1):81–92.

Hauser, Richard, and Irene Becker. 2000. Changes in the Distribution of Pre-Government and Post-Government Income in Germany, 1973–1993. In *The Personal Distribution of Income in an International Perspective*, edited by R. Hauser and I. Becker. Berlin: Springer.

Hehir, J. Bryan. 1980. Human Rights from a Theological and Ethical Perspective. In *The Moral Imperatives of Human Rights: A World Survey*, edited by K. W. Thompson. Lanham, Md.: University Press of America.

Held, David. 1987. *Models of Democracy*. Stanford: Stanford University Press.

Henkin, Louis. 1992. Human Dignity and Constitutional Rights. In *The Constitution of Rights: Human Dignity and American Values*, edited by M. J. Meyer and W. A. Parent. Ithaca: Cornell University Press.

———. 1995. *International Law: Politics and Values*. Dordrecht: Martinus Nijhoff.

———. 1999. Kosovo and the Law of 'Humanitarian Intervention'. *American Journal of International Law* 93 (4):October.

Henry, Charles P. 1996. Introduction: On Building a Human Rights Culture. In *International Rights and Responsibilities for the Future*, edited by K. W. Hunter and T. C. Mack. Westport: Praeger.

Herdt, Gilbert, ed. 1994. *Third Sex, Third Gender: Beyond Sexual Dimorphism in Culture and History*. New York: Zone Books.

Herskovits, Melville J. 1972. *Cultural Relativism: Perspectives in Cultural Pluralism*. New York: Random House.

Hewlett, Sylvia Ann. 1980. *The Cruel Dilemmas of Development: Twentieth-Century Brazil*. New York: Basic Books.

Hicks, Alexander M., and Joy Misra. 1993. Political Resources and the Growth of Welfare in Affluent Capitalist Democracies, 1960–1982. *American Journal of Sociology* 99 (3):668–710.

Hinsch, Bret. 1990. *Passions of the Cut Sleeve: The Male Homosexual Tradition in China*. Berkeley: University of California Press.

Hobart, Mark, ed. 1993. *An Anthropological Critique of Development: The Growth of Ignorance*. London: Routledge.

Holdrege, Barbara A. 2004. Dharma. In *The Hindu World*, edited by S. Mittal and G. Thursby. New York: Routledge.

Horsefield, J. Keith, ed. 1969. *The International Monetary Fund 1945–1965: Twenty Years of International Monetary Cooperation, Volume III: Documents*. Washington, D.C.: International Monetary Fund.

Howard, Rhoda E. 1984. Women's Rights in English-Speaking Sub-Saharan Africa. In *Human Rights and Development in Africa*, edited by C. E. J. Welch and R. I. Meltzer. Albany: State University of New York Press.

———. 1993. Cultural Absolutism and the Nostalgia for Community. *Human Rights Quarterly* 15: 315–38.

———. 1995. *Human Rights and the Search for Community*. Totowa, N.J.: Rowman and Littlefield.

———. 1999. Gay Rights and the Right to a Family: Conflicts between Liberal and Illiberal Belief Systems. In *Innovation and Inspiration: Fifty Years of the Universal Declaration of Human Rights*, edited by P. R. Baehr, C. Flinterman and M. Senders. Amsterdam: Royal Academy of Arts and Sciences.

Huber, Evelyne, and John D. Stephens. 2001. *Development and Crisis of the Welfare State: Parties and Policies in Global Markets*. Chicago: University of Chicago Press.

Hungerford, Thomas L. 2008. Income Inequality, Income Mobility, and Economic Policy: U.S. Trends in the 1980s and 1990s. Washington, D.C.: Congressional Research Service.

Huntington, Samuel P. 1968. *Political Order in Changing Societies*. New Haven: Yale University Press.

Huntington, Samuel P., and Joan M. Nelson. 1976. *No Easy Choice: Political Participation in Developing Countries*. Cambridge, Mass.: Harvard University Press.

Ikenberry, G. John. 1992. A World Economy Restored: Expert Consensus and the Anglo-American Postwar Settlement. *International Organization* 46 (1):289–321.

Independent International Commission on Kosovo. 2000. *The Kosovo Report: Conflict, International Response, Lessons Learned*. New York: Oxford University Press.

Innocent III. 1969 [c. 1200]. *On the Misery of the Human Condition*. Translated by M. M. Dietz. Indianapolis: Bobbs-Merrill.

Ishaque, Khalid M. 1974. Human Rights in Islamic Law. *The Review of the International Commission of Jurists* 12:30–39.

Ishay, Micheline. 2004. *The History of Human Rights: From Ancient Times to the Globalization Era*. Berkeley: University of California Press.

Ishwaran, K. 1980. Bhakti Tradition and Modernization: The Case of *Lingayatism*. *Journal of Asian and African Studies* 15 (1–2):72–82.

Jackson, Robert. 2000. *The Global Covenant: Human Conduct in a World of States*. Oxford: Oxford University Press.

Jackson Preece, Jennifer. 1998. *National Minorities and the European Nation-State System*. Oxford: Oxford University Press.

Johnson, Harry G. 1962. *Money, Trade, and Economic Growth*. Cambridge, Mass.: Harvard University Press.

Jordan, Mark D. 1997. *The Invention of Sodomy in Christian Theology*. Chicago: University of Chicago Press.

Kallen, Evelyn. 1996. Gay and Lesbian rights Issues: A Comparative Analysis of Sydney, Australia, and Toronto, Canada. *Human Rights Quarterly* 18 (February):206–23.

Kamir, Orit. 2002. Honor and Dignity Cultures: The Case of *Kavod* and *Kavod Ha-Adam* in Israeli Society and Law. In *The Concept of Human Dignity in Human Rights Discourse*, edited by D. Kretzmer and E. Klein. The Hague: Kluwer Law International.

Kant, Immanuel. 1930. *Lectures on Ethics*. Translated by L. Infield. London: Methuen.

——. 1981 [1785]. *Grounding for the Metaphysics of Morals*. Translated by J. Ellington. Indianapolis: Hackett.

——. 1983 [1793]. On the Proverb: That May be True in Theory, but is of No Practical Use. In *Perpetual Peace and Other Essays*, edited by T. Humphrey. Indianapolis: Hackett.

——. 1991 [1797]. *The Metaphysics of Morals*. Translated by M. Gregor. Cambridge: Cambridge University Press.

Katz, Jonathan, ed. 1975. *Government versus Homosexuals*. New York: Arno Press.

Kelly, Nathan J. 2004. Does Politics Really Matter? Policy and Government's Equalizing Influence in the United States. *American Politics Research* 32 (3):264–84.

Kennan, George F. 1985/86. Morality and Foreign Policy. *Foreign Affairs* 63:205–18.

Kennedy, Stetson. 1959. *Jim Crow Guide to the U.S.A.: The Laws, Customs and Etiquette Governing the Conduct of Nonwhites and Other Minorities as Second-Class Citizens*. London: Lawrence and Wishart.

Keohane, Robert O. 1982. The Demand for International Regimes. *International Organization* 36 (2):325–55.

Khadduri, Majid. 1946. Human Rights in Islam. *Annals* 243.

Klostermaier, Klaus K. 2007. *A Survey of Hinduism*. 3rd ed. Albany: State University of New York Press.

Kohl, Jurgen. 1981. Trends and Problems in Postwar Public Expenditure Development in Western Europe and North America. In *The Development of Welfare States in Europe and America*, edited by P. Flora and A. J. Heidenheimer. New Brunswick, N.J.: Transaction Books.

Kolenda, Pauline. 1978. *Caste in Contemporary India: Beyond Organic Solidarity*. Menlo Park, Calif.: Benjamin/Cummings.

Krasner, Stephen D. 1982. Structural Causes and Regime Consequences: Regimes as Intervening Variables. *International Organization* 36 (Spring):185–206.

Kraus, Franz. 1981. The Historical Development of Income Inequality in Western Europe and the United States. In *The Development of Welfare States in Europe and America*, edited by P. Flora and A. J. Heidenheimer. New Brunswick, N.J.: Transaction Books.

Kraynak, Robert P. 2003. 'Made in the Image of God': The Christian View of Human Dignity and Political Order. In *In Defense of Human Dignity: Essays for Our Times*, edited by R. P. Kraynak and G. Tinder. Notre Dame: University of Notre Dame Press.

Kristeller, Paul Oskar. 1972. *Renaissance Concepts of Man and Other Essays*. New York: Harper and Row.

Kritsiotis, Dino. 1998. Reappraising Policy Objections to Humanitarian Intervention. *Michigan Journal of International Law* 19:Summer.

Kuefler, Matthew. 2001. *The Manly Eunuch: Masculinity, Gender Ambiguity, and Christian Ideology in Late Antiquity*. Chicago: University of Chicago Press.

Kuhn, Dieter. 2009. *The Age of Confucian Rule: The Song Transformation of China*. Cambridge, Mass.: Belknap Press of Harvard University Press.

Kuznets, Simon. 1955. Economic Growth and Income Inequality. *American Economic Review* 45 (March).

Lakatos, Imre. 1970. Falsification and the Methodology of Scientific Research Programmes. In *Criticism and the Growth of Knowledge*, edited by I. Lakatos and A. Musgrave. Cambridge: Cambridge University Press.

———. 1978. *The Methodology of Scientific Research Programmes*. Cambridge: Cambridge University Press.

Langlois, Anthony J. 2005. The Narrative Metaphysics of Human Rights. *International Journal of Human Rights* 9 (3):369–87.

Lau, M. P., and M. L. Ng. 1989. Homosexuality in Chinese Culture. *Culture, Medicine and Psychiatry* 13 (4):465–88.

LeBlanc, Lawrence J. 1991. *The United States and the Genocide Convention*. Durham: Duke University Press.

Lee, Manwoo. 1985. North Korea and the Western Notion of Human Rights. In *Human Rights in an East Asian Perspective*, edited by J.C. Hsiung. New York: Paragon House.

Legesse, Asmarom. 1980. Human Rights in African Political Culture. In *The Moral Imperatives of Human Rights: A World Survey*, edited by K. W. Thompson. Washington, D.C.: University Press of America.

Leipziger, Danny M., and Vinod Thomas. 1997. An Overview of East Asian Experience. In *Lessons from East Asia*, edited by D. M. Leipziger. Ann Arbor: University of Michigan Press.

Leupp, Gary P. 1995. *Male Colors: The Construction of Homosexuality in Tokugawa Japan*. Berkeley: University of California Press.

Lewis, Jon E., ed. 2003. *A Documentary History of Human Rights: A Record of the Events, Documents and Speeches That Shaped Our World*. New York: Carroll and Graf.

Lewis, Mark Edward. 2007. *The Early Chinese Empires: Qin and Han*. Cambridge, Mass.: Belknap Press of Harvard University Press.

Lewis, Milton. 2007. A Brief History of Human Dignity: Idea and Application. In *Perspectives on Human Dignity: A Conversation*, edited by J. Malpas and N. Lickiss. Dordrecht: Springer Netherlands.

Liebich, Andre. 2008. Minority as Inferiority: Minority Rights in Historical Perspective. *Review of International Studies* 34 (2):243–63.

Lillich, Richard B. 1967. Forcible Self-Help by States to Protect Human Rights. *Iowa Law Review* 53.

Lindholm, Tore. 1999. Article 1. In *The Universal Declaration of Human Rights: A Common Standard of Achievement*, edited by G. Alfredsson and A. Eide. The Hague: Martinus Nijhoff.

Lipset, Seymour Martin. 1959. Some Social Requisites for Democracy: Economic Development and Political Legitimacy. *American Political Science Review* 53 (1):69–105.

Liu Shu-Hsien. 2003. *Essentials of Contemporary Neo-Confucian Philosophy*. Westport: Praeger.

Lo, Chung-Sho. 1949. Human Rights in the Chinese Tradition. In *Human Rights: Comments and Interpretations*, edited by UNESCO. New York: Columbia University Press.

London, Leslie. 2008. What Is a Human Rights-Based Approach to Health and Does It Matter? *Health and Human Rights* 10 (1):65–80.

Lorberbaum, Yair. 2002. Blood and the Image of God: On the Sanctity of Life in Biblical and Early Rabbinic Law, Myth, and Ritual. In *The Concept of Human Dignity in Human Rights Discourse*, edited by D. Kretzmer and E. Klein. The Hague: Kluwer Law International.

Luard, Evan. 1981. *Human Rights and Foreign Policy*. Oxford: Pergamon Press.

Macartney, C. A. 1934. *National States and National Minorities*. London: Oxford University Press.

Machan, Tibor. 1999. *Private Rights and Public Illusions*. New Brunswick, N.J.: Transaction Publishers.

Machan, Tibor R. 1989. *Individuals and Their Rights*. La Salle, Ill.: Open Court Press.

MacIntyre, Alasdair C. 1988. *Whose Justice? Which Rationality?* Notre Dame: University of Notre Dame Press.

———. 1990. *Three Rival Versions of Moral Enquiry: Encyclopaedia, Genealogy, and Tradition*. Notre Dame: University of Notre Dame Press.

Macklin, Ruth. 2002. Cloning and Public Policy. In *A Companion to Genetics*, edited by J. Burley and J. Harris. Oxford: Blackwell.

Malpas, Jeff, and Norelle Lickiss. 2007. Introduction to a Conversation. In *Perspectives on Human Dignity: A Conversation*, edited by J. Malpas and N. Lickiss. Dordrecht: Springer.

Mandelbaum, David. 1970. *Society in India*. Berkeley: University of California Press.

Mangalpus, Raul. 1978. Human Rights Are Not a Western Discovery. *Worldview* 4 (October).

Margalit, Avishai. 1996. *The Decent Society*. Cambridge, Mass.: Harvard University Press.

Marglin, Frederique Apffel, and Stephen A. Marglin, eds. 1990. *Dominating Knowledge: Development, Culture, and Resistance*. Oxford: Clarendon Press.

Maritain, Jacques. 1943. *The Rights of Man and Natural Law*. New York: C. Scribner's Sons.

Marks, Stephen P. 1981. Emerging Human Rights: A New Generation for the 1980s? *Rutgers Law Review* 33:435.

Markus, R. A. 1988. Introduction: The West. In *The Cambridge History of Medieval Political Thought c. 350–1450*, edited by J. H. Burns. Cambridge: Cambridge University Press.

Marshall, T. H. 1950. *Citizenship and Social Class and Other Essays*. Cambridge: Cambridge University Press.

———. 1981. *The Right to Welfare and Other Essays*. New York: Free Press.

Maslow, Abraham. 1970. *Motivation and Personality*. New York: Harper and Row.

———. 1971. *The Farther Reaches of Human Nature*. New York: Viking Press.

Mawdudi, Abul A'la. 1976. *Human Rights in Islam*. Leicester: Islamic Foundation.

Mbaye, Keba. 2002. *Les Droits de l'homme en Afrique*. 2nd ed. Paris: Editions A. Pedone.

McClatchy, V. S. 1979 [1921]. Assimilation of Japanese: Can They Be Moulded Into American Citizens. In *Four Anti-Japanese Pamphlets*, edited by V. S. McClatchy. New York: Arno Press.

McHale, John, and Magda Cordell McHale. 1979. Meeting Basic Human Needs. *Annals* 442.

Meckled-Garcia, Saladin, and Basak Cali, eds. 2005. *Legalization and Human Rights*. London: Routledge.

Mei, Y. P. 1967. The Basis of Social, Ethical, and Spiritual Values in Chinese Philosophy. In *The Chinese Mind: Essentials of Chinese Philosophy and Culture*, edited by C. A. Moore. Honolulu: East-West Center [University of Hawaii] Press.

Meyer, John W., John Boli, George M. Thomas, and Francisco O. Ramirez. 1997. World Society and the Nation-State. *American Journal of Sociology* 103 (1):144–81.

Meyer, John W., and Ronald L. Jepperson. 2000. The "Actors" of Modern Society: The Cultural Construction of Social Agency. *Sociological Theory* 18 (1):100–120.

Meyer, Michael J. 2002. Dignity as a (Modern) Virtue. In *The Concept of Human Dignity in Human Rights Discourse*, edited by D. Kretzmer and E. Klein. The Hague: Kluwer Law International.

Miller, David. 2011. On Nationality and Global Equality: A Reply to Holtug. *Ethics and Global Politics* 4 (3):165–71.

Miller, Richard W. 1986. Democracy and Class Dictatorship. *Social Philosophy and Policy* 3 (3):59–78.

Mittal, Sushil, and Gene Thursby, eds. 2004. *The Hindu World*. New York: Routledge.

Moggridge, Donald, ed. 1980. *The Collected Writings of John Maynard Keynes, Volume XXV: Activities 1940–1944, Shaping the Post-War World, The Clearing Union*. Cambridge: Cambridge University Press.

Monshipouri, Mahmood. 1998. *Islamism, Secularism, and Human Rights in the Middle East*. Boulder: Lynne Rienner.

Morgan, Rod, and Malcolm Evans. 1999. *Protecting Prisoners: The Standards of the European Committee for the Prevention of Torture in Context*. New York: Oxford University Press.

Morgenthau, Hans J. 1954. *Politics among Nations: The Struggle for Power and Peace*. 2nd ed. New York: Alfred A. Knopf.

——. 1979. *Human Rights and Foreign Policy*. New York: Council on Religion and International Affairs.

Morris, Bruce R. 1967. *Economic Growth and Development*. New York: Pitman Publishing.

Morsink, Johannes. 1999. *The Universal Declaration of Human Rights: Origins, Drafting, and Intent*. Philadelphia: University of Pennsylvania Press.

Mott, Luiz R. B. 1996. *Epidemic of Hate: Violations of the Human Rights of Gay Men, Lesbians, and Transvestites in Brazil*. San Francisco: International Gay and Lesbian Human Rights Commission.

Moussalli, Ahmad. 2001. *The Islamic Quest for Democracy, Pluralism, and Human Rights*. Gainesville: University Press of Florida.

Munro, James. 2011. The Relationship between the Origins and Regime Design of the ASEAN Intergovernmental Commission on Human Rights (AICHR). *International Journal of Human Rights* 15 (8):1185–1214.

Murphy, Sean D. 1996. *Humanitarian Intervention: The United Nations in an Evolving World Order*. Philadelphia: University of Pennsylvania Press.

Mutua, Makau. 1995. The Banjul Charter and the African Cultural Fingerprint: An Evaluation of the Language of Duties. *Virginia Journal of International Law* 35:339–80.

——. 2001. Savages, Victims, and Saviors: The Metaphor of Human Rights. *Harvard International Law Journal* 42:201–45.

Muzaffar, Chandra. 1999. From Human Rights to Human Dignity. In *Debating Human Rights: Critical Essays from the United States and Asia*, edited by P. Van Ness. London: Routledge.

Nambiar, Satish. 2000. India: An Uneasy Precedent. In *Kosovo and the Challenge of Humanitarian Intervention: Selective Indignation, Collective Action, and International Citizenship*, edited by A. Schnabel and R. Thakur. Tokyo: United Nations University Press.

Nanda, Ved P. 1992. Tragedies in Iraq, Liberia, Yugoslavia and Haiti: Revisiting the Validity of Humanitarian Intervention under International Law—Part I. *Denver Journal of International Law and Policy* 20.

Nanda, Ved P., Thomas F. Jr. Muther, and Amy E. Eckert. 1998. Tragedies in Somalia, Yugoslavia, Haiti, Rwanda and Liberia: Revisiting the Validity of Humanitarian Intervention under International Law, Part II. *Denver Journal of International Law and Policy* 26:827–69.

Nardin, Terry. 2002. The Moral Basis of Humanitarian Intervention. *Ethics and International Affairs* 16 (1):57–70.

Nathan, Andrew J. 2001. Universalism: A Particularistic Account. In *Negotiating Culture and Human Rights*, edited by L. Bell, A. J. Nathan and I. Peleg. New York: Columbia University Press.

Nexon, Daniel H. 2009. *The Struggle for Power in Early Modern Europe: Religious Conflict, Dynastic Empires, and International Change*. Princeton: Princeton University Press.

Nickel, James W. 1997. Group Agency and Group Rights. In *Ethnicity and Group Rights*, edited by I. Shapiro and W. Kymlicka. New York: New York University Press.

——. 2006. *Making Sense of Human Rights*. 2nd ed. London: Blackwell.

——. 2008. Rethinking Indivisibility: Towards a Theory of Supporting Relations between Human Rights. *Human Rights Quarterly* 30:948–1011.

Niebuhr, Reinhold. 1932. *Moral Man and Immoral Society: A Study in Ethics and Politics*. New York: C. Scribner's Sons.

Novak, Michael. 1999. Human Dignity, Human Rights. *First Things* 97:39–42.

Nussbaum, Martha C. 1994. Platonic Love and Colorado Law: The Relevance of Ancient Greek Norms to Modern Sexual Controversies. *Virginia Law Review* 80 (7):1515–651.

——. 1997. Capabilities and Human Rights. *Fordham Law Review* 66:273–300.

——. 2000. Aristotle, Politics, and Human Capabilities: A Response to Antony, Arneson, Charlesworth, and Mulgan. *Ethics* 111 (1):102–40.

——. 2003. Capabilities as Fundamental Entitlements: Sen and Social Justice. *Feminist Economics* 9 (2–3):33–59.

——. 2011. Capabilities, Entitlements, Rights: Supplementation and Critique. *Journal of Human Development and Capabilities* 12 (1):23–37.

Ordonez, Juan Pablo. 1994. *No Human Being Is Disposable: Social Cleansing, Human Rights, and Sexual Orientation in Colombia*. San Francisco: International Gay and Lesbian Human Rights Commission.

Osiatynski, Wiktor. 2007. Needs-Based Approach to Social and Economic Rights. "Paper prepared for the Salzburg Global Seminar" http://www.salzburgseminar.org/documents//412Osiatynski16082003.pdf.

Otto, Dianne. 2001. Defending Women's Economic and Social Rights: Some Thoughts on Indivisibility and a New Standard of Equality. In *Giving Meaning to Economic, Social, and Cultural Rights*, edited by I. Merali and V. Oosterveld. Philadelphia: University of Pennsylvania Press.

Palley, Claire. 1991. *The United Kingdom and Human Rights*. London: Stevens and Sons / Sweet and Maxwell.

Palma, Gabriel. 1977. Dependency: A Formal Theory of Underdevelopment or a Methodology for the Analysis of Concrete Situations of Underdevelopment? *World Development* 6 (July/August).

Pannenberg, Wolfhart. 1991. *Systematic Theology*. Vol. 2. Grand Rapids, Mich.: William B. Eerdmans.

Parekh, Bhikhu. 1999. Non-ethnocentric Universalism. In *Human Rights in Global Politics*, edited by T. Dunne and N. J. Wheeler. Cambridge: Cambridge University Press.

Parent, William A. 1992. Constitutional Values and Human Dignity. In *The Constitution of Rights: Human Dignity and American Values*, edited by M. J. Meyer and W. A. Parent. Ithaca: Cornell University Press.

Peach, Lucinda Joy. 2001. Are Women Human? The Promise and Perils of 'Women's Rights as Human Rights'. In *Negotiating Culture and Human Rights*, edited by L. S. Bell, A. J. Nathan and I. Peleg. New York: Columbia University Press.

Penna, David R., and Patricia J. Campbell. 1998. Human Rights and Culture: Beyond Universality and Relativism. *Third World Quarterly* 19 (1):7–27.

Pflugfelder, Gregory M. 1999. *Cartographies of Desire: Male-Male Sexuality in Japanese Discourse, 1600-1950*. Berkeley: University of California Press.

Pogge, Thomas W. 2001 [1995]. How Should Human Rights Be Conceived? In *The Philosophy of Human Rights*, edited by P. Hayden. St. Paul, Minn.: Paragon House.

Pollis, Adamantia. 1992. Human Rights in Liberal, Socialist, and Third World Perspective. In *Human Rights in the World Community: Issues and Action*, edited by R. P. Claude and B. H. Weston. Philadelphia: University of Pennsylvania Press.

———. 1996. Cultural Relativism Revisited: Through a State Prism. *Human Rights Quarterly* 18 (2).

Pollis, Adamantia, and Peter Schwab. 1980. Introduction. In *Human Rights: Cultural and Ideological Perspectives*, edited by A. Pollis and P. Schwab. New York: Praeger.

Preis, Ann-Belinda S. 1996. Human Rights as Cultural Practice: An Anthropological Critique. *Human Rights Quarterly* 18 (2):286.

Puta-Chekwe, Chisanga, and Nora Flood. 2001. From Division to Integration: Economic, Social, and Cultural Rights as Basic Human Needs. In *Giving Meaning to Economic, Social, and Cultural Rights*, edited by I. Merali and V. Oosterveld. Philadelphia: University of Pennsylvania Press.

Raaflaub, Kurt A. 2001. Political Thought, Civic Responsibility, and the Greek Polis. In *Agon, Logos, Polis: The Greek Achievement and its Aftermath*, edited by J. P. Arnason and P. Murphy. Stuttgart: Franz Steiner Verlag.

Ratti, Rakesh, ed. 1993. *A Lotus of Another Color: An Unfolding of the South Asian Lesbian and Gay Experience*. Boston: Alyson Publications.

Rawls, John. 1955. Two Concepts of Rules. *Philosophical Review* 64:3–32.

———. 1971. *A Theory of Justice*. Cambridge, Mass.: Harvard University Press.

———. 1996. *Political Liberalism*. New York: Columbia University Press.

———. 1999. *Collected Papers*. Cambridge, Mass.: Harvard University Press.

——. 1999. *The Law of Peoples*. Cambridge, Mass.: Harvard University Press.

Reiff, David. 1999. A New Age of Liberal Imperialism? *World Policy Journal* 16(2):1-10.

Reilly, Niamh. 2009. *Women's Human Rights*. Cambridge: Polity Press.

Renteln, Alison Dundes. 1988. Relativism and the Search for Human Rights. *American Anthropologist* 90 (1):56–72.

——. 1990. *International Human Rights: Universalism versus Relativism*. Newbury Park, Calif.: Sage Publications.

Ringer, Benjamin B. 1983. *"We the People" and Others: Duality and America's Treatment of Its Racial Minorities*. New York: Tavistock Publications.

Rioux, Marcia H., Lee Ann Basser, and Melinda Jones, eds. 2011. *Critical Perspectives on Human Rights and Disability Law*. The Hague: Martinus Nijhoff.

Rishmawi, Mervat. 2010. The Arab Charter on Human Rights and the League of Arab States: An Update. *Human Rights Law Review* 10 (1):169–78.

Risse, Thomas, Steven C. Ropp, and Kathryn Sikkink, eds. 1999. *The Power of Human Rights: International Norms and Domestic Change*. Cambridge: Cambridge University Press.

Rittberger, Volker, and Peter Mayer, eds. 1993. *Regime Theory and International Relations*. Oxford: Clarendon Press.

Rodgers, Gerry, Eddy Lee, Lee Swepson, and Jasmien Van Daele. 2009. *The International Labour Organization and the Quest for Social Justice, 1919–2009*. Geneva, Switzerland: International Labour Office.

Ronayne, Peter. 2001. *Never Again? The United States and the Prevention and Punishment of Genocide since the Holocaust*. Lanham, Md.: Rowman and Littlefield.

Roosevelt, Franklin D. 1938. *Public Papers and Addresses of Franklin D. Roosevelt*. Vol. 1. New York: Random House.

——. 1950. *Public Papers and Addresses of Franklin D. Roosevelt*. Vol. 10. New York: Harper and Brothers.

Rosanvallon, Pierre. 1995. The History of the Word "Democracy" in France. *Journal of Democracy* 6 (October):140–54.

Ross, Susan Deller. 2008. *Women's Human Rights: The International and Comparative Law Casebook*. Philadelphia: University of Pennsylvania Press.

Ross, W. D. 1930. *The Right and the Good*. London: Oxford University Press.

Rostow, Walt. 1960. *The Stages of Economic Growth: A Non-Communist Manifesto*. Cambridge: Cambridge University Press.

Rowen, Henry S., ed. 1998. *Behind East Asian Growth: The Political and Social Foundations of Prosperity*. New York: Routledge.

Ruffin, Patricia. 1982. Socialist Development and Human Rights in Cuba. In *Towards a Human Rights Framework*, edited by P. Schwab and A. Pollis. New York: Praeger.

Ruggie, John Gerard. 1982. International Regimes, Transactions, and Change: Embedded Liberalism in the Postwar Economic Order. *International Organization* 36 (2):379–415.

Runciman, W. G. 1990. Doomed to Extinction: The *Polis* as an Evolutionary Dead-End. In *The Greek City from Homer to Alexander*, edited by O. Murray and S. Price. Oxford: Clarendon Press.

Sachweh, Patrick. 2008. The 'Moral Economy' of Social Inequality: A Study of Popular Views about Poverty and Wealth. Paper presented at Stanford Center on Poverty and Inequality conference, Work, Poverty and Inequality in the 21st Century, Stanford University, August 2008

Sachs, Wolfgang, ed. 1992. *The Development Dictionary: A Guide to Knowledge as Power*. London: Zed Books.

Safrai, Chana. 2002. Human Dignity in a Rabbinical Perspective. In *The Concept of Human Dignity in Human Rights Discourse*, edited by D. Kretzmer and E. Klein. The Hague: Kluwer Law International.

Said, Abdul Aziz. 1979. Precept and Practice of Human Rights in Islam. *Universal Human Rights* 1 (1):63–80.

Sajó, András. 1996. Rights in Post-Communism. In *Western Rights? Post-Communist Application*, edited by A. Sajó. The Hague: Kluwer Law International.

Samnoy, Ashlid. 1990. *Human Rights as International Consensus: The Making of the Universal Declaration of Human Rights, 1945–1948*. Bergen: Department of History, University of Bergen.

——. 1993. *Human Rights as International Consensus: The Making of the Universal Declaration of Human Rights, 1945–1948*. Bergen: Chr. Michelsen Institute.

——. 1999. The Origins of the Universal Declaration of Human Rights. In *The Universal Declaration of Human Rights: A Common Standard of Achievement*, edited by G. Alfredsson and A. Eide. The Hague: Martinus Nijhoff.

Schabas, William A. 2009. *Genocide in International Law: The Crime of Crimes*. 2nd ed. Cambridge: Cambridge University Press.

Schachter, Oscar. 1983. Human Dignity as a Normative Concept. *American Journal of International Law* 77:848–54.

Schalow, Paul Gordon. 1989. Male Love in Early Modern Japan: A Literary Depiction of the 'Youth'. In *Hidden From History: Reclaiming the Gay and Lesbian Past*, edited by M. B. Duberman, M. Vicinus and G. Chauncey. New York: New American Library.

Schlesinger, Arthur, Jr. 1979. Human Rights and the American Tradition. *Foreign Affairs* 57 (3):503–26.

Schmitt, Arno, and Jehoeda Sofer, eds. 1992. *Sexuality and Eroticism Among Males in Moslem Societies*. New York: Harrington Park Press.

Schwarzenberger, Georg. 1955. The Standard of Civilisation in International Law. *Current Legal Problems* 8:212-234.

Sen, Amartya. 1981. *Poverty and Famines: An Essay on Entitlement and Deprivation*. New York: Oxford University Press.

——. 2004. Elements of a Theory of Human Rights. *Philosophy and Public Affairs* 32 (4):315–56.

——. 2005. Human Rights and Capabilities. *Journal of Human Development* 6 (2):151–66.

Senarclens, Pierre de. 2003. The Politics of Human Rights. In *The Globalization of Human Rights*, edited by J.-M. Coicaud, M. W. Doyle and A.-M. Gardner. Tokyo: United Nations University Press.

Sharma, Arvind. 2003. *Hinduism and Human Rights: A Conceptual Approach*. New Delhi: Oxford University Press.

——. 2005. *Modern Hindu Thought: An Introduction*. New Delhi: Oxford University Press.

Shell, Susan M. 2003. Kant on Human Dignity. In *In Defense of Human Dignity: Essays for Our Times*, edited by R. P. Kraynak and G. Tinder. Notre Dame: University of Notre Dame Press.

Shelton, Dinah. 2008. *Regional Protection of Human Rights*. Oxford: Oxford University Press.

Shue, Henry. 1979. Rights in the Light of Duties. In *Human Rights and U.S. Foreign Policy*, edited by P. G. Brown and D. Maclean. Lexington, Mass.: Lexington Books.

———. 1980. *Basic Rights: Subsistence, Affluence, and U.S. Foreign Policy*. Princeton: Princeton University Press.

———. 1984. The Interdependence of Duties. In *The Right to Food*, edited by P. Alston and K. Tomasevski. [The Hague?]: Martinus Nijhoff.

Shultziner, Doron. 2004. Human Dignity: Functions and Meanings. *Global Jurist Topics* 3 (3).

———. 2006. A Jewish Conception of Human Dignity: Philosophy and Its Ethical Implications for Israeli Supreme Court Decisions. *Journal of Religious Ethics* 34 (4):663–83.

Siegel, Richard L. 1985. Socioeconomic Human Rights: Past and Future. *Human Rights Quarterly* 7 (3):255–67.

Slater, Jerome, and Terry Nardin. 1986. Nonintervention and Human Rights. *Journal of Politics* 48 (1):86–96.

Smith, Rhona K. M. 2003. *Textbook on International Human Rights*. Oxford: Oxford University Press.

Stacy, Helen. 2004. International Human Rights in a Fragmenting World. In *Human Rights with Modesty: The Problem of Universalism*, edited by A. Sajó. Leiden, Netherlands: Martinus Nijhoff.

Stewart, Frances. 1985. *Basic Needs in Developing Countries*. Baltimore: Johns Hopkins University Press.

Stiefel, Matthia, and Marshall Wolfe. 1994. *A Voice For the Excluded: Popular Participation in Development*. London: Zed (in association with the United Nations Research Institute for Social Development).

Stowell, Ellery C. 1921. *Intervention in International Law*. Washington, D.C.: John Byrne.

Suganami, Hidemi. 1984. Japan's Entry into International Society. In *The Expansion of International Society*, edited by H. Bull and A. Watson. Oxford: Clarendon Press.

Sulmasy, Daniel P. 2007. Human Dignity and Human Worth. In *Perspectives on Human Dignity: A Conversation*, edited by J. Malpas and N. Lickiss. Dordrecht: Springer.

Sunstein, Cass R. 2004. *The Second Bill of Rights: FDR's Unfinished Revolution and Why We Need It More than Ever*. New York: Basic Books.

Svensson, Marina. 2003. *Debating Human Rights in China*. Lanham, Md.: Rowman and Littlefield.

Tabandeh, Sultanhussein. 1970. *A Muslim Commentary on the Universal Declaration of Human Rights*. London: F. T. Goulding.

Tai, Hung-Chao. 1985. Human Rights in Taiwan: Convergence of Two Political Cultures? In *Human Rights in an East Asian Perspective*, edited by J. C. Hsiung. New York: Paragon House.

Tan, Hsien-Li. 2011. *The ASEAN Intergovernmental Commission on Human Rights: Institutionalising Human Rights in Southeast Asia*. Cambridge: Cambridge University Press.

Tatum, Dale C. 2010. *Genocide at the Dawn of the Twenty-First Century*. New York: Palgrave Macmillan.

Thomas, Daniel C. 2001. *The Helsinki Effect: International Norms, Human Rights, and the Demise of Communism*. Princeton: Princeton University Press.

Thomas, George M. 2010. Differentiation, Rationalization and Actorhood. In *New Systems Theories of World Politics*, edited by M. Albert, L.-E. Cederman and A. Wendt. Houndmills: Palgrave Macmillan.

Thompson, Simon. 2006. *The Political Theory of Recognition: A Critical Introduction*. Cambridge: Polity.

Thornberry, Patrick, and Maria Amor Martin Estebanez. 2004. *Minority Rights in Europe*. Strasbourg: Council of Europe.

Tilley, John J. 2000. Cultural Relativism. *Human Rights Quarterly* 22 (2):501–47.

Tinder, Glenn. 2003. Facets of Personal Dignity. In *In Defense of Human Dignity: Essays for Our Times*, edited by R. P. Kraynak and G. Tinder. Notre Dame: University of Notre Dame Press.

Todaro, Michael P. 1994. *Economic Development*. 5th ed. New York: Longman.

Tomuschat, Christian. 2003. *Human Rights: Between Idealism and Realism*. Oxford: Oxford University Press.

Trencsényi, Balázs, and Márton Zászkaliczky, eds. 2010. *Whose Love of Which Country? Composite States, National Histories and Patriotic Discourses in Early Modern Central Europe*. Leiden, Netherlands: Brill.

Tyagi, Yogesh. 2011. *The UN Human Rights Committee: Practice and Procedure*. New York: Cambridge University Press.

UNESCO, ed. 1949. *Human Rights: Comments and Interpretations*. New York: Columbia University Press.

United Nations Development Programme. 1997. *Governance for Sustainable Development: A UNDP Policy Document*. New York: United Nations Development Programme.

United States National Resources Planning Board. 1943. *National Resources Development Report for 1943*. Washington, D.C.: National Resources Planning Board.

Van Beuren, Geraldine. 1998. *International Law on the Rights of the Child*. The Hague: Kluwer Law International.

Van Dijk, P., and G. J. H. van Hoof, eds. 1998. *Theory and Practice of the European Convention on Human Rights*. The Hague: Kluwer Law International.

Vasak, Karel. 1984. Pour une troisième génération des droits de l'homme. In *Studies and Essays on International Humanitarian Law and Red Cross Principles in Honour of Jean Pictet*, edited by C. Swinarski. The Hague: Martinus Nijhoff.

———. 1991. Les différentes catégories des droits de l'homme. In *Les Dimensions universelles des droits de l'homme*, edited by A. Lapeyre, F. de Tinguy and K. Vasak. Bruxelles: Émile Bruylant.

Vincent, R. J., ed. 1986. *Foreign Policy and Human Rights*. Cambridge: Cambridge University Press.

Vizard, Polly. 2007. Specifying and Justifying a Basic Capability Set: Should the International Human Rights Framework Be Given a More Direct Role? *Oxford Development Studies* 35 (3):225–50.

Vizard, Polly, Sakiko Fukuda-Parr, and Diane Elson. 2011. Introduction: The Capabilities Approach and Human Rights. *Journal of Human Development and Capabilities* 12 (1):1–22.

Waaldijk, Kees. 1994. Standard Sequences in the Legal Recognition of Homosexuality: Europe's Past, Present, and Future. *Australasian Gay and Lesbian Law Journal* 4 (4):50–72.

Wai, Dunstan M. 1980. Human Rights in Sub-Saharan Africa. In *Human Rights: Cultural and Ideological Perspectives*, edited by A. Pollis and P. Schwab. New York: Praeger.

Wallace, Rebecca, ed. 1997. *International Human Rights: Text and Materials*. London: Sweet & Maxwell.

Waltz, Susan. 2001. Universalizing Human Rights: The Role of Small States in the Construction of the Universal Declaration of Human Rights. *Human Rights Quarterly* 23 (1):44–72.

——. 2002. Reclaiming and Rebuilding the History of the Universal Declaration of Human Rights. *Third World Quarterly* 23 (3):437–48.

——. 2004. Universal Human Rights: The Contribution of Muslim States. *Human Rights Quarterly* 26 (4):799–844.

Walzer, Michael. 1977. *Just and Unjust Wars: A Moral Argument with Historical Illustrations*. New York: Basic Books.

——. 1980. The Moral Standing of States: A Response to Four Critics. *Philosophy and Public Affairs* 9 (3):209–29.

——. 1994. Comment. In *Multiculturalism: Examining the Politics of Recognition*, edited by A. Gutmann. Princeton: Princeton University Press.

Washburn, Wilcomb E. 1987. Cultural Relativism, Human Rights, and the AAA. *American Anthropologist* 89 (4):939–43.

Weisstub, David N. 2002. Honor, Dignity, and the Framing of Multiculturalist Values. In *The Concept of Human Dignity in Human Rights Discourse*, edited by D. Kretzmer and E. Klein. The Hague: Kluwer Law International.

Weiner, Myron. 1987. The Goals of Development. In *Understanding Political Development*, edited by M. Weiner and S. Huntington. Boston: Little Brown.

Weiss, Thomas G. 1999. Principles, Politics, and Humanitarian Action. *Ethics and International Affairs* 13 (1):1–22.

Wheeler, Nick. 2000. *Saving Strangers: Humanitarian Intervention in International Society*. Oxford: Oxford University Press.

Whelan, Daniel J. 2010. *Interdependent Human Rights: A History*. Philadelphia: University of Pennsylvania Press.

Whelan, Daniel J., and Jack Donnelly. 2007. The West, Economic and Social Rights, and the Global Human Rights Regime: Setting the Record Straight. *Human Rights Quarterly* 29 (4):908–49.

White, Gordon, and Roger Goodman. 1998. Welfare Orientalism and the Search for an East Asian Welfare Model. In *The East Asian Welfare Model: Welfare Orientalism and the State*, edited by R. Goodman, G. White and H.-J. Kwon. New York: Routledge.

Wilson, Richard. 1997. Introduction. In *Human Rights, Culture and Context: Anthropological Perspectives*, edited by R. Wilson. London: Pluto Press.

Witte, John, Jr. 2003. Between Sanctity and Depravity: Human Dignity in Protestant Perspective. In *In Defense of Human Dignity: Essays for Our Times*, edited by R. P. Kraynak and G. Tinder. Notre Dame: University of Notre Dame Press.

Wolfson, Evan. 1991. Civil Rights, Human Rights, Gay Rights: Minorities and the Humanity of the Different. *Harvard Journal of Law and Public Policy* 14: 21–39.

Woodward, C. Vann. 1966. *The Strange Career of Jim Crow*. 2nd ed. New York: Oxford University Press.

World Bank. 1992. *Governance and Development*. Washington, D.C.: World Bank.

Wright, John T. 1979. Human Rights in the West: Political Liberties and the Rule of Law. In *Human Rights: Cultural and Ideological Perspective*, edited by A. Pollis and P. Schwab. New York: Praeger.

Yao, Grace Y. 2011. *Grounding Human Rights in a Pluralist World*. Washington, D.C.: Georgetown University Press.

Yates, Steven. 1995. 'Righting' Civil Wrongs: Toward a Libertarian Agenda. In *Liberty for the 21st Century: Contemporary Libertarian Thought*, edited by T. R. Machan and D. B. Rasmussen. Lanham, Md.: Rowman and Littlefield.

Zakaria, Fouad. 1986. Human Rights in the Arab World: The Islamic Context. In *Philosophical Foundations of Human Rights*, edited by UNESCO. Paris: UNESCO.

Zechenter, Elizabeth M. 1997. In the Name of Cultural Relativism and the Abuse of the Individual. *Journal of Anthropological Research* 53:319–47.

Zhang, Dainian. 2002. *Key Concepts in Chinese Philosophy*. Translated by E. Ryden. New Haven: Yale University Press; Beijing: Foreign Languages Press.

Zivi, Karen. 2012. *Making Rights Claims: A Practice of Democratic Citizenship*. New York: Oxford University Press.

Index